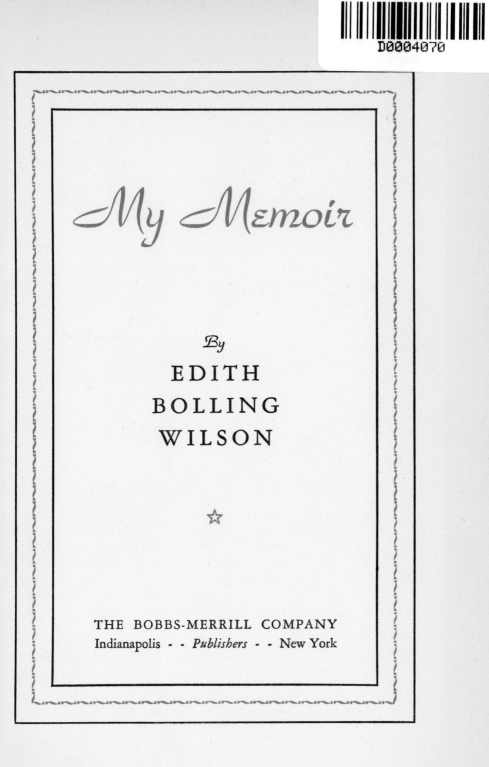

My Memoir

By
EDITH BOLLING WILSON

☆

THE BOBBS-MERRILL COMPANY
Indianapolis - - *Publishers* - - New York

FIRST EDITION

PRINTED IN THE UNITED STATES OF AMERICA

A part of this work has been published in the *Saturday Evening Post*
under the title AS I SAW IT.

PRINTED AND BOUND BY
Braunworth & Co., Inc. · *Builders of Books*
BRIDGEPORT, CONN.

MY MEMOIR

LIST OF ILLUSTRATIONS

FOREWORD

On the train in Washington, D. C.,
starting to Saratoga Springs, N. Y.,
August 14, 1927.
For many years I have been urged by editors and friends to write
of the deep experiences it was my great privilege to share with my
husband, Woodrow Wilson, in the White House and during the
World War, and, by a caprice of fate, at foreign courts during the
Peace Conference of 1918-19.

Although I have never written a line for publication, I have decided to yield to these importunities and dedicate a month's leisure
from home to making a record of facts, many of which I am sure have
not heretofore appeared in print.

Armistice Day, 1937.
That "month" has stretched itself to more than ten years, for only
today has the last word of my memoirs been written. In the interim
I have circled the globe, been several times to Europe, and had a
delightful sojourn in Mexico City.

October 11, 1938.
After another year of consideration, and helpful criticism from
close friends, I have today signed the contract for publication of my
manuscript. Among these friends I would be ungrateful not to
mention Mr. Bernard M. Baruch, Mr. Ray Stannard Baker, Mr. Paul
E. Lesh, Mr. D. Laurance Chambers; and notably Mr. Marquis
James—for his advice and assistance in preparing the manuscript for
publication, and my brother, John Randolph Bolling, who compiled
and edited the *Chronology of Woodrow Wilson,* and who has given
me not only his informed and patient aid but relieved me of the
burden of all routine work, correspondence with editors, proof-
reading, and endless other details, in the more than ten years in
which this book was written.

I claim no reader's attention with the idea I will reveal official secrets; for nothing is further from my thought. But I *have* revealed the truth concerning personal matters which has been often distorted by the misinformed. And if I take the public into my confidence about these matters, it is because the high office which my husband held robs them of a private character and makes me feel that they belong to history.

E. B. W.

© *From a Photograph by Arnold Genthe, N. Y.*

CHAPTER 1

I WAS born in Wytheville, Virginia, on Monday morning, October 15, 1872, at nine o'clock—the hour set for the convening of the Circuit Court of which my father was judge. Father used to laugh and tell how the opening of the Court was delayed so he could be on hand to greet me. Consequently, as he always said, I began my career by "keeping gentlemen waiting."

There is a tradition regarding the seventh child, and I suppose, like other traditions, it varies. But certainly it brought me luck and deep happiness. There were eleven of us and, as I shall refer to my brothers and sisters so frequently in this narrative, I shall here introduce us all by name, beginning with the oldest: Rolfe, Gertrude, Annie Lee, Will, Bertha, Charles, Edith, Randolph, Wilmer, Julian and Geraldine. Of these Charles and Geraldine died in infancy.

We lived in an old brick house in the center of this small southwestern Virginia town which was named for George Wythe, a signer of the Declaration of Independence. Though the house was shabby and inadequate, material deficiencies were repaired by understanding, sympathy and love, making it to us healthy, happy youngsters in every sense a home. My father and mother had been born and bred in the eastern part of Virginia where, "before the war," meaning the Civil War, there were slaves and abundance. Mother had her own maid, Father his man, in those spacious times. But with the ending of the war, the old order passed, and they found themselves, like thousands of others, with everything swept away, and unable to live on a plantation with no one to work it and no money.

I remember so well hearing my father tell of the breaking up of the plantation. Many of the older negroes had stayed on after the emancipation and looked to him to provide for them just as before. He called them together and said: "You are now free; you don't belong to us any more, and you will have to work to provide for

1

yourselves." The poor things could not comprehend and stood silent. So he added: "We even have no food to give you." At this they said: "Go 'way, Marse William; you know we are hungry, and you are just joking with us." He knew they really were hungry, so he decided to humble his pride and go to Lynchburg, Virginia, where the Federal Government had officers in charge, and ask for food for "the wards of the nation."

Every horse had been taken by the Yankees, and only a mule left. He told old Uncle Moses to hitch the mule to the wagon, and together they drove into Lynchburg. The gentleman in charge of the commissary was both courteous and understanding when Father told him of the plight of the negroes. At once he gave orders to load the wagon with bacon, flour, sugar and coffee, insisting that the food be used by the family as well as the negroes.

There was great rejoicing in the cabins at the sight of food, but neither my grandmother nor my mother nor my aunt would touch it. My father told them the greatest treat would be real coffee for which, during the last months of the war, they had used parched corn as a substitute. Not even this treat would tempt these unreconstructed ladies, who said Yankee coffee would choke them.

When the family was ready to leave the plantation, and the negroes came to say goodbye, old Henry begged to be taken along. This was hard to refuse. For four years Henry had been the guardian of the household silver and other valuables, except Mother's diamond engagement ring which she had wound inside a ball of yarn. During the war my grandfather, Dr. Archibald Bolling, had opened his house as a military hospital, my mother, my aunts and my grandmother acting as nurses. As anaesthetics were not allowed to come through the Federal lines, Mother described the sufferings of the men as terrible.

Among the wounded men brought in was a young German, Rudolf Teusler, who spoke almost no English. By the time he was well enough to leave he had fallen desperately in love with my aunt, Mary Jefferson, and she with him. The fact that he had espoused the Confederate cause appealed to her, for she was a Rebel, as we were called, to the end of her life. This, and his suffering for the cause, made a romantic combination she was unable to resist for, in spite of the protests of my grandparents, they were married, and when the war was over he took her to Germany to live. There she learned his tongue and spoke it as fluently as she did English.

My father, having graduated in law at the University of Virginia, hoped to establish himself in the practise of that profession. With an invalid mother, a young and inexperienced wife, two babies and no money, this was a grave problem. The one light in a dark world was the knowledge that at Wytheville they could at least have a roof over their heads. For there, on Main Street, was an old house which my paternal grandfather (then dead) had taken in payment for a debt. The family arrived only to find this haven untenantable, as it, too, had been used as a Confederate hospital. But in time it was scrubbed and patched up and they moved in to make the home in which nine more of their children were born.

After the war father formed a law partnership with General William Terry, to whom he had gone to school when a small boy, and who had married a relative. General Terry was a brave Confederate soldier, and had taken over the original "Stonewall Brigade" when General Jackson was promoted to higher commands. I remember a story which my father told in a most fascinating way of a time during the war when General Terry had been so severely wounded that he could not walk, and was in danger of capture. He sent for my father. Early one morning, a messenger came to say that the Federal troops were coming down the mountain to take the little town of Wytheville. As the General was too badly wounded to sit his horse, my father got him into an old carriage, drawn by a pair of horses that were hardly able to drag it, and drove out of one end of town as the Federal troops came in at the other. The carriage was seen and pursued by two or three cavalrymen. Just before the latter came in sight, the roads forked. When the old darky driver asked which road to take, my father said "the left." This was a side road. The cavalrymen assumed the carriage had gone on the main road, and so went that way for some distance. When they found their mistake, the carriage was so far away that they gave up the pursuit. My father would laugh and say: "That is just how near they came to capturing a Confederate General." The fugitives stayed in the woods all day, while the enemy looted and burned the town, setting fire to a Presbyterian church where the Confederates had stored some ammunition. Early the next morning my father took General Terry's field glasses and saw the blue line of soldiers going slowly back up the mountain.

Many such war stories and much laughter brightened that crowded old house in Main Street. In addition to our own numerous family both of my grandmothers lived with us; also an unmarried sister of my mother, and a widowed sister, Mary Teusler, whose war-time romance I have mentioned. My Aunt Mary Jefferson, or "Jeff" as we called her, and her husband had returned from Germany to live in Georgia. With one son, Rudolf, Junior, who was a little younger than I, she had come to make her home with us after her husband's death. Thus from my earliest recollection we were a large household, with many guests at meals. I now wonder how Mother, with so many little children, with untrained and indolent servants and the long division of a slender purse, ever got things done. But, bless her heart, she was always equal to it, and was as young and gay as we were. So often since she has said, "They were the happiest days of my life"; and she and Father certainly made them so for all of us.

My Grandmother Bolling was also a very important factor in our lives. An unusually capable and dominant person, to whom an obstacle meant only something to be overcome, she used to say with scorn: "I hate a *can't;* anyone can do anything they try to." And she proved it. I wish I could give you the mental picture I have of her. She was small, very thin, and stooped, due to an injury to her spine, received when, as a very young woman, she was thrown from a horse. She always wore black dresses, made exactly alike: a very full skirt (six widths of material), over a small set of hoops; these were gathered at the waist line to a long, straight bodice, buttoned down the front. A very full bishop-sleeve, with cuffs matching the crêpe collar fastened with a hair brooch in front, and a snowy white cap, completed her costume. She wore gold-rimmed spectacles, and white aprons when she worked, and this was almost all the time for she had been brought up in the old school which believed literally that we had to account for every idle moment. She never relaxed her vigilance. When it grew too dark on winter afternoons for more exacting work, she would pick up her knitting, which was always near her, and through the darkness, or the fitful flames from the big wood fire that heated her room, you could hear the click of the steel needles as she knitted the finest silk or wool socks and stockings.

This picture is not complete without the background of her own room where she spent so many years. On account of the injury to her back she rarely left the house, and then had to be carried in my father's arms and put into a carriage. On these rare occasions she wore a large black shawl and a quaint black silk bonnet, shirred over all the top, and tied on over the white cap with broad black silk strings.

Her room was the center of the house, and was big and square. On the floor in winter was a Brussels carpet, with bouquets of crimson roses; in summer, a spotless white matting. In one corner of the room was a huge four-poster bed, with a trundle bed underneath on which some of us as children often slept. Then there were a mahogany wardrobe; an old chest of drawers with tiny mirror and three drawers set on top; a washstand, couch, big open fireplace with shiny brass dogs; a candlestand on which was her student's lamp; several chairs, her own particular throne being a rocker over which was spread a dog-skin beautifully tanned and dressed. It had belonged to a dog she had loved, and she kept this skin to the day of her death. Near the fireplace, in a corner, stood her sole leather trunk, very tiny for these days, and studded with brass nails with heads as big as quarters. They were always kept polished just as when she "used to pack this and have it strapped on the back of the carriage and take William Holcombe [my father] and Mary Jefferson [my aunt] and drive over to Montpelier and spend a week."

But to me the real treasure chest was another tiny trunk which I still have. It is about the size of a doll's trunk, and she filled it with all her personal treasures, including love letters from my grandfather when he was a medical student in Philadelphia, before they were married. These letters were sealed with wafers and had cost twenty-five cents to mail. There were also odd bits of ribbon, trinkets, and the little souvenirs we all love and keep because they visualize to us the days that are dead and make our pulses throb again.

Perhaps I have given too much canvas to the tiny lady who sat enthroned on a dog-skin and who used a very long staff when she walked. But this same lady was a distinct personality, and to her I owe a very loving debt of gratitude. She was as strong in her likes and dislikes as she was in every relation to life. She simply did, or did not, like you—and there was the end of it, and no compromise.

Of my two oldest sisters, like the men in the Bible, "the one was taken and the other left." And the same way with the sister only three years older than I—she took me, and had nothing to do with Bertha.

This preference was not all a bed of roses for it entailed staying in the four-poster at night, and waiting on her at any and all hours. It meant washing, ironing and remaking the elaborate white caps, which were fresh every other day, and, what was to me the greatest hardship of my young life, taking care of the cages for twenty-six canary birds, and acting as providence for them in births, deaths and the raising of their broods.

This care was not left to the haphazard discretion of a child but was done every day under her personal supervision and direction, and never allowed to be slighted. Personally, the only real fun I ever got out of the canaries was when we would find a young one that had been crowded out of the flannel-lined nest and lay stark and hideous on the floor of its cage awaiting burial! Then my brother Will, who became a doctor and has healed so many sufferers, would act as high priest. We would put the little dead bird in a spool box, place that in our red wagon, and have the interment in the Bird Cemetery we had laid out in the garden by the stable. We would go to the marble yard and get a chip cut from a big slab and write on it the name and the date of the death of the deceased.

These duties which I have described also had their generous compensations. If you basked in the light of Grandmother Bolling's approval—no inconsiderable asset when compared with her displeasure—you were given access to all she had, physical, material or spiritual. For myself I can truly say she taught me nearly everything I know. She was never too sick or too tired or too busy to help me. From her I learned to read and write. She even tried to teach me French, which she had learned to read by herself. The Bible she knew from cover to cover, and we read it together morning and night. She taught me to knit, to sew, to embroider, hemstitch and crochet, and to cut and fit dresses.

I laugh now when I recall the perfect confidence with which I undertook, at the age of fourteen, to make two suits of clothes for two boys who were older than I and who came to my sister Bertha's Sunday School class up in the mountains. They said they could not come to the church in town because they had no suitable clothes. My sister told this at supper one night, and I said to Father: "If you will get us the cloth, Bertha and I will make them suits of clothes." I remember now the twinkle in his eye when he said, "All right, I'll get it tomorrow." The work over those suits equalled, I am sure, at least three and a half times the labours of Hercules. Even that, though, was excelled by the courage of Jim and Bill Jones who wore them, and marched bravely up the church aisle to the font where my father and sister met them and stood as their sponsors in baptism. Afterwards, when my sister asked one of them, in Sunday School class, who were his sponsors in baptism, he said he did not know. When she said, "Oh yes you do. Who stood for you when you were baptized?" he replied: "I remember now; it was John the Baptist."

Having already described my Grandmother Bolling, I must try to picture the contrast between her and my mother's mother, Grandmother Logwood, who was very tall and erect. She told us that when a little girl she was never allowed to sit touching the back of her chair; it was considered as inelegant to do so as for a lady to show her ankle. In consequence of this early training she sat as straight as an arrow and carried herself with the dignity of a queen. She had very dark hair and fine brown eyes.

Her room was always a haven, and before her big wood fire she would sing old songs to us in the evenings. I remember one called "Lord Ullin's Daughter," where the hapless daughter had eloped with her lover in a boat which was swamped in angry waters. When her father discovered her plight he ran to the shore only to see the tiny craft storm-tossed beyond reach. To this day I remember the thrill I always received at the verses:

> "... One lovely hand she stretch'd for aid,
> And one was round her lover.
>
> "'Come back! come back!' he cried in grief,
> 'Across this stormy water;
> And I'll forgive your Highland chief,
> My daughter!—Oh my daughter!'"

Of course the boat went down and the hapless pair were drowned, for in those strict days even poems and songs must point a moral.

I never again expect to taste anything comparable to the cocoanut balls Grandmother Logwood used to make for us at Christmas, or anything so good as her pralines of pecan nuts and brown sugar.

One of our great joys was to give entertainments where all the household would assemble as an audience. We would regale them with tableaux or plays, the latter usually written by my cousin, Rudolf Teusler. One tableau I loved was called "The Soldier's Bride" where, standing on a red cushion, I impersonated the bride with a discarded lace curtain over my head, and beside me was my brother Will, with a toy gun in his hand and an old Confederate cap on his small head.

If only that vivid imagination which is the birthright of every child could last! The wooden gun and an old lace window curtain served as the magic carpet on which we mounted to other worlds where life was filled with romance.

At Christmas-time Will, Bertha and I always formed a "Club" for our united gift buying. We had a Constitution and a Board, my brother acting as president, Bertha as secretary and I as treasurer. This honour came to me for the exceedingly practical reason that I had more financial influence than either of the others with my banker, who was Grandmother Bolling.

The autumn I was born an old friend, Mrs. Stuart, had arrived to spend a few days in the house as a guest. She stayed four months (as was often the custom in the South) and when she left, my mother told me she took me in her arms to say goodbye and when she put me back in the cradle said: "I have put a Christmas present in the baby's hand, and don't let her forget me." This gift was a tiny ten-dollar gold piece which my Grandmother Bolling took to keep for me. When I was older I was told of this fortune, and it continued to be an Aladdin's lamp for me until I was almost grown for, whenever I needed anything, I would go to my grandmother and say: "Please give me my ten dollars as I have to have such and such a thing." She would always reply: "Oh, I hate for you to spend that; can't you get along with what you have?" Of course I couldn't "get along," so the dear old lady would put her hand in her ample pocket and take out a worn black pocketbook from which she would hand me the necessary amount, saying: "This will get what you need." Usually it was a little less than I had asked for, but I learned this very early

Sallie White Bolling, 1843-1925
Mother of Mrs. Woodrow Wilson. From a daguerreotype.

William Holcombe Bolling, 1839-1899
Father of Mrs. Woodrow Wilson. From a daguerreotype.

and allowed for the discount. Thanking her I would say, "Oh, I am so glad I can still keep my gold piece"; and truly old Mrs. Stuart was never forgotten, as my grandmother kept her memory bright by acting as my banker. Often she would add enough to my small deposit to round out a dollar, thus increasing my principal.

I still have a little memorandum book containing the record of our "Club," in which are listed the gifts for each member of the family with cost opposite—all written in cramped, childish writing. Then appears this funny "minute" of the meeting held December 24th, 1879: "Motion before the house—how to get Edith out without waking Grandma?"—meaning that as I slept in Grandmother Bolling's room how could I get up at daybreak, as we felt we must do on Christmas morning, without disturbing the old lady. Alas, the "minute" does not record how it was to be done.

About this time the first wedding I recall took place, the bride being Mother's half-sister who had always lived with us, and to whom we were devoted. After I was grown she used to laugh and tell me this story: She was away when I was born, and upon her return several months later she was eager to see "the new baby," so Mother held me in her arms to show me off, and my aunt exclaimed: "Oh, Sister, she is the ugliest child you have ever had." My mother indignantly replied: "She is no such thing, but even if she is she is so sweet and good you forget it."

But to return to the wedding. The groom was General James G. Field who was twice her age and a widower with four children. The General had lost a leg in the 'sixties, and of course to such romantic youngsters as we were these stern facts were terrible disappointments, for we had pictured the storybook hero, handsome and young. Though the old General was a fine man he was far from a beauty and his grey hair and beard made him seem to us a Methuselah!

Shortly after her marriage my aunt begged her mother, from whom she had never been separated, to come and make her home with them where they lived in Albemarle County, Virginia. It was a tragic day in our young lives when my Grandmother Logwood left, bringing the first realization on my part that life does not always flow on evenly with no changes. Now her cheery room seemed strangely empty; no merry songs or exciting stories; no big crackling fires with chestnuts roasting in the ashes—just silence! But, as happens in childhood, other interests soon filled the void, and we ceased to miss her.

So life went on until the summer before I was thirteen. I had never been out of that little town of Wytheville, Virginia. The blue circle of the mountains bounded my world and, outside of a very limited acquaintance with other children, the four walls of our old house, and the picket fence of our own yard and vegetable garden beyond, had been spacious enough for the healthy development of body and mind. I had never been to school. My Grandmother Bolling and Father had taught me all I knew, Father wrestling with arithmetic when he had time, and she doing the rest. There was generally a governess in the house for the older children, but I was terribly shy and begged to go on as I had begun, with my grandmother, and was allowed to do so.

On this eventful night in May, I was sleeping in the big four-poster bed in Grandmother's room. As she had grown too feeble then to climb into it, she slept in a small bed, and needed much care in the night. I used to make a game of counting the times she would call me to wait on her, and sometimes it was thirty-nine or forty in a night. I think it was for this reason that Father planned to take me on a trip.

As I say, I was fast asleep, and vaguely conscious of someone standing by me holding a light. I opened my eyes to see Father with a candle, guarding it carefully from the deep lace valance which hung from the tester above the bed. He had on his dressing gown and whispered so as not to waken Grandma: "How would you like to go with me tomorrow to the University of Virginia?" I was so excited I thought I was dreaming, but he went on and said: "Come over in your mother's room and we can plan the whole trip."

There was of course no more sleep for me that night; the train left at eight-thirty in the morning and everything had to be got ready. As I had never travelled in my life naturally I had nothing to travel with, and I think Mother, with all her resourcefulness, was a little dubious of the results of a hastily collected equipment. Miss Curtain, the dressmaker, was then making a dress for one of my sisters and Mother said that if it were finished I should have it. The idea that it might not fit never occurred to me, or the fact that what would suit a young lady of twenty-three might look queer on a child of thirteen.

Left to right: Bertha Bolling, age 5; Edith Bolling, age 2; William Archibald Bolling, age 7. Edith objected to posing until they gave her the orange which she holds in her hands.

Such speculations were for more sophisticated children, my only anxiety being that it might not be finished. But it was, and when old John, our man of all work, returned with the parcel under his arm, there was no cloud in the sky. With numerous other contributions from other members of the family I was ready, and when I stepped on the train that spring morning the grass in the valleys, just touched by the sun of the new day, was no greener than I.

We reached Charlottesville that afternoon and went to the hotel. My father was on the Board of Visitors at the University of Virginia and had to attend a meeting every morning. Before leaving on the first day he told me he would see Dr. Randolph and ask if I could go up and stay with his daughters while he was busy. Dr. Randolph came back to the hotel with him and said we must move to his house to stay. His daughters were a good deal older than I, but they were ideal hostesses and took me up to Monticello which was, in those days of bad roads and heavy family carriages, quite a trip, and consumed most of the day. Father could remain only three days, but he arranged for me to go with Mrs. Shackelford, the Doctor's married daughter, to Orange Court House, Virginia, where I was to spend the night and then go *alone* to Gordonsville, Virginia, about twenty miles, to visit my aunt—the one who had lived with us before her marriage and who now presided over a lovely old house, called Windsor, in Albemarle County.

It was a real adventure—going alone on a train. It proved a unique one as well, for the train plied only between the two places, and moved—or stood still—according to the courtesy and chivalry of its commander, old Captain Scott. He knew everyone, loved them all and accommodated everybody.

When Mrs. Shackelford put me on the train, she said: "Captain, this is Judge Bolling's little daughter, and I know you will take good care of her." The old gentleman took off his big white straw hat and bowed like a cavalier, saying: "As if she were my own, madam." After that, he put the straw hat up in the rack and replaced it with his badge of office, a dark *blue* cap, that being his one concession to uniform, and the train puffed its way slowly out of the station. He seated himself beside me and began to talk. When we had been going some minutes he suddenly rose and gave several vigorous pulls at a cord which ran above our heads, and the train as suddenly stopped. He stuck his head far out of the window and called to a man following a plow. When the man came near, the old Captain bawled at him: "I brought out that gear you broke yesterday, and I'll drop it off for you." They talked and joked, and after about twenty minutes we started off again on our tour. This was my first ride on a *private car and special train,* for it carried only one coach and was called "the jerkwater." I recalled it to my husband when we were making a long swing around the circle in the President's Campaign for Preparedness prior to our entry into the World War. He sighed and said: "What a lot of care and responsibilities I have brought to that little girl." I told him to be with him was worth it all, and beguiled him with describing the station at Gordonsville, as I recalled it on that first glimpse. It was full of people changing from the Richmond to the Washington train, and fortifying themselves with legs of fried chicken from the big trays that were carried on the heads of tall black negro women. Dressed in calico dresses and big white aprons the chicken vendors smiled as only darkies can smile, revealing the generous white teeth and something of the happy-go-lucky nature of the negro of the South.

Among all these new and unfamiliar faces I was glad to discover my aunt, running to welcome me as I descended from my "jerkwater special." In a trice we were in the big family carriage which lurched and swayed over heavy dirt roads through a country that seemed flat, after our mountains in southwest Virginia.

I had a lovely visit of several weeks there.

CHAPTER 2

IN the autumn of 1885, my oldest sister, Gertrude, was married to Alexander Hunter Galt, of Washington, D. C. On my fifteenth birthday I went off to boarding school—to Martha Washington College, in Abingdon, Virginia. This school was chosen because I was eager to learn music, and an excellent teacher was there. The professor was a friend of my oldest brother, Rolfe, then in a bank in Abingdon.

The school was under the direction of a man whom Dickens could have chosen for the head of Dotheboys Hall and been content to take as the epitome of all that was narrow, cruel and bigoted. He starved us almost to death, and gave us no heat in our bedrooms, or in the music rooms, where our fingers became so stiff with cold they would refuse to strike the keys.

As I had never been to school except to my grandmother, the routine and endless restraints were difficult, but I worked awfully hard. In spite of this, and the undernourishment, I grew apace. When I went home for the Christmas holidays, I had shot up like Jack's beanstalk until everything I wore was too short. I got a new grey silk Henrietta dress whose long tight-fitting lines so emphasized my slenderness that the girls called me the grey spider. The following June when I came home again I had reached my present stature of five feet, nine inches. I was then nearly sixteen, and on the threshold of my first serious love affair.

The man was about thirty-eight. He had come to Wytheville during the winter, representing some Northern capitalists. He was a New Yorker and had money. He kept fine horses and entertained in a much more elaborate style than our modest townspeople were accustomed to. I met him on the first night of my arrival at home. He had come to call on my older sister, and, as he told me afterwards, fell in love with me as soon as I entered the room. From that time on I saw or heard from him every day. I was still such a child that, at

13

first, I thought his gifts of candy and flowers, and his moonlight picnics on top of the mountain, where we all went in old-time hacks, represented merely acts of kindness of an older man to a child. For to sixteen, thirty-eight looks very old.

I did not go back to school the next winter because I was so thin and so subject to terrible colds that I was directed to stay at home and live out in the open air. By Christmas I began to realize that a new element had come into my life, and that romances were not all in books. Of course it was an imitation love, and I wonder now why my father and mother worried over it, for it was nothing but a fascination on my part, though desperately serious on the man's.

In the spring I again visited my aunt in eastern Virginia, which visit was broken by another exciting and unexpected trip, this time to Richmond. The equestrian statue of General Robert E. Lee was to be unveiled in Richmond on Decoration Day, I think it was, and his old soldiers had been asked to come and march, wearing the old Confederate grey uniforms. My aunt's husband, General Field, was to go. His old uniform was brushed and pressed and we drove into town three miles to see him off. About the station the crowd was dense, and special trains, like troop trains, were going through every few minutes with bands playing and flags waving, and every inch of space taken up, and not even standing room left, for it seemed that the entire South was going to pay this tribute to its loved leader. As I have said before, my aunt was the General's second wife, and as young as his children. She became more and more enthusiastic as the trainloads of friends passed—all calling out to us that we had better come along.

After we had waited three hours, a train arrived in which some space was still to be had. When the General was ready to get on, he said: "Well, madam [as he always called my aunt], I wish you were going along." To the surprise of everyone she answered: "Well, I am." Then she turned to me and said: "Come on and go with me. We can buy some toothbrushes and dream robes in Richmond. We must not miss this historic occasion." All I needed was a word, and in another minute we were off. She got a seat on the train, but I stood up all the way. When we reached Richmond the General went off to join his regiment which was quartered as guests of the city. My aunt and I found every hotel packed, and absolutely nowhere to sleep.

Moreover it was piping hot, and carriages could not be had at any price. We went into the first shop to buy a parasol. The only one left was flaming red, and so we bought that and started out again. We had gone a block when a familiar voice said, "Well, where did you-all come from?" We turned to find an old friend who had visited us in Wytheville, and who took us right to her lovely old-fashioned cool house on the Hill, where we stayed three days.

This was my first visit to a city, and it seemed to me a seething mass of humanity and distractions.

The next winter I went off to school again, this time to Powell's School in Richmond, where I had a very happy year and where, in two months, I had entirely recovered from my fascination and entered heart and soul into anything that came along.

The school was small—only about thirty girls as boarders. My roommate was Lucy Day, who afterwards married Senator Tom Martin of Virginia, and in the room next us were Maria Lee Evans, of South Carolina, who married Senator Gary of that State, and Mamie Fauntleroy from Virginia. We four formed the closest friendship, which has lasted ever since, though the circle has been broken by the death of Mrs. Martin.

To any girl who had the good fortune to go to Powell's School I need not tell of the privileges all had, for it was like one big family, and Mr. Powell was father, counsellor and comrade to each of us. Everything was on the honour system. No teacher was permitted to spy or report on any girl, and the *esprit de corps* was so fine that a girl who broke a rule would almost invariably admit it at Saturday morning "Confession." This rite was held immediately after breakfast in the Study Hall. Mr. Powell acted as high priest, and I can see him now seated at the end of the room in a big chair, holding on his lap the Book of Roll Call. With all of us facing him from our desks, he would call each name from A to Z, and instead of saying "Present" we would call out the offences we had committed during the week; and woe betide the girl who said "Nothing to confess" if the rest of us knew it to be untrue!

For small oversights, such as leaving lights burning in practise rooms, or failing to put things in order, we were usually only admonished; but for holding midnight parties, cutting Study Hall, or real defiance of reasonable laws, we had to pay in various ways.

Before the end of the school year, I think early in May, we were thrown into the deepest gloom when Mr. Powell was so badly injured in a streetcar accident that a leg had to be amputated. We were all told to pack and leave as quickly as possible, as his life hung in the balance. It was a personal sorrow to each of us, for we all loved him, and the first great sorrow to touch my happy, carefree life. I recall now the ache and helplessness that seemed to grip each one of us as we tiptoed about that silent house, hoping, yet fearing, to meet the doctors and nurses, lest they tell us of the lost fight.

When I left, I did not realize that I was leaving my school days behind. But so it proved, for the next winter there were the three younger boys to be sent to school, and the expense was too great for me to have another year away.

That winter I visited my married sister who lived in Washington, D. C., and spent four months with her. A new world was opened to me. I had never before been to the opera, and very little to the theatre. Through many good friends of hers we went several times a week, and I was fascinated by the glamour of it. Just the week before I was to go home, Adelina Patti came to Albaugh's Opera House for only one night. Both my sister and I felt we could not stand it not to go. But the tickets were five dollars apiece, which we could not afford, and our one hope was that someone would ask us as his guests. But the days passed and no one did, and finally—on the date itself—we gave up all hope.

My sister's house was on G Street, between Nineteenth and Twentieth, where, instead of a streetcar, there was what was known as the Herdic Line. The herdics were long vehicles, like busses, with a door in the back and seats along the sides, and were drawn by over-worked, lean old horses. The driver was the conductor as well, and beside him was a little box for the fares. If a passenger wanted change there was a slit like a letter box through which he poked his bill, and the horses were jerked to a standstill while the driver searched through various pockets to extract the proper change. This process greatly impeded the progress of the vehicle and therefore no schedule could be counted on.

I have explained these details in order to visualize for you the heartbreaking delay which attended my rapture when I was, at the last minute, really invited to hear Patti. We were at dinner, and I had been for a long walk, getting in too late to change my dress. I had on a dark green plaid cloth which I had worn as a school dress the year before. The telephone rang and a friend of my brother-in-law said two tickets had just been given him. He wanted me to have one and his wife the other—if I could join them in ten minutes; otherwise they could not wait, for all Washington would be there and we could not get in. I flew on wings of happiness to get my coat. My sister said, "You certainly are not going in that worsted dress when everybody else will be in full evening attire." I replied, "I certainly am, for no one knows me and I don't care anything about that if I can only hear Patti." So my brother-in-law said, "Well, come on," and we rushed to catch the herdic. It seemed ages before one came lumbering along. Then it stopped at every block for passengers, none of whom ever had the right change and we would have to wait for the usual search to be made by the driver for coins.

At last we reached the corner where our friends were waiting. We ran the two intervening blocks, for the announcement had been made that no one would be allowed to enter after eight o'clock. But—we got there, and literally had to be pushed through the crowds. Our seats were in the front row, and reaching them was an adventure. When we turned to face that brilliant audience I am afraid my friend was a little ashamed of me in my dark school dress, for she had on evening clothes. But I laughed and told her I should never be seen, and I am sure I never was—as I sat there in a world of my own, drinking in the liquid, exquisite notes of the "Jewel Song" from *Faust,* "Coming Thro' the Rye" and "The Last Rose of Summer."

I got back home in a sort of dream, to find my sister, her husband and Norman Galt, a cousin of the latter, sitting around the dining-room table having a chafing-dish supper of oysters. It was a shock to me to think of anyone being able to eat when there was so much beauty in the world that I had been living in.

I know now that I was still very much of a child, for it did not occur to me that Norman Galt's frequent visits were in any way due to his interest in me. He was about nine years my senior, but he seemed much older, and I never gave him a thought. He sent me flowers and candy; but I was used to that—as all Southern girls were—and felt it only a natural attention. When I was going back home, he said he was thinking of coming down to Virginia in the summer, with my sister and her husband. I said: "Why don't you? I think you would enjoy it." I meant that and nothing more. I knew he was very lonely at home, for his mother had died a few months before, and he and his father lived alone in a big brownstone house on H Street, where we had been for very formal dinners, and where the sense of loss and sorrow still lingered.

He did come that summer. The next winter I went back to Washington, but not until I had been there two months did I realize that Norman was in love with me. We were the best of friends, and I liked him immensely, but I did not want to marry anyone. However, his patience and persistence overcame me, and after four years of close and delightful friendship we were married, and I went to Washington to live.

We stayed with his father until we could afford a house of our own. We got a tiny one, but all we wanted, and there we spent six very happy years. We were so ecstatic over it, because it was our own, that Norman's father always spoke of it as "the Palace," and came often to see how "the Palace" was getting on.

We moved in the day before Thanksgiving, with all our things in place, and my father and mother arrived in time to take the first meal with us, and see all the simple but sweet furnishings—with the *new* still on them. All my family were devoted to Norman, and no one could have been lovelier than he to each and every one of them. He was sound in his judgments, and unfailing in his eagerness to help the younger boys and do everything he could for anyone I loved.

The first year there was hardly a cloud on our horizon. But when we had been married less than two years, death claimed first Norman's brother-in-law, a delightful man, and then, in twenty-four hours, his father. These two deaths were quickly followed by the hopeless invalidism of Norman's oldest brother, Charlie, who was a bachelor and for whom Norman assumed all responsibility. Then my own adored father died very suddenly, and his going left a void in my life that still throbs with pain. To every one of us he was not only a father, but a comrade—who shared our joys and sorrows, who understood our complexities, and taught us all we knew of *fine* principles and real Christianity. From my earliest recollection, he had never been too greatly occupied to listen and to help us in any-

EDITH BOLLING, AGE 13

thing, great or small. We went to him with childish troubles, and, as we grew older, sought his advice on graver things. Our love affairs were always confided to him, and when we were grown and went to parties, it was he who sat up for us until two or three in the morning. In winter he always had a big open fire blazing a welcome to us, and we would all sit around it and tell him of the things that had happened.

The reason Mother could not share these cozy talks was that all day she watched over us and kept things going in a household where there were nine children, an invalid grandmother and endless guests who used to visit for weeks or months at a time. So Father kept the watch at night, and if we were not going out he would read aloud to us—Dickens, Shakespeare or some book of the day. On such occasions we usually met in my grandmother's room where, with the candlestand by him on which stood the student's lamp he had used at the University of Virginia, Father in a big chair unfolded to us this world wherein Shylock demanded his pound of flesh, or Hamlet soliloquized, or Jack Bunsby told Captain Cuttle "she'd capter him agen," or dear old Betsey Trotwood seemed to sweeten life with her own wholesome personality. Grandmother would knit as he read, and I always associate his beautiful voice with the click of the fine steel needles.

My father was one of the few good readers I have ever heard. We were all Episcopalians, and he was the lay reader at our little church, where everyone used to ask: "Is Judge Bolling going to read the service on Sunday? Because, if he is, I don't want to miss it." When I was a tiny child the rector was threatened with tuberculosis and advised to go farther south for a year. He came to Father, as everyone did when in trouble, and said he did not know how he and his young wife would live without the church salary. Father said he himself would keep the church open for a year, and would send the rector his salary just the same. He did this, in addition to all his own work, reading sermons that famous men had preached. Moreover he continued the elementary religious instruction of us children at home. Father believed Sunday School a splendid thing but not intended for children who could be taught at home. We were always taught in groups of three, and, when the oldest one was confirmed, the third was just as well prepared. So it happened that when my brother Will was fourteen, and ready for confirmation, I was ready to be presented to the Bishop at the age of nine.

When the list was given to Bishop Whittle he said I was too young, and could not be included in the class. But he said he would like to see me to tell me this himself. So I was sent for, and with beating heart I went. I was small for my age. The old Bishop, looking very austere, took me in his lap and began his questions. Alas, if I were asked them today, I could not answer half of them. But then, owing to my father's teaching, the Bishop could not stump me. Finally he put me down and said: "Tell your father, little girl, you are the best prepared candidate I have examined, and I *want* you in the class tomorrow."

All this gives an idea of what the death of such a father meant to us; in addition was the sorrow of breaking up our old home which had never been closed for a day in thirty-odd years and which up to that time had seemed to me as fixed as the planets.

But Mother said she could not stay there without Father. Grandmother had died a few months before and we were all married or away except my sister Bertha and the two younger boys. So, after Father was laid to rest, Annie Lee, Wilmer and I stayed in Wytheville long enough to tear up the roots of our old home. The blood of our own hearts dropped with them.

This was in July, 1899, and, when I got back to Washington, Mother and Bertha came to visit us. In the winter they went to stay with Annie Lee, who lived in Tennessee, and my youngest brother, Julian, came to us to go to school for a year. The following year Mother moved to Bridgeport, Connecticut, to make a home for Randolph, Wilmer and Julian, who were in business there. They took a small house on Fairfield Avenue where all the old things from Virginia were transplanted and where for five years they made a centre around which we all gathered whenever we could and found much happiness in being together again. However, the climate was severe in winter, and despite the unfailing kindness of their new friends, Mother longed for the South. As Washington was the home of Gertrude, my oldest sister, as well as myself, they all came there, and Norman gave all the boys places in his jewelry business, known for over a hundred years as Galt's. He was then the sole owner.

I have not yet given a picture of my gentle mother. She was very lovely physically, and had the purest spirit I have ever known. Her presence was a benediction, and no one ever heard her say an unkind thing. I always think of her when I read "Charity suffereth long and is kind," for she lived that precept every hour of her life. She was married before she was eighteen. My father being older, and she of a timid nature, from the first she deferred to him in everything. But after a decision was made, she stood by it with all the loyalty and gallantry of a trained soldier carrying out the commanding officer's directions.

She had in all eleven children, and raised to maturity nine of us. All this was done with the slenderest means, with inadequate servants, and despite personal privations. But *she* was always adequate, and radiantly happy. She and my father were necessarily apart a great deal, for he was much absent from home, first as judge of the Circuit Court, and then as attorney for the Norfolk & Western Railroad Company. They never failed to bridge the distance with daily letters, and I have often seen Mother with a baby on her lap, and another tiny child at her knee, seated at a table, or beside a windowsill, writing her daily letter in a beautiful round hand, each character formed as though for engraving.

She and my grandmother made nearly everything we all wore. How the old Domestic sewing machine used to spin under Mother's tiny foot on the treadle! She would sing as she sewed, and was never too busy to stop and help us with French or music or anything except arithmetic or algebra. On these subjects she would say: "Wait until your father comes. I never bothered with figures."

She was educated when young ladies played the guitar, read French, embroidered and sang to the accompaniment of the harpsichord.

From this sheltered, busy life, with the care of a big house, she came to Washington to a small apartment with nothing to do, and with only her memories to haunt the empty days. But she never repined, only saying that she would have to depend on us now that Father was gone, and we must not expect her to decide things, for it made her nervous and unhappy. And it was to us all the greatest privilege to shield her and her gentle spirit from anything that chilled or wounded it.

Three years passed and then, in January, 1908, after a brief illness my husband died, and I was left with an active business either to maintain or to liquidate, upon which all of my income was dependent. I had had no experience in business affairs, and hardly knew an asset from a liability. My husband had not even had the business all by himself long enough to pay off his indebtedness to his father's estate and his uncle from whom he had bought it, and to the brother whose share he also had bought.

I was immediately faced with the decision whether to continue the business alone, take in a partner, or close it up for what I could get. Aside from my own problems, there was the responsibility I felt to employees who had been with the firm for twenty or thirty years. Also there were my own three brothers, who would be without positions, and on whom Mother and my sister Bertha, who was unmarried, depended for contributions to their support. I spent sleepless nights, not knowing which was the wise course to take, and having, moreover, much advice from friends and relatives, no two of whom ever gave the same counsel.

Amid this mass of confused opinion, I decided to pin my faith to the man who had served my husband and his father, and had been a faithful steward. His name was Henry Christian Bergheimer. I am proud to acknowledge here the debt I owe to him, for he dedicated all that was in him to me and my service, and by his own integrity and ability steered my ship through difficult waters that were often muddied by criticism and lack of co-operation from those who served under him.

I made him manager, without bond, and tried to learn from him, instead of interfering with his authority. In all of this I was advised and guided by Mr. Nathaniel Wilson, who was not only my lawyer but my honoured and valued friend, and to whom too I wish to pay a tribute of affection and grateful admiration.

With these two staunch allies I decided to continue the business, and for many years we three worked together. My own part was small, for it consisted chiefly in holding up the hands of my advisers. But we had long and technical conferences, and I was kept in touch with the conduct of everything—with all we made and all we owed; and I set for myself the minimum amount I could live on and never exceeded it, in order to leave every cent in the business until we had paid for it. Mr. Bergheimer did exactly the same thing, paying himself a nominal salary, and saying he did not deserve any more until the business could make it.

The name of Galt's on a piece of paper had always been as good as a bond. We were offered all the credit we wanted, both from banks and from business houses from whom we bought goods. But credit meant paying interest on money borrowed, so we did not take it, except to save discounts on bills, and thus kept our friends and our independence and asked no favours.

I continued to live in the house at 1308 Twentieth Street, N.W., to which we had moved two years before my husband's death and which we rented from his father's estate. The house had been built by Mr. Galt, Senior, for another son when he had married many years before. Another house was built for my sister-in-law, Mrs. Reginald Fendall, by her father at the time of her marriage; and he had always said he would do the same for each of his children. But when we were married he did not feel that he could afford it. I mention this only because it is due to my husband to say that he worked for everything that was his and that the business would not have been continued but for him; it was not handed to him on a silver platter by any means.

CHAPTER 3

*A*FTER Norman's death each of my brothers and sisters offered to come and live with me, but I felt it was wiser to meet the future alone and not to disorganize their lives by making them feel my dependence. In 1910 I took my sister Bertha abroad with me. This was my third trip to Europe. We sailed on the Red Star Line for Antwerp, but had no very definite plan as to where we would go from there. On the boat we met some very nice people, Mr. and Mrs. Fessenden, from Connecticut, who told us they were going to a little town called Middelburg, in Holland, which they had heard was absolutely unknown to tourists and where you saw the simple life of the people undramatized for the travelling public. They suggested that we go with them.

As Middelburg was a comparatively short journey from Antwerp, we said we would join them there. First I wanted a little while at the delightful Hotel St. Antoine in Antwerp where I had stayed before. This pleasant place, with its courtyard where we could dine outdoors, and its excellent French cuisine and service, formed a retreat in which to rest after a sea trip, and afforded an atmosphere of quiet and dignity which I loved. You would be waked often in the early hours by the great Cathedral chimes across the way only to be lulled to sleep again by the accumulated stillness that followed the chiming of huge bells.

In Middelburg we found our friends of the boat, and to our delight we four were the only guests in the hotel excepting native people who had come for the great annual event of the Week of Butter Market. The big open square that formed the lungs of the village was transformed into a great mart, with stalls or booths where rosy-cheeked Dutch women, wearing a sort of yoke across their shoulders from which polished brass scales were suspended by long chains, sold rolls of golden butter weighed thus on their own sturdy shoulders. They wore full black skirts, tight bodices and half sleeves so snug-fitting that it seemed as if their strong arms would burst through. Their little caps were of white net or lace, with elaborate gold pins pendant over their ears. The costumes were completed by wooden sabots which made a clang unlike any other sound I have ever heard.

In the centre of all this activity was a street merry-go-round—the wonder and delight of the children. As to dress, the little girls were small replicas of their mothers and the cutest little things one ever saw—so shy they clung to one another's hands until they formed long queues of dimpled, happy faces under their fascinating white caps. When we treated them to a ride on the merry-go-round, the contraption did not stay put long enough to get all the babies aboard before it would start again. With half of them on the revolving disc and half on the ground, they would not let go one another's hands—the result being a succession of little black figures rolling off, round-eyed and amazed, but never crying; rather up and at it again on the next round.

Certainly I think that village was the model for the advertisement of Spotless Town. At the Grand Hotel, where we stayed, everything but the frame of the bed was removed from our rooms to the garden each day for an all-day airing. The floors were waxed and polished every day, windows washed, and all linen fresh. As we were literally *cleaned* out of the rooms for the day, we had much time to observe our neighbors in the little street outside—the main street of the town on which the shops and better residences faced. Here every morning the entire fronts of the houses were scoured by hand with soap and water; all signs, such as drugstores and barber shops have, were taken down and scoured. The cleansing process was completed late in the afternoon by a corps of women who got down on their knees and washed the cobblestones one by one. Do you wonder that we stayed six days to witness this remarkable performance—wondering if it could go on day after day, or if it were done only to impress us; and, if the latter, trying to tire them out? But our friends had been there a week ahead of us and said it was certainly the daily custom of that unique little town, and so we finally had to leave them to their spotless fate and carry with us only another memory of a privileged experience.

From Middelburg we went to Munich where we found the hotels packed with tourists on account of the Passion Play, and every hotel charging a fixed rate far in excess of the normal one. We wanted to stay several weeks for the music and beauty of the wonderful city, but we did not want to present most of our money to the hotel proprietors. So we looked up the address of Frau Glocker, of whose pension we had heard good report. It was just beyond the Vierjahreszeiten Hotel, and well located on the Maximilian Strasse. There were four long flights of stairs to mount, with no lift, but, when we presented ourselves to Frau Glocker, we were distressed to learn she had not *"eine Betl"* left in the house. The old lady was a character, and the place homelike and attractive, and we felt it would be a real experience to become her paying guests. As we were eager to stay we asked if she knew any other place she could recommend. She apparently liked us, too, but had the idea that, being Americans, we would not be satisfied with simple surroundings. So she hesitatingly suggested that if we would not mind *very* simple rooms she might be able to take care of us across the street where she had rented an apartment over the theatre and put Frau Sopher, her housekeeper, in charge. She said we could come over to her apartment for meals; and that if we were content with this, we could each have a single room, opposite a large bathroom. Few people took baths, she said; and added that on account of the water tax, she had to charge a mark, or twenty-five cents, for a bath. If we would pay that it would be really like a private bath. The room and three meals would be seven marks, or a dollar and seventy-five cents, apiece a day, the mark extra for a bath making it two dollars.

So we crossed to the Schauspielhaus and rang a bell at a huge door beside the main entrance, and awaited our fate, which appeared in the form of dear old Frau Sopher who for weeks after was to be our willing slave, friend and adviser. When, from her own immaculate rooms on the ground floor, she touched a button which released the great doors, we saw a winding stone stairway, apparently having no end, as it coiled up and up. She welcomed us with ceremonial dignity and said her mistress had telephoned her to show us the rooms, which, after we climbed up one hundred or more steps, she did. They were neat and foreign-looking, the outstanding furniture being enormous porcelain stoves built in stacks for the heat to radiate through. They resembled nothing so much as a succession of white trays decreasing in size as they ascended, and the total effect was like some gigantic tombstone—which was not a very gay suggestion. But we didn't mind. Besides the stoves there were just the essentials—bed, washstand, table, and a mirror on the wall; by the stove a clothespress and two chairs. It was all so clean it shone. When we were established I found my stove invaluable for, by putting a folded towel in the trays, I used them for all my toilet requirements, and found it a sort of game to locate each thing as I needed it.

Frau Sopher did not speak a word of anything but German, but in that she was educated far beyond her class in this country. She could discuss the German authors and poets—Heine being her favourite—with real appreciation. She adored my sister, who spoke excellent German, having been taught by my aunt who, as I said early in this narrative, married a German and afterwards maintained herself by teaching his mother tongue.

My own German was sketchy, but I could understand a good deal, and when Sopher would knock on my door each morning and say: *"Der Bad ist bereit,"* I knew I would find the bath just the right temperature, with plenty of towels on hand.

After a few days she told us it was no trouble to give us breakfast in our rooms, and thus save us the long descent and ascent on Glocker's side. So from then on she brought us dainty trays of her own pretty china, with hot dripped coffee, toast and eggs, or *Schinken* (ham) broiled just to a crispy toothsomeness.

We went to the opera which began at four in the afternoon, and had an intermission of an hour for dinner, to resume and last until ten o'clock. On these days when we got back we always found a tempting cold supper awaiting us, prepared by the same faithful old hands.

Even though we were together, it was a real adventure to return to our sky parlours over the theatre, for we would get a cab and say to the driver: *"Die Schauspielhaus, Maximilian Strasse."* The driver would look at us pityingly, as though we were crazy Americans, and say: *"Ach nein, es ist sehr spät."* My sister would reply in her best German: "Yes, we know, but we live there." Then I am convinced he would conclude we were indeed crazy, and the best thing to do was to humour us before we became violent. So we would proceed. Arriving we would dismount, produce a key big enough to have opened the Bastille, and approach the forbidding door—always conscious of the amazed gaze of the cabby. The door would open and one tiny electric light would go on. We would get inside, locking the great doors behind us, and be in the eerie light which only emphasized the inky darkness beyond its feeble ray. But with true Teutonic thoroughness the thing was perfectly worked out mechanically for, as we climbed up the steps, where the light grew faintest we would find a button on the wall which, when pressed, lighted another bulb ahead and extinguished the one below; and so on, around the corkscrew curves, button after button lighted a beacon towards which we pressed until the journey was complete and we stood breathless, perhaps, but triumphant, before our own doors. The whole thing always reminded me of a Sunday School book given us when we were children, called *Out of Darkness into Light.* Had I been a Bunyan I could have made an allegory of this spooky groping—up, up— always following the Light. After a few days we felt more at home and arranged to go to Oberammergau for the next Sunday. When we went to make arrangements we were told that many people refused to stay at the house of Zwink because he took the part of Judas and therefore was called by that name by the townspeople. This prejudice seemed absurd, particularly as Judas' daughter, Marie, took the part of the Virgin Mary. So I said we would not hesitate to stay there.

We went on Saturday, reaching the picturesque little village late in the afternoon. It lay among the encircling hills in its simplicity and beauty. The outstanding feature of the landscape was the great peak that outstrips those around it, and on the point of which flamed a gigantic cross of light, giving to the stranger who approached in religious mood a suggestion of the sensations of the Wise Men as they followed the Star which led them to the Great Miracle in the little town of Bethlehem.

Like many others, I suppose, we approached the Passion Play with divided feelings as to whether or not it would seem sacrilegious. But as soon as one met the actors and got into the atmosphere of the town, the doubt vanished; for the people seemed dedicated and trying to shape their own lives on high principles, feeling the responsibility of being the living interpreters of reverent history.

It is twenty-eight years since that time, and yet, as I write today, the impressions are as vivid as though made yesterday. The beauty of the scenes, the harmony of music and colour as the old Bible story unfolded, form an illusion of my having lived through that time myself.

After this exalting experience Bertha and I wound up our travels with a delightful sojourn in London and sailed for home.

In the early summer of the succeeding year, 1911, occurred the death of an elderly friend, Mr. James Gordon, whose passing has had a deep effect on my life. Mr. Gordon was a picturesque Scotchman who had married in Virginia and as a mining engineer made and lost several fortunes. Before his death he had asked if I would look out for his only child, a motherless daughter of seventeen. I then knew this girl only slightly. She was lovely to look at, very intelligent and, like me, lonely. So we decided to take each other on faith and go to Europe together. We stayed five months. Thus began a friendship which has lasted through many years and many vicissitudes, unmarred by a single misunderstanding. Her name is Alice Gertrude, which girlhood chums had shortened to Altrude, and so she shall appear, and appear rather often, I imagine, in the pages of this story.

Altrude Gordon and I were not long running into a puzzling and amusing experience. Tiring of the crowds and the big hotels at Ostend and similar places, we consulted our trusty Baedeker to see if he recommended, or "starred," any small hotels or pensions in Brussels. Finding two stars accorded Bernard's Private Hotel, I telegraphed for accommodations and, receiving a favourable answer, we took a train which put us in the Belgian capital early in the afternoon.

When we drove up in a little fiacre we thought the cabman must have gone to the wrong place, for even the street seemed deserted, the blinds in all the houses being drawn and no sign of life anywhere. But when the cab drew up in front of a large house, which was apparently closed, the front door opened and a servant advanced for our luggage and assumed charge of everything. There being no lift, we were shown up two long flights of steps to the third floor where we found charming rooms overlooking a garden. They were exquisitely clean, with dainty white curtains under gay chintz, and everything homelike and comfortable. After unstrapping our bags, the butler asked in French: "At what hour will Madame have dinner?" I replied, at eight o'clock, whereupon he bowed and withdrew.

After getting freshened up, we decided we would go for a little walk and investigate our surroundings. We opened our door—for our rooms connected—and the same man was evidently waiting for us. He silently accompanied us to the front door, which he opened, and bowed us out. The house seemed full of closed doors on every side, and there was not a sound.

Deciding that we would find the other guests at dinner, we roamed around, as one loves to do in a new European city, until time to dress. When we returned to the hotel, again the front door was opened by the same ubiquitous man who bowed us a welcome.

We dressed for dinner, and at eight a tap on the door announced: *"Madame, le diner est servi."* We were escorted downstairs by our butler host and ushered into a charming little dining room opening onto the garden. One table, and one only, was set—for two. A perfect meal was served by our butler. No other guest or servant appeared. The meal over, our man opened the great doors connecting with a cozy sitting room where we found the English and American papers and magazines and where he brought us our coffee. Not another human soul appeared, and we began to wonder what sort of place this could be. We stayed downstairs until ten-thirty, when we arose to go upstairs and, before we could reach the door, it was opened from without and there stood our "shadow" waiting to precede us upstairs to open our door and bow a good night to us.

It all seemed so queer that I am not ashamed to say I decided to put the furniture against the doors during the night, for I was sure we would be bowed into bed at night and out again in the morning. The next day exactly the same order was observed, and then I felt certain that we must be in some queer place which could not be as perfect as it seemed, though the cuisine would have tempted an epicure, the service was faultless, and the whole tone of the place dignified and distinguished.

Yet I told Altrude we must stay on until we found the skeleton which must inhabit a closet behind one of those closed doors—which we passed and repassed many times each day. So we stayed for two weeks, making short daytime excursions to Bruges, Ghent, and so on, and returning to rest in what had assumed almost the aspect of our own home. For after the first few days, when the table was furnished with only ordinary china and silver, new and superb old pieces of silver appeared, and rare china and plate; and still we appeared to be the only ones to enjoy all this luxury.

At last we felt we must go on to Italy. So we notified our factotum that we would be leaving in two more days, when, to my surprise, he begged that if possible we stay until the third day, for then the proprietor would be at home and he would so like for him to see us. So we stayed—still rolling furniture against the doors every night.

When the third day arrived, and the proprietor with it, he told us he was just starting for a holiday when my telegram came. He was going to answer us to say the hotel was closed, but his head man had begged to be allowed to take us as he and the chef were to stay. The proprietor agreeing, the head man had put away all the nicer things until he saw whether or not we were of the sort to appreciate nice things. So our mystery was solved.

From there we went for lovely, dreamy weeks on Lake Como, at Belagio, where we got a boat by the day for a song and our nice old boatman would row us across the lake where we would debark and roam up the hillsides to the shrines hidden in the vineyards, or to a tiny church perched on a hilltop growing rosy pink in the setting sun. Or our boatman would take us to a tiny place for tea where we would read and lounge, while he lay in the boat smoking his pipe and smiling up at us as we sat above him on a rock.

Finally we went to Lugano and there met a Mr. and Mrs. Lombard whose home, Château Trevano, is known to many musicians and artists, and there we were offered charming hospitality. The house itself held historic interest, for there, in its white marble theatre, was given the first performance of Gounod's *Faust;* and in the same theatre the present owner conducted an orchestra of his own—for the pleasure of his friends summoned from far and near to enjoy the concerts he generously provided.

At last we drifted back to Paris, where, like most Americans, we meant to end our trip. It was early October, and we found the city full of charm and snap, with houses being opened, and the French people returning to submerge the Americans who earlier in the summer swarm in such numbers that they appear to possess the city, and certainly do possess the shops and the big couturières. Like all the rest of American femininity, Altrude and I invested almost our last penny in dresses and hats, allowing a scant margin to pay hotel bills, tips and so on before sailing in about another week. Neither of us was eager to get back to Washington and to an empty home. So when a cable came saying our business matters had been delayed until January, we decided we would stay until December, and return just in time for Christmas.

Accordingly we cabled for money to be sent through the American Express Company. Knowing our funds should arrive in two days at the most, we gaily went forward with our plans for a two months' stay.

We were then at the Crillon Hotel. We decided it was too expensive for a longer stay, however, and so found quarters at a hotel on the Rue de Rivoli. Though the move took most of our remaining capital, we engaged a French teacher to give us an hour's lesson every day, and resolved to spend certainly another hour a day in the Louvre studying the pictures. On the third day after cabling, we began to think it queer that no money had come. After that we took a cab each morning and afternoon and rode to the American Express office to see if our funds had been authorized. We soon knew the men in the banking department, and when we walked in they would immediately shake their heads and say: "Sorry, nothing today." This went on, day after day, until we began to view our diminishing assets with alarm.

We had friends to whom we could have confided our distress, but a foolish pride forbade our asking the favour of a loan. We decided to take a late breakfast, and have an early dinner, thus cutting out one meal a day; then, instead of getting cabs twice a day to go to the Express office, we went only in the early afternoon, and walked. But whether we walked or rode, the answer was the same: an unwelcome negative.

We were embarrassed by this, fearing the Express people would think us imposters. So we began going every other day, making our inquiries so casual that we hoped it would seem of small matter whether the money came or not. We next decided to have only a frugal tea in the afternoon and omit dinner. But even this economy helped little. Finally we became so sensitive towards the men at the Express office that I told Altrude she must not go there again; I would go alone and save her the mortification. So I plodded alone every other afternoon to receive my usual depressing answer until one day the clerk said he had received an inquiry from the United States Express office asking if he knew of two ladies who were expecting funds. The United States Express had had money waiting for them for two weeks, without an inquiry. The American Express official remarked that this might be the money we were expecting. I tried not to let him see the joy and relief his suggestion brought me, as I asked where the United States Express office was. When he said: "Oh, just across the way—in the next block," I think I *ran* over there and asked breathlessly if they had money waiting for two ladies— giving our names. A man said yes, those were the names, but could I get someone to identify me, and he was closing in a few minutes.

I realize now that I was very inexperienced, for I felt if he closed the office without paying me the amount, it would certainly never open again. So I said, "No, I have no one to identify me, beyond the fact that I have told you who I am. You can look at me and know that whatever I say is the truth. I must have my money tonight, though you can keep my friend's until tomorrow, when she will come for it." The man evidently decided I was too green to be a crook. "Oh, well," he said, "I'll take a chance."

That night Altrude and I celebrated the end of our spell on half rations with a *real* dinner at Voisin's.

Often since we have laughed over the days in Paris when we were too poor to buy a meal, and munched cakes of chocolate to keep up our strength and courage.

The next summer—1912—I was abroad again, with my sister Bertha. That was a Presidential election year, but so little was my interest in political affairs that I could hardly have told who the candidates were. I was in Paris on election day, and when the local papers announced the victory of Wilson and Marshall I was glad because the Democrats had won, but beyond the fact that they were Democrats, Messrs. Wilson and Marshall were little more than names to me.

The night after the election we had some guests to dine at Prunier's, the famous fish restaurant. Among them were a Mr. and Mrs. X., formerly of Princeton, where Mr. X. had been a professor under Woodrow Wilson. Naturally the assembled company singled him out to ask many questions of the President-Elect and his family.

Mr. X's responses were not flattering. In fact, said Mr. X., so little did he admire Woodrow Wilson as president of Princeton that he, X., had left the University on that account. Nor did he seem to like Mr. Wilson's daughters much better than he did their father.

If the reader will pardon me I shall now jump ahead of my story. Some eighteen months after the dinner at Prunier's I was driving in Washington with Mr. Wilson and his daughter Margaret. This was shortly after our first meeting. I laughed and told them that I had heard some very unflattering things said of them by a man they used to know. Then I mentioned his last name, and Mr. Wilson quickly said, "You don't mean so and so"—giving his full name. I said, "Yes." He asked: "Why, where in the world did you know him?" I told then how we had met Mr. X. and his wife in Paris and how kind they had been to us, and he said: "Oh, I see; well, his wife is a fine woman and I am sure you enjoyed her."

Years passed and in the early part of the submarine tragedies of the World War this same man, his wife and daughter were passengers on the *Sussex* when it was torpedoed. The daughter was injured. Another daughter, married and living in Washington, appealed to me for information concerning her family. Mr. Wilson sent personal messages for detailed reports of these particular passengers, and asked that everything possible be done for their relief. We kept the daughter in constant touch with them through the State Department. The girl was grateful and understanding. Not so the father. He sent a hostile cablegram to Mr. Wilson, demanding that Germany pay for its destruction of American life.

Now to go back to the dinner in Paris. What Mr. X. said about Woodrow Wilson interested me, and I have always wondered why. I had no interest in Princeton, and little interest in whoever might be President of the United States. Permanent residents of Washington, who are not in politics, are likely to acquire that rather unusual state of mind. Having seen a number of Presidents—at a distance, of course—I did not have the interest that would be normal to a person living in a part of the country where a President is a rare sight. Still, as I say, I was sufficiently stirred by Mr. X.'s recital to recall the one and only time I had ever laid eyes on Woodrow Wilson.

It was in Philadelphia, I think, in the year 1909. My sister, two friends and I were staying at the Bellevue-Stratford for a few days.

As we left the dining room after dinner one evening, the hotel manager had bowed to us, saying: "I wonder if you ladies would be interested in looking in the ballroom for a few minutes. The president of Princeton University is addressing the alumni at a Princeton dinner. I cannot take you in, but you can look through the door." That was my first glimpse of Woodrow Wilson.

CHAPTER 4

*R*ETURNING from abroad early in November, 1912, I found the newspapers filled with articles about the President-Elect, his family, his writings and so on. What is more, I found an ardent Wilson partisan right in the family. My sister-in-law, Annie Litchfield (Mrs. Rolfe E. Bolling), had read and studied everything she could find about the new leader. She had been at the Baltimore convention all day and every day and night, had worked in the campaign, and was altogether absorbed in the man, the Party and the platform—to such an extent that I, fresh from Europe and uninformed of all these vital particulars which she had at her finger tips, found her a little boring!

By and by, March blew itself in, and Annie Litchfield returned to visit me during the week of the Inauguration.

She talked nothing but Wilson, Wilson, Wilson—until, in desperation, I would get a copy of *The New Freedom,* a compilation of the President-Elect's speeches, read it aloud to her and ask how she thought such and such things could be accomplished? She had so studied every word that all she needed was a question to set her going. I wish I could recall some of her eloquence.

On the morning of March 4, 1913, she was up early, ready to start for a long day "down on the Avenue," and could not believe her ears when I said I was going to stay quietly at home; that I had seen both McKinley's and Roosevelt's Inaugurations, and that they were all alike. "All alike!" she snapped. "This is a Democrat, and a great man. I'd go even if I had to stand on the sidewalk in the crowd. The idea—when you have that wonderful balcony of your own, at Galt's—not to go!" I felt that I had sunk in her estimation, and would have to do something to reinstate myself, and the very next night my opportunity to do so came unexpectedly.

She and I were alone at dinner, and I happened to pick up the evening paper. My eye caught a headline. "Listen," I said, "the *Star*

36

says the President and his party will go to the theatre tonight."
Thereupon my sister-in-law answered: "Well, then, so will we."
"But," I said, "it does not say which theatre—and we have no tickets."
"Never mind," was her sturdy response; "I'll telephone the *Star* and
find out."

Dinner was forgotten while the newspaper office was called, but
alas! they said they could not give out such information. She was
furious but, nothing daunted, she said: "Very well, I will call the
Baltimore *Sun;* I know those men and they will tell me if they
know."

The *Sun* did not have the information but promised to call the
press room at the White House and, if they learned anything, to call
us back. It was eight o'clock when the telephone rang, and the word
came: "The National Theatre, to see Billie Burke." My little electric
car was at the door, and in two minutes we were in it, rounding
Dupont Circle. Those were the good old days of quiet streets, with
little traffic, and as I parked the car near the main entrance of the
theatre the police held up their billies in salute, since the White House
car was approaching.

We rushed in, and I told Annie I would ask the doorkeeper whom
I knew to let her inside the house where she could see the President
arrive while I tried to get some tickets. The old fellow at the ticket
window, who had been there for years, entered into my anxiety to
buy tickets "for an out-of-town friend" who was eager to see the
President. He gave me two seats right under the Presidential box,
and we got into our places while the audience stood awaiting his
coming.

That evening one of the audience saw nothing of the play, for
Annie unblushingly turned to face the box and, as I told her, stared so
at her hero I thought he was bored, for he looked tired and retreated
behind his programme several times for a good yawn.

On our return home, my guest definitely hinted that before her
visit was over she would have a great surprise for me; and, sure
enough, on the following Saturday she came down to breakfast
waving a letter triumphantly in the air. "Now see what I have done
for my skeptical hostess," she cried. "I have arranged for you to meet
the President. After that I know you will rave over him as much as I
do." Continuing, she said: "I wrote to him and said I was only in

Washington for a brief time; that I had worked for him during the campaign, and was an ardent admirer, and could I bring a friend and just pay my respects to him at the office. Here is a letter from Mr. Tumulty giving me an appointment for two o'clock today, and *I* will take you." "Not if I know it," was my unappreciative answer. "I have lived in Washington seventeen years and never been inside the White House. Why should I bother a tired, busy man to shake hands with me? I would feel like an idiot going in there." "Are you really serious?" she asked incredulously. "And do you mean you will not take me down there?" "Of course I will take you down, and ride round the block while you go in. I have tickets to take you to the matinée at Poli's, so it will fit in beautifully."

To her disgust I stuck to my plan, and conveyed her, in her best bib and tucker, to the steps of the Executive Offices; then circled the block, as far as Fifteenth Street, where the crossing policeman always held up the traffic for me, allowing me to cross, and giving me a salute.

While my sister-in-law is making her momentous call may I relate a little story about this same crossing police official? He had been stationed for years at Fifteenth Street and Pennsylvania Avenue. I was the first woman in Washington to own and drive an electric car and this policeman constituted himself my special protector and guide. So we had become firm "bowing acquaintances." I did not even know his name until years later when I was living in the White House. There I got a pathetic letter from him, recalling the many times he "had held up things for me at Fifteenth Street," and saying he had been sent " 'way over northeast" where he *never* saw *me* (the subtlety of this compliment!), and would I not like to have him guard me at the White House.

The letter was so naïve, and the man had always been so courteous to me, that I took it to my husband, to know if it was all right for me to recommend him for a transfer. I knew how Mr. Wilson detested people trying to get jobs by influence in place of merit; so I was surprised when he said, with a twinkle in his eye: "I think you could write to Major Pullman [then Chief of Police] and put before him the qualifications of your man—that he let pretty ladies break laws at dangerous crossings, etc.—for the force sadly needs such a cavalier." Then he added: "You can tell him I will feel safer here

Left to right: Edith Bolling, holding parasol; Annie Lee Bolling; Mrs. Rolfe
E. Bolling, a sister-in-law; Bertha Bolling. Photograph made in Wytheville, Va.,
summer of 1890.

with such a disinterested guardian, and be glad to see him appointed, if consistent with his record." He *was* appointed, and, years after when, as a private citizen, I would drive to the White House to leave a card, I would solemnly be saluted by my old friend, smart in his blue uniform and shiny brass buttons.

But to return to that afternoon in March, 1913. A little after two o'clock I picked up my outraged guest and took her to the matinée. She could talk of nothing but her interview with the President, and of my inexplicable attitude.

The spring of the following year this same Wilson enthusiast visited me again, at the time Sir Moses Ezekiel's beautiful memorial to the Confederate dead was to be unveiled in Arlington Cemetery. The President was to make the address. Annie Litchfield was a member of the United Daughters of the Confederacy, under whose auspices the ceremony was held. The afternoon of the unveiling came with every promise of good weather, until people began to crowd into the grounds of Arlington, the lovely old home place of our beloved General Lee. Ominous clouds suddenly appeared, and great peals of thunder rolled back and forth, accompanied by a high wind that seemed to gain new strength as the clouds got blacker and blacker. All would have been well, and the ceremonies finished before the storm broke, had not an overzealous chairman, who was to introduce the President, felt that the world was waiting for the words that were dropping from his lips. He spoke for a full hour. As I had only my little open electric chariot, and the wind was strong enough to sweep away so light a car, I urged that we leave and try to make shelter before we were drenched. But no; the President was to speak. "Wild horses could not tear me away until I hear him," said my guest. "But," she considerately urged, "you go, and I will come back with friends." I therefore left, and got home just before there was literally a cloudburst, and wind so strong that tops were ripped from automobiles and many light cars overturned.

Hours passed, when finally my anxiety regarding my sister-in-law's fate was relieved by her return; but I cannot picture her state of wreck! She had gone out in spring array—new crêpe dress, lace hat with wreath of pink roses, and a large boa of crisp tulle, a new and smart accessory of that season. Alas! The crêpe dress had shrunk nearly three inches, showing a petticoat that had *stretched,* dropping low underneath. The hat was like a bathtub, and the roses, now white, floated in a sort of saucer that the crown formed, and each rose was a little cup of rain water. The tulle boa was a flat, sticky mass, a pitiful halo for a face down which little streams trickled. Her shoes were soaked and muddy. When I exclaimed at her appearance the answer was: "Well, I heard him, and it was worth it all!"

That night she and I were going to the Corcoran Art Gallery to a reception given in honour of Sir Moses. So we had to have a hasty dinner, to be ready to start. When she went to change before dinner we found that even her stays were dripping wet. She had brought no others with her, and mine would not answer. My faithful old Susie was summoned from her kitchen and told to heat irons, and while we were at dinner the stays were ironed as dry as possible.

How many times we have laughed over these irresponsible days— and how far back they seem!

As I have told about the times I did not meet the President, or hear him speak, it is only fair to own that I did hear and see him once after a definite effort on my part. It was the first time that he addressed the two Houses of Congress in joint session. Of course this created tremendous interest, for it had not been done since the days of John Adams—the usual custom being to send a written message which the Clerks of the House and Senate droned out.

But even the unusual ceremony did not prepare us for the tremendous throngs of people who stormed the Capitol for admission. My dear mother having said a day or so before that she would like to go, I had airily replied: "Well, I will take you, with the greatest pleasure, and we will get Hunter to get us tickets." Hunter was my oldest sister's husband, and for years had been a court reporter. Strange to say, Hunter did get two tickets; but his wife also wanted to go, and two tickets would not admit three persons. However, I volunteered to take them up and if there was a crowd I would not go in, but wait outside. In this nonchalant fashion we joined the marching throng in the corridors and finally arrived at the door of the House gallery, some twenty minutes before it was opened.

On duty was a nice old doorkeeper who kept begging people not to crowd, but to wait patiently until the door was opened. As my mother was not able to stand long, I asked him if he would not like to give her his chair while he was standing trying to control the crowd. He said, "Certainly," and, after thanking him, I offered him some candy. At this he looked at me with a skeptical eye, and said: "Lady, have you got a ticket to get in here or are you trying to wheedle me into letting you in without one?" This was a new point of view, for the candy was offered in appreciation of his courtesy to Mother. But I saw what he meant and told him frankly that I did *not* have a ticket; that the other two ladies did, and that I was not trying to corrupt him, but intended staying outside to wait for my friends—so he could take the candy with a clear conscience, for it was in no sense a bribe.

He took it. Just then the signal was given to open the doors. The old doorkeeper looked at me, and then beyond, at the hundreds of people crowding behind us. In the same quizzical tone he said: "How are you going to stay *out* with that crowd pushing you *in* the minute these doors open?" With that he opened them, and we were swept in, and on, and on, to the very front where in the gallery on the right side I found myself next to the big clock on the front row, immediately above the Speaker's rostrum. In a few minutes I was looking down on the tall, slender figure of Woodrow Wilson, President of the United States.

A photograph of that scene was taken, and a copy sent to the President, which was framed and hung in the upper hall at the White House. Later (on one of my first visits to the White House) Mr. Wilson showed me that photograph—along with many other interesting pictures. I told him the story just related, and pointed out myself tucked away in a corner above his head. He said—well, never mind what he said. To quote Kipling, "That's another story," and one that must stay locked in my own heart.

A few weeks after my adventure in the House gallery, Washington and all its concerns were out of mind, for Altrude Gordon and I were aboard the steamer *Minnetonka* bound for Europe once more. The *Minnetonka* was the choice of Altrude's cousin and guardian, Mr. Pat F., who accompanied us. "Cousin Pat" suffered from hay fever and he wanted a slow ship and a long ocean voyage. He got both, but no relief from hay fever. The *Minnetonka* carried a large shipment of cattle. Hatches were opened to give them air. The hay the cattle ate apparently contained the very elements to set "Cousin Pat" to sneezing and weeping.

He disappeared into his cabin and did not show up for a meal in the dining room for two days. His first complaint was against *us* for selecting a boat which carried only first-class passengers and cattle. At this Altrude offered a mild protest, as Cousin Pat himself had done the selecting. Altrude was not a very good sailor and cayenne pepper had been recommended to her as a fine thing to tone up the stomach. As she spoke to Cousin Pat she gave her food a generous sprinkling of red pepper, which a wanton breeze carried straight to the sensitive nostrils of our sufferer. Flinging down his napkin with every epithet he could utter between sneezes, Cousin Pat vanished from view, and we hardly saw him again during the crossing.

We landed at Tilbury Docks, London, at night and my happiness was destroyed for weeks by the pitiful plight of the cattle being forced down a long gangplank onto the smaller boat far below us. The incline was steep, and at the far end of the gangplank they had to make a last steep step off in the pitch darkness, not knowing where they would find a footing. Men on either side prodded and pushed them. Their poor eyes were pathetic in their fright.

All night long I stayed on the deck watching those miserable animals. Towards morning I spoke to a deck hand: "Why do you want to scare them to death making them step off that way into empty space?" He jauntily replied: "Well, you see, it ain't much to them. They are all to be slaughtered anyhow."

We were to stay in London for several weeks as it was Cousin Pat's first time in Europe and he was keen to see all the historic things. Our first day was plain sailing; he liked it, and his ills abated on dry land. The second day we were to escort him to the Tower of London, and, as I had been there many times before, I took my fountain pen and some writing paper in my bag to write some letters while the others went through the Tower.

On reaching the entrance I was surprised to be told that on account of the outrages committed by the Suffragettes no one was allowed to carry anything in his hand; purses and bags must be sealed and checked at the gate. I took out the paper and fountain pen and asked if I could take them with me. The officer solemnly examined the pen and handed it back, saying: "Thank you, I see no harm in that." I found a nice shady corner on one of the side entrances and settled myself to write. Deep in a letter, I suddenly became aware of being watched. I looked up to find a tall Britisher in a crimson-coated uniform, holding a gun, standing above me. I was so surprised that involuntarily I said: "What's the matter?" and before he replied I realized I was the centre of a circle of onlookers. He said: "I am here to watch you; we don't trust women these days." It was the day of tight skirts, so I could not have concealed a bomb had I tried, but it was so funny that even the soldier smiled when two others joined him and the three stood over me until my friends returned, which, in the circumstances, seemed hours to me. I rose to join them, observing, "Well, there are my friends, I am glad to say." One of the soldiers remarked to another: "Not half so glad as we are." But to me they saluted and, shouldering their arms, escorted us to the gate where I said: "Thank you for your good care." By nightfall, Cousin Pat was disgusted with England. He had seen all and more than he wanted, and nothing compared with the good old U.S.A.

Still, he wanted to have a look at Paris. Here again, first impressions were satisfactory; he liked the gaiety of the streets of Paris. Of course he pitied the inability of the French to talk a real language— but, still, they would learn some day. So that night we had a really agreeable person at dinner, and the next two days were bearable. On the fourth day it rained. When we met at lunch heavy gloom hung over our cavalier, and he, like Rachel weeping for her children, refused to be comforted and said he was going out alone.

At dinner, however, he was in such a jovial mood we wondered what had happened. As the skies had cleared we got one of the old-time open fiacres and went for a drive in the Bois. We stopped at one of the restaurants there and got back about midnight. As we were parting for the evening, Cousin Pat said: "Well, I'll tell you all goodbye, for this afternoon I went to the office and exchanged my sailing for the fastest boat back to God's country. I am leaving to-morrow morning at eight!" And so ended our seeing Europe with Cousin Pat.

Thus liberated, Altrude and I fled to the château country, taking with us a Frenchwoman from whom we had had lessons in Washington, and who had returned to Paris for the summer. She turned out to be highly temperamental and about as difficult as Cousin Pat. She had friends in the Pyrenees Mountains, and we were to keep her with us until we reached them. After a stay in Tours at the delightful little Hôtel de l'Univers which Henry James describes in his *Little Tour in France,* we worked our way slowly to the Pyrenees, stopping in small villages off the beaten track among the people who were neither French nor Spanish but Pyrenees peasants. One day, driving in an open carriage, we seemed alone in the world. There were no signs of life anywhere, just a road climbing up, up, skirting the edge of sheer cliffs, where, on one side, you looked what seemed to be miles above, and, on the other, the same distance below. At a hairpin turn we were amazed to see on the road above us an old woman, a very small boy and a two-wheel cart drawn by a tiny donkey. They were trying to lift a big cow with a broken leg into the cart. Considering the weight of the cow the feat was an impossibility. The sight was pathetic but comical, for the little boy was in the cart trying to pull the cow in by the tail, and the old woman was struggling with the helpless cow's body.

The boy and the donkey were so small, and the cow and the woman so big, that it was obvious that if the impossible should happen and the woman get the cow in the cart, donkey, cart and boy would all turn a somersault and land down in the valley below.

We felt sorry for them and I told our *cocher* to go and help the woman while we held his horses. He assured me his horses were *very* wild and would certainly bolt. I insisted, however, and Altrude stood at their heads while Mademoiselle, the driver and I tried to lift the cow. At my suggestion the donkey was led out of the shafts of the cart to permit the bed of that vehicle to drop to the ground. Then we all shoved and pulled when—*voilà!*—in went the huge bulk of the cow. At that instant a shriek from Altrude announced the disappearance of the donkey which was tearing down the road at a two-forty gait. The old woman burst into tears and curses, saying we had lost the only thing she had left in the world, for *"la pauvre vache avec la jambe cassée"* was all she owned, and without the donkey she could not save the cow. But she forgot her goatlike little boy! Without a word he had dashed down the cliff and after a breakneck descent headed off the donkey. We last saw the poor little animal pulling valiantly cart, cow, woman and boy—all content with some silver we had given the boy. We went on our way wondering if the good Samaritan had felt any real gratification.

Late that evening we reached the house of a friend of Mademoiselle's. It was already dark in the tiny hamlet which clung to the sides of the mountains and all we could see was a miniature cottage outlined against the black cliff above, and springing from the side of the cliff a waterfall of such force that it thundered in our ears and gleamed white in the shadow. Everything was as primitive as possible, our beds being bags filled with straw placed on homemade frames tied across with ropes. The water was conducted into the house by its own force through wooden troughs and dumped into a crude tank. The flame of a candle cast deep shadows into the corners of the room and made us feel very, very far away from home. However, after an application of the icy water from a tin basin, we were ready for supper and descended to a plain, but clean, room, which served as kitchen, dining room and lounge. A table with a red cloth, two candles, and some flowers, looked very dainty—set away from a big fireplace where a spit turned mechanically and the light from the fire made copper pans and skillets gleam. The chef was in white, and his waxed moustache bore testimony to his tendency to be a dandy.

The supper was a revelation. There was first an omelette, such as none but French hands could create, for *"make"* would be an inadequate word to describe such a work of art. Then *pâté de foie gras,* in slices as we serve ham; and last a chicken braised on the spit, potatoes in cream, and *fraises des bois,* with a pot of cream, and coffee like nectar. When I tell you this was all prepared before our eyes, and served by one of the most exquisite creatures I have ever seen, you can imagine our astonishment. Madame was a typical French beauty: hair like the raven's wing, creamy magnolia-petal skin, dark, tragic eyes, and an air of mystery that fascinated me.

Later, when I expressed this to Mademoiselle, our guide, she told me a strange story. Her friend had always been very beautiful; she lived in Paris, and had fallen madly in love with a Turkish diplomat. He married her and took her to his own country where, to her horror, she found she was only one of a harem. Finally she escaped through the friendship of his chef, who was our present host. Hidden away in these mountains, they were happy, except that they longed for their beloved Paris.

After several days in this delightful place we left Mademoiselle with her friends and went by train to Biarritz. Nothing could offer sharper contrast with this primitive life in the vastness of the mountains than a fashionable place such as Biarritz. One had to rub one's eyes to be sure it was the same earth. In the one all was simple and stripped to the bone; in the other the very quintessence of luxury and artificiality—the resort of the idle rich, with sated appetites and blasé tastes. But, with it all, Biarritz is a beautiful spot which defies the human element to rob it of its charm.

We had telegraphed to reserve rooms at the hotel which had been one of the palaces of Napoleon III, and we arrived about five one heavenly afternoon in an open fiacre piled with our hand luggage, much of it unshapely owing to queer things we had acquired in our trip through the mountains. A great bed of heliotrope, whose perfume made the air delicious, greeted us in front of the hotel; and above this, on a perfectly manicured lawn, in coleus, was the Napoleonic crest with "N. & E.," for Napoleon and Eugénie.

We ourselves must have had a very bucolic air, for at the desk a supercilious clerk, in frock coat and puff tie, looked us over critically. At first he "feared he had nothing," but finally discovered one room up under the roof. Of course we did not want that. Then he asked: "For how long would you desire to remain?" To which I replied: "That would depend on how we like it." Then he said they did have a large double room with balcony and bath which was promised whenever some old patrons arrived, but he could let us have it for a few days for twenty-five dollars a day. I told him the price was absurd and that we would go somewhere else. He then asked, in hurt tones, what we had *expected* to pay, and almost sobbed aloud when I said ten dollars a day. We got the room at my price, though, and a really charming one it was with a balcony that tempted one to sit and dream and live only for the beauty in the world. As he was disappearing he said if we would give him the slip for our trunks he would have them brought up. "Oh," said I, "we have no trunks." At which our servitor bravely overcame a desire to faint, and retired speechless.

After several luxurious days we crossed the border to San Sebastian, in Spain, another lovely spot; then on to Burgos to see the great cathedral. The following day, we planned to go to Madrid, but alas, we reckoned with little knowledge of Spanish railroad etiquette which, it seemed, was to run trains into the station but, if they were filled, not to open the gates so other passengers could embark. The trains which came through from Paris were all sold out. In consequence the gates were never opened. We were told at the hotel that the best thing would be to return to Paris and get a reservation straight through to Madrid. "But," we said, "we are already halfway, and it is a long and expensive trip back to Paris." "Yes, that is so, and it is a pity," said our informant, adding, as if to make everything quite logical: "But the hotel here is expensive, too."

After three days of waiting, and each time going to the station with the hope that we could get a place on a train, a funny little Spaniard arrived at my door wearing a porter's cap and no other insignia of service but a bland and childlike smile. "You want go Madrid?" he said. "Truss me. I drive for Johnny Wanamaker, New York. I get train for you tonight." He did; but a local non-corridor compartment, where we were locked in for fifteen hours with two Spaniards, father and son, one German and two birds in a tiny box. I sat bolt upright all night holding Altrude against my shoulder.

We arrived in Madrid at 6:00 A. M., and that same afternoon went to a bull fight because we were told that a certain famous toreador, whom we must not miss, would be on hand.

The scenes in the streets were colourful: picturesque costumes; mounted picadors swaggering up and down; ladies with their lace mantillas and garlands of flowers; crimson and yellow and black displayed everywhere. We reached the arena in time to see a cousin of the King, in his absence, throw the key to open the gate for the bulls to rush in.

Fans waved, lace fluttered in the breeze, and the play began. Many times we followed the instructions of a Spanish friend, who had told us: "You will please not to look when the horses get killed; put your fan before your face." This was all very well; but unless you kept your fan before your face all the time you could not shut out the cruelty and horror of seeing helpless animals, goaded into fury, try to tear one another to pieces. We stayed through the deaths of innumerable horses and of five bulls—none of which had any real fight in them, but were driven like sheep to be slaughtered. Then we fled and went home to bed too sick to speak of what we had seen.

Madrid has many other things to charm and interest, though. The hotel at which we were staying was also the residence of Mr. F. F.

Dumont, the American Consul, and acting chargé in the absence of the American Minister. Through his kindness and Mrs. Dumont's we attended a number of affairs, including parties given for President Poincaré of France who was making a visit of State to the King of Spain.

While abroad one does a number of things one never does at home. My appearance at official affairs is an example. In Washington, with such affairs going on all around me, like many another permanent and unofficial resident of the capital I had never attended one. But in Madrid I must confess that I was really glad to go.

From Madrid we progressed to Toledo, to Seville and Granada, seeing most of the things that travellers see, and on to Algeciras and Gibraltar. There we conceived a desire to cross to Tangier, and, if possible, go a little way into the interior of Africa. On being told it would be unwise for two women to go alone I sought that friend to tourists, Thomas Cook, and asked for a guide. Cook's promised us a reliable man, accustomed to just such duties.

On the appointed morning we met our guide at the dock. He was a gigantic Moor in native costume, with earrings in his ears, and his face scarred from smallpox. A little bit overawed by this huge creature, I asked: "And what is your name?" With a beguiling grin he answered: "Mohammed, Missie"; and from that time we were friends. He waited on us hand and foot, and when Altrude got seasick he said he had a nice place for her to lie down out on the deck, and guided her to an improvised couch covered with his own cloak or burnoose. In a little while she did feel better. "What am I lying on?" she asked, sitting up. Mohammed's reply almost bowled her over again, for, lifting up the cloak, he displayed a great pile of dead rabbits. Beaming upon her, he replied: "Rabbits, Missie."

There is no harbour at Tangier and the boats stop outside where the passengers are transshipped to tiny little rowboats, each manned by villainous-looking natives who charge enough to make it necessary to bargain with them before one embarks. Of course Mohammed saved us from this, but it was a terrifying experience to get into the little boat, for the waves were high and it would rise up on the crest of one only to be swept quickly twenty feet away and wallow in the trough of the sea before coming up again. The trick was, I found, to jump when you saw the boat coming up. Mohammed went first, taking with him our hand luggage that our hands might be free. Then when he shrieked over the noise of all the bargaining: "Jump, Missie," I jumped, and landed in long dirty arms which steadied me until I got my balance. Then Altrude came next, and I held my breath until she was beside me. I expected her to be ill from the way the boat rose and fell, but I think we were both too scared to have any thought beyond the longing to be again on solid ground.

We were in Africa two days which, for me, was time enough. In the Market Space in Tangier we saw women and men with awful snakes wrapped around their arms and bodies. They would make the creatures stick their heads 'way out and try to touch you. Our guide said we must see a famous cemetery outside the city, and as it was too far for us to walk he would arrange for us to ride. He appeared at the hotel mounted on a splendid horse, followed by five of the tiniest donkeys I have ever seen. Each of these patient little beasts was saddled with a queer chair seat made of wood with a little rail around three sides, and covered with red cloth. From this chair were suspended red cords which supported a sort of running board on which one's feet rested. Altrude, three Virginia friends whom we had met, and I took our places on these funny things. With his burnoose drawn up over his head to shield him from the sun Mohammed looked very picturesque, and we, like his meek and unimportant womenkind, followed single file in his train. The streets were so narrow that often our funny saddles bumped against the walls when we turned a corner. The houses were mostly one story, the outside walls a beautiful sky-blue which tended to soften the glare of the sun.

In the evening we went to several of the places to see the native girls dance. I hardly know what to call the resorts, for they were unlike anything of the sort in this country. One entered a small, unpretentious-looking house, and went upstairs, to find a spacious interior where musicians seated on the floor played on queer instruments. Opposite them were many mats or cushions upon which we and the rest of the audience were seated. Coffee in tiny cups was served. Mohammed directed us to take the coffee, but not to drink it. After some time the door opened into another apartment which contained a rude stage on which the dancers appeared. Most of the dancing was vulgar and uninteresting. When this became evident our guide would suggest our leaving and trying another place. At last we found a really lovely Spanish dancer, who was grace itself; but it had grown late, and by this time our friends from Virginia, weary of sightseeing, had left us to return to the hotel. We started back ourselves about one A. M.

As we walked down the narrow, silent street, we heard in the distance a rhythmic beating of cymbals and a drum when, to our great surprise, our guide took us each quickly by the hand, saying: "Run, Missies, run!" Without knowing why, or whither, we all ran for blocks until we reached a street where we beheld a fantastic cortège which he explained was a wedding procession. It was entirely a male affair. First came young boys, almost naked, carrying flares to light the way. Back of them were the musicians beating their slow and solemn rhythm on strange-looking instruments. These were followed by a horse on whose back was mounted a tall cone-shaped sort of thing in which the poor bride was concealed. The motion of the horse caused his burden to sway from side to side, and one of the surrounding company of men was kept busy righting it. Mohammed explained that the bride was being conveyed to the home of her future husband whom she most likely had never seen. There she would be carried in over the threshold, in this case by his friends who escorted her. Then they would stay and celebrate with the bridegroom all night, but would never see the bride. It seemed so horrible to me to think of such a fate awaiting any woman— disposed of by her family and left to the mercy of a stranger—that I could not get her out of my thoughts.

Columbus could have been no happier to set foot on the New World than we were to return his visit and reach Spanish soil again after our forty-eight hour expedition into Africa. Shortly thereafter we sailed from Gibraltar for home, and though I could not have guessed it then, that was my last glimpse of Europe for more than five years.

CHAPTER 5

*I*NSTEAD of going abroad, as usual, I spent the summer of 1914 in Maine with my time-tried travelling companion, Altrude Gordon. An affair of the heart and the great and complicating affairs of the White House had a hand in this decision, though these matters concerned me only indirectly, as the friend and confidante of Altrude Gordon. Cary Travers Grayson, the White House physician and long a valued acquaintance of mine, had become a serious suitor for Altrude's hand. Although they seemed to me much in love, the young lady professed herself unwilling to make a decision controlling her future.

So we decided to go to Maine, where, in the wilderness solitudes, Altrude could think things over. Maine was chosen because of its proximity to Cornish, New Hampshire, where the summer White House was to be established. Dr. Grayson was expected at Cornish. Possibly he could slip away now and then, join us in Maine and assist Altrude in her thinking, amid surroundings more conducive to reflection than the formal and busy life of Washington.

A walking and canoeing trip in the Rangeley Lake region, where two friends from Boston were to join us, was agreed upon. But first Altrude and I stopped off at Kineo, where we had expected a flying visit from Cary Grayson. However, a crisis in Europe was developing and Dr. Grayson wired: "Detained in Washington. Hope to come next week." Next week it was the same story, and the week after that the same. We were due to join our friends, a brother and sister, at Jackman, in the northern part of the state, and could wait no longer. Leaving trunks behind and dressed in stout walking boots and camp clothes, and with our baggage reduced, as we thought, to the unalterable minimum, we entrained for Jackman.

The hotel there was primitive, but clean. As the first day of our expedition involved an overland "carry" of ten miles we retired early. Scarcely had we done so when the clouds which had been gathering all day broke and the flood that descended on the tin roof sounded as I imagine his flood did to Noah in the Ark. At six in the morning when we rolled out it was still raining. Of course I thought we could not start. Our two guides said only tenderfeet stopped for a shower. On a two weeks' trip we must expect wettings and we might as well get the experience early.

Opening our packs to get out raincoats we asked the guides to look over our equipment and see if they could suggest anything to add. The faces of those guides were studies. "Naw," one said, "but a good deal to shed." On a carry we would have to shoulder our own packs, and the lighter the better. About half of the irreducible minimum with which we had left Kineo was rejected.

So we started, with the water pouring down our backs and the landscape obscured by sheets of rain. But by noon the sun had appeared and we got out our fishing lines and the guides showed us how to whip a stream. We caught enough fish for lunch, which our escorts cooked marvellously. Around a good campfire we dried ourselves and felt well rewarded for the discomforts of the start. At nights we made permanent camps, as they are called, sometimes staying several nights in the same one. In the daytime we travelled, by water or on foot, over a great many miles of country. We went through blueberry thickets waist-high, where the fruit was ripe, cool and covered with a bloom of frost. Sometimes we would startle a deer that was enjoying the berries as much as we were. Incidentally, those guides had done right in paring down our baggage. But for that I do not think I should be writing these lines, for one mile in Maine equals ten in Virginia.

Except for one thing we were sorry when our two weeks were up: Cary Grayson had not appeared. War had stricken Europe, the President's wife had died, and no one of the White House entourage had been able to leave. I think we would have stayed longer but for the necessity of getting back to Kineo to retrieve our trunks before the hotel closed.

We reached that sophisticated place looking like tramps, and I confess that a good bed was welcome after a fortnight of sleeping on pine boughs. On our second day there I ate some cold chicken for lunch and by evening was miserably ill with ptomaine poisoning. The hotel was in the throes of closing and I was told that the regular house doctor had gone. About all his young assistant could think of to do was to tell Altrude that he doubted if I would live. Naturally the girl was terrified, which simplified matters none. For three days I was too desperately sick to lift my head. Guests came in to express their sympathy. One of them, a Mr. Lippincott, of Philadelphia, I remember most kindly. "My child," he said, "I am older than you. It is impossible to get a doctor here, and I would feel responsible if I let this matter go on. Therefore I have gone to the general store, where they sell everything, and bought you these. They are put up by Wyeth, pharmacist, of Philadelphia. You can be sure of their preparations. I advise you to take these as directed until you are strong enough to get the boat to Boston." Then he produced a tiny dark bottle filled with large brown pellets marked "Cholera Cure."

I swallowed the things and told Altrude to arrange for us to take the boat the following morning. By superhuman effort I made it, in the fullness of time reaching Washington. Having seen me home, Altrude Gordon went to New York to visit friends, leaving Dr. Grayson longing for someone to talk to about her, and I was the natural one. During the period of my convalescence he came to see me every day. He told me much of the happenings in Europe; of the possibilities of graver and graver complications as far as the United States was concerned; of the heartbreaking loneliness of the President since the loss of his wife. Two of the President's daughters, Mrs. Sayre and Mrs. McAdoo, had their own homes. The other, "Miss Margaret," as Dr. Grayson always called her, not liking Washington or the social responsibilities that devolved upon her position, was away most of the time. Miss Helen Bones, the President's cousin, who had come to them as a sort of personal secretary to Mrs. Wilson, had been ill and was desperately lonely as she had no intimate friends in Washington.

One day, when I was almost well, Dr. Grayson asked me if he could bring Miss Bones to see me, adding: "I know you would like each other, and I feel sure you can help me get her well; for what she needs is outdoor exercise, and I can't get her to walk. If, after you know her, you would take her walking, it would do worlds for her." I said: "My dear Doctor, as you know, I am not a society person. I have never had any contacts with official Washington, and don't desire any. I am, therefore, the last person in the world able to help you." He protested that as they were in mourning there was no entertaining at the White House; that the poor little lady was starving for companionship. I said, "Wait until Altrude comes back. Take her as your assistant and Miss Bones will then be able to plan things so you can see Altrude and, in turn, she can help Miss Bones."

So the days passed until one morning Dr. Grayson telephoned to know if I were going to be at home, and if so' could he run in. He came in a White House car with Mrs. McAdoo and Miss Bones. They asked me to join them in a ride through the park. The day was perfect, and I went gladly, and found them both full of charm, easy to know, and thoroughly unspoiled. When we got back they said they would come again soon—which they did in a day or two. As we learned to know one another, we found much in common, and it came about that Helen Bones and I began to take long walks together. We would take my little electric and go to Rock Creek Park where, in those beautiful days of few motors, we would park it under a tree and tramp along the lovely bridle paths and then return to my house to have tea and sit before the fire in my library and talk. Naturally she often mentioned the President, or "Cousin Woodrow" as she called him, telling of her devotion to him, of his unfailing sweetness to her, and all about his and Mrs. Wilson's family connections. She told of the other young relatives they had sent to school or college, just as they had done for her. Her own mother having died when she was a little girl, the President's mother took her into their home. So throughout her life she had known and loved him and "Cousin Ellen," as she called the late Mrs. Woodrow Wilson.

These talks gave me a very intimate insight into the man whom the world judged cold, or a human machine, devoid of emotion. But beyond the natural interest inspired by all who sit in high places, I felt he was too remote for me ever to have an opportunity to know and assay for myself. Nevertheless, my imagination was fired by the picture Helen gave me of a lonely man, detached from old friends and associations—the fate of official life—uncomplainingly bearing the burden of a great sorrow and keeping his eye single to the responsibilities of a great task.

By a curious coincidence it was exactly at this time that my lawyer, Mr. Nathaniel Wilson, a Republican in politics and no relation to the President, developed a great intellectual interest in him. He read

EDITH BOLLING, 1892
On her first visit to Washington, D. C.

everything the President had written, and passed the books on to me, saying he thought I should read them not only to keep in touch with affairs of the Nation, but also because of their literary merit.

Here I must pause to introduce the reader to Mr. Nathaniel Wilson, who at that time was president of the Metropolitan Club in Washington, and for years the head of the legal profession in the capital. He was a lovable old man who had lived much within himself and who gave me generously of his rich store of knowledge. Our relation was one of friendship rather than of lawyer and client; and he was a good deal of a dictator, too. His pet abomination being a telephone, he resented one ringing in a house where he was. As my house, 1308 Twentieth Street, was a small one, and I lived alone but for two maids, my 'phone was my watchdog and rang on each floor, unless I could remember to cut the bells off before he arrived. Many a lecture I have had from him telling me how unworthy of my dignity it was to allow young men to telephone me instead of writing a proper note; and many a time, when he would come to spend an evening, if I was called to the telephone he would leave in high dudgeon. But the funny part was that in a day or so he would apologize for his anger, and have someone in his office *telephone* to say that if I was at leisure he would call.

I think the dear gentleman had me very much on his mind, for in many ways he showed his anxiety to find for me some objective in life. He would sit and look at me, and say: "My, my! You have a destiny, but what it is I cannot determine; you should be preparing yourself for something that is to come." I would laugh and tell him I knew he meant I was only a cumberer of the ground. This I admitted, saying that I appreciated the prosaic quality of my life, destined to be spent, like millions of others, in a backwater of commonplace. To this he would reply: "Well, it is your own fault; you have potentiality, and some day you will be sorry you wasted these years when you might be fitting yourself for what is coming."

Alas, that prophecy came true. I might have fitted myself to be a wiser, abler helper to my future husband in the duties that crowded the years almost at hand.

I could write many pages of this rare friend who dared tell me my faults as well as pleasanter things, and whose counsel was always a shield and buckler. When I first told him of my friendship with

Helen Bones he warned me to beware of people in high places; but he followed our friendship with deep interest.

On a brilliant afternoon in March, 1915, Helen Bones and I went for one of our customary walks. Instead of using my little electric car she said we must go in the White House automobile to the park and let the car wait while we walked. We had a long tramp and found the paths muddy. When we started back in the car I said: "I will have your boots cleaned when we get back to my house so you won't have to arrive at the White House with such muddy ones." She replied: "We are not going to your house. I have ordered tea at the White House this afternoon, and you are to go back with me." I said: "Oh, I couldn't do that; my shoes are a sight, and I should be taken for a tramp." "Yes, you can," she answered, "for there is not a soul there. Cousin Woodrow is playing golf with Dr. Grayson and we will go right upstairs in the elevator and you shall see no one. I have had tea with you every time and Cousin Woodrow asked me the other day why I never brought my friends back there. He really wishes I would have some one in that lonely old house."

I agreed to go, following her plan to get in the elevator and ascend to the second floor. But what she had not arranged was the greeting we received when we got out of the elevator. The President and Dr. Grayson, just returned from golf, with boots as muddy as ours, were rounding the turn of the hall. We met face to face. We all laughed at our plight, but I would have been less feminine than I must confess to be, had I not been secretly glad that I had worn a smart black tailored suit which Worth had made for me in Paris, and a tricot hat which I thought completed a very good-looking ensemble.

The two gentlemen, I am sorry to say, were not so well attired. Their golf suits, as I found out later, were made by a cheap tailor the President had known years before and whom he was trying to help by giving an order. They were *not* smart.

This was the accidental meeting which carried out the old adage of "turn a corner and meet your fate."

Helen explained she had brought me for a tête-à-tête tea, but if they would like to come she would invite them. So, after they had changed, and we had got the mud off our shoes, we met round a glowing fire in the oval sitting room on the second floor and had an hour of delightful talk. They asked me to dinner, but I declined.

I did not see the President again until several days later when I dined at the White House, though meantime Helen and I had several walks together. Then on April 7, 1915, Helen called me on the telephone to ask if I would go for a drive with her instead of walking. If so she would send the car for me and I could pick her up as she was detained and could not get off as early as she had hoped. When I reached the White House I was amazed to find the President ready to go with us. He insisted upon sitting in the front seat by Robinson, the chauffeur, and having Mr. Murphy, the Secret Service agent, occupy one of the chairs, leaving Helen and me alone on the back seat of the big open touring car.

The President seemed very tired and desirous of rest. Though Helen and I chatted like magpies, we let him be quiet; and I don't think he spoke from the time we left until our return about five-thirty. Then they both begged me to come back and dine with them, as they were entirely alone. So I went, and after a quiet little dinner we three sat around the fire and discussed books, and he read aloud several delightful things. He was one of the best readers I have ever heard, and he loved books and good English so that his own keen apprecia-tion and enthusiasm added beauty to them. In reading aloud he would close a book and give some explanation of an involved pas-sage, saying: "Don't you think there he meant so and so?" or, laugh-ingly, "If I had written that when I was a boy my father would have made me rewrite it until I really said what I meant!"

That night he told me of the unusual relationship between him and his father, and of the infinite pains the latter took with his training and education, saying that even when he was a very young boy his father made him a partner in his thoughts and would discuss every subject with him, elucidating as he went. Then his father would ask: "Do you thoroughly understand that?" When he would fall into the trap and say, "Oh, yes," his father would turn the tables: "Very well then, write it out and bring it to me so I can see that you do." Thereupon the boy would find many points he had not under-stood. When the paper was presented the father would read it and say: "What did you mean by that; did you mean such and such a thing?" Again the affirmative answer, whereupon the paper would be handed back and his father would say: "Well, you did not say it, so suppose you try again and see if you can say what you mean this time, and if not we'll have another talk and a third go at it." "Many times," the President said, "I have had even a fourth and fifth 'go at it' before my father thought it really conveyed what I could easily have told him, but what, when I tried to write, became obscure and involved."

This intimate picture of his childhood, and the admiration he had for his father, immediately established a bond of sympathy between us, for I had so exactly the same reverence for my own father. So we stopped the reading and talked of our childhood hours, and found many things in common regarding the South, the poverty of all our own people after the Civil War and the faithfulness of the old negroes to their masters and mistresses. I told him of an old servant who had belonged to my grandfather and who after the emancipation had drifted to Texas to live, but who made the long journey back to Virginia every few years to see her people, as she called my grand-mother and my father. I remember our distress at hearing, through a Texas paper, of her death by accidental drowning. All Southern children were taught to call the old slaves "uncle" or "aunt," by way of respect; so we always called this old woman "Aunt Silvey." Imagine our surprise a few months after reading of her death to see her appear hale and hearty, wearing as usual her red bandana. She was always smiling and bobbing, and when she appeared my father said: "Why, Aunt Silvey, we heard you were drowned." She curtsied and said: "Law, Marse William, I heerd that too, but soon as I heerd it I knowed 'twa'n't so."

The evening ended all too soon, for it was the first time I had felt the warm personality of Woodrow Wilson. A boylike simplicity dwelt in the background of an official life which had to be content with the husks of formal contacts when starving for the bread of human companionship.

Thereafter I never thought of him as the President of the United States, but as a real friend. That evening started a companionship which ripened quickly. He, Helen and I often went for motor rides after dinner. They would come for me and we would have the best sort of time. We talked over the things which were rapidly develop-ing in the conduct of the War. From the first he knew he could rely on my prudence, and what he said went no further. When problems confronted him, which they did in every hour of those tragic years, it seemed to clarify things for him to talk to us as we sped along in the cool April night through the darkness with faithful Murphy on the front seat and the Secret Service car following close behind us.

On April 28, 1915, I got the first note I ever received from him. Here it is:

"My dear Mrs. Galt,

"I have ordered a copy of Hamerton's 'Round My House' through the bookseller, but while we are waiting for it I take the liberty of sending you a copy from the Congressional Library. I hope it will give you a little pleasure. I covet nothing more than to give you pleasure,—you have given me so much!

"If it rains this evening would it be any fun for you to come around and have a little reading,—and, if it does *not* rain, are you game for another ride? If you are not in when this gets to you, perhaps you will be gracious enough to telephone Margaret. Your sincere and grateful friend

"WOODROW WILSON."

My reply follows:

"My dear Mr. President:

"How very good of you to remember my desire to read 'Round My House' and take the trouble to send to the Congressional Library to gratify me. I can think of nothing more restful than to come and have you read to us, or in case it clears, go for another ride, *but* (that word that so often destroys plans) I have promised my dear Mother to spend this evening with her, so cannot give myself either pleasure."

On April 30th the book came with a note and that night Altrude Gordon, Dr. Grayson and I were to dine at the White House. Late in the same afternoon a corsage of golden roses came to me with the President's card, and at 7:45 Dr. Grayson arrived to escort me in the White House car, and we stopped at 1600 Sixteenth Street, N.W., to get Altrude. She was highly excited as she had received pink roses as a corsage from the President, and in consequence had decided at the last moment to change her costume to suit the colour of the roses. When we got to her house she was only starting to dress.

Poor Dr. Grayson! All anxiety for her to make a first delightful impression, knowing that the President was always most punctiliously prompt himself, and expected other people to be, he was dismayed to find that we should be late. Imploring me to "make her come on," he said he would turn his back while "she put on the *finishing* things in the car." Altrude consented, and we had a merry time getting the final things done in the few blocks to be covered before we got to the White House gate. But the flowers were put on, having been tried first at the side of the shoulder, then at the waistline, and finally back on the shoulder.

My own dress was a princess black charmeuse Worth had created for me, with a panel front of jet forming a very slender line. The golden roses with gold slippers made all the colour I wore.

After a very happy evening we departed early as the President, Dr. Grayson and Helen Bones were leaving for Williamstown, Massachusetts, where the President's daughter, Jessie Sayre, and her husband made their home, and where their son Francis was to be baptized on the following day.

They returned to Washington May 3rd, and the next day I again dined at the White House. The President's sister, Mrs. George Howe, and her daughter, Mrs. Cothran, had arrived the day before. The latter's little girl Josephine, then a baby, accompanied them. It had turned suddenly warm and after dinner we all went out on the south portico where coffee was served. Dr. Grayson was at dinner, but left almost immediately, and Margaret, Helen, Mrs. Howe and Mrs. Cothran walked down in the grounds, leaving me alone with the President.

Almost as soon as they were gone he brought his chair nearer to mine and, looking directly at me with those splendid, fearless eyes that were unlike any others I have ever seen, he said: "I asked Margaret and Helen to give me an opportunity to tell you something tonight that I have already told them." Then he declared his love for me, speaking quietly but with such emotion the very world seemed tense and waiting. This is almost too sacred and personal to relate, but it was so simply and characteristically done that it belongs to history as representing the man.

It came to me as almost a shock. Not having given a thought to such a development, I said the first thing that came to my mind, without thinking it would hurt him: "Oh, you can't love me, for you don't really know me; and it is less than a year since your wife died."

"Yes," he said, "I know you feel that; but, little girl, in this place time is not measured by weeks, or months, or years, but by deep human experiences; and since her death I have lived a lifetime of loneliness and heartache. I was afraid, knowing you, I would shock you; but I would be less than a gentleman if I continued to make opportunities to see you without telling you what I have told my daughters and Helen: that I want you to be my wife. In the circumstances of the spotlight that is always on this house, and particularly on me as the Head of the Government, whoever comes here is immediately observed and discussed; and do what I can to protect you from gossip, it will inevitably begin. If you can care for me as I do for you, we will have to brave this; but as I cannot come to your house without increasing the gossip, you, in your graciousness, will have to come here. It is for this reason I have talked to the girls about it, so that they can safeguard you and make it possible for me to see you. They have all been wonderful about it, and tell me they love you for your own sake, but would anyway for mine."

We talked on for more than an hour, and I told him if it had to be yes or no at once it would have to be no. Finally we agreed that, as neither of us was a child, in spite of the public gaze we were entitled to continue the friendship until I should decide one way or the other. I tried to say how deeply I appreciated the manliness which had prompted him to tell me frankly the situation.

At ten o'clock I arose to go, for I never stayed late. The rest of the party joined us and the President and Helen took me home. We were very silent on the drive, being too deeply stirred to talk. I still keep the dress I wore that night—a white satin with creamy lace, and just a touch of emerald-green velvet at the edge of the deep square neck, and green slippers to match.

The following morning Helen came, and we went to Rock Creek Park for a walk. She said nothing about the night before until we sat down on some stones in the deep of the wood to rest. Then she let her eyes flash fire at me, as she said: "Cousin Woodrow looks really ill this morning." Bursting into tears, she added: "Just as I thought some happiness was coming into his life! And now you are breaking his heart." I tried to explain, but she would not listen, and cried more. Then, suddenly, a big white horse appeared through the trees and Dr. Grayson on his favourite "Kelly" came into view. Seeing Helen in tears he stopped and said: "Why, what is the matter?" Helen lied unblushingly, saying she had fallen over a log and hurt herself so she could not help weeping. I don't think he believed her, but he pretended to and rode on.

His coming broke the strain, for I was beginning to feel like a criminal, and guilty of base ingratitude. I told her I was far from being the ogre she thought me; that I should indeed be worthy of all her indignation if I were to consent to something I did not feel; that no one in the world would so quickly resent pity as the President; and that I felt I was being fair to us both in promising him that for the present things should go on exactly as they had done—until I had time to recover from the shock of the night before and to re-adjust our positions; for up to that moment I had never thought of him except, first, as the President, and second, as a perfectly delightful new friend—who was as lonely as I was and longing for companionship. I said that I recognized I was playing with fire where he was concerned, for his whole nature was intense and did not will-ingly wait; but that I must have time really to know my own heart.

"Of course," I told her, "there is a glamour around the man as President. There is the deep admiration I feel for the man himself and the flattering assurance he stresses that he needs the help I could give him in so many ways. But I am sure I am right in standing off from all these and trying to sift my own feeling free of each circum-stance. To do this I must see him, and I am honest enough to add that I *want* to see him; and now that my eyes are open it may seem unwomanly to go on with the informal dinners and long rides that have filled these past weeks. But as he says he cannot come to me as he wants to, in the circumstances I will go to him; and this must satisfy even you."

Just before this eventful night I have mentioned I had accepted an invitation to join the President's party and go to New York on the *Mayflower,* from which he was to review the Atlantic fleet. Of course I had looked forward to it with the keenest delight. The party was to include the President's sister, Mrs. Howe; her daughter and little granddaughter; also Margaret, Helen, Mr. Tumulty, Dr. Grayson and Altrude Gordon. We had all planned and discussed it so much that for me to drop out for no apparent reason I knew would cause comment. On the other hand I questioned whether it was the dignified thing to do—after knowing the truth. But having declared I would continue our friendship, I reasoned this was living up to that bargain. And so we all set sail, a very merry party, late in the afternoon.

The night was clear and the Potomac River like silver. After dinner we were all on deck, when gradually the party drifted off in twos and I was alone with the President. He had been unusually quiet during dinner, and I sensed that something was troubling him. He said: "Let's lean on the rail instead of walking, as I want to talk to you. I am very much distressed over a letter I had late today from the Secretary of State [William Jennings Bryan] saying he cannot go on in the Department as he is a pacifist and cannot follow me in wishing to warn our own country and Germany that we may be forced to take up arms; therefore he feels it is his duty to resign."

At that time I knew only the side of the "Great Commoner" that stood for his extreme views on free silver which had split the Democratic Party in 1896; and also that many persons did not take him seriously. So it seemed to me that, far from being a calamity to have him resign, it was a real benefit. When the President paused and asked me what I thought the effect would be, I unhesitatingly said: "Good; for I hope you can replace him with someone who is able and who would in himself command respect for the office both at home and abroad."

We talked a long time as we stood there, and I told him that years before I had seen a play called *Rosemary* in which Maude Adams had taken the part of a very young girl eloping with a boorish young lover in an old-fashioned coach which broke down at the country estate of a fascinating bachelor. The bachelor was played by John Drew. The elopers had to beg hospitality for the night, and next morning the host, already charmed by the beauty of the bride-to-be, surprised the lovers in the midst of a violent quarrel. The girl tried to end the spat with a kiss which her suitor sullenly refused. Upon this the host demanded that the sullen suitor give the girl what she asked. I remembered John Drew's tones when he said: "Kiss her, sir, and [aside] thank God for the chance." "This," I said, "is apropos of Mr. Bryan's suggestion to resign, and my advice is, 'Take it, sir, and thank God for the chance.' "

This made the President smile, but I saw that he was deeply troubled. He went on to say that he had thought of appointing Robert Lansing, and when I exclaimed: "But he is only a clerk in the State Department, isn't he?" Mr. Wilson replied: "He is a counsellor of the Department, and has had a good schooling under old Mr. John W. Foster, his father-in-law, for whom I have great respect. I think he would steer Lansing, and the combination would be of great help to me. If I get an older man he is apt to be rigid and have precedents by which to steer, and in these days old diplomacy cannot function; the world is changing so rapidly that we have got to change with it, or be left far behind. Mr. Foster is ripe in experience, and we would have the benefit of all he can give us, I am sure; and Lansing, on the other hand, is, I think, good material to meet these new conditions."

We had a quiet night, reaching Chesapeake Bay early next morning to find a violent storm raging; and from there until we got to New York our party went down like a row of nine pins. First Mrs. Howe, Mrs. Cothran and Josephine, her daughter, were too ill to get up. The maid who had been taken along to care for Josephine was the sickest of all. I shared a room with Altrude Gordon and had to help her dress and get on deck to see if the air would restore her. On our way up I stopped at Helen's room only to have her say: "Just let me alone; I am desperately sick." From there I went to Margaret, who said in her plucky way: "Oh, I'm all right, but I just think I will stay in bed and not move!"

When I came up on deck Altrude was lying flat on the floor, white as a sheet. Seated beside her was Dr. Grayson and, naval surgeon though he was, he looked almost as ghastly as the girl. Just as I reached them the President approached from the forward part of the boat, looking fit as a fiddle, for he loved the sea. "Why, Grayson," he said, "do get a rug or something to put over Miss Gordon, for she can't stay there like this." As he spoke, I happened to be looking at the dear Doctor, and I am sure his face was scarcely less tragic than that of some wretch hearing his death sentence; for he was so sick himself he knew to move was to court trouble. But there was nothing else a gentleman could do, and he did it like a gentleman; simply gathered himself together for a spring and went below before anything happened! In a few minutes a steward appeared with a rug which he flung over Miss Gordon, and then retreated, for he, too, was ill.

Poor Altrude mourned: "Oh, please don't bother about me!" So I covered her up and said: "I think I will see if I can get you a little brandy and ice." The President said: "I will tell Brooks [his valet] to get it for you. I have to go below to do some work, and I will send it right up by him." I waited with Altrude, but as nothing happened I thought I would go in the dining saloon and see if there was any brandy aboard. There I found Brooks, another wretched sailor, trying to hold up his head long enough to manage the tray with the ice on it while he got the bottle of brandy open. Seeing how hopelessly sick he was, I said: "Give it to me, Brooks, and you go and lie down." This he did without protest, and I pulled the cork and started back to the deck. But just as I reached the hatch the boat gave an awful lunge which made the world seem to turn upside down for me and I grew blindly sick. So I lay down right where I was, still clutching the quart of brandy, and, holding the bottle upright on my chest, I closed my eyes to try to steady myself. In a few minutes I was startled to hear the President's voice above me, saying: "Why, are you hurt?" "No," I said. "I am only sick, but I will be all right in a minute." We could not help laughing at the funny picture I made. He told me that he had gone back to the deck to see about Miss Gordon only to find the Doctor recovered and in command, and that they had taken her to her room.

By this time I was over my queer spell and so continued to our room where I found the Doctor much restored and Altrude able to swallow a few drops of brandy.

When lunchtime arrived the only ones to appear were the President, Mr. Tumulty and I. The dining-room boys were all so ill they could hardly serve us. All went well through the soup course, but the next was spring lamb with green peas, and when the latter were handed Mr. Tumulty he turned the same shade of green as the peas and fled—never to reappear until we were tied up in the Hudson River. Thereupon both Margaret and Mr. Tumulty declared that immediate engagements in Washington made it necessary for them to return by train.

We had a gorgeous day in New York. The President spoke at a luncheon, reviewed a parade and attended a dinner. Mrs. Josephus Daniels, wife of the Secretary of the Navy, gave a dinner for the ladies, on the U.S.S. *Dolphin,* the boat used by the Secretary. She had the wives of the officers commanding the fleet, and several interesting New York women; and a very charming hostess she was. A launch took us from the *Mayflower* to the *Dolphin* and was to call for us as soon as the dinner the officers were giving the President was over. When the launch came alongside the *Dolphin* we were all amazed to see the President and his aides. He came aboard to greet Mrs. Daniels and her guests, which pleased them very much.

The day of the review of the fleet was a perfect one, and we were all up early. By ten o'clock the officers who had been asked aboard the President's yacht began to arrive. The President went on the bridge, and the boat steamed slowly down the river, pausing a little as each warship passed and fired a salute, and the band played the National Anthem. I have to confess the continued roar from the guns became deafening, but the fleet was decorated with signal flags and the long vista we had from the deck made a wonderful picture.

The review took all morning, and afterwards a luncheon was served and we returned to our anchorage. Then the official party left and many of the officers of the fleet came alongside in their launches to pay their respects to the President and say goodbye.

Soon after this we set sail for home, minus several members of the party. The return trip was in a complete calm, and we anchored off the Virginia shore in the Potomac River and went in small boats to General Lee's birthplace, Stratford Hall. The noble old house, though in desolation and decay, was filled with the romance of its former dignity as the cradle of a great man.

Reaching Washington early the following morning, the entire party drove to the White House for breakfast, after which I went home. Even now it is impossible to analyze those days of doubt as to my own feelings, for not to have loved and honoured Woodrow Wilson when once privileged to know him is incomprehensible. When he offered me his love so royally I confess my amazement that I ever hesitated. In justice to my intelligence, though, I must honestly say that this was largely because he was President of the United States. There was the fear that some might think I loved him for that; then the terrible thought of the publicity inevitably entailed; and the feeling that I had no training for the responsibilities such a life held. Oh, so many things swarmed in my thoughts; and yet each time I was with him I felt the charm of his presence. He would fascinate me by the direct and simple way he discussed his hopes for the legislation he was having enacted—all the problems which confronted him and the fears, even then, that the fires of war raging in Europe might leap the Atlantic and involve our own country. This would send me home more and more torn by the will to love and help him, and yet unconvinced that I could really help, and unwilling to take all he had to offer without giving largely in return.

I say "send me home," for there, again, was another situation to meet and overcome—as it is a privilege almost unknown for a President to call on his friends. They invariably pay him the respect of calling on him; and whenever he goes anywhere he is attended by six or eight Secret Service men, and it is as ceremonious as the opening of Parliament. So, to see him at all without the most unwelcome publicity, we had to arrange for a drive together, when always Helen Bones or Margaret Wilson would go with us; and then I would go back with them to the White House for tea, or dinner. But that could not be repeated too frequently, for we did not want gossip excited. The only other means of communicating was by letter. Almost every day we would keep in touch through faithful little Helen who would come for our walk and bring me a line from the "Tiger" as she lovingly named him. She said he was so pathetic caged there in the White House, longing to come and go, as she did, that he reminded her of a splendid Bengal tiger she had once seen— never still, moving, restless, resentful of his bars that shut out the larger life God had made him for.

CHAPTER 6

THUS went by the early summer days of 1915, each one incomplete that gave no opportunity for us to meet. One night when I went to dinner at the White House the President said he would like to know my sister Bertha of whom I spoke so often. Margaret asked if I would bring her on Wednesday afternoon at five for tea. I knew it would give Bertha pleasure, as it certainly would me; so I took her. When we arrived neither Margaret nor Helen had got back from another appointment, and so we waited on the lovely south portico (so filled with memories of that night in May), where the kettle was boiling on the tea table. After we had been there about fifteen minutes the President came over through the arcade, from the Executive Offices. Astonished to find us alone, he made apologies for Margaret and Helen, saying he knew they had been unavoidably detained. Then he looked despairingly at the steaming kettle, and said he had never made tea before, but having tackled all sorts of new jobs since coming to Washington, he supposed he could do that. So taking up the caddy he poured nearly all that it contained into the tea pot, making a beverage more like lye than tea. All the while I sat apart and watched him with amusement while he kept up a delightful flow of conversation with my sister.

I know one of us should have offered to make the tea, but my sister always says she is more afraid of a teakettle than any man can be; and I did not want to assume the part of hostess in the circumstances. So he sent out S.O.S. signals in vain, until at last he said: "Let's adjourn to the garden where all the summer things are in their glory." There he quoted that lovely poem by Thomas Edward Brown, "My Garden":

"A Garden is a lovesome thing, God wot!
    Rose plot,
    Fringed pool,

> Fern grot—
> The veriest school
> Of Peace; and yet the fool
> Contends that God is not—
> Not God! in Gardens! when the eve is cool?
> Nay, but I have a sign:
> 'Tis very sure God walks in mine."

Finally the girls arrived. They had gone to a party in the country and on their return the chauffeur, trying to make a short cut home over a new road, had lost the way. But I had to tell them we had had a mighty good time without them, and that it was time for us to go.

A little while after this the summer exodus from Washington started. The President again rented the Winston Churchill home, Harlakenden House, at Cornish, New Hampshire. Both Margaret and Helen asked me to come for a visit. Again I hesitated to accept; but after careful thought I decided to go, for the President would be there but little and when he was we could have a real opportunity to know each other in a normal, natural way. Both he and Margaret begged me to do this, and it was arranged that Helen and I should motor up in the big touring car, spending one night in New York and there doing some shopping before proceeding to Greenfield, Massachusetts, for the second night, and so on to Cornish on the third day. We started on June 21, 1915, a marvellous morning, Mr. Jervis, one of the Secret Service men, going with us.

We paused at Princeton, New Jersey, for two or three hours, and Helen showed me all the places so intimately connected with the President: his own house, in Library Lane; '79 Hall, built by his class; Nassau Hall, where hung an awful portrait of Mr. Wilson, done by his friend Fred Yates, at the time he was president of Princeton University; Prospect, the house where he lived, and other places so familiar to me through his love for them. The whole place was eloquent of him, and I knew how he longed to show it to me himself.

Next morning in New York we got through our modest shopping by eleven and decided to leave at once. The roads were so good that we reached Greenfield very early where we had dinner and then, as the moon was full. we thought that instead of spending the night there we would go on to Cornish. Alas, we reckoned without knowledge, for the concrete roads we had been speeding over suddenly ended and we found ourselves in sand nearly up to the hubs, where we could make no time. As we toiled labouriously along, the night air in the mountains got like ice and we shivered with cold. We were dressed for June motoring in Washington, but not in the Vermont and New Hampshire mountains. However, there was nothing to do but roll up in rugs and go on.

Very tired, and very cold, we reached our haven at two A. M. where we found the housekeeper up with a warm fire and a hot supper to welcome us; and a request from the White House to call up *at once* upon arrival as several messages had been sent to Greenfield, and later to Harlakenden, to know what had happened to us. So Helen telephoned to Mr. Rodier at the Executive Offices, to tell him we were not lost.

It was too late to see the house that night, or to do anything but get a hot bath and go to bed. But there was ample opportunity the next day, for poor little Helen was completely done up from our trip and could not lift her head from the pillow. After seeing that she was better left alone, I wandered through the big house by myself and found it very lovely and comfortable. It was like an English country house, long and low, with a charming out-of-doors dining room at one end, opening off the formal dining room, which was architecturally balanced on the opposite side by a sunny terrace overlooking the Connecticut River. There was a long music room opening on the terrace, with many deep-set windows and a great fireplace.

The cozy room I liked best of all gave off this great room in which there was always a glowing fire, books, big easy chairs, and a couch upholstered in English chintz. Nearly the entire end of the room was glass, one tremendous piece set in a moulding. Thus the view of Ascutney, the high mountain that dominates the landscape, was framed in a picture I shall never forget.

The entrance to the house was through a large hall furnished with refectory tables, heads of elk and other animals, very formal Venetian chests and long seats—picturesque, but not homelike. The second floor contained many bedrooms and sleeping porches. After my survey of the house I returned to my own sweet room, where I wrote my impressions of the place to the President, and to my mother, apologizing to the former for giving him anxiety over us the day before.

In a few days Margaret arrived; also the Sayres with their first baby, then about six months old, and the house was buzzing with life.

Cornish is a charming spot, a mecca for artists and cultivated people. The chief rivalry among these delightful folk seemed to be who could make the loveliest garden. Whenever my thoughts turn back to that wonderful summer, there seems about it all a halo of gorgeous colour from the flowers, and music made by the river where nearly every day we walked when the President was there. He was like a boy home from school, when he could steal a week-end away from Washington and come there to the peace and quiet of the hills. When we walked we would try to forget that lurking behind every tree was a Secret Service man. We would go, always a car full of us, on long motor rides through that lovely country, exploring new roads and sometimes very bad ones, getting back in the late twilight for tea on the terrace, or stopping at a picturesque little teahouse en route; then a late dinner, after which the best part of the day would come.

With the curtains drawn to shut out the cold night air, we would gather before a fire, and together read the latest dispatches sent from Washington, from Europe, from Mexico, from everywhere. The President would clarify each problem for me, and outline the way he planned to meet it. Or if, happily, nothing was pressing, we sometimes read aloud, and discussed the things we both loved. Such times were rare, but when they came they seemed a real diversion for him.

Dr. Grayson, the girls and Frank Sayre decided to read aloud the President's *A History of the American People,* and would collect in the music room where first one and then the other would read. We sat in a little room adjoining and they would frequently call in through the open door to comment on some condition where history seemed to be repeating itself, or ask some question, until, one night, the President said: "Do you youngsters realize that I have taught most of my life, and that right now I am in the midst of so much history in the making that I cannot turn my mind back to those times? Besides, I have never been proud of that History. I wrote it only to teach myself something about our country." Turning to me, he added: "You know it was first published in *Harper's Magazine,* in four or five instalments. When they offered me a thousand dollars for it I thought it meant the entire thing and accepted it. So when, on the appearance of the second instalment, they sent a check for another thousand dollars, I returned it saying they had overlooked the fact they had already paid me. Imagine my surprise to get the check back again with the delightful news that it was a thousand dollars for each instalment. Whereupon I took all the family to England for the summer, for it was like a windfall." That last word reminded him to ask, as he often did: "Do you know the interesting derivation of that word windfall? I looked it up once and it comes from an old English custom that tenantry on great landed estates must never cut the trees, but that all timbers brought low by the wind or other cause were theirs by right. Such wood was designated in law as 'windfall.' "

These happy days would end all too quickly when Mr. Wilson, accompanied always by Dr. Grayson, would leave us and go back to Washington. From there I had long, delightful letters from him every day until he could come again; and his letters kept me *en rapport* with the stirring things with which each day was crowded.

The house up there seemed dead until he came again. Helen and I would drive or walk every day. The nearest village was Windsor, Vermont, to enter whose sacred precincts it was necessary to cross a toll bridge. There was a special arrangement whereby cars from the "President's Cottage," as it was called, paid the toll by the month. One day when we were walking we wanted to go into the village and had no money with us. We borrowed a dollar from one of the Secret Service men, as the old woman who kept the tollgate was a dragon, and we did not want to ask favours of her. So we approached her and tendered our silver cartwheel. Without so much as looking at us she handed back ninety-five cents. Helen said: "What is the charge for crossing the bridge on foot?" She snapped back: "Two cents." Following this lead Helen said: "Well, you gave me only ninety-five cents when it should have been ninety-six." "No," said the dragon; "it is two cents for one person to cross, but five cents for two together." This illuminating information explained much to me then and since concerning Vermont thrift!

The old woman was a character. People who had been there for years told us she had never been seen even to nod her head to anyone crossing the bridge, and for her to speak was unknown. So we decided to play a game and see who could break down her defence and make her acknowledge a presence. As we passed we would all say "Good morning," or "Good afternoon"; but never a sound came from those hard old lips. At last, just a few days before my visit was to end, the President, Helen and I drove in to Windsor. We halted on the bridge and he leaned out and lifted the Scotch cap he always wore when driving in the open car and said in that delightful voice that never failed to thrill me: "I am afraid we give you a great deal of trouble going back and forth so much." "Naw," she said, "it's my job." And for the first time she turned and looked at him, and, something in her responding to what he gave out, *she smiled!* When we drove on, Helen and I exclaimed, and the President said: "Poor old woman. Her smile reminded me of what some fellow said about another's face; that it was like 'the breaking up of a hard winter.' I think I understand how grim you must be if 'it is only your job' you are doing and you see nothing bigger ahead."

Soon after this the day came when I was to leave. Two friends of mine from Geneva, New York, Mr. and Mrs. Hugh L. Rose, were coming in their car for me and we were to motor to the Jersey coast for a week with my mother and sister Bertha and then go to Geneva where I would remain until September.

Those days in Cornish had brought the banishment of any doubt of my love for Woodrow Wilson, but had not overcome my reluctance to marry him while he was in the White House. I told him if he were defeated for re-election I would marry him, but if not I felt still uncertain of assuming all the responsibility it would necessarily bring. So the day arrived when my friends were to come to Harlakenden for luncheon, and then we were to start immediately on our journey. The day dawned clear and beautiful, and after breakfast we went on the terrace where the pouch with official mail was always brought, and where each morning we worked together on what it contained.

We followed this routine as usual, until it was finished, but there was lead in our hearts. Then we went for our favourite walk along the river. It was dreadful to leave with no definite promise beyond what I have written; but so it had to be; and after a formal lunch the entire household gathered at the front door to see us off, and as we sped down the driveway I looked back to see his figure alone, in his white flannels, outlined against the darkness of the open door.

Those were two very long months, July and August, 1915, which I spent visiting the Roses in Geneva. My determination to wait for the result of the 1916 election was weakening. Though I tried to keep to what I then deemed to be a wise decision, Mr. Wilson's letters told in every line his need of the sustaining power of love—though never consciously, for he scorned what is said to be akin to love, that is, pity.

I was glad when September came and I was back in my own tiny house in Washington where I could think things out alone, and did not have to be entertained. I found the house a bower of flowers with, what was much more important to me, a note of welcome and the confirmation of a plan made before I left Cornish that I should come that night to dine at the White House and we would go afterwards for a motor drive, where we could talk aloof from other eyes and ears.

When I arrived for dinner both Helen and Margaret welcomed me at the door, but the President had had to see the Secretary of War on an urgent matter. So we sat in the Red Room and talked while we waited for him. Helen said she thought the strain of things was telling on him dreadfully, and both the girls frankly stated that they felt it largely my fault. Just at that moment he came in from the Blue Room, looking so distinguished in his evening clothes, and with both hands held out to welcome me. When I put mine in them and looked into those eyes—unlike any others in the world—something broke down inside me, and I knew I could, and would, go to the end of the world with or for him.

He had changed, his eyes seemed pools of tragic suffering. Such moments are too tense to last, and this one was broken by the commonplace announcement from the butler that dinner was served. Here we renewed the delightful sense of comradeship we four always had together, and told of all the happenings of the weeks since we had parted. After dinner Margaret had to hurry off to some engagement, so faithful little Helen joined us for our ride. We took a very long one, and the President told me of the increasing danger of our

28 April. 1915 ——

My dear Mrs. Galt,

I have ordered a copy of Hamerton's "Round My House" through the bookseller, but while we are waiting for it I take the liberty of sending you a copy from the Congressional Library. I hope it will give you a little pleasure. I can't think anything more than to give you pleasure,—you have given me so much! If it rains this evening, would it be any fun for you to come around a have a little reading,—and if it does not rain, are you game for another ride? If you are not in when this gets to you, perhaps you will be gracious enough to telephone Margaret.

Your sincere and grateful friend,

Woodrow Wilson

FACSIMILE OF FIRST NOTE RECEIVED FROM WOODROW WILSON

being unable to keep out of the War; of the domestic complications, and of the continuing difficulties with Mexico. When we were returning through Rock Creek Park he turned and said: "And so, little girl, I have no right to ask you to help me by sharing this load that is almost breaking my back, for I know your nature and you might do it out of sheer pity." I am proud to say that despite the fact that Mr. Murphy, of the Secret Service, and Robinson the chauffeur were on the front seat, and Helen beside me on the back seat, I put my arms around his neck and said: "Well, if you won't ask me, I will volunteer, and be ready to be mustered in as soon as can be."

Of course the ride was prolonged, and we three were like children as we mapped out plans. For there seemed no reason to postpone things any longer.

On the next morning, September 4, 1915, Margaret and Nell were told of our engagement. The only question now was when to take the country into our confidence. I thought it best to wait a year, when the Presidential campaign should be over and when, no matter what the result, I promised I would marry him. I was convinced the Republicans would win, and had a sort of stubborn pride to show the world that it was the man and not the President I loved and honoured. Mr. Wilson strongly protested this delay, and said he needed me, which made it hard to hold to my own conviction.

Then suddenly something happened which changed the entire situation, and might have changed the current of our lives. I was alone in my house for dinner and had promised later in the evening to go for a drive in the park with the President and Dr. Grayson. About eight o'clock the Doctor arrived alone, looking worried and upset. He said the President had sent him to tell me something which he could not bring himself to write.

It was this. Colonel House was at the White House, having just returned from a conference with Secretary McAdoo. They both had been told in confidence of our engagement and, the Colonel said, they had sounded out a few people, particularly newspaper men, who told them the gossip was that should the rumours concerning our engagement be true, Mrs. Peck was going to come out against the President, saying she had letters from him which would be compromising; and that all the old whispered scandals of the 1912 campaign would be revived. To this the President had replied it was his duty as a gentleman to protect me from such backstairs gossip. For himself or his political fortunes, it made no difference—that this campaign of slander had been futile before, and if tried would be again. But the publicity would hurt and involve me in a way he had no right to ask. So he had set himself to write and tell me but, to quote Dr. Grayson: "He went white to the lips, and his hand shook as I sat watching him try to write; his jaw set, determined no matter what it cost him, to spare you; but after a long time he put the pen down and said: 'I cannot bring myself to write this; you go, Grayson, and tell her everything and say my only alternative is to release her from any promise.'"

The little Doctor choked as he repeated this. For myself I was silent, unable to comprehend such a situation. At last the Doctor rose to go, asking: "What shall I tell him?" I answered: "Tell him I will write."

When he was gone, I sat for hours thinking, thinking, when, as suddenly as the blow had fallen, its weight lifted, and I saw things in their true proportions. It was our *lives* that mattered, not politics, not scandal. If I did not care enough for the man to share his misfortunes, his sorrows, then it was a futile love! I would glory in standing by when the world scoffed and doubted, for in the end he would triumph and vindicate my trust.

I lighted my desk light and wrote from my heart:

> "1308 Twentieth Street.
> "Sept. 19—1915

"Dearest—
"The dawn has come—and the hideous dark of the hour before the dawn has been lost in the gracious gift of light.

"I have been in the big chair by the window, where I have fought out so many problems, and all the hurt, selfish feeling has gone with the darkness—and I now see straight—straight into the heart of things and am ready to follow the road 'where love leads.'

"How many times I have told you I wanted to help—and now when the first test has come I faltered— But the faltering was *for* love—not lack of love. I am not afraid of any gossip or threat, with your love as my shield—and even now this room echoes with your voice—as you plead, 'Stand by me—don't desert me!'

"This is my pledge, dearest one, I will stand by you—not for duty, not for pity, not for honour—but for love—trusting, protecting, comprehending love. And no matter whether the wine be bitter or sweet we will share it together and find happiness in the comradeship.

"Forgive my unreasonableness tonight (I mean last night, for it is already Sunday morning), and be willing to trust me.

"I have not thought out what course we will follow for the immediate present for I promised we would do that together.

"I am so tired I could put my head down on the desk and go to sleep—but nothing could bring me real rest until I had pledged you my love and my allegiance.

"Your own

"EDITH."

I sent this letter early that morning. The day passed with no word or reply. This I could not understand but I felt the evening would bring the explanation. But the next day and the next followed, and I felt humiliated and hurt. About noon of that third day Dr. Grayson came. Grave anxiety marked his chiselled features. Without even shaking hands he said: "I beg that you will come with me to the White House. The President is very ill, and you are the only person who can help. I can do nothing." He added: "I know it is a lot to ask after what you have both been through, but it is a desperate situation. Neither Miss Margaret nor Miss Bones is here, so I will have to act as chaperone." "Did the President ask you to come?" I asked; and he said: "No, I told him I was coming, and he said it would be unfair to you and weak in him to ask it." Then Dr. Grayson added: "If you could see him you would not hesitate. He looks as I imagine the martyrs looked when they were broken on the wheel. He does not speak or sleep or eat."

I had to think! So I left him and went to my room. Could it be my letter had fallen into alien hands? Could he think I was of such base metal I could not stand an acid test? Did he still care, or did he doubt? Then I remembered what I had written: "I will stand by."

So I went, and the Doctor and I were strangely silent as we drove through the familiar streets; and when we left the elevator on the second floor of the White House, he went quickly to a door which he opened and beckoned me to follow.

The curtains were drawn and the room dark; on the pillow I saw a white, drawn face with burning eyes dark with hidden pain. Brooks, the coloured valet, was by the bed. No word was spoken, only an eager hand held out in welcome, which I took to find icy cold, and when I unclasped it we were alone.

Strangely in these tense moments things are understood with no need of words. I never asked why he had not answered my letter, only had it reached him. He said, "Yes."

Three months later, the day after we were married and were sitting before the fire in our cozy suite at Hot Springs, Virginia, my husband asked to make a confession of something that had lain heavy on his spirit. I laughed and said: "Well, I promise to absolve you." He drew from his pocket the letter which I had written in the early hours of that September morning. The seal was unbroken, the envelope worn on the edges from being so long in his pocket. He said: "I think I am rarely a coward; but when this letter came that Sunday morning after a sleepless night, I could not open it, for I felt the world slipping from under my feet. I was so sure, with your horror of publicity and all the rest of it, that this was the end, and you would never see me again, that I could not bring myself to face the written words; so I put it here, where it has been ever since. Now with you beside me I *want* to open it, remembering no matter what the hurt it holds that you came like an angel of light to heal my wound."

We read it together and what he said need not be told here; only that he begged that the letter never be destroyed.

Years afterwards, when I asked Colonel House to tell me where he got such an unjust impression as he gave the President about Mrs. Peck, he said he had never heard anything about it from anybody; that he and Secretary McAdoo had planned it between them because they thought at the time that a second marriage of the President might prevent his re-election. Colonel House concluded his story: "In that I was mistaken, for I think you have been a great asset." When I asked Mr. McAdoo about it, he said that it was entirely "the Colonel's idea"! This shifting of responsibility between Colonel House and Mr. McAdoo was a matter I never mentioned to my husband because I knew it would make him see red.

Now to go back a way. After much thought Mr. Wilson and I decided to announce our engagement on October 7, 1915, giving the news to the representatives of the press assigned to the White House. The President phrased the announcement and asked Mr. Tumulty to give a copy to each man.

It was after dinner on the evening of the sixth. I entered the study at the White House just after Mr. Tumulty had left. The focal point of this intimate room was the flat-top desk, a gift to this Government from Queen Victoria. On it stood the green-shaded student's lamp that Mr. Wilson had used while studying law at the University of Virginia. He loved to work under that lamp which was lighted every night. In the years to come that desk grew very familiar, made sacred to me by the hours which he spent there; and while never cleared of work, for fresh demands came to it every hour of the day, it always gave the impression of perfect orderliness. The desk is a double one, very large, with stacks of small drawers at each corner, and a deep central drawer on each side between the stacks. The President had given strict orders that anything of immediate importance from the State, War or Navy Department should be put at once in the central drawer on the opposite side (next the door as one entered the study) from where he sat. He never went in or out of the room without looking in that drawer to see if there were things which he should act on at once. In later years I assumed that supervision for him, particularly during the War, when things moved so swiftly that even a half-hour's delay might be serious. So no matter where I was, or what I was doing, I would go to this receptacle every little while and often find it too full even to close. And many a time, when we planned a free evening together, The Drawer, with all the problems sealed in big linen envelopes bearing an ominous red square clipped in the corner—which meant *"Immediate and Important"*—would end all hope, and we would settle down to work instead of to rest and read, as we had hoped.

But I have wandered far away from that October night when I stood by the desk and leaned over the President's shoulder to see how the announcement looked typed for the press. I am glad that I paused there, for that serene evening in the study, with a fire crackling on the hearth, and the blinds drawn, was the last quiet time we were to have together in the White House for so many months and years to come.

Next morning I was plunged into a maelstrom of kindly curiosity—

publicity of every sort, and contacts with every description of person, from real friends and charming acquaintances to self-seekers and cranks. Before eight o'clock telephone and door bells were ringing, and when I heard some one coming up to my room I thought it was the maid with the breakfast tray. But not at all; it was a lady whom I knew, but who had never had access to my bedroom, and who "just could not wait to tell you how wonderful it was." My poor servants were as unprepared as I for what was before us, and could not cope with persons like this woman.

Hardly had I recovered from this episode when some one I really wanted to see called, and I went downstairs to the drawing room. I had been there a few moments, when a ring at the bell announced another caller. I told the maid to say that I wished to be excused. She opened the door and, *sans cérémonie,* in rushed a man I knew very slightly, did not like, and to whom I had always been "Mrs. Galt." He caught me in his arms and kissed me, saying: "I always knew you would do something big, and this is the biggest thing yet. My wife is out of town but I am sure she will come immediately back so as to be at the wedding." He cast down a cluster of flowers and went as he had come, leaving me speechless. I felt that the world had suddenly gone mad.

The next thing that stands out in that day of readjustment to a new life was the arrival of a tiny black dachshund, just about two weeks old, poor little thing! His neck was encircled by a red, white and blue ribbon, tied in a huge bow, through which was fastened a big card stating: "My name is America." This seemed the last straw, and if the little beast had not been so utterly miserable, it would have been funny. The dog was too young to keep, so I returned it next morning with a courteous note expressing appreciation but adding it would be impossible to keep it as I was leaving for Philadelphia early the following day. Another gift, which I still cherish, is an original drawing by C. K. Berryman, the talented cartoonist of the Washington *Evening Star*—a Cupid standing beneath a big tree on the White House lawn.

The history of October 7, 1915, would not be complete without mention that it was the first time the President felt he could call on my mother without exciting curiosity. So he went that afternoon to see her, and later she, my sister, brother and I dined at the White House.

The only other guests were the McAdoos, and we had a jolly evening all to ourselves.

The following day the President was to go to Philadelphia for the opening of the World Series in baseball. Mr. Wilson had asked Mother and me to join the party. The day was radiant. It was our first appearance together since our announcement, and along the route crowds gathered to greet us. Upon reaching Philadelphia we had an escort of police. No matter how accustomed one grows to the deference paid the great office of the Presidency, it never ceases to be a thrilling experience to have all traffic stopped, the way cleared, and hear acclaims from thousands of throats. So, in this first experience where I shared the acclaim, I was excited as any child.

The Mayor of Philadelphia was at the box to greet us. We found a charming welcome everywhere, and people tried in the nicest way to express their interest in and approval of me. This was trying in some respects, but I was so content and happy that even the natural curiosity of strangers did not seem an intrusion. The following day Mother and I dined at the White House. The next morning I drove to Baltimore to do some shopping. That evening, October 10th, was the first time the President dined with me alone in my own home.

By this time letters and telegrams were coming to us both from all over the country. Of course the majority of those from strangers went to the White House, but I was inundated by letters of every sort including delightful ones from old friends, many of whom I had known since childhood. Then there were requests for everything from money, photographs, automobiles and advice to discarded clothing. One letter stated the writer was 5 feet, 8 inches tall; weight 140; hip measurement 40; bust 38; very attractive; only needing up-to-date clothes to be a beauty.

The days were too full for us to see each other with regularity, so we had a direct telephone line installed from the White House to my house. It did not go through the exchange, but connected one instrument with the other. By this means we could talk over things that needed immediate conference. On the days when we had no time for a visit the President would send me by messenger foreign and domestic information so I could keep in touch with his work. These always bore a pencilled line of comment or explanation.

Often he would be so keen to know what the morrow would bring that he would say: "Well, if there is anything very important I will call you and Helen into executive session." And many times Helen would come early in the morning to see me and tell me the results of some decision he had made the day before; what the newspaper men said; what the effect on the country had been; how Germany had reacted to it. If it were possible, the President himself wrote a few lines to keep me in touch with his thoughts, and I sent him my suggestions or comments.

This became later a daily means of communication. They were vivid letters from him—often only a few lines—but how perfectly they brought me his anxieties, his sense of personal responsibility for the welfare of the people of the country, and his eagerness to have the point of view of one as remote as I from the great moral issues at stake.

In this way I followed day by day every phase of the mosaic which he was shaping into a pattern of statecraft, and we continued this partnership of thought and comradeship unbroken to the last day of his life. It was a rare privilege, and except for formal interviews with officials I always "sat in" when one or two people we knew came to discuss policies. In that way I was never a stranger to any subject, and often able in small ways to be of help.

It had been a custom for Mr. Wilson to join some of the members of the Princeton Class of '79 at a dinner each year, but since he had become President the practise had been discontinued. I begged that it should be revived and a dinner given at the White House. This was done shortly after the announcement of our engagement, and I was elected an honourary member of the class.

Our second trip together was on November 27th when we went to New York for the Army and Navy football game at the Polo Grounds. According to a time-honoured custom the President occupies a box first on the side of the Army; then during the intermission between halves the Admirals of the Navy cross the gridiron to pay their respects to the Commander in Chief and escort him to a similar box on the side of the Navy.

On this day, as we crossed the field, there was a perfect ovation. Every one seemed to be our friend.

Among the gifts which came at the time our engagement was announced was a large nugget of gold from the people of California

DRAWING ROOM WHERE CEREMONY WAS PERFORMED

with the request that part of it be used for our wedding ring. It was such a charming letter that we decided to accept the gift and the suggestion. I say "accept the gift," for we both felt it to be the part of good taste not to have wedding invitations but to send announcement cards after the ceremony. For in that way we would announce to the public that we did not expect gifts. Otherwise every official would have felt it was incumbent on him to send the President a gift, and neither he nor I desired any. We remembered the unkind criticism of President and Mrs. Taft when they had sent out thousands of invitations for the celebration of their Silver Wedding, and how they were embarrassed by receiving gifts from people or corporations whose fortunes were controlled by the Government. But the nugget of gold from an entire State was, after all, not so intrinsically valuable, and it had a romantic appeal which we loved. So, the plain gold band that Woodrow Wilson placed on my finger on December 18, 1915, and which has never been off, was fashioned from the nugget with as little alloy as possible. We found that the ring required so little metal there was still a good deal left. Later we used some of it to make a scarf pin for the President. This scarf pin was a reproduction of the official seal of the President of the United States and was enamelled in natural colours; it was so small it was never in the least conspicuous; he rarely dressed for the daytime that he did not wear it.

It was characteristic of Woodrow Wilson that on the day he left office, March 4, 1921, after wearing the scarf pin to the Capitol whither he had accompanied Mr. Harding for his Inauguration, he took the pin out of his scarf, put it away and never wore it again.

While Governor of New Jersey he had a pin of the Governor's seal. After he left office that, too, was put away.

But I must finish this little history of the California gold nugget. Again there was some left, and this we had made into a seal ring, with "Woodrow Wilson" wrought, as a seal, in the shorthand characters which he used in his personal memoranda. The characters were copied exactly as written by him. We both liked the idea of each having a ring of the same mining, and the seal was a very convenient one for especial use. Years after, when the Treaty of Versailles was signed in that gorgeous Hall of Mirrors in the Palace of Versailles, after the name "Woodrow Wilson" appears the seal from this ring which he was wearing on that eventful day, June 28, 1919.

We had decided to have a very quiet wedding in my own house with only the two families present. So many of my friends told me: "Oh, you should be married in the White House; it would be so historic." But I told them we preferred simplicity to historic background, and that nothing would induce me to be married there.

That settled, the next thing to decide was the ceremony. I being an Episcopalian, and the President an elder of the Presbyterian Church, it seemed proper for both faiths to be represented. I decided to ask the rector of St. Margaret's Church, where I had a pew at that time, and Mr. Wilson's pastor of the Presbyterian Church to share the ceremony prescribed by the Episcopal prayer book. So Dr. Herbert Scott Smith, of St. Margaret's Church, Washington, D. C., and Dr. James H. Taylor, of the Central Presbyterian Church, Washington, D. C., were asked.

I had previously expected a Bishop to perform the ceremony, explaining to him that I could not ask his wife to be present as I was asking no one outside our immediate families, and as she did not live in Washington it would not seem a discourtesy to omit her. He replied that he and she perfectly understood the matter. He was to be my guest at the old Shoreham Hotel, and he was to arrive two days before the date of the wedding. Imagine my surprise and indignation the morning of December 16th to receive a letter from the Bishop stating he and his wife had arrived at the Shoreham where they had found the reservations made for them, and where they were most comfortable; that they were sailing in a few days for England where it would cause his wife "much chagrin to acknowledge to her titled friends that she had not been asked to the marriage of the President where her husband had officiated"; so she had decided to come with him, and would, he felt sure, be welcome at the ceremony.

The moment I finished re-reading this document—for I could not believe I had read it aright the first time—I walked straight to my desk and wrote my answer. I thanked the Bishop for letting me know of the embarrassing situation his wife found herself in regarding my wedding, but I reminded him that several weeks before I had explained why I could not include her in the wedding party. It was impossible to change or add to my list, and so the only other course was to excuse him from his promise to perform the ceremony, which I was doing at once.

Having signed this I rang the private telephone to the White House and fortunately found the President alone in his study. I read both letters to him. He was far more tolerant than I, saying of course he agreed with me that it was a preposterous thing the Bishop had done, but that after all his office demanded respect. Moreover, we should consider the gossip it would cause. "Why not wait and think it over a little?" he said. But I was hurt to the quick that a head of our church should have so affronted the President of the United States. I said: "No, this letter goes to him right now. I will postpone our wedding rather than be bludgeoned into a thing of this kind." "Yes," came the voice over the telephone. "I was afraid of that. But, after all, the poor fellow has enough to stand with a wife like that."

The letter was dispatched, and Dr. Smith was asked to act in the Bishop's stead. He was very fine about the whole thing. On December 16th, Mr. I. H. Hoover, head usher of the White House, got our marriage license.

The day of our wedding was clear, but we had had a light snow the day before which made the air crisp and bracing. My house was turned over to decorators and caterers. Mr. Hoover had offered to relieve me of all the detail in these matters. So I can comment on them without the hint of bad taste for he ably took command and the results were very lovely. The house was small, only two rooms deep. Every piece of furniture was removed from the lower floor, which consisted of a small drawing room, with bay window, where the ceremony was performed; a dining room, and an entrance hall. The ceremony was set for 8:30 P. M. Apropos of this, Mr. Wilson was amused when, that morning, Mr. Hoover came to him and said: "Mr. President, I will be on hand tonight as usual to tell you when it is time for the ceremony." "Do you think I will need that, Hoover?" he asked.

The President reached my house a half-hour before the time for the ceremony, coming alone except for the escort of the Secret Service. He ran upstairs at once to my sitting room on the second floor, and punctually at the stroke of the clock, Hoover tapped on the door and solemnly announced: "Mr. President, it is eight-thirty." We smiled at each other as we both said "Thank you," and went downstairs together.

In the course of the ceremony when the minister asked, "Who giveth this woman to be married to this man?" my mother stepped forward and put my hand in that of Mr. Wilson.

Following the ceremony we had a buffet supper, and left soon afterwards. Going down the steps to the waiting motor we found that the streets had been roped off for a block in every direction so that no spectators were near. We were in the motor, and off, before the crowd at a distance realized that we were leaving.

I wore a plain black velvet gown with a velvet hat trimmed with goura, and had lovely orchids. The President wore a cutaway coat and grey striped trousers. We had no attendants. His daughters, Margaret, Jessie and Nell, were there; also Mr. McAdoo and Frank Sayre; Mrs. Howe, the President's sister; her daughter, Mrs. Cothran; Dr. Stockton Axson, the first Mrs. Wilson's brother, who had given me the loveliest welcome when our engagement was first told to him; my lovely mother, and all of my sisters and brothers and their husbands or wives; Dr. Sterling Ruffin, an old friend and the Bolling family physician; Dr. Grayson, and Altrude Gordon, who was my house guest at the time; and the brother and sister of my first husband, who also rejoiced in our happiness. Added to these were a few devoted old servitors of the various households, who stood in the hall, and when we were leaving called, in the mellow Southern voices of the negro: "God bless you, Miss Edith and Mr. President." Mother's old cook, who had belonged to my grandfather, always called me "Miss Ether." Her parting words, as we went down the steps which were taking me to a much larger life, were: "Take Jesus with you for your doctor and your friend!" Many times since I have thought that if I could take Him with as simple and childlike faith as this fine old negro woman did, the new life with its broader opportunities could have been more useful to others and more enriched for myself.

We were to take the train at the little railroad station in Alexandria, for Hot Springs, Virginia. We had a lovely drive over in the moonlight with the world lying white with snow around us. As our plans had been kept secret, the people gathered at the station in Washington were disappointed. We slipped quietly over to Alexandria with only the Secret Service men who went with us to the private car where Brooks, the President's valet, and my maid had preceded us. The railway car was filled with flowers. On a table some dainty sandwiches and fruit were arranged; and so we left about midnight for our two weeks' holiday.

When we reached Hot Springs next morning, the limousine from the White House was waiting for us, and we drove quickly to the Homestead. The mountains were white with snow, and the air from them crisp and biting; but it came to me as a real touch of welcome from *home,* for my whole early life had been spent in that stimulating climate.

Our suite at the hotel was charming; a large living room, with English chintz-covered furniture; a wood fire; windows overlooking the golf course, and flowers everywhere. We had a private dining room where the delicious meals were served; two bedrooms with baths, and rooms for the servants. All the new magazines were on a big table. The whole place justified the name *Home*stead, and the management did everything to promote our comfort and ensure us privacy.

We played golf in the mornings, and took long motor trips in the afternoons. Mr. Wilson had known that part of the country years before, so it was great fun adventuring to rediscover old roads and places he had loved. When the roads would get too bad for the heavy car to negotiate, we often got out and walked.

We started early one morning to drive to White Sulphur Springs to spend the day, but ran into heavy roads which made our progress slow, though it was possible, until we reached a stream so swollen that the chauffeur said he was afraid the water would overflow the car. We decided to get out and let him try it, and if he could make it we would cross on a tree which had fallen across the stream. If he could not, we would return in the Secret Service car and send him help. We stood in the road and watched the big Pierce Arrow lunge and plunge in the current but finally emerge triumphantly on the other side. Then came our turn, for the old tree which was to form a bridge for us was slippery and wet, and very rotten in places; but by forming a sort of human chain—the five Secret Service men, the two chauffeurs and ourselves—we steadied one another and with a real thrill of adventure reached safety.

Of course we were late, having taken hours to go; but we had lunch, walked around to old haunts and over part of the new golf course, and started back. By this time the water in the stream had gone down, and we were able to drive over; but even so we did not get back until nearly nine P. M., having started at eight in the morning. Now, I am told, the roads are so good that it is hard to believe such a distance could have taken thirteen hours.

When Christmas came, just a week later, we found in the dining room of our suite that morning a great tree with glowing lights and tinsel, and the assurances of the thought and good wishes of the guests in the hotel. Also an invitation from the management to a moving picture to be given in the lounge that afternoon. We decided to go, and so notified them, and at their request we had a little informal reception first where all the guests were presented, among them Lord and Lady Aberdeen, of Scotland. The latter was the only person who insisted upon being received in our own suite.

We had hoped to stay away three weeks; but, alas, on January 3, 1916, came news which made an immediate return to Washington necessary; and we reluctantly turned our faces homeward. At the White House we found a family party still gathered for the holidays: the Sayres, Mrs. Howe, her daughter and granddaughter Josephine besides Margaret and Helen. They gave us the most royal welcome, and had everything in festive array.

CHAPTER 7

THE suite at the White House traditionally used by the President and his wife is in the southwest corner. It consists of two large bedrooms, each with bath, and a small dressing room. We always had an open fire in these sunlit rooms, where we breakfasted alone, and so started each busy day quietly, with no servants in attendance after the big tray was brought and the small table laid. Anything to be kept hot was put on the hearth before the fire. I loved this little touch of home, for lunch and dinner were always shared with the rest of the family and the multitude of guests and relatives who constantly came and went.

Under direction of my brother Richard Wilmer, the faithful Susan (my cook, maid and personal attendant for twenty years) had done much of the work incident to closing my small home at 1308 Twentieth Street. The furnishings of my own room were moved into the White House. My bedroom there was so enormous that it could easily accommodate the pieces I brought, and I felt more at home with some of my own things around me. I took there also my piano and books. But the thing that caused much merriment to Helen and Margaret was the arrival of my Wilcox & Gibbs sewing machine, for they both said: "When do you think you will ever have time to sit down and sew on it?" Truly they were right, at that time, for the twenty-four hours never seemed to have minutes enough to encompass all the things the wife of the President must do. But in a little over a year when we entered the World War, the wheels of that machine seldom were idle as we turned out in stolen moments pajamas, surgical shirts, etc., for the Red Cross.

I tried to arrange my own appointments to correspond with those of the President, so we might be free at the same times. We found that we both could work better with the happy prospect of being together afterwards. Tasks pressed so, particularly for him, that it

89

was necessary to have a daily programme, and to keep to it. Ours was this:

Breakfast at eight o'clock sharp. Then we both went to the study to look in The Drawer and possibly, if nothing had "blown up" overnight, there was time to put signatures on commissions or other routine papers. These I always placed before my husband, and blotted and removed them as fast as possible, for there were so many every day that it was a comfort to try to keep abreast of them and permit no accumulation.

Pardon cases were studied before he signed them. They often arrived in stacks. I can see them now with their grim, grey backers, on which would be written by the Attorney General: "Reviewed and pardon denied." These always seemed terrible, and the President never accepted this recommendation without himself reading and weighing all the bulky evidence which accompanied the application. Those which bore this inscription: "The Attorney General recommends pardon," or reprieve, or commuting of sentence, were less carefully gone over; for the President's feeling was that he could safely grant leniency where the Attorney General recommended it, and save his own time for other things.

By nine o'clock Mr. Charles L. Swem, the President's private stenographer, would arrive. If I could spare the time I would linger to hear the dictation in answer to the mail which he brought, representing such a wide field of subjects. It was a delight and an education to hear the lucid answers that came with apparently no effort from a mind so well-stored.

Later I would turn to my own mail with a decided sense of anticlimax. Mostly it concerned requests for help, or suggestions as to how I could assist the cause of woman suffrage, or could influence the President to declare war, or insist that he appoint to an office some relative of the writer who had voted for Mr. Wilson. I do not mean there were never delightful letters, for there were; but very few in comparison with the hundreds of others. To go back to our daily routine:

Leaving the study I would see the housekeeper, usually stopping at the door of the little office which adjoined her room and where all the domestic business of the household was transacted. She had a book in which, after consulting the cook, she wrote out the menus

PHOTOGRAPH OF PAINTING MADE BY A. MULLER-URY
Painted just after Mrs. Wilson went to the White House, in 1916.

for the day, which I looked over, and suggested anything I wished changed. Then I would tell her as far as I could how many we would be for lunch and dinner, and how many people would have tea; for often, when I had officials, Margaret would have her friends in another room, and Helen hers in still another.

Then I would go to my mail. My secretary, Miss Edith Benham, had her desk and several telephones at the end of the big west hall outside my room. Here we worked for hours, not only on letters, but over lists for dinners, lunches and receptions; and answered the requests from Senators and Representatives wishing constituents invited to the White House. These lists might have grown to such proportions the house could not have accommodated them; but in each instance where the request had to be refused, a courteous note of explanation and regret was sent. Daily I learned new things, for instance that when the President dines out—which he does officially only with the Vice President and members of the Cabinet—the hostess submits in advance a list of prospective guests for White House approval. At first it gives one a funny feeling to tell a lady, in effect, whom she can and whom she cannot invite to her table—but I discovered that they were quite used to it, and after a while so was I.

From my vantage point in the big window-seat I could always see the President when he left his study to go to the Executive Offices. He would signal to me and I would leave all the puzzling questions and walk over with him. If the day were fine we would go through the garden; if not, under the sheltered arcade, and there have a brief moment together.

Then I would return to my job and not see him again until lunch, which we seldom had without guests; and even then, unless they were strangers and the meal a formal one, we used the little dining room as more homelike. However, this was always a time of recreation, for no business was ever discussed. We talked of books and permanent things that the present unrest could not disturb.

The Cabinet met two days a week, usually at two-thirty in the afternoon, and sometimes there would be a brief interval between lunch and that business. But when Congress was in session this short time was usually filled with receiving members who had to be consulted about legislation, or some one of the Cabinet who wanted to talk over things in his department before the others came.

Before dinner we sometimes could go in the motor for a little breath of air; after dinner, occasionally, to the theatre. More often there would be work to do and I would take my book, or unanswered letters, or other work, and sit in the study while the President studied or used his typewriter; for his was the habit of doing very confidential correspondence himself. Messages to Congress, relations with foreign governments, exchanges of notes and so on, through the State Department—all these things were done in those quiet hours together in the study, the President working under the old green-shaded student's lamp. Often it was long after midnight before he finished. Then he would look up with a smile and say: "You don't know how much easier it makes all this to have you here by me. Are you too tired to hear what I have written?" Who could have been weary with such an inspirational love? Overburdened as the days increasingly became during those years of war, these evenings come back to me now in all their richness of complete happiness.

My first public appearance as the wife of the President was at a reception to the diplomatic corps. There were 3,328 guests. I wore a white gown brocaded in silver with long white tulle drapery, then known as "angel sleeves." It was thrilling, the first time, to greet all the Cabinet in the Oval Room upstairs and then with the President precede them down the long stairway, with the naval and military aides forming an escort, the Marine Band playing "Hail to the Chief," and the waiting mass of guests bowing a welcome as we passed into the Blue Room.

On January 11th came the first State dinner to the Cabinet; then on January 14th the Vice President and Mrs. Marshall gave a dinner for us at the Willard Hotel. It was a lovely affair. The days in between were crowded with duties and pleasures. Almost every afternoon I would receive different Ambassadors and Ministers with their wives who had written for appointments to call. It seemed a little more of a courtesy to them and the countries they represented to receive them severally rather than in groups; so my secretary and I worked out a plan to ask them thirty minutes apart, for a perfectly informal cup of tea before an open fire in the Red Room. We would begin at four for the first; four-thirty for the second, and so on at half-hour intervals until six, leaving time between to have the tea table rearranged. Often the butler would be waiting with fresh cups and plates to rush right in if we overlapped our time. We always tried to find out beforehand a little of the background of the guests. When they were recently arrived and did not speak English with ease, I would try to make the interview as brief as seemed courteous to relieve them of any embarrassment. By these little informal tea parties a bond was established which became personal, as well as official, and instead of their being only a matter of routine we really enjoyed these varying and interesting contacts.

The next big event of the social season was a great ball given for us by the Pan-American Union in its beautiful building. It was a very gracious courtesy from one America to another, and I am not alone in saying it was one of the most elaborate and beautiful functions ever given in Washington. My favourite flower was, and is, the orchid; and knowing this, all through our friendship and engagement the President had sent orchids to me. I had worn them so constantly they were known as "my" flower. So imagine, if you can, the tropical beauty of the table laid in a great room in which many lights brought out the exquisite beauty of form and colour; orchids of every variety and shade, massed like a garden abloom, in the centre of which was a miniature pool reflecting the flaunting glory of the flowers. I still like to pause and revisualize that scene: the diplomatic corps in court uniforms with orders blazing on crimson and blue coats; women in trailing gowns and many jewels; the Marine Band splendid in scarlet coats; and every one smiling a welcome as we were escorted through the crowded rooms.

I had chosen a black velvet gown with long train of silver over blue, and carried a big fan of unusual design on the order of the ceremonial fans used in the Far East. It was made of grey feathers mounted on a stem of intricate mosaic work in various shades of blue.

The following day we left Washington again, this time not for a honeymoon, but for a hard tour through the West on what became known as "the President's Preparedness Campaign." For Mr. Wilson felt it his duty to go to the country and inform them of the possibility that we might be drawn into the conflict in Europe, and of the necessity of preparing for it.

Our first stop was New York City, then Pittsburgh, where, after a night on the train, we arrived in time for breakfast at the Schenley Hotel. Here I had my first experience with "the local committee." This body is made up of the outstanding citizens of the community, headed by the mayor or other official who acts in that capacity. Usually they send an advance guard of two or more (usually more) who board the President's train several stations ahead of where he is to speak. Their function is to inform him of local conditions; how it would be well if he could say a word about Smith or Jones who is running on the State ticket; how it would help the Party if he would stress this policy and soft-pedal that, and so forth. These gentlemen usually were first met by Mr. Tumulty at the train platform and then presented to the President. When the business of the day was over, he would present them to me.

Every station through which the train passed was crowded with people, and if we paused they always begged the President to speak. If there was time he did; if not, he would appear on the platform and greet them. As we were to be in Pittsburgh all day, and there was an endless succession of people clamouring for audiences, Dr. Grayson and I slipped through a back door of the hotel and took a drive.

We went on to Cleveland, Milwaukee, Chicago, Des Moines, Kansas City and St. Louis, everywhere finding the people interested in what the President said, but almost apathetic regarding the possibility of war. They seemed to feel the Atlantic Ocean a barrier that nothing could overcome, and that there was no reason for anxiety. Despite the warmest of welcomes everywhere, the reaction to his messages of warning was disappointing to Mr. Wilson.

In Chicago at the Blackstone Hotel, after an exhausting day of excitement and addresses, the President went to bed earlier than usual. My room was separated from his by a big sitting room, and I was writing letters when I heard a loud knocking at his door. This surprised me, for always, in travelling, the Secret Service men sit in the hall, guarding the President's room and never allow strangers to approach it. Therefore I went quickly to investigate and found Dr. Grayson. He said: "Oh, Mrs. Wilson, I just came to see if the President is all right." "Certainly," I said; "I think he is asleep unless your knocking has awakened him." He hesitated a moment and then said: "May I just come in and see?" This struck me as very strange, so I asked: "What is the matter; have you any bad news?" "Not a thing; I just know he was pretty tired and want to see if he needs anything."

We found my husband asleep and did not disturb him. I learned next morning that some poor fellow had fallen from a window just over the room occupied by the President and been instantly killed. The Secret Service men feared he might have been trying to get in the window below with some evil intent, but this was never proved. Nevertheless, after this every hotel room was searched by a Secret Service man before the President could enter.

Writing the words "Secret Service" recalls the funny idea of my coloured Susan when the President used to come to see me before we were married. She always announced with ceremony: "The President and his Silver Service." But when I told her it was not "Silver" Service but "Secret" Service, she amended it to "The President and his Secretive Servants," and beyond that she refused to budge!

Returning to Washington, early in February, 1916, we settled down to a routine of work and entertaining and being entertained by the members of the Cabinet which went on unbrokenly except for an occasional holiday on the *Mayflower*. We would leave late Friday night, or Saturday afternoon, and slip down the Potomac for the week-end. These were red-letter days, for quiet hours were balm after the turmoil of a busy week, and the commander of the *Mayflower,* our good friend Captain "Bob" Berry, always saw to everything to add to our pleasure and comfort. He would be notified by telephone at what time we would come aboard; so when the limousine would reach the gate of the Navy Yard there were Marines standing at attention. At the gangplank the Commandant of the Yard and his aide would greet us. At the top of the gangplank the commander of the *Mayflower* and the officers of the ship stood at salute and the crew was drawn up at attention while the band played the National Anthem.

This little ceremony over, all hands went quickly to work to untie from the dock and get away. We loved getting into steamer coats and sitting on deck bundled in rugs in the comfortable wicker chairs. The shore receded and for a brief time we forgot Washington.

If we sailed in the afternoon we always found tea prepared, with the cake, made of pecan nuts, of which I was specially fond. The chef was a master hand at pastry. This personage, an old Chinaman, had been on the boat a great many years and he loved to make things which were delicious but too rich for daily diet. So we often suggested a simple menu.

Even on a holiday work was carried along. The President's typewriter was never left behind, for it was more essential to him than any other piece of baggage. The faithful Brooks, the President's valet, and my maid always went down ahead of us. When we arrived everything was unpacked and in order. Even the "office" would be established.

We usually stayed on deck until we passed Mount Vernon, for we loved the formal tribute which was always paid to our first President. Officers and crew assembled on deck, two sailors holding the lines which control the flag at the prow of the boat. When abreast the tomb, the colours were dipped, and the bugler stepped from the line in which the band was formed and sounded "Taps," while the bell tolled solemnly. Everyone on board stood at salute, my husband removing his hat and holding it across his breast. Then "The Star-Spangled Banner" was played, and the gracious assurance of respect and remembrance was over.

We both liked studying the charts to see if we could find some little tributary of the river to explore. After Mount Vernon was passed we usually went to speak to old Captain Luckett, who had been the pilot of the *Mayflower* ever since it had become the President's yacht, and who would have been heartbroken to have the boat sail without him. Then we would go to the chart-room where often Captain Berry would join us and we would try to find a new port.

Later when the United States had entered the War, we had an amusing result of one of these explorations. Finding on the chart a tiny speck marked Tangier Island, we asked if we could stop and inspect it. Captain Berry said we should reach that part of the river very early next morning, and he would send the launch over to see what the conditions were. In the morning he reported the water about Tangier Island too shallow for the launch but feasible for a rowboat which would take us to a small fishing village. Accompanied by two of the officers and the Secret Service staff, we transshipped to the tiny boat, landed on a wooden "dock" and made our precarious way over a single plank which led to dry land at one end of the small street that composed this quaint little town. On either side were neat little one-story houses, each with a tiny front garden, surrounded by a picket fence. The yards contained the family graves marked by simple headstones. We walked the entire length of the village, and, although by this time it was nearly noon, we saw only closed doors and drawn blinds; not a person in sight. It truly seemed a city of the dead.

Curious to know the reason for this, after returning to the dock, the President said: "Let's go back again and see if we can find out what this means." About the nearest houses we found no sign of life as before, but at the far end of the street our return had taken the inhabitants by surprise. The people were all outside. But the moment they saw us they sped back into their houses and closed and locked the doors. Only one old man stood his ground, peering at us through his glasses. My husband lifted his cap. "Good morning, sir," he said. "I hope we are not disturbing your quiet homes here." The old fellow stood agape and, slowly removing his own hat, he said: "Isn't this the President?" When Mr. Wilson replied, "Yes, I have that honour, sir," the old man broke into a hearty laugh and said: "Well, sir, I want to shake your hand, for we all think a lot of you down here." After a hearty handshake he continued to laugh and then told us that early that morning they had seen a big ship anchor outside in the river, then some men in uniform put out in small boats for their island. This gave them great alarm for they decided that the officers were Germans coming to blow up the island. They had been greatly relieved, however, when the men did not land and thought they were safe—until a second time the same boat put out and headed for their abode. Then the people held hasty counsel and decided, as they had no means of defence, they had better shut their doors and windows and pray.

The old fellow added: "Well, sir, when I saw your lady with you I kinder felt she wouldn't be with Germans; so I thought I'd just stay out here and she would see there was no harm in me." Then he begged to go and tell his friends. In a moment the street was filled and every one wanted to shake hands with the President.

They were a sturdy, happy people who lived by fishing. Even the tiny children seemed as much at home in their boats as a duck is in water.

We often went back to see our friends after that, and bought crabs or fish for our Sunday luncheons. This little village is worth a visit, for I know of none other like it. Without a horse or motor on the island, it seems removed from the modern world.

On the Sundays we were at home we went alternately to the Episcopal and Presbyterian churches. Often we would dine or go for Sunday night supper with my mother, for it was a real holiday to have a family party and no formality. If this was not practicable, owing to house guests, we would reverse the order, and my mother, brother and sister would come to us.

Saturdays we tried to keep as free as possible. If we succeeded we would take long motor rides, sometimes going as far as Harper's Ferry for dinner at the Hill Top House where a courteous old coloured man would be at the door to welcome us, always saying: "Suppose you want fried chicken and corn bread, sir?"

On March 26, 1916, we had a message saying a little girl had been born to Jessie and Frank Sayre. She was named Eleanor, and was a fine baby.

The next events that stand out were Easter, and the egg-rolling in the White House grounds on Easter Monday. All the families of the Cabinet were invited, and many friends with their children. It is really an unusual sight—the thousands of youngsters, white and black, all with gaily coloured baskets filled with eggs and rabbits; all moving towards the south portico where the President came to greet them, and where we stood for many minutes watching the kaleidoscope of colour.

In May, 1916, we went to Charlotte, North Carolina, for the celebration of the anniversary of the Mecklenberg Declaration of Independence. It was a boiling hot day; one of those sudden descents of summer that cause unexpected discomfort. The ceremonies were in the open to accommodate the thousands of people from all over the State who had poured into the town. A large wooden platform or stage had been put up, with no cover, not even an awning; and rows of chairs placed to seat the official party, all facing a blazing afternoon sun. The hapless Marine Band had been summoned from Washington, and they wore the thick, red uniform coats of winter weight. It was terrible for them. Fortunately for me, I was wearing a thin white dress and a large straw hat—which did afford a little shelter.

PRESIDENT AND MRS. WILSON LEAVING D. A. R. HALL, WASHINGTON, D. C., APRIL 17, 1916

The front of the platform was draped in bunting, and a table, with ice water and glasses, placed before the Mayor of Charlotte who was to make the address of welcome and introduce the President.

This dignitary arose—and I can see him now as though it were yesterday—! He was about five feet high and wore a frock coat which must have belonged originally to an ancestor who was a giant; for the tails of the coat just escaped the ground, and the sleeves were of proportionate length. Nothing daunted by this handicap, the little man began, and as he warmed to his subject the sleeves were pulled above his elbows, the coattails would be lifted nearly as high as his head, and after holding them there a few minutes the hands would release them only to come down with forensic force on the table where the pitcher and glasses would jangle their contribution to the uproar. On and on he went—thirty, forty, fifty minutes—when suddenly the members of the Marine Band began to succumb. They dropped like flies, and the valiant little Boy Scouts tried to lift and carry them to some blessed shade.

The speaker would look at the prostrate forms, but, with a debonair flirt of his coattails, attack another paragraph of the pages of typed matter before him. Hardly had the band received first aid when women all around me began to faint, and the Scouts, with perspiration pouring down their boyish faces, came to tender their services.

Up to this time it had been funny, but I suddenly found myself as hot from anger as I had been from the sun; for the man had no right to punish other people so. At last he stopped, for lack of breath, I think, and sat down, looking more like a vanquished prize fighter than anything I can think of; for both cuffs had slipped their moorings, and one was open. His hair was standing on end, and the necktie had sought sanctuary under his left ear.

My husband's address was calm and mercifully short.

Soon after our return from this trip the lawn parties began. And we were lucky in having beautiful days for them, for they had to be arranged too far ahead to forecast the weather. But it seemed always so in those years of official life whenever the President spoke or received out-of-doors; the gods protected him until it became a slogan—"Regular Wilson Weather." I think the only exception was the dedication of the Confederate monument at Arlington, which I described some pages back. The lawn parties are very informal and picturesque functions—made gay by the brightly coloured marquee for the refreshments, the airy dresses of the women and the army and naval officers in their uniforms. The President and I stood under one of the large trees where Colonel Harts, military aide, and Captain Berry, naval aide, made the introductions. After we had greeted everyone there was always time for some talks with old friends while we moved about the grounds.

I think, at last accounts, I left the reader a little in doubt as to what would be the ultimate conclusion of the courtship of Cary Travers Grayson. He and Alice Gertrude Gordon—Altrude to those who read this book—were married at St. George's Chapel in New York, on May 24, 1916. Helen Bones, my brother Randolph, Mr. Wilson and I arrived in New York in the afternoon, with just comfortable time to change our clothes at Mr. Charles R. Crane's apartment and repair to the chapel. The Cranes were out of town. They had Russian servants who understood no other language, which created a dilemma for Nell McAdoo whom we joined at the apartment. She had had some white slippers dyed to match the dress she was to wear at the wedding and sent to Mr. Crane's. Nell asked in her best French, then in German, then in English, if her slippers were there. To all three queries she received blank looks. So we all tried the sign language, showing the servants my slippers, which were grey, and then her dress which was rose colour. Nothing happened. Nell was in despair. She said: "I just can't go with no shoes to match my costume." We were just starting to make a search through the place when Mr. Crane's lovely daughter arrived in time to save the day. For the slippers were there, but had been put away with hers.

The wedding was simple and dignified, with only the close friends of the bride and groom around them. The bride had planned no attendants, but just before the ceremony she asked me if I would come to the church and stand beside her. Fortunately I had worn a pale grey taffeta, and a big grey hat made of tulle; so I did not mar the effect of the white decorations, and the bride's white loveliness, by having dark clothes. We went from the church to the bride's apartment for a few minutes where we left the happy pair and caught a train back to Washington, arriving at midnight.

On Memorial Day, May 30, 1916, we went to Arlington where my husband spoke. Several others preceded him and while they were speaking he proposed that we learn all the lines of the "Star-Spangled Banner" which was printed in full on the programmes. We did it, and on our way home said the words over to each other. Had we known the thousands of times we were to hear these words during the coming years of the War we would have been even more intent on learning them.

On June 2, 1916, we went on the *Mayflower* to Annapolis, for the graduation of the midshipmen. This was the first time I had been there for these ceremonies. It is a beautiful and moving sight—all these slim young cadets in white uniforms receiving their diplomas from the hands of the President of the United States, or the Secretary of the Navy, before they spread over the world with their promises to defend their country. On June 13th we were at West Point's commencement exercises—another wonderful and colourful spectacle.

The day after we got back the President headed the Preparedness Parade in Washington which was one of a nation-wide series. After leaving him at the Peace Monument, where he joined the line of march, I returned to the reviewing stand which had been erected in front of the White House. How young and vital he looked as the line of marchers swung around Fifteenth Street where we could see them. He wore white flannel trousers, a blue sack coat, white shoes, white straw hat, and carried an American flag about a yard and a half long. What a picture, as the breeze caught and carried out the Stars and Stripes! They were walking at a good pace, and the crowds which lined the Avenue cheered to the echo. At Executive Avenue the President left the parade and came to the stand to review the rest of it, staying until time for a hurried lunch, after which we drove to the Monument grounds where he addressed the people.

CHAPTER 8

THAT summer of 1916 was crowded with every sort of thing. First on the list was the ever-encroaching menace of the War in Europe. Then came the Presidential campaign. The changes time brings! Four years before I had been blithely touring abroad, catching, with indifferent ears, only the faintest echoes of the partisan struggle across the waters at home. I had never met a President of the United States and never expected to. I had never voted, nor expected to.

Now not a day passed without consultations with the men in charge of Democratic headquarters, and with party leaders from far and near. Chief of these, naturally, was Mr. Vance C. McCormick, the national chairman, of whom we both became so fond, and who proved so able and so true a friend. Then there were the threatened railroad strikes all over the country, and the constant effort to reconcile the railway brotherhoods and the executives of the roads.

The days were never long enough, so we decided to start them at 5:00 A. M. and try, as my husband said whimsically, to "steal up on them in the dark." I felt that with their already long hours, it was unfair to the servants to serve breakfast so early. I told the cook and butler to fix things for us, and leave them in the icebox in the pantry, and I would cook some eggs and make coffee on the electric burner. Never once did they allow me to do it, and at 5:00 A. M. our breakfast was served just as it formerly had been at eight o'clock.

A scourge of that terrible summer was infantile paralysis, which all over the East fastened its deadly grip on little children in the twinkling of an eye. The McAdoos had taken a house at Spring Lake, New Jersey, where Nell was established with her baby daughter, just a year old. She became panic-stricken for fear the disease should descend upon her baby. Knowing that Shadow Lawn, the place we had rented near Asbury Park, was surrounded by very large grounds, where the gates could be closed and the baby isolated, she

102

moved there to await our coming. First one thing, then another, detained us in the heat of Washington. We did not get away until September, and then only because my husband declined to use the White House, the Nation's property, for a political purpose. September 2nd was the date fixed for the formal ceremony of notifying the President of his nomination to succeed himself. He said that as this could not be held in the White House we would go to Shadow Lawn, in New Jersey, the State whose citizens had elevated him to public life.

Though the gentlest person in the world, and devoted to "Miss Eleanor," as he called Mrs. McAdoo, Dr. Grayson was furious when her telegram came saying she had moved the baby and herself and nurse to Shadow Lawn. "Mrs. Wilson, this is a dreadful thing Miss Eleanor has done," he said. "The President is bound to be there next week. Suppose this baby should develop this awful germ right there where he is bound to go. She can stay only a few days anyway because when the President is there the house will be swarming with people of every sort, and she could not be in a worse place." As I recall it, Dr. Grayson took matters in his own hands and telegraphed Mrs. McAdoo and advised her to take the baby farther north.

On September 1st we moved into our new quarters, the party consisting of Helen Bones, Altrude and Dr. Grayson, Mr. Tumulty, my brother Randolph, my husband and me. As we drove up to the house not a light was seen in a single window, which we thought strange. Then out of the gloom came merry voices. Margaret and some friends from New York who had just arrived had taken the wrong turn in the drive and landed at the garage, which they thought a very queer-looking house, although even it was of tremendous proportions. Then, happily, the lights came on—there had been power-plant trouble, we learned—and we had our first glance at the inside of the house we had been trying to get to all summer. The first impression was awful. We entered a room which looked more like a lounge in a summer hotel—very large, with a staircase, wide enough for an army abreast, opposite the front door. This staircase ended in a big platform on which rested a grand piano. Then the stairs parted to run in opposite directions as if each was ashamed of the other. These flights of steps led to a gallery on which the various bedroom suites opened.

The lower floor consisted of this vast lobby, a formal drawing room, a library whose only claim to the title consisted of a New York telephone directory neatly tucked away behind velvet curtains that covered elaborately ornamented book-stacks; a large and ornate billiard room with lights hidden behind armour, and much crimson as to curtains and walls; a formal Pompeian dining room, and— blessed simplicity—an out-of-doors dining room done in white and green.

The worst thing in the house was a white marble statue in the centre of the "lobby." It must have weighed tons, or we would have had it removed. So we draped it as much as possible.

These, as I have said, were first impressions; but the bedroom suites were charming and homelike, with splendid, spacious baths for each one. So later, when we got settled, we were happy and comfortable at Shadow Lawn. The grounds were so large we could have privacy. A small house, built for the little daughter of the owners, contained a bedroom, playroom, dining room and a wee bath. All was simple and what any child would love. On the big house were acres of porches. I think there were seventeen complete sets of porch furniture, each different, and whenever I passed from one to another I felt as though I were being escorted through a furniture store.

Our favourite retreat away from all this was a second-floor sitting room furnished entirely in white wicker and chintz. It opened on a porch made to represent the deck of a steamer, and was not ornate.

By ten o'clock in the morning the Notification Day crowd began to assemble. Special trains brought delegations, each with its band. For days carpenters had been at work putting up long rows of seats. In addition, hundreds of chairs were distributed about, until the vast lawn was an improvised open-air theatre, facing the front of the house where a speakers' stand had been added to the broad porch.

We had asked the Notification Committee, and many friends, to a standing lunch. I think several hundred accepted. Others lunched on their trains or found the sandwiches and coffee served on the grounds sufficient to stay them. The day had dawned grey but by noon the wind shifted and the sun came out brilliantly—"Wilson Weather" again. Senator Ollie James of Kentucky made the notification speech, and was never in better form or happier mood. Then came my husband's speech of acceptance, which had been carefully prepared. He reiterated his dedication, if re-elected, to the duties of his high office, as a servant of the whole people.

Next morning we were on our way to Kentucky to dedicate the beautiful marble shrine at Lincoln's birthplace. For me it was a pleasant trip, with my husband and the inimitable Senator John Sharp Williams of Mississippi swapping stories, but not a very restful one for the President who was beginning to show the effects of the summer's strain. I was charmed by the situation of the shrine, and, I must confess, by my husband's tribute to his great predecessor. Little did I suspect how near to us were those hideous burdens of war which had weighed Lincoln down. Back to Washington for two days to sign the bills and attend to multifarious details that go with the adjournment of Congress. Dr. Grayson said to me that the President must "slow up," and take some time for golf, or he could not keep going. The next stop was Atlantic City. The salt air was refreshing, but a Suffragette meeting, a charity concert and people, people, people, drained away the benefit of it all, so we motored back.

Next morning my husband was too sick with a headache to get up until after lunchtime when we were to receive the Governor of New Jersey and Mrs. Fielder. As they left, a telegram came saying that Mrs. Howe, the President's sister, who had been ill, was much worse. In the morning we set out for New London, Connecticut, Mr. Homer Cummings riding part of the way with us. We were three days at a hotel, and then the *Mayflower* was ordered up from New York. On board, the President could get some relief from the constant press of visitors. On the fourth day Mrs. Howe's physician, Dr. Edward P. Davis, of Philadelphia, came aboard. Dr. Davis and my husband were classmates at Princeton, but it was to me the Doctor spoke, urging that the President leave. "He is under terrific strain, and there is nothing he can do. His sister may live for weeks, and she may go any minute. The President cannot even be in her room. I will stay and do what I can, but I do not answer for the consequences if he does not get away and have some let-up."

At Shadow Lawn stacks of work awaited my tired husband. With Mr. Swem, his capable stenographer, he settled down to it without the loss of a moment. I loved to watch them work together. As Mr. Wilson spoke and Swem wrote, a panorama of the world's affairs passed before me. I often sat amazed at the problems a morning's mail brought, and said a prayer of thanks I did not have to solve them.

In the briefest time the letters, typed and ready for signatures, were back on the desk, with the ones that were pressing signified by a square of red cardboard clipped to the top. I always watched for these, and, when a free moment came, put them before my husband and blotted the signature—after removing one to place another. We loved doing this together, and he so often said: "When you are here work seems like play." Had I not done these little services, how many precious hours with him I should have missed!

After two days at Shadow Lawn, a telegram announced Mrs. Howe's death. We made ready for the long journey to Columbia, South Carolina. There she was buried from the little church in which she had been married; and we left her in the churchyard under a canopy of flowers brought by old friends. Before leaving Columbia, we went to the house where my husband had lived as a boy, and which has since been made a memorial to him. It is a simple and typical Southern home.

Now the campaign began in earnest. As long as Congress was in session, and we had to stay in Washington, my husband felt he could do nothing personally; for he refused to use the White House as a campaign centre. But Shadow Lawn was for the time being our home, and we could, with perfect propriety, do as we pleased. After the heat of Washington, and the long journeys to Kentucky and to South Carolina, it did seem peace indeed to drop anchor in this comfortable big house, with the protecting acres shaded by fine old trees. But every day brought people to see us, either on business or pleasure. The night we got back from South Carolina, Mr. Vance C. McCormick arrived saying he regretted to intrude at such a time but there were questions about the campaign that should be discussed. The next night Mr. Walter Hines Page, our Ambassador to England, came. The following day, being Saturday, there were again special trains bringing crowds of people. The President spoke, clarifying the eight-hour legislation. Colonel House came as an overnight guest, arriving just as Mr. Page was leaving. Sunday brought more arrivals but by afternoon all were gone. The Graysons, having settled in a little house near by, left Mr. Wilson and me to enjoy alone one of the rare evenings when we could relax, and my husband read aloud as we sat before a wood fire.

This could not last. Next morning we were off again at nine for Baltimore, where the President addressed a meeting of grain dealers. There was a real ovation when he rose to speak. As I sat on the stage where I could watch the faces of the men in the audience, I was impressed by their attention and eager interest. Mother and my sister Bertha returned to Shadow Lawn with us. Our queer house fascinated them.

Besides the regular work, the study was piled high with commissions to be signed. The officer personnel of the Army was being recommissioned, and the signing of so many thousand documents was no light task. The President was asked to review some units of the New Jersey National Guard. So we drove over to Sea Girt, and he mounted a horse and, accompanied by Colonel Kennedy, as military aide, rode up and down the lines, looking very stunning, I thought. When he came back to the car he laughed and told a story of a similar review when he was Governor of New Jersey and had jestingly discussed his attire with the reporters. One paper quoted him as saying: "It seemed queer to ride a horse wearing a high hat and cutaway coat." Whereupon another paper commented: "We have never seen a horse wearing a high hat and cutaway coat, but if the Governor says so, we agree with him that it was a very incongruous sight."

We returned from Sea Girt in time to see the Young Men's Democratic Club of New York, fifteen hundred strong, march through our gates with bands playing. My husband made his first "political" speech of the campaign to them. He had been urged to do it by his advisers. Personally, I liked the other kind he had been making very much better.

So autumn and the campaign wore on and when there was as much as five minutes between appointments we would tackle the army commissions. They stood in stacks several feet high. We had a large table especially for them, with blotters and everything ready. I would place and blot them as fast as he would sign; and we made a sort of game of it, seeing how many we could do in stated moments. We tried to do at least one hundred a day, but even then the stacks never seemed to grow less, for new ones came each day. Later, when the War came to us, the law was changed relieving the President of signing the commissions of officers below the rank of captain.

We tried to get in a drive every day, or some golf at Spring Lake. Our accommodating Secret Service men usually acted as caddies, but one day two rather elderly men begged to carry our bags. When my bag fell to the lot of the older of the two, I saw he was terribly put out because he did not get the President's. As I played in my very worst form, he became more and more bored, and finally I thought to placate the old fellow by asking his advice. When I had a very near approach to the green, I said, in my most beguiling way: "Do you think I can reach the green with the midiron?" "Yes, if you hit it often enough," he replied.

I like to pause as I write to refresh my spirit with the memory of the few comparatively serene days we were able to spend in the quiet of the shaded, cool lawn, or in the big house, where, with many of our loved ones around us, we could almost resume the ways of private life. The McAdoos were close enough for us to see them nearly every day. Margaret was there most of the time, and the Frank Sayres several times. My dear mother, and my sister Bertha, were also there for a visit; and Helen Bones nearly always. The Graysons, whose house was close by, were constantly in and out. When business interviews and conferences were out of the way pleasant people would stay to lunch or dinner with us. Then there was always delightful conversation and a matching of wits, for never was there a time at our table when the men talked "shop." That was an unwritten law, for my husband craved and needed that brief respite from affairs of State or the exigencies of politics. Even when things were tense and liable to snap, we tried to forget for the time we were at table, and I am sure it was a wise decision. Alas, though, how these temporarily banished problems rose to smite us when we left the table! For day after day, at the White House, the faithful Hoover, the head usher, would be poised as we crossed the threshold of the dining room, saying: "Mr. President, the Secretary of War—or the Navy—is waiting to see you in the Green Room. I have just put three communications with a red tag on them in The Drawer. Senator Blank telephoned to ask if you could see him before four." And so on, ad infinitum. Often we would be talking over such interesting things that we longed to continue, but could not.

Early in October Mr. Henry Ford lunched with us, and I remember his saying he had made a collection of very thin watches. We were at the table at the time and, with the naïveté of a little boy, he disgorged his pockets to show us his treasures, laying them before me in a line. Watches thin as a knife-blade; one with an inset of rubies round the edge; one with sapphires; one entirely of platinum, as I remember it—and he fairly glowed with pride when we admired them.

Another day old Mr. Jacob Schiff lunched with us, and I still recall with regret an unfortunate oversight of that day. He had written my husband asking for an appointment. The letter was dated from New York. In replying, Mr. Wilson said: "Suppose you lunch with us on Tuesday and we can talk afterwards regarding the matter." After he arrived I inquired after Mrs. Schiff, asking: "Where is she now?" His reply was: "My dear lady, she was at your door fifteen minutes ago when she came to fetch me." Of course we had no idea that she had been with him, and, it was worse to find they had a house only a few miles away. I know they understood, but we were both so sorry.

On October 3rd we left on a special train for Omaha. The crowds at every station seemed to grow in numbers the farther west we got. At Chicago we were joined by several Senators from the West. I particularly remember Senator Walsh, of Montana; also Mrs. Bass, Chairman of the Woman's National Democratic Committee.

We reached Omaha in the morning, and up to that time I had never seen more people packed into a given space than every street held. We went to the Commercial Club where my husband spoke after a luncheon. From there we drove in open cars sixty blocks to review a pageant, and I was especially interested in the Indians who took part in it.

At last we reached our hotel where the rooms reserved for us were bowers of flowers. I remember one lovely basket from the "working girls"; a cookbook from an organization of Jewish women; and a beautifully woven basket from an Indian tribe. We changed our clothes and went to a swine show, which was for us a unique experience. One great swine weighed 1115 pounds, and was a sight for the gods. As usual, we were escorted by representatives of the newspapers. Wherever we went this army, like Mary's little lamb, "was sure to go." The correspondents must often have grown weary. So it seems that Mr. Louis Seibold of the New York *World* gave himself a holiday and did not go to the swine show. When his fellow scribes returned they told him what he had missed, and told especially of this 1115-pounder, in which he refused to believe. That night when we had all attended a big dinner at the auditorium and had got back on the special train to start home, I had a request from Mr. Seibold to ask if he and three other newspaper men could come into our car for a few minutes. I couldn't imagine what they wanted, for we were all tired after a very full day; but I said I would be glad to receive them. When they arrived, Mr. Seibold, the spokesman, said they had asked him to believe they saw a pig weighing 1115 pounds, and he declined to do it. Knowing I was a truthful person, he had said if I confirmed the story he had nothing else to say, but if not—

Well, I did confirm it, and after a pleasant little talk they said good night. Next morning on the train I received from Mr. Seibold the cutest little toy pig, pure white with a pink nose. Around his neck was a violet ribbon, tying a great cluster of fresh violets. I have him yet, and he sits in silent meditation by my fireplace until some-one picks him up and squeezes him. Then he emits a squeak that is very piglike.

That afternoon after leaving Chicago we asked the newspaper men into our car to tea, and had a lot of fun over the "swine." The morning I had spent writing notes to thank all the nice people who had sent me flowers and other things. I always tried to do this myself instead of having my secretary do it.

At Shadow Lawn next morning, my old friends Mr. and Mrs. Hugh L. Rose arrived in a new car in time for lunch. It was Satur-day and another crowd was arriving by train and marching into the gates by the time lunch was over. My husband addressed them, and we invited all the special friends in to tea.

Sunday was a welcome day of rest, and we all went to St. John's Church at Long Branch. Other guests arrived unexpectedly to lunch but left early, and we drove up to Atlantic Highlands and had the afternoon to ourselves.

On Tuesday Helen and I went to New York to shop for the day. When we got back I found that Mr. Lansing, the Secretary of State, had arrived. There had been disturbing news of another U-boat disaster. Mr. Lansing spent the night and he, my husband and I had a long, serious talk before going to bed.

Next day we were again on the road, this time to Indianapolis. Most of the afternoon we worked. We reached our destination about the following noon, and my husband made an address at a luncheon. Then we went to a stand to review an automobile parade sponsored by the Good Roads Association, where Mr. Wilson made another speech. From there we went to the fairgrounds where he spoke again and was given a gavel made from a plank of an old road. My brother Will from Detroit joined us for the day, and we were sorry to leave him when we started back late that afternoon.

We reached Shadow Lawn just in time for the usual Saturday delegations. This time they came from Pennsylvania. Mr. A. Mitchell Palmer, afterwards Attorney General of the United States, headed them and made a very nice address. Among the guests for tea were Dr. and Mrs. Simon Baruch, the father and mother of Mr. Bernard M. Baruch who was to distinguish himself during the War by his brilliant service as the head of the War Industries Board, and whom the President and I learned to count as a friend and counsellor, and to regard with personal affection.

Next day when I awoke I found my husband dressed for the day and at my bedside making shorthand notes for an address. He gave me a glowing smile and, when I exclaimed at my being so lazy, he said: "You have forgotten what an important day this is in my life, your birthday; so I had to get up early to greet it." He put in my hand a small package which contained a little platinum brooch.

The next day we had an October birthday dinner party which included Nell and Mac, my sister Bertha, Helen Bones and Dr. Grayson, all October children. We wore our best bibs and tuckers and made a merry evening of it.

Two days later we went to Chicago, my mother and sister going as far as New York with us where they were to visit my oldest brother Rolfe until our return. We also made another trip to Cincinnati, and before the end of October one to Buffalo, returning by way of New York for a sort of climax to the campaign. There we spent a very busy day, ending with a tremendous meeting at Madison Square Garden. The crowds were so dense it was impossible, even with the help of hundreds of police, to get near the entrance of the building. They stretched for blocks, and, after a battle, we went to the opposite end of the building, climbed a fire escape and got through a window. When the meeting opened, and my husband rose to speak, the cheering went on for half an hour. That was only the first of three such ovations. As soon as we could get out of the Garden we went to Cooper Union where there seemed to be just as many people. After the President had spoken there, we went outside to a sort of impromptu stand and here he addressed thirty thousand who could not get in either of the buildings.

We were glad when it was over and we could return to the *Mayflower,* which was lying near East Twenty-third Street. Margaret and Helen were with us, and we steamed slowly towards Atlantic Highlands during the night, to reach home early the next morning. Another speech at Shadow Lawn on the following Saturday closed the hectic 1916 campaign.

On that day, in addition to the usual crowds from New York and elsewhere, two hundred and fifty Princeton people came, many of them old friends. We asked them all to stay to tea, and found them very interesting and delightful. As usual, some of the old friends stayed and dined with us.

When I awoke the next morning I tried to picture to myself how in this brief time since we were married, less than eleven months, my whole life had changed; and how much happiness had been crowded into those busy months. This was Sunday, November 5th, and the election was to be on the following Tuesday. I had never felt that we could win the majority of the electoral votes, for while the masses seemed for my husband, there was so much money in the hands of the Republicans. In addition, the Mexican policy was still being attacked, and the war in Europe was bringing new and greater problems every hour. All this was summed up as I lay there that Sunday morning and turned things over in my mind before any of the household were stirring. I began to speculate on what we would do when we should leave the White House, which I calculated would be in just four more months.

It had been a wild night. A sudden downpour of rain, followed by high winds, had made it impossible to sleep. While I was going over these questions in my thoughts, the door gently opened and I saw my husband standing there already dressed. Seeing me awake he came in and said: "I was hoping you were awake because I want to make the speech to you which I intended making yesterday, but someway could not get it out. It was this!"

He then brought out clear as crystal his programme for the future. Alas that I cannot repeat it, for it was destined to be put aside on account of the War, and so forever lost.

When he finished, I told him that I had been mapping out what we would do after he had been defeated and we could live our own lives. He stood up and, looking down at me, said: "What a delightful pessimist you are! One must never court defeat. If it comes, accept it like a soldier; but don't anticipate it, for that destroys your fighting spirit."

Later in the day we went for a ride, taking Mother and my sister with us. I remember the ocean was wild and majestic, with great angry waves breaking on the rocks. On Monday, November 6, 1916, I find recorded in my "Line-a-day Book": "At 2:30 a delegation headed by Mr. Paderewski arrived to ask W. to set aside a day to help the Poles. I knelt in the hall above and heard all they said. Mr. P. ended with a beautiful tribute to my husband and expressed his utmost faith in him and his sincere desire to help these suffering people."

I shall never forget Mr. Paderewski's face as he stood pleading the cause of his country. It was so fine, so tragic, so earnest. As I knelt there above them I felt I was witnessing through his eyes all the suffering and degradation of his countrymen. His hair was like a nimbus around his head. To have seen together these two men who were making the world better and happier is a memory I shall always cherish.

November 7, 1916, Election Day, dawned radiantly clear, and we had a very early breakfast together and drove to Princeton to vote. Although we got there a little before nine o'clock, we found crowds of students—and photographers—gathered to give us welcome.

While my husband was in the old engine house voting, I sat in the car laughing with the boys who had pushed and jostled good-naturedly to get a glimpse of the President. When he came out they cheered him again. That was as near as I ever came to voting at the polls for a Presidential candidate. New Jersey had not then granted the suffrage to women. In 1920 we voted by mail, and following that, after Mr. Wilson's death, I lost my right to vote, being a resident of the District of Columbia.

From Princeton we had a beautiful drive home, and reached there before eleven o'clock. The rest of the day we worked as usual. Late in the afternoon Frank Sayre arrived, having gone to his old home in Pennsylvania to vote, and then come on down to spend the night with us. He and Dr. Grayson were the only guests at dinner, after which we all gathered in the upstairs sitting room to await the news of the election. The telegraph company had offered to run in a special wire so we could get the returns, but my husband said he did not care for it, and we would get the news by telephone from the Executive Offices.

We decided to play a game of Twenty Questions, but before we began, Dr. Grayson said he thought he would run in to Asbury Park and see what the news was at the Executive Offices, and would telephone us. An hour had passed without news, when, about ten o'clock, Margaret jumped up, saying: "Oh, there's the 'phone." A tactless friend in New York was calling to condole with her over "your father's defeat." Margaret was breathless with surprise and resentment, and spluttered out at him: "Why, he is not defeated. What are you talking about?" This reply was amazing, for he had said: "The flashlight from the New York *Times* building—white for Wilson, red for Hughes—has already flashed red, conceding the election to the Republicans." But Margaret stood her ground and valiantly declined to accept this as final. "Impossible," she said. "They cannot know yet. In the West they are still at the polls."

As soon as the friend rang off, we called the Executive Offices, only to find the same report, and Mr. Tumulty beyond speech in his impenetrable gloom.

How did I feel? Well, not so hopeful or so indignant as Margaret; and not so encompassed by gloom as Tumulty. All along I had felt in my bones that the Opposition was too rich and too strong for us. Hard and bitter as it was to see my husband torn from his work towards the great and liberal objectives he held for his country, and which he had so feelingly outlined to me at dawn on Sunday morning, I had long been secretly preparing an armour against the arrow of defeat. This armour met the test. I found real consolation in the thought that, at last, we should be alone together.

CHAPTER 9

SITTING in the living room at Shadow Lawn on the evening of Election Day, 1916, we had finished our game of Twenty Questions when Dr. Grayson returned from the temporary White House offices at Asbury Park to confirm the cheerless news we had received by 'phone. Indeed, the battle seemed lost. My husband was the least disturbed member of the party. He agreed with Margaret that it was too early to be assured of anything, adding, however, that Republican claims of victory and Democratic concessions of defeat seemed soundly based—on the overwhelming majorities against us in the populous East and Middle West.

Then he appeared to put the matter from his mind. This was in keeping with a lifetime habit: when one thing was finished, turn to the next, without exulting or without repining. He listened while we all expressed our feelings, and then said: "Well, I will not send Mr. Hughes a telegram of congratulation tonight, for things are not settled." Then, for a few minutes, he looked very grave. "There now seems little hope," he said, "that we shall not be drawn into the War, though I have done everything I can to keep us out; but my defeat will be taken by Germany as a repudiation of my policy. Many of our own people will so construe it, and will try to force war upon the next Administration." Then he said: "Well, as we got up so early, what do you say to having a glass of milk and going to bed?" Suiting the action to the word, he called the butler who brought up sandwiches and ginger ale, etc., and milk. After taking only the latter, at 10:30 he said good night and went off to bed, adding: "I might stay longer but you are all so blue."

I lingered a few moments to finish my glass. As soon as he was gone the girls burst into rage that the country had not stood by him or comprehended what he was doing for it. Turning to me they said: "What do you feel?" I tried to say candidly what I have already said to my readers. Naturally I felt a keen sense of disappointment; any one would. But I had never felt we could win and therefore was not

115

shocked as they all seemed to be. And away back in my mind was the thought of personal freedom for my dear one, and for myself, which the relinquishment of this burden would bring.

I felt I must not linger to talk, but go and see if there were any way to assuage his natural feeling of being discredited. I found him already in bed, and he said: "Well, little girl, you were right in expecting we should lose the election. Frankly I did not, but we can now do some of the things we want to do." I sat on his bed, thinking he would want to talk; but in a few minutes his hand, which was holding mine, relaxed, and he was sleeping that quiet sleep which characterized him. There was never a sound of breathing, or a motion of the body; it was really rest; a suspended animation which, if he were ill, always alarmed me.

In the coming years when every nerve was tense with anxiety during the War, and the burdens resting on his shoulders enough to crush the vitality of a giant, there would come days when he was incapacitated by blinding headaches that no medicine could relieve. He would have to give up everything, and the only cure seemed to be sleep. We would make the room cool and dark, and when at last the merciful sleep would come, he would lie for hours in this way, apparently not even breathing. Many a time I have stolen in and leaned over him to listen—to see if he really were alive. Sometimes this sleep would last for five, six, or even eight hours. He would awaken refreshed and able at once to take up work and go on with renewed energy.

To go back to November 7th. I could not sleep, feeling that all the things he had accomplished would be marred because they were only a part of the whole pattern of reform he had started. There was a tremendous record of accomplishment: the Federal Reserve Bank system; the tariff; the Panama tolls; the eight-hour law; and so on. But still much more to be done which was dear to his heart. In spite of his quiet acceptance of what he thought to be the verdict of the people, I knew he was hurt. I was still wide awake when at 4:00 A. M. Margaret knocked at my door; she said she had just talked to Mr. Vance McCormick at Democratic headquarters in New York and he told her better news was coming in, and he had not given up hope. She said: "Shall we wake Father and tell him?" "Oh no," I said, "do let him sleep."

She decided to go in to New York for her music lesson, and if she found things really any different she would telephone me. So she got off at eight, and at breakfast we read the papers, with Mr. Hughes' picture and all the family history of himself and of Mrs. Hughes. The usual day's routine went on—the dictation of the mail; the clearing up of work that needed attention. Two old Princeton friends, Dean Fine and Mr. McAlpin, had written the week before to know if they could see Woodrow, and we had asked them to lunch. They arrived half an hour late and full of apologies, which were rather vague. As they had asked for an appointment with the President, we felt there might be something they wanted to discuss privately. So the rest of us withdrew, after the coffee was served in the "lounge," as I always called that huge hall.

Later my husband told me what happened. He waited for them to open the subject of their visit, and talked for nearly an hour; but nothing developed, and finally he said: "Well, it is delightful to see you fellows, but what was it you especially wanted to see me about today?" Whereupon they looked at each other, both visibly embarrassed. At last Dean Fine said: "I am sorry to say the real object of our visit cannot be accomplished, for we thought when we wrote we would come over and congratulate you on your re-election."

Then the whole mournful story came out. They had arrived at the gate only five minutes late, and had sat there before coming in trying to think of some reason for their visit that would sound plausible, for they hated to tell him the truth. My husband said they were so tragic, and so embarrassed, that he laughed heartily and told them they were taking it much harder than he was; but he loved them for it and it was like old Princeton days to talk it over with them.

Margaret got back about 4:00 P. M., but she knew nothing definite, and after dinner we again awaited news. As nothing of certainty came we all turned in about eleven o'clock.

The next day was our last at Shadow Lawn. I find this entry in my diary:

"Thursday, November 9: Got up about 8; found no one knew a thing more than the night before. Margaret had to go to New York and we spent the morning receiving telegrams and winding up things at Shadow Lawn. Played golf at Spring Lake, and when we were on the 8th tee Dr. Grayson arrived with news from Headquarters that they thought California was safe and if so that meant Democratic victory. The Doctor and Altrude were leaving at 4:30, and he was so excited and nervous she said he could neither eat nor sleep."

At 8:30 that night we left, still without more definite news, to motor to Sandy Hook where dear Captain Berry was waiting for us with the launch. He was keyed to concert pitch over the election. On the *Mayflower* everything was *filled* with flowers. We sat on deck until 9:30 P. M. when Margaret went to bed, and the rest of us walked around the deck. Presently the marvellous lights of New York came into view. In the harbour we stopped to put off our old Chinaman, the cook, who was very ill. Captain Berry had sent for a tug to take him to the hospital. It seemed pitiful when the poor, thin old body was tenderly lowered on a stretcher, and then his box of possessions after him; and in a few minutes the tug was only a speck of red light in the darkness.

I suppose the suspense and strain were making my nerves queer, for I felt so weepy over the old Chinaman that I don't know what would have happened had not an orderly come at that moment with a handful of wireless messages. We went into the smoking room under the light to read them. They all told of new gains in the West, but the issue was still uncertain.

The following is from my journal:

"Nov. 10, 1916: Up at 7:30. Brooks brought a wireless that seemed to make victory certain. All through these days Mr. Wilson has been calm and undisturbed, but I can see the strain is telling, so I will be doubly glad when it is settled. We had a happy little breakfast by ourselves in the main cabin; then I rushed below to tell the girls [Margaret and Helen] the last news. At 9 o'clock [A. M.] we got to Rhinecliff [N. Y.] where we had a special train awaiting us with our familiar car, 'The Mayflower.' "

There were great crowds both at the boat and the train, and one lady rushed forward and presented me with a fragrant cluster of violets, saying: "These with all the happiest wishes for our next

President and Mrs. Wilson, and Senators Overman and Smith of Georgia, on way to U. S. Capitol, March 5, 1917

President and his wife." This was really the first time I had felt certain that, in spite of all the reports to the contrary, the people had stood by my husband, and that he was re-elected. When we got on the train it was massed with flowers, and there were cheering throngs of people everywhere.

We had a comfortable trip, and reached Williamstown, Massachusetts, at 1:30 in the afternoon. Frank Sayre met us, and we found Jessie waiting at the door of their attractive house. We had gone there for the christening of their little daughter who was named Eleanor Axson for her grandmother. This little ceremony took place in the church, and went off with dignity and simplicity, the baby behaving beautifully. Afterwards we went to tea with Dr. Harry Garfield, president of Williams College.

We walked back to Jessie's home in the early twilight in time to dress for a family dinner party which consisted of ourselves and Frank's brother and aunt. After dinner a crowd of students from Williams College came to serenade the President. Dr. Garfield, who was with them, made a graceful little address of congratulation to which my husband replied. Just after this a delegation from North Adams came with many banners and red fire, and there were more speeches.

The next night we arrived at the White House, glad, in more ways than one, to be settled again. Colonel House gave us a ludicrous account of the senior Mr. Henry Morgenthau's big dinner on the night of the election. It was planned as a "victory dinner," but the guests began to call for liquids to assist them to swallow the bitter news that the Republicans had won. He said Vance McCormick literally aged before their eyes, turning a greenish yellow, but that he never gave up his fight and cheered them all with his optimism. Next day my diary contained a graver note: "Long talk about affairs in Europe between Woodrow and Colonel House; latter does not think things as serious as W. does."

Busy days followed. Nearly every evening there were long conferences in the study with either the Secretary of State or the Secretary of War. I was worried, too, over my dear mother, who did not seem well, and was unhappy in her new apartment. Presently she, Bertha and my brother Randolph moved to the Powhatan Hotel. Mother felt she could not keep house without her faithful old Mathilda, who was sick and not able to work. This old coloured woman was like a member of our family. She had been a slave of Mother's father. When a little girl, she had fallen asleep in front of an open fire. Her dress caught and she was so terribly burned the doctors said it was impossible for her to live. But my grandmother took her in to "the big house" where she nursed her, and dressed the wounds for months, and saved her life. Mathilda was just a little older than Mother. They had played together as children, forming one of those ties which often happen in the South. When the Civil War made Mathilda free, her one fear was that "Miss Sally" (my mother) could not keep her. This proved to be true, for, when the old plantation was abandoned, Mother said they did not have food to give Mathilda, or money for her railroad fare to Wytheville. That parting was one of the many heartbreaks of the period. Thirty-five years later, when Mother was living in Washington, Mathilda walked back into our lives as though she had always been there, becoming cook and general factotum.

My husband, too, was weary and unwell—reaction from the strain of the campaign. The mountain of mail awaiting us on our return to Washington was, for him, but an incidental labour. So also was the terrific pressure for appointments which left him no minute to himself that did not represent a battle and a disappointment for someone. In time stolen from sleep the really important duties of the Presidency must be performed. The first thing was the annual message to the Congress, which must be ready early in December. But a graver problem was the European situation. Germany's disregard for its pledge not to sink vessels without warning, given at the time of the destruction of the *Sussex* the spring before, the President feared could lead but to one thing: war. Colonel House did not share this view. The President began turning over in his mind a proposal to make another mighty effort for peace—for the whole world. He proposed a note to the belligerents of both sides to try to pave the way to a negotiated peace. Colonel House opposed the idea, which troubled my husband for he valued House's counsel.

I find in my diary:

"My dear one felt so wretched he went back to bed soon after breakfast and I sent for the Doctor. I had lunch sent to his room for us both, but he ate little, falling asleep soon afterwards. Slept the entire afternoon while I worked at desk and nearly caught up with letters. Had dinner upstairs and read and talked and had rare evening together."

The next day our patient was better, but when Dr. Grayson arrived he said he thought we should give up going to New York for the Army and Navy football game. So we cancelled the orders for the train. Helen and I sent off our tickets for others to enjoy, and I spent the morning with Miss Benham working out a programme for the formal dinners and receptions for the winter. After lunch my husband and I worked in the study together, and at six o'clock, while he had a massage, I walked alone for an hour. That night, both of us being too tired to work, we turned on the electric piano and sat in the firelight and listened to some of the music from the operas.

"November 25, 1916," reads my diary: "Woodrow still not well; helped him in study until 12; he is writing what he says 'may prove the greatest piece of work of my life'; and oh if only it is so, for it will mean so much."

This was the projected peace note to the Powers. Two days later Colonel House came down from New York and had a long session with my husband in the study. He pronounced the note "wonderful," but suggested delay in dispatching it, saying that public opinion in France and in England should be prepared in advance.

On December 2nd we went to New York for the ceremony of the illumination of the Statue of Liberty. It was a perfect night, cool, with a new moon and many stars. From the bridge of the *Mayflower* we beheld the sombre outlines of the statue, quite dark, and flanked on either side by battleships. Suddenly out of the darkness above appeared a spot of light, and we could hear the hum of a motor. The light came nearer and at length we could see the open plane, piloted by Ruth Law. "As Miss Law sped along," reads my diary, "she dropped white fire, making the plane look like a giant comet." At a word from the President rockets went up from the *Mayflower,* and the statue was flooded with light. The flaming torch in her hand blazed forth—to quote Mr. Wilson—"a symbol of that which is to make the world alight when all men, everywhere, have Liberty."

At a dinner at the Waldorf-Astoria my husband spoke feelingly of peace, which he said could come only with liberty, and that there could be no liberty so long as small groups determined the destinies of peoples. The reception accorded these words sent the President back to Washington determined to strive the harder to bring peace to Europe.

On December 5th the President read his annual message to the Congress. The scene was impressive, as it always is. Scarcely had he begun to speak when a group of Suffragettes in the gallery unfurled over the rail a large banner of their colours, yellow and white. The President took no notice. The audience did not appear even to see it, most of them being too intent on the President's words to observe the incident. A guard quietly removed the banner, not a word being said by anyone.

On December 12th, a surprising development occurred in the European situation, affecting profoundly Mr. Wilson's peace plans and putting in motion a train of events that was to change the daily lives of all Americans. Germany offered to discuss peace. But the offer was couched in arrogant terms and was predicated on the military situation of the moment, then most favourable to the Central Powers. This called for a revision of the President's contemplated note, and for new consultations, while news of the Allies' reception of the German proposal was awaited. That night, with much else on our minds, the winter's formal entertaining began with the dinner for the Cabinet. The White House was full of overnight guests, most of whom left the following day while my husband considered a message from our Embassy in Berlin hinting that should the Germans' peace offer fail they would declare a ruthless submarine campaign. In a last effort to avert impending calamity, the President reworked his peace note to the Powers. I sat with him in the study.

That the Allies would reject the German overture was a foregone conclusion. To keep hope for peace alive, on December 18th the President's note to the belligerents was dispatched. It was our first wedding anniversary, and snowing when we awoke. My husband gave me a beautiful pendant of diamonds surrounding a black opal, the opal being my birthstone. In the afternoon we went to the golf course, but it was too cold to have much fun. Changing our clothes, we went to the Corcoran Gallery for the exhibition of paintings by

American artists. One of his real joys was pictures, and usually we bought one at the American exhibit. This year, however, there was nothing we thought we could live with.

Two days later the Secretary of State, Mr. Lansing, in discussing the President's note with newspaper men, mentioned "the possibility of our being forced into the War." The headlines were enormous. "Woodrow dreadfully worried," my diary says. "He asked Lansing to make a second statement to correct the wrong impression, which he did, but it was a great blunder in the face of all Woodrow has done to present his note without causing friction."

Amid these events my husband and I squeezed in one little Christmas shopping tour together. At Becker's leather store a clerk was so shy that he could hardly articulate. Showing the President a bag with a removable watch he said: "You could take it out and make a wist wrotch out of it." He tried the sentence again, with the same result, and was about to retire in confusion when my husband said: "A capital idea. I have always wanted a wrist watch and never have had one. I think I'll take the bag to get the watch." The poor man beamed at him.

On Sunday, the day before Christmas, we went to St. Margaret's Church, and after lunch walked over to the Treasury Department steps to hear children sing carols. That night we all trimmed a tree in the Oval Room on the second floor so that little Josephine Cothran and Jessie's baby could have a real Christmas. And the older people enjoyed it as much as the children.

My gift from my husband was something I had wanted for years, a lovely gold mesh bag. Christmas morning we all had breakfast downstairs and then went up to the tree which was already ablaze with light, and the room glowing with real Christmas cheer, to which the big open fire added its wealth of colour.

From all this happy scene I ran off to St. John's Church to communion and then to the Powhatan Hotel to bring greetings to Mother. The rest of the day was filled with people coming and going. The climax was the family gathering for dinner—the two families, making in all twenty-two people. The dear old house was filled with flowers, many of them gifts from friends, and the table brilliant with the Christmas poinsettias. After dinner we decided to have charades, and, as all three of the Wilson girls have real histrionic talent, they were loads of fun. We used the upstairs hall for a stage and the bedrooms on either side as dressing rooms.

I remember particularly how lovely Nell looked that night in a new sapphire-blue velvet worn for the first time, and the horror we all felt to see her come on the stage, on her knees, with her train tucked over her arm, a handkerchief tied around her head, like a pirate, and a knife in her teeth. I wish I could recall the word this was to illustrate. It has eluded me, but the memory of her beauty and her utter obliviousness to her lovely gown are very vivid.

The party broke up late. The last guest had gone and we were saying good night in the hall upstairs, when my sister-in-law, Rolfe's wife, fell as a rug slipped on the polished floor. We wanted to send for the doctor, but she would not hear of it. She went off to bed, but not to sleep, for she had broken a small bone in her wrist.

The next night the Grayson household came to dinner, bringing several holiday guests. Colonel and Mrs. Harts also were there, and after dinner Colonel Harts gave us his lecture on Washington, and its future development, illustrated by lantern slides. January 5, 1917, was Mother's birthday. We had a family party for her, and as the Christmas house party had broken up, family life was adjourned after this for the programme of official entertaining.

The previous season I had inaugurated a custom of morning meetings with the Cabinet ladies to establish closer personal relations among us and to discuss problems arising from those bugaboos of official life, precedent and precedence. We met at twelve o'clock and it was always an agreeable hour. This year we all seemed so engaged that I felt these meetings, which had already accomplished their object, only one more burden on busy women. To get their own households regulated, to look after children and the everyday demands was enough to occupy any woman's morning. So the regular meetings were discontinued with the understanding that should anything out of the ordinary arise we would have a special session.

I was moved to make this suggestion largely on account of Alice Wilson, daughter of the Secretary of Labor and Mrs. William B. Wilson. They were no relation to my husband. Mrs. Wilson being an invalid, everything in a household of nine children devolved upon Alice who was the oldest. In addition she acted as her father's secretary. The patience with which this courageous girl bore the trials of her mother's affliction was a touching and painful thing to see. On the day of our last meeting Mrs. Daniels, the wife of the Secretary of the Navy, had driven up in a new limousine. Cabinet officers had formerly used victorias and horses. Mrs. Daniels was as excited as could be over the new acquisition, and invited us all to go downstairs and see it. The limousine looked stunning, but personally I regretted seeing the horses go.

The Suffragettes, campaigning for national legislation to give the ballot to women, as certain States already had done, about this time began to picket the White House. They stood on either side of the gate with great banners and transparencies bearing "Votes for Women," and several pointed comments regarding the President. One bitterly cold day while they were there, we were going in to lunch when Mr. Wilson's eye caught the yellow gleam of the Suffragette banner. He shivered at the thought of women standing in the icy wind for hours and said to the head usher: "Hoover, go out there and ask those ladies if they won't come in and get warm, will you? And if they come, see that they have some hot tea or coffee."

Hoover returned very quickly, saying: "Excuse me, Mr. President, but they indignantly refused."

CHAPTER 10

O N January 11, 1917, Colonel and Mrs. House arrived from New York in time for tea. Ostensibly they had come down to attend the first of the Cabinet dinners, the Secretary of State's, which was to be given that evening. Actually my husband wished to go over with the Colonel his next contemplated move in the threatening international situation.

Both the Central Powers and the Allies had declined to act on the President's peace overtures of December 18th. This had been anticipated. Before the rejections came Mr. Wilson was turning over in his mind an idea for one more effort to stop the War before we should be drawn in or before deepening national hatreds should make a durable peace impossible, regardless of which side should ultimately score a military victory. My husband had finished the first draft of his proposed statement of the case. It was addressed not to belligerents alone, but to all peoples, in an appeal to the conscience and common sense of the world. The President asked for "peace without victory," on the ground that any other peace would rest on quicksands. Given a conqueror's peace, the vanquished would only go to work to try to even the score some day. The President asked the belligerents to make, and the Powers of the world to preserve, a rational, give-and-take peace—an idea which later he was to develop into the League of Nations.

Before dressing for dinner my husband and the Colonel spent an hour in the study going over the text of the appeal. Our visitor emerged glowing. I find recorded in my diary: "Mr. House was wild about it and says it is the greatest thing he [my husband] has ever done." The Colonel's own diary, as later published, calls it "a noble document and one which I think will live." Naturally, we were pleased by our visitor's comments and went off to the Lansings' dinner in a happy frame of mind. There the subject was not mentioned, for, mindful of the Secretary's blunder in connection with the December peace note, the President had not as yet taken Mr. Lansing into his confidence.

The destiny of the world seemed to depend then—as, in truth, I believe it depends now—on the ultimate acceptance of the principles Mr. Wilson had in mind. This was never far from his thoughts as we moved through crowded days. The round of official entertaining, which always has its trying aspects, began to seem trivial indeed. The dinner of the Secretary of the Treasury and Mrs. McAdoo was the next big affair, which really proved a diversion in two respects. First was the novelty of being formally received by one's daughter. The other was a little joke the fates and the *couturiers* played on three of the ladies: Mrs. Pitney, wife of one of the Supreme Court justices, Mrs. Williams, wife of the Comptroller of Currency, and me. We appeared in velvet dresses made from exactly the same model. Fortunately the colours were different, one being blue, the second green and mine black with silver. Comparing notes we found one had come from Baltimore, one from Boston and one from New York. All were copies of a Worth gown.

After the dinner we went to the ball for the Children's Hospital of Washington because the receipts for this fine charity were always swollen by the attendance "of the President and the First Lady of the Land." I quote this phrase in order to say that the practise of calling the President's wife the "First Lady" was always a disagreeable one to me. I think that if some clever person would start a little crusade against it in the newspapers it could be ridiculed to death.

My journal for January 20th contains quite an account of the impressive funeral ceremonies for Admiral Dewey, concluding: "After this W. and I went to the study where I read his peace note aloud to him while he copied it on his typewriter."

Two days later we were abroad early for a round of golf in Virginia. At 12:45 I was in my place in the gallery of the Senate to hear my husband read his peace message. That night I wrote: "It is so just and conclusive that more and more I feel that he is inspired and that he must attain all he is striving for, for the good of the world."

Next night was the Congressional reception, always the largest formal affair of the season. The time-honoured custom at State receptions had been for members of the Cabinet and other privileged guests to stand "Behind the Line," meaning behind the long receiving line

which consisted of the President, his wife and the ladies of the
Cabinet ranged in order of official precedence. There was always a
scramble for the honour of being asked "Behind the Line" with the
result that so many won that distinction the poor women in the line
were constantly buffeted about and the trains of their dresses used
as rugs. Cabinet officers would spend most of their time trying to
act as buffers between the crowd and their wives. We decided to do
away with the sacred "Behind the Line," substituting a background
of palms and ferns. It worked like a charm and measurably reduced
the fatigue of the reception.

How good, when all this was over, to relax with my husband
before a fire and read the editorial comment on the peace address.
The reaction was good, and my spirits rose. Twenty-one years have
passed since that evening, and I am happy to note that critics more
disinterested than I regard that document as one of Mr. Wilson's
finest State papers.

Alas for the immediate results. On January 31st, nine days after
his appeal, Germany's formal answer was received: a declaration of
unrestricted submarine warfare.

I felt a sense of impending climax to the series of crises to which I
had been exposed. At two in the afternoon of February 3rd my husband delivered before the Congress an address which, after a terrific
day, he had laboured until midnight to complete. In this way the
country formally received the news of the severance of diplomatic
relations with Germany. Within an hour after the President had
ceased speaking, Count von Bernstorff was given his passport. Mr.
Lansing said that he received it very solemnly, saying he had done
all he could "to prevent this."

Congressmen and other officials and leaders descended upon the
White House, counselling everything under the sun. My husband
asked me to let him see the programme of official entertainments,
hoping that a few might be cancelled to save time. On second
thought he said that such a course might unduly alarm the country;
so the next night we dined at the Secretary of the Navy's—on fried
chicken, ham, corn bread and beaten biscuit. At the Daniels' one
could count on the good old Southern dishes.

Sunday, February 25th, we did not go to church. As my husband
needed a complete rest, he stayed in bed most of the morning and

in the afternoon we went for a drive. At dinner my brother Randolph came in to say that our sister, Annie Lee, was critically ill and about to undergo an operation. What a shock this was! Annie Lee had just left us, and was expected to return in a few days from her home in Roanoke, Virginia, with her husband, Matthew H. Maury, and their two little girls, to attend the Inaugural ceremonies. After a two weeks' visit she had left us looking the picture of health, with her snow-white hair, her radiant colour—which was natural—and dark eyes. It had been lovely to have her and I was always glad when we could snatch a few minutes for a real home talk.

Next morning Kurzman's representative arrived from New York with their models from which we selected our dresses for the Inauguration. Mother, Nell McAdoo, Helen and Bertha were with me. Everything was unpacked in the Rose Room and by the time we had made our choices it was time to go to the Capitol where the President asked Congress for legislation to arm merchant ships to safeguard our rights on the seas. "A very solemn address," my diary records, "and we came home feeling that a cloud was obscuring the sun— both from the dangers confronting our country and from personal anxiety concerning Annie Lee."

Well we might, for a few hours later a message came that Annie Lee was dead. The blow to Mother was so great that the doctor said she could not go to the funeral. I moved her over to the White House while the others went.

Pressing days. With the House twenty to one for the armed ship bill, twelve stubborn Senators, taking advantage of the unlimited debate rule, started a filibuster to defeat it. On March 2nd the President spent most of his day at the Capitol fighting for his bill. "Only one more day," I wrote in my diary, "to get it through."

March 3rd dawned with wretched, rainy weather. The filibusters remained obdurate. At 4:30 I dragged the President from his desk for a walk between showers. We stopped for a moment at the Corcoran Gallery, where the pictures always refreshed his mind. The White House was filling up. Colonel and Mrs. House arrived during our walk and we returned just in time to greet Mr. Vance McCormick and his mother. She was a lady of the old school, full of fun and wit combined with dignity. Her snowy cap, collar and cuffs reminded me of my Grandmother Bolling, at whose knee I learned so much that has stood me in good stead through life. As I thought of the morrow I could not but reflect how greatly in need of those teachings I should be in the trials that seemed upon us.

March 4th falling on Sunday, the oath of office was taken without formality. At 11:20 we reached the Capitol in a pouring rain, accompanied by Mr. McCormick. Mr. Tumulty, Mr. Rudolf Forster, Mr. Young and Pat McKenna from the Executive Offices awaited us in the President's Room. Cabinet members, Senators and Representatives swarmed in and out while the President signed bills—all but the ship-arming bill, which the filibusters had defeated. At 11:40 Chief Justice White came in and began chatting with me. The committee which ordinarily waits on the President to say that Congress has adjourned, "having finished all business," decided not to go through that form, as the statement would be manifestly untrue. So the adjournment was announced only by the ringing of a bell and the Clerk of the Senate's saying to the Chief Justice: "It is now twelve o'clock." My husband arose, standing beside the littered desk where he had been signing papers. The Clerk handed him the Bible he had used four years before, and also when he became Governor of New Jersey. The Chief Justice administered the oath.

This simple ceremony (I was the only woman present) was more to our taste than the formal Inauguration which followed on Monday, March 5th. Though the day came in darkly, at ten o'clock the sun appeared, which I prayed might be an augury of the lifting of the cloud of war. The heavy escort of Regular troops and Secret Service men which attended us during the procession to the Capitol had a look of grim preparation—as indeed was the fact, for letters had been received threatening the President's life. After the formalities at the east front of the Capitol we started back to the White House. One warning letter contained the details of a supposed plot by which a bomb was to be thrown from the roof of a house overlooking the route. Consequently soldiers and Secret Service men had been detailed to all roofs. Just beyond the Peace Monument there was an unaccountable halt in the procession and suddenly *plump!* something fell in my lap. *The bomb!* I thought. Happily, only a clump of flowers had been thrown from a window.

At noon on March 7th the President came in from the Executive Offices so wretched with a cold that I telephoned Dr. Grayson with the result that he ordered his patient to bed. He remained abed, or in the house, for ten days. The seclusion rested and restored him somewhat, freeing him from profitless interruptions for the contemplation of more important matters.

The armed ship bill having been defeated by the Senate filibuster, Mr. Wilson asked the Attorney General for a ruling as to whether he could, without authorization from Congress, arm our merchant ships against submarines. The Attorney General ruled that the President possessed this power. Whereupon the Secretaries of State and the Navy were asked for details on procedure in carrying out an armed ship policy. They replied in long memoranda which I read to the President as he lay in bed. Mr. Lansing, especially, saw no hope for peace and urged that we proceed on the theory that we should soon be at war with Germany. This was on the 8th and 9th. The 11th, Sunday, found Woodrow better and I had Mother, Bertha and Randolph to dinner. To amuse my husband I suggested that he and Randolph try the ouija board. They did, and who should announce himself as present but Lord Nelson, saying he wished to discuss submarine warfare. We were all interested by what he said, for it was entirely logical.

The following day, March 12th, the President gave the order to arm the ships. At ten that night Dr. Grayson arrived. Seated before the fire in my room he gave us the reactions he had heard from navy men and others. All favourable.

From my diary:

"March 13, 1917: W. did not get up until lunch-time; he still feels wretched. There is a streetcar strike in the City [Washington] and a [national] railroad strike threatened to begin on Saturday. W. saw several people and telephoned others to see if it could be averted.

"March 14, 1917: Still raining. W. in bed until one, but seemed better.

"March 15, 1917: Thrilling news from Russia regarding an almost bloodless Revolution. Overthrow of the Government and taking control by the people."

The tidings of the Czar's abdication, contained in a dispatch from Ambassador Francis, and the hope for a democratic Russia, seemed to give new strength to the President's conception of a war against autocracy. Immediate preparation was made to recognize the new Russian Government.

Other measures having been unavailing, on March 16th the President publicly appealed to the railroad executives and to the brotherhoods to compose their differences in "this time of national peril." On the 18th the strike was called off, but the 19th brought word of the sinking of three American ships by German submarines. "The shadow of war," reads my diary, "is stretching its dark length over our own dear country."

On March 21st the President summoned Congress to meet in extraordinary session on April 2nd to consider "grave questions of national policy." This meant war.

My diary: "March 30, 1917: Perfect day, but W. felt he must work on his message to Congress. So we closed the door and gave orders no one was to disturb him. We lunched alone and I took him for an hour's ride in the park."

Mr. Wilson was at work on his War Message, evolved as he evolved nearly all his State papers, first making a draft in shorthand, then correcting it in a combination of shorthand and longhand, then typing a fair copy on his own Hammond typewriter. On this day while he worked I decoded some cipher messages that had come for him.

The Message was finished on Sunday, April 1st, after we had returned from services at Mr. Wilson's church. The President had asked Frank I. Cobb, editor of the New York *World,* to come down. He simply wanted a friend to talk to. Due to a delay in receiving the invitation, Mr. Cobb did not arrive until one in the morning. The President was waiting up. They talked for an hour or so.

"April 2, 1917: Momentous day. Congress convened at 12 noon; called in special session to declare war. The House did not organize in time for the Message to be delivered until 8:30 P. M. When we reached the Capitol the crowd outside was almost as dense as Inauguration Day, but perfectly orderly. Troops were standing on guard round the entire building which stood out white and majestic in the indirect lighting which was used for the first time this eventful night. When I reached the gallery, after leaving my husband in the room always reserved

for him, I found every seat taken and people standing in every
available place both on the floor and in the galleries. My mother
and Margaret and I sat on the first row, and I could hear people
breathing, so still was this great throng. When my husband
came in and all rose to their feet my very heart seemed to stop its
beating . . ."

After the first applause there was utter silence as the President
read—until he pronounced the words: "We will not choose the path
of submission." Whereupon Chief Justice White, an ex-Confederate
soldier, rose to his feet and cheered. The response from the galleries
and the floor was deafening.

When the reading was over my husband waited for me to extricate
myself from the gallery. Through cheering multitudes we drove
slowly home in silence. The step had been taken. We were both
overwhelmed.

At three o'clock in the morning of April 6th the House adopted
the War Resolution. At noon I took the President for an hour's walk,
after which we sat down to lunch with Helen. While at the table
Mr. Forster, of the Executive Offices, brought in a printed copy of
the Resolution, signed by the Vice President and the Speaker of the
House. We all left the table and went into the ushers' room for the
President to sign. I asked him to use a gold pen he had given me.
Present also were Mr. I. H. Hoover, the head usher, and Mr. Starling
of the Secret Service. When my husband had written his name,
Hoover pressed a button to notify the Navy Department and Mr.
Forster lifted the receiver of a telephone, which he held in his hand
to give the news to the reporters waiting in the Executive Offices. At
two o'clock Woodrow left for a Cabinet meeting. The evening we
spent alone.

CHAPTER II

I AM told that the longest hours of work observed in the army training camps were those for young officers, where reveille sounded at 5:45 in the morning and the working schedule closed at 9:00 P. M. This working day was criticized by some as too long, on the ground that men not driven to the point of constant fatigue would be capable of better work. That is a subject on which I am not competent to pass. But if such a schedule were, indeed, too burdensome for healthy men in their twenties and thirties, I think the same observation would apply to the White House wartime routine. There the day began at five. Before six the President was at his desk, and often he was there at midnight.

People descended upon the White House until their coming and going was like the rise and fall of the tides. To achieve anything amid such distractions called for the most rigid rationing of time. Otherwise the result would have been chaos, at a time when order and system were indispensable if the vast and scattered resources of the country were to be harnessed, co-ordinated and thrown effectively against the enemy.

I know that the emotional drain and the work combined were too much for me, and after we had been in the War just eight days I had to take a day off in bed. At dinnertime the President came to my room. He read me a paper he had prepared, appealing for the co-operation of American industry. When he had finished I asked if he should not include the railroads. "I had forgotten them," he said gravely. "My brain is just too tired to act." I called the girls—Margaret Wilson and Helen Bones—and told them they must make Woodrow go with them to the theatre. They went, and on their return all three trooped into my room. My husband seemed a different person for the relaxation.

After that experience I needed no one to tell me what my most important war-work would be. Talking the matter over with Dr.

134

OPENING OF AIRMAIL SERVICE, MAY 15, 1918

Left to right: President Wilson; Secretary of the Navy Josephus Daniels; Mrs. Wilson.

Grayson, I was told by him that the President should have some new form of exercise to supplement his golf. Naturally the Doctor, who was raised in a saddle, suggested riding. Accordingly I said to my husband that *I* would like to take up horseback riding. Woodrow said that he would see Grayson at once and have him pick a mount for me. Results tumbled upon me quicker than I had anticipated when, the next afternoon, I was bidden to be ready to ride at five o'clock with Dr. Grayson *and* my husband. By borrowing Margaret's breeches, Nell McAdoo's coat and Altrude Gordon's boots I was ready on time. Of course the Secret Service men went too, and, although we might not have made very promising candidates for the cavalry, we had lots of fun.

Thereafter our rides became a regular thing, and I think about the only piece of wearing apparel I bought that summer was a riding habit. This small self-denial was in keeping with a pledge duly signed. A few days after the declaration of war the Cabinet ladies and I had subscribed to a pledge "to reduce living to its simplest form and to deny ourselves luxuries in order to free those who produce them for the cultivation of necessities. We have decided to omit the usual entertaining and to eliminate largely our social activities to enable us to give more time and money to constructive preparedness and relief work. In the management of our domestic economy we pledge ourselves to buy simple clothing and food and not demand out-of-season delicacies. We make an appeal to all women of America to do everything in their power along these lines not only as individuals but organizations to hasten the end of the struggle and win the War."

Further to help in the production of food, wartime gardens were started. In Washington the Government turned over unoccupied ground for that purpose to any civilian who wanted to grow vegetables. Edith Benham, my secretary, took over one of these tracts, and, in addition to her secretarial work, tended it early and late with wonderful results.

The Government ploughed the land, and staked it off, but the individual did the rest. Perhaps to this generation it will be hard to visualize the Potomac Drive from where the road goes under the railroad trestle, all the way to Hains Point, as one vast truck garden. There, in place of the present deep blush of the Japanese cherry blossoms, one would see happy, intent faces blushing from the sun or from toil unusual to ladies whose white hands had formerly fluttered over nothing more weighty than teacups.

When the Food Administration was organized under Mr. Herbert Hoover I signed the following pledge:

"I am glad to join you in the service of food conservation for our Nation, and I hereby accept membership in the United States Food Administration, pledging myself to carry out the directions and advice of the Food Administrator in the conduct of my household insofar as my circumstances permit."

Along with other signers I received a card which was displayed in a window of the White House. The design was in red, white and blue; and how familiar this circle of blue, with spears of white wheat, became during those anxious months. The humblest cottage, hidden deep in the country, displayed it as proudly as did the mansion. Often I have seen my husband's eyes fill with tears at the sight of one of those cards or of a Red Cross emblem. "I wish I could stop," he would say, "and know the people who live here, for it is from them that I draw inspiration and strength."

On one of the early days of the War the former President, Mr. William Howard Taft, called on my husband in connection with matters of Red Cross administration. Curiously, while they discussed important matters downstairs, Helen Bones, Edith Benham and I were upstairs doing our first stint of Red Cross work. Previously I had called at the local headquarters and volunteered our services in the capacity of seamstresses. Margaret had already embarked on a concert tour which she concluded in June, turning over the receipts, about $10,000, to the Red Cross. The sewing machine I had brought to the White House after my marriage was moved into a small room next to Helen's, which thereafter was the sewing room. We had goods and patterns and began that day cutting out and basting pajamas. This little "unit" operated throughout the War, indistinguishable from tens of thousands of others. Mother and my sister Gertrude often came to lend a hand. Despite interruptions I tried to do my share. I remember one evening when I had the rare pleasure of having four of my brothers to dinner. I persuaded Helen to take

Woodrow to the theatre while I sewed and the boys played billiards.

The khaki of our Army and the blue of our Navy uniforms began to give colour to the streets of Washington; and to these soon were added the varied hues of the uniforms of the Allies as their official Commissions reached these shores to discuss the tying in of our efforts with theirs. First to come were the British, headed by the distinguished and distinguished-looking Mr. Arthur Balfour. A cultured man of the world, easy to know, he gave the impression of an absorbed interest in the person to whom he was speaking—which is always flattering. His refined face was war-worn and weary. I remember taking him to the south portico to see the gardens. He said the flowers cheered him, and, after the gloom and shadows of London, to see our lighted streets, lighted houses and gleaming white buildings was like being transported to another world. He wondered if we appreciated half we had. The magnitude of our preparations for war and the buoyant spirit of our people worked a great change in Mr. Balfour. Before he returned his cheeks were ruddy and he looked a new man. At a dinner to the principal members of the Mission Helen and I were the only women among fifty men. That night I confided to my diary that Major General Bridges looked "stunning" in his field uniform and that among the younger members of the party who came in after dinner was an "aviator who has brought down seven German planes. Looks little more than a boy, and is very lame, poor fellow."

The French, headed by M. René Viviani and Marshal Joffre, followed the British in a few days. Of all the honours heaped upon him the amiable old hero of the Marne made the most of a Virginia ham we sent him. He said he only wished his wife were here to taste it; so we gave him another to take home. My husband came into the dining room while Helen, Mr. Young of the Executive Offices and I were puzzling our heads over the seating arrangements for the formal dinner for the Mission. He offered to help, and soon had us laughing—all except dear old Mr. Young, who I thought would burst from suppressed merriment. But the old gentleman's idea of dignity would not permit him to laugh out loud in the presence of a President, and he had served many. M. Viviani, who spoke no English, took me in to the dinner. On the other side of me sat Ambassador Jusserand, and beyond him "Papa" Joffre, who spoke only French. I tried to sustain a conversation in their language but my tourist French was in bad working order that evening and M. Jusserand had to help me over the hard places.

The Italian, Belgian, Russian and Japanese Missions followed in order. There was particular public enthusiasm for the Belgians and for the representatives of the new republican Russia. We ourselves felt a sort of a tie to the Russians when, shortly before, Nona McAdoo was married to a young attaché of the Russian Embassy. When the Russian Commissioners presented themselves at the White House to pay their first call they had to pass through a line of Suffragette pickets carrying a banner saying that President Wilson was deceiving the Russians. If he truly believed in democracy how could he deny women the vote? I was indignant, but apparently no less so than a crowd of onlookers who tore the picketers' banner down.

A little later, on our return from the noon wedding of Elizabeth Harding, daughter of the president of the Federal Reserve Board, the Suffragettes displayed a banner so outrageous that the police arrested them. Imagine our surprise when Dudley Field Malone, whom my husband had appointed Collector of the Port of New York, defended these women. Nevertheless, they were sentenced to sixty days in the workhouse. I was blazing with anger at Malone's conduct, and my husband was deeply hurt. He suggested pardoning the women, though not because Mr. Malone had defended them. He said they must not be made martyrs. Mr. Tumulty opposed the pardon but the next day, after a round of golf with Dr. Grayson and me, the President signed the paper.

The visit of the Russians raised hopes that, at last, the great resources of that country would make themselves felt against the enemy. My husband was not so sanguine about this. One afternoon my brother Randolph and I were motoring with him when he remarked that he did not like the news coming out of Russia. "I feel certain," he said, "that they will soon be in a state of revolution." "You don't mean very soon, do you?" asked my brother. "Alas, yes I do," was his reply, which startled both of us. "It would not surprise me to find a dispatch when I get back to the White House saying the [Kerensky] Government has been overthrown and that the Bolsheviks are in command." About ten days later we had just finished dinner at the home of the Secretary of the Interior and Mrs. Lane when the awful news came of the murder of the Czar and his family. The President arose, saying he felt sure all shared his feeling that this was no time for festivity as a great menace to the world had taken shape that day. The party broke up immediately.

Small things as well as large brought home the changes going on about us. Miss Benham was sad, but proud, when her fiancé, Admiral James M. Helm, received orders to report for duty at Mare Island. We had him to tea before he left, and found him an excessively shy and likable man. The deck of the *Mayflower* was braced for the mounting of guns, and its commander, Captain Berry, was in a state of distraction over the fate of his application for a transfer to a destroyer in the war zone. Frank Sayre dropped into town, crazy for an overseas post with the Y.M.C.A. McAdoo said he would like to resign from the Cabinet and raise a regiment. However, it was decided that in this war there should be no such personal regiments or divisions. A draft law was written, placing all on the same level of obligation. Ex-President Theodore Roosevelt wanted to raise a division, and came in person to solicit the President's permission. On the same day that my husband (after much thought and consultation in which politics had no part) made public the decision vetoing Colonel Roosevelt's proposed command, he proclaimed June 5th as Registration Day for the draft, and orders were given placing General Pershing in command of our troops that were to go abroad.

Later, when the draft was enlarged to include all males between eighteen and forty-five, Mr. Wilson drew the capsule containing the first number from the bowl. It was number 322. Mr. Gilbert, one of the White House guards, said that his son held that number: "I give the best I have to help you, Mr. President." My husband could hardly trust himself to speak. Taking Gilbert's hand in a firm grasp he said in a muffled voice: "God grant he may come back to you!" That prayer was answered, for he did come back.

One summer day we dropped down the river in the *Mayflower* on what appeared to be a usual week-end cruise. Though the news had not appeared in the papers, the fleet was at anchor in York River. The President said that he wished to go aboard the flagship and talk informally to the officers. We were in York River in the morning, passing along the line of ships. At Mr. Wilson's request the Presidential salute was omitted. On the deck of the *Pennsylvania* my husband was literally surrounded by eager faces, many of them so very young. Bareheaded, he talked to them; and it was one of the most inspired utterances I ever heard him make. He appealed to what was noble and heroic in their natures. He emphasized the opportunity for service for each of them, no matter how lowly his station. He urged them to use their brains to discover a means to end this awful conflict and promised them his ear at all times. It came from his heart, and I think it went to theirs. The response, when he had finished, was of a quality different from ordinary applause. In all there was something very solemn about that day.

About this time Mr. Edward N. Hurley, Chairman of the Shipping Board, asked me if I would rename the eighty-eight German ships in our ports which the Government had taken over. I requested a list of the original names and the tonnage of each vessel. I was in the study, where my husband was working under the old green-shaded lamp, when the list came. When I saw the tonnage of the *Vaterland* I exclaimed, and read it aloud. He looked up: "Well, that one is easy, for it would *have* to be the *Leviathan.*" He also named the smallest one, which became the *Minnow.* The original names of the *President Lincoln, President Grant, George Washington* and *Amerika* were retained, with the "k" changed to "c" in the last.

That left eighty-two to work on. The task did not seem so hard. But when I found that five Lloyd's registers must be consulted to avoid duplications, I ran into complications, never dreaming that there were so many ships in the world. I started to use the names of American cities, rivers, lakes, mountains and so on, and was surprised to find that most of them had been previously used. So I returned to the Indian names, which had really been my first idea, but discarded because most of them were long and hard to spell. There seemed, however, no recourse. This, rather than the fact that I myself am of Indian descent, explains the use of Indian names.

With the first eighty-eight out of the way Mr. Hurley asked me to name the new ships that were coming off the ways. There were hundreds of them. I sent to the Library of Congress for Indian dictionaries and pressed my brother Randolph into service. We tried for short and pretty names, and exhausted the supply very soon. After struggling with the jawbreakers I would get up a list of a hundred names. Randolph would go to work with Lloyd's and scratch out forty as already used. Trivial as it may seem, as the War went on, and other duties increased, this work of naming the ships became a genuine burden. I would finish one list, take a deep breath, send it in to Mr. Hurley and receive, with his note of thanks, a longer list of new and nameless ships.

The summer of 1917 was extraordinarily hot. Anyone familiar with Washington's normal summer weather can, then, imagine my delight when, on September 7th, my husband came in from the office at noon with the news that he could get away for a few days' rest in a cooler clime. We lost no time. We quietly boarded a train at midnight, reached New York unannounced next morning and drove, unrecognized, to the Twenty-third Street wharf where Captain Berry awaited us with a launch. In five minutes we were aboard the *Mayflower* which, with her new guns and gun crews, had the look of a sure-enough warship. It was raining, but we did not mind—so long as it was cool. We took to our cabins and simply rested as our boat moved up Long Island Sound towards New London. We anchored off that port at six, and Captain Berry and Mr. Murphy, head of the Secret Service, went ashore to telephone Margaret to have dinner with us. The weather had cleared and we sat on the fantail deck and watched the sun set in a sea of gold. At 7:30 Margaret arrived, bringing Jessie, and Madge Elliott, her mother's sister. We were so glad to see them, and had the jolliest kind of an evening.

Setting sail again next morning we passed through the Cape Cod Canal and went on to Gloucester, where Colonel and Mrs. House took us for a motor ride. Homeward bound, we passed through the canal again, which was lined with people. Standing on the bridge we acknowledged their cheery greetings. At the southern end of the canal we found, to our surprise, three torpedo boats waiting to convoy us. On one a sailor in white wigwagged that an officer wished to come aboard with an important message.

He arrived in a small boat and spoke to Captain Berry who rejoined us on the bridge looking very serious. A German submarine, he said, had been sighted off Nantucket Light on the day before. As it was known that the President's boat was in these waters he said he thought it safer for us to put back into the canal. The suggestion, he said, came from the Navy Department, and was, to him, an order.

My husband said he did not feel at all anxious and had no idea of going back into the canal. He asked how long it would take to get to New London. I could see that Captain Berry was worried. "I could not reach there before five o'clock," he said. "The best I can make is fourteen knots an hour." It was then eleven in the morning. My husband said: "Please present my compliments to the officer and thank him for his message, but let's get under way for New London as quickly as possible."

The day was as clear as crystal and the sunshine like gold. With a lookout aloft in the crow's nest, the gun crew on deck at its guns, and the torpedo boats surrounding us, we were soon off at as rapid a clip as the *Mayflower* could make. When I went down from the bridge I found Susan, my coloured maid, with her eyes fairly popping out with fear. Every time the engines made a noise she thought we were blown up. I tried to calm her, but I think she spent six miserable hours until we dropped anchor in the harbour of New London, and sent ashore for Margaret to come to dinner.

Next day we went in the launch as far as we could, and then in a motor boat, up the Connecticut River to Lyme. Madge Elliott joined us at Miss Florence Griswold's where Woodrow had once spent a summer years before. Miss Griswold, a quaint little lady of the old school, had a very definite personality. For years her house had been a resort for artists. Many of her doors bore witness of their work in paintings of near-by landscapes. From there we went, by motor boat, to call on some old Princeton friends, Professor and Mrs. Vreeland. They would not hear of our leaving before lunch; so we stayed and had an informal happy time, returning by way of Lyme to see the Sir Christopher Wren Church.

Once more aboard the *Mayflower* we found a telegram from Jessie begging us to visit her at Siasconset, on Nantucket Island. The submarine scare having evaporated, we sailed at midnight without our formidable naval escort.

The harbour on Nantucket is at the village of that name, a picturesque old whaling port, separated by the length of the island from Siasconset where Jessie's cottage was. Covering the distance in an old yellow surrey with two horses, we were soon on the beach where Woodrow built a wonderful fort of sand for the children. After dinner, we sat around the fire until 8:30, and then started back to Nantucket. So dense was the fog that we could not see the horses.

This did not at all disturb our driver, an old man who kept up a running fire of conversation. He would let his horses go at a fast trot, then suddenly pull them up short, take his long whip from the stock, and drop the butt end down on the ground. Then he would touch the butt to his lips. At last the President asked: "Taking soundings, Captain?" "Yes, President," replied the old fellow. "I know the taste of every foot of this ground. I can tell where I am, fog or no fog." Sure enough he brought us on schedule into Nantucket where the launch was waiting.

The fog continued throughout the night, but the sun burnt it off in the morning and the day was crisp and beautiful. We spent it on the top deck where my dear one read aloud while I was busy knitting.

We anchored off New York next morning, and I went ashore to shop while Woodrow was busy with mail which had come aboard. Mother and Bertha were in New York, visiting my brother Rolfe and his wife. That evening we all went to the theatre. The audience gave my husband a wildly enthusiastic welcome. He was so pleased, because he felt that it meant that the people approved his handling of the War. That night when we returned to the *Mayflower* Captain Berry was not there. He had driven to Bernardsville, New Jersey, to see a small daughter, born during our cruise.

After a jolly lunch on board next day with the proud and happy Captain Berry and Colonel and Mrs. House, we took the three o'clock train for Washington. In our absence Hoover, the head usher, had had my room repainted and done over. With flowers everywhere and a bright fire burning, for the evening was cool, it looked so sweet and homelike. Much piled-up work awaited my husband, but the machinery for administering the multiple concerns of a nation at war was moving more smoothly now. Nine days of rest had done wonders and we both felt so refreshed that work seemed a pleasure.

That was our last cruise with Captain Bob Berry. He got his destroyer, the *Manley,* destined for immediate North Sea service. When he came one evening at teatime to say goodbye, I felt that we were losing a member of the family. The entry in my diary for that day closes with a prayer: "May God take care of him and all the thousands of others who are risking their lives for their country!"

This will be my last quotation from that diary, which I soon became too busy to keep.

CHAPTER 12

A FEW days after returning from the invigorating cruise off Massachusetts I heard that our dear old Mathilda was very ill. This former slave had served my mother until about a year before the time of which I write. Infirmities of age obliging her to retire, Mathilda had since lived, comfortably provided for, among friends of her own race in Washington. Her retirement, as much as anything else, had decided Mother to give up housekeeping and live in the Powhatan Hotel.

My sister Bertha and I were soon at Mathilda's side. The poor old soul was unconscious. There was little we could do. In a few hours she died. Thus took flight a true Christian spirit. Though Mathilda could not read or write she knew her Bible through and through, and practised its precepts as carefully as any person I ever knew. That night I went to bed with a heavy heart, and awoke with a high fever, aching all over. Dr. Grayson was away on a Liberty Loan speaking tour with Mr. McAdoo. I sent for Dr. Sterling Ruffin, who pronounced my ailment grippe. As Dr. Grayson would be gone for a month, Altrude came to stay at the White House.

I was in my room more than two weeks. Woodrow would come and read to me when he could, but I was always fearful that he would catch that dreadful germ. My dressing-room windows faced the State, War and Navy Building. During my convalescence, as, indeed, all during the War, I seldom went to bed without looking across the way at the lights gleaming from every window. They seemed to send a message of friendly assurance that here they were, standing by to finish the job. No matter how late the hour those lights were always there. Often I have shut off my own lights and stood a long time watching. Always there were figures moving back and forth, as busy men went from office to office; and in the telegraph and decoding rooms there was never an end to the work. When news from abroad arrived late at night, the Secretary of War would come to confer with the President, and they would both look so grave and so tired. My own heart was heavy with theirs, but these lights across the way always cheered me, and after watching them I would go to bed feeling more hopeful.

The more I think of the calm poise of the President, and his patient and unfailing optimism during those days, weeks and months, the greater he seems to me. No matter what the burden was, he never complained. He was always ready to help even in trifling matters on which I would ask his judgment, and always accessible to any who had a claim on his consideration. His expression, in one of his speeches, that he had "a one-track mind" has been so often quoted that I mention it only to demonstrate my point. He could get off the official "track" and run on his personal "track" as completely as though the two were closely parallel. When he left his desk or office, he apparently closed that door in his mind, and was ready to play; then he would play with the abandon of a boy. Frequently, at night, we would go to the Oval Room upstairs after dinner and he would put a record on the Victrola and say: "Now, I'll show you how to do a jig step." He was light on his feet, and often said he envied Primrose, the minstrel dancer, and wished he could exchange jobs.

Mr. Wilson enjoyed vaudeville and was a regular patron of Keith's Theatre. No matter how foolish the skit, he said it rested him because it took his mind off responsibilities and refreshed his spirit to see light-hearted people who "took on no more at their hearts than they could kick off at their heels." Particularly he enjoyed the tap dancing, and Primrose always pleased him. The manager of the theatre, Mr. Roland S. Robbins, and his assistant Mr. Chevalier, always met us at the entrance and escorted us to our box.

Returning from a performance, or for that matter any recreation, my husband would go to his study for a look at The Drawer. Though it may have been bare when we departed, often he would find it filled again. He would sit down beside his green-shaded lamp and take up one paper after another—and so work until the small hours. Approval was designated by "Okeh, W. W." on the margin of a paper. Someone asked why he did not use the "O. K." "Because it is wrong," Mr. Wilson said. He suggested that the inquirer look up "okeh" in a dictionary. This he did, discovering that it is a Choctaw word meaning "It is so."

After a long White House reception my husband loved to get upstairs and twist his face about as an actor does in playing character parts. His muscles were so flexible, and he had such control over them, he could make his ears move and elongate his face or broaden it at will in a perfectly ludicrous way. He said that after hours of polite greetings and "smirks," commonly called smiles, his face needed resting just as other muscles of the body needed exercise.

So often we talked of what we would do when he should be emancipated from the burdens of official life. A bicycle tour of Europe was mentioned. My husband loved cycling. When at Princeton he used to go abroad during the summers and wheel alone over the roads of Scotland, England and the Continent, stopping at little wayside taverns and striking up acquaintance with farmers, townsmen and all manner of folk. He used to laugh and tell of one time, in Scotland, when on a Sunday he pedalled up to a little kirk to attend the morning service. The pious Scottish elders looked askance at the stranger's cycling knickerbockers. He was led to a closed-in pew where this strange and un-Sundaylike garb would not be a distraction to others. Seating him there, an elder took from his pocket a large key and solemnly locked Professor Wilson in. Not until the service was over and everyone else had left the church was the pew door unlocked and the bicycling worshipper permitted to depart.

He yearned for more experiences of that kind. Bicycles were luxuries in southwestern Virginia when I was a girl, and so I had never learned to ride. My husband said the deficiency was easily remedied, and one day there arrived at the White House a brand-new Columbia wheel. Where to take my lessons was a problem. Obviously not in the White House grounds whose paths are clearly visible from the surrounding streets. At length Mr. Wilson had it: the White House basement. It is commodious, and with some clearing away a space sixty feet long was provided. My husband and a couple of the Secret Service men used to go down with me at night. I fell off several times and nicked the enamel on the new wheel. Though I did not master the cycling art we made up for that in laughter and had such hilarious good times that it was genuine recreation for all concerned. Being a country girl at heart, what I needed was more room, and so the cycling lessons were deferred until we should be free to resume them out of doors, a day, which, alas, never came.

One Sunday during the summer of 1917 the President suggested that we drive quietly over to Virginia and attend the service at Pohick Church, which was the place of worship of George Washington. When we arrived the little edifice was well filled. Mr. Wilson, my brother Randolph and I were escorted to the Washington pew, given prayer books and left to ourselves. The service over, we were accompanied to the door by a member of the vestry and permitted to depart without any of the crowding which usually attends the appearance of a President in public. Also I was impressed by the large congregation, for it was raining.

Afterwards Mr. Jervis, one of the Secret Service men, asked how I had enjoyed the service. When I told him my impressions he said: "May I tell you a story?" This is the story:

Knowing our plans Mr. Jervis had reached the church at 9:30, finding it closed and not a soul about. At the nearest house he inquired whether there was to be a service. The man did not know but said that the preacher was holding Sunday School at his own house and that Jervis might inquire of him. At the minister's house Mr. Jervis found a young man instructing a group of barefoot little girls and boys. Jervis asked the man whether there would be a service at the church, because the President had intended to come. "The president of what?" asked the clergyman. "Of the United States," replied Jervis. The minister looked at his caller sorrowfully. "Young man, are you ill?" he asked.

Jervis showed his badge, adding that the President and Mrs. Wilson were due in an hour. The badge was convincing. The minister clapped his hands. "Children, Sunday School is dismissed. All of you run home and tell your fathers and mothers the President is coming to church and I want a good congregation to welcome him." Then he turned to Jervis. "Young man, I must shave. You run over to the church and tell the sexton to ring the bell—vigorously." The children scattered in every direction. At the church Jervis found the old sexton opening the door. He gave the minister's message. The sexton's mouth stood open for a minute. Then he said: "Here, you ring that bell. It's just outside in a tree. I got to go home and shave."

My birthday was on the 15th of October, and my husband's gift was a ring set with a black opal, my birthstone. Unfortunately I had to spend the afternoon receiving, for my illness had put me behind with my list. Among those who came was the new Greek Minister whom, of course, I liked because of the things he said about my husband. The President's high principles, he said, had sanctified the War, making it a thing of inspiration rather than greed, and Europeans were beginning to appreciate this. Following him were the Russian Ambassador and Madame Boris Bakhmeteff; in three months she had learned to speak English very well. As they left, the British Ambassador and Lady Spring-Rice came to present the Lord Chief Justice and Lady Reading. Lord Reading was here as a special commissioner of his Government to deal with financial questions.

Two days later John Singer Sargent came to arrange to paint Woodrow's portrait. We had a general turn around the Rose Room to get things just as he wished them. The room has a north light from two large windows. The great four-poster bed was draped with dark curtains the housekeeper brought from the attic chest to form a background. Then a platform was to be erected so the sitter would be on a level with the artist's eyes. Then a chair that would "paint well" was requested. We toured the house and finally he found the chair in a corner of the upstairs hall.

All this trouble I thought worthwhile if only we could have a fine portrait. At length Sargent said: "You know, Mrs. Wilson, I have never been so nervous over a portrait in my life." I looked at him in perfect astonishment. "Why, what do you mean?" Sargent put his hands on the back of the chair he had chosen for the portrait and leaned his weight on them without replying. I added: "That is surprising from the great Sargent." I recall his curious expression as he turned and faced me, saying: "Well, I only hope I can do it."

All this struck me as peculiar, for surely painting a portrait was nothing for Sargent to be nervous about, despite the unusual chain of events that had brought him to Washington. Early in the War, I think in 1915, Sargent had donated a canvas at a sale in London for the benefit of the Red Cross, with the understanding that he would paint the portrait of the purchaser or anyone designated by him. The canvas was bought by an Irish gentleman, Sir Hugh Lane, who in the following year lost his life in the sinking of the *Lusitania*. He left his collection of paintings to the National Gallery in Dublin, and as he had made no suggestion regarding the Sargent canvas, his executors took a popular vote in the British Isles to determine who should be the subject. Mr. Wilson's name was on a majority of the ballots. So Mr. Sargent came to this country to paint the portrait for the National Gallery, where it now hangs.

While he was at work my cousin Rudolf Teusler, whom the reader may recall as a childhood playmate of mine in Wytheville, Virginia, arrived from Japan. He was a physician, distinguished as the head of St. Luke's Hospital in Tokyo. On the outbreak of war Rudolf had cabled Mr. Wilson offering his services in any capacity. Later he was attached to the expeditionary force in Siberia. One day during his visit with us, Mother, Helen Bones, Rudolf, the President and I were driving out to the American University Camouflage Camp and asked Mr. Sargent to go along. The officers who showed us about were delighted at our amazement when an unoffensive-looking stone would roll aside and from under it would emerge a soldier. The commandant said that he had been less successful in disguising shell holes in open country, where it might be necessary to place men as lookouts. Mr. Sargent said quickly: "Line them with black velvet. It absorbs light and reflects nothing." I am sure it would have done what he said, but the idea of carting black velvet about on the front seemed a trifle impractical.

The artist had lunch with us several times. I found him extremely courteous and well-bred, though uninteresting. My husband said he never worked harder than he did to entertain Sargent while he posed. For all this, the finished portrait was a disappointment to me. I think it lacks virility and makes Mr. Wilson look older than he did at the time.

It was not until a long time afterwards, however, that I got what may be a clue to the artist's nervousness on the day of our meeting. This came from Mr. Henry White. Mr. White said that Sargent had told him that the night before going to the White House he had dined at the home of Senator Henry Cabot Lodge. Lodge had said that he was delighted to hear that Sargent was to do President Wilson's portrait, as it presented a great opportunity for the artist to serve his Party. Everyone knew Sargent's ability to find in human beings the counterpart of animals, and thus reveal some hidden beastly trait. Lodge said that he knew there was something sinister hidden in Wilson which he looked to Sargent to reveal to the world.

Then, Mr. White told me, the painter turned to him, adding: "I have therefore studied the man and tried to probe his very soul. I could find nothing hidden or unworthy."

I tell this story exactly as Mr. Henry White told it to me. Unfortunately all three men—White, Sargent and Lodge—are dead, but perhaps there are others still alive who know of it.

Late in October Colonel House sailed for Europe at the head of a Mission which included General Bliss, the Chief of Staff, Admiral Benson and representatives of the civilian war-making agencies. They were to attend two or three important Interallied councils looking not only towards the proper utilization of the growing American effort but to some general revisions of strategy. With close to a million men in training for the armed forces ashore and afloat, with Regular Army and National Guard troops moving to France, with money credits flowing like water into the Allied exchequers and the industrial forces of the Nation regimented under the able direction of Mr. Bernard M. Baruch, the war-worn Allies began to take on new hope. You could see it in the faces of their representatives in Washington.

Ordinarily the President's foreign communications were handled by the code room in the State Department but he and Colonel House had a private code known, so far as I am aware, only to them and to me. It was used in matters requiring the greatest secrecy, Colonel House himself coding and decoding messages and I performing that service for my husband. While the American Mission was on the sea the Allies suffered two staggering blows—the Italian defeat at Caporetto and the uprising of the Russian Bolsheviks who had occupied Petrograd and put the Kerensky Government to flight. When Colonel House reached England things had changed so unexpectedly and so greatly for the worse that all military plans and programmes must be revised. The situation was graver than it had been since 1914.

The President had accepted an invitation to address the convention of the American Federation of Labor at Buffalo. Just as we boarded a train at 6:15 in the evening, a message arrived from Colonel House which my husband and I sat down at once to decipher. We read that at the moment the situation in Allied councils was too uncertain for any definite statement. Parliamentary crises confronted both the

French and British Governments. The conferences the Americans had come to attend had been postponed pending clarification of the situations at the front and at home.

With this unsettling news we reached Buffalo in the morning where the President delivered his prepared address, exuding perfect confidence in victory. Before noon we were rushing back to the capital. Next day came a cable which took me three hours to decode. Colonel House said that the President's Buffalo speech had made a good impression and had helped the spirits of the Allies. They needed help. Colonel House described the Italian situation as "desperate." Reports from Russia were more hopeful, however. Kerensky was fighting to regain Petrograd. Possibly resistance to Germany in the East might not collapse, after all. But in any event England, France and Italy were too far spent to do more than hang on, awaiting help in the spring from the Americans, and possibly the Russians.

In a few days the Russian bubble burst. Kerensky's troops were beaten and their leader vanished. The Bolsheviks, in power, sued for an armistice. Italy seemed a military liability rather than an asset. America was the Allies' last and only hope.

During this eventful week occurred the death of Mr. Warren Young of the Executive Offices. I pause now, as I did in 1917, amid more stressful scenes, to pay a tribute to the memory of this rare public servant. He was one who, without obtruding, supplied that drop of oil to the machine which must grind on day by day, week by week and year by year. Few who see the results heed the hand that supplies that drop of oil, lacking which the machine will not grind without friction. Among other duties Mr. Young had for many, many years kept for the wife of each President a scrapbook of programmes of musicales and balls, luncheon and dinner menus, newspaper clippings and so on, recording the social history of each Administration. The one he made for me is before me. As continued by Mr. Young's successor, Mr. Rockwell, it forms a part of my reference library for this book.

On one of these crowded days the President received a beautiful oil painting of a little Armenian girl holding in her hand a white anemone, the national flower of her people. She was dark, with lustrous large eyes, and wore a lovely native costume of vivid green wrought with many colours. On the frame was a bronze tablet, which I copy, for the picture still hangs in my home:

"L'ESPÈRANCE Presented to WOODROW WILSON, President of the United States, November 27th, 1917, by Mrs. Hovsep Pushinan as an expression of thanks for the hope and gratitude his efforts to help suffering Armenia have inspired in the hearts of all Armenian women."

L'espèrance. . . . The whole world seemed to be looking to America.

On November 28th, in the first real snowstorm of winter, I went downtown to start my Christmas shopping and stopped at my lawyer's office. That afternoon my brother Wilmer brought the papers for me to sign relinquishing the little house at 1308 Twentieth Street, N.W., so long my home. I would have liked so to keep it, for sentimental reasons. Alas, I could not, and so signed away my one-fourth interest in it, closing another chapter in my life.

Thanksgiving Day we attended a service at the Methodist Church where Bishop McDowell preached. He paid a tribute to the President which brought an enthusiastic response, such as one seldom hears in a church. On the way home Woodrow was very solemn. He said he appreciated such praise, but that it sobered his spirit to think of all that was expected of him.

Praise, though he enjoyed it as any normal person does, invariably affected my husband thus. It gave him far more concern than the threats of assassination which he constantly received. Occasionally such letters came to me. "Don't bother over that," Woodrow would say. "No one who is going to commit such an act is going to write about it beforehand; and I firmly believe that as long as a man is useful in the world he will survive. So dismiss this as one person at least we do not have to concern ourselves with."

And I did dismiss such things, feeling not the least anxiety—over physical danger or my husband's ability to lead in his great task. Looking back, I wonder at my calm, and can ascribe it only to something I got from him. Just as cowardice is contagious, so trust in one we love dissipates fear. The only fear Woodrow Wilson knew was the fear of God should he fail in his own duty. Praise was more likely than threats to bring him to realize this.

For the opening of the Third Liberty Loan the President and I went to Baltimore. After a long drive through the city we reached a beautifully decorated grandstand where Mayor Preston, of Baltimore, said to me in a whisper: "Mrs. Wilson, I want to apologize to you for the absence of my wife. I have received anonymous letters saying this stand will be blown up today, so I would not let her come. Of course *I* had to." "Certainly, Mr. Mayor," I answered, "in such circumstances she is most excusable." Whereupon, wiping the cold sweat from his brow, he said: "I knew you would understand, but I did not tell the President because I did not want to make him nervous, as we may be blown up at any moment." The supposition being, I suppose, that the wife of the President was free from nerves! With no credit to myself, that happened to be the case.

My greatest alarm during the day was caused by George Creel, director of the Committee on Public Information. He had started from Washington by airplane the moment we had boarded the train. He was to meet us at the station in Baltimore and so demonstrate the superior speed of airplane travel, then a great novelty. When we arrived Mr. Creel was not on hand, and until I got word of what had happened I was far more concerned about him than I was about being blown up by a bomb. The plane had made a bad landing, resting on one wing and leaving pilot and passenger marooned in the cockpit until a ladder was fetched so they could climb down.

But I am getting ahead of my story. Late in November, 1917, the President went to work on his annual message to Congress. Far into the nights I would sit with him, often decoding Colonel House's cables or coding Woodrow's replies, as he wrote at his desk.

The message was delivered on December 4th. The Joe Wilsons came over from Baltimore for the day, arriving just as we got in from Virginia where I had insisted that the President go for nine holes of golf—the first exercise he had had for days. On our arrival at the Capitol, several Capitol police and Secret Service men were necessary to clear a path to the gallery. In earlier pages I have tried to describe a similar scene, and will not repeat myself. However, that ceremony never failed to give me a thrill: the Vice President and the Cabinet, the Justices of the Supreme Court in their black gowns, occupying the front seats; behind them the Senate and House members at their desks; Secret Service men at each door and surrounding the rostrum; reporters lining the press gallery.

Exactly as the hands of the big clock in the chamber pointed to the hour of noon came the announcement:

"The President of the United States."

After the applause he began to speak.

"Our present and immediate task is to win the War, and nothing shall turn us aside."

A declaration of war against Austria-Hungary, as well as against Germany, was recommended.

"With victory an accomplished fact peace will be evolved, based upon mercy and justice—to friend and foe."

Despite the many times we had gone over every word together so that I could repeat them almost line by line, the sentences came out in new colours and sank into my consciousness. With Russia out of the War, with Rumania crushed and Italy virtually beaten, all in the space of two months—I retained an unshakable faith in America's ability to win.

On December 16th I finished my first knitted trench helmet, and that afternoon the President's cousin, Captain Woodrow Woodbridge, recently commissioned at the officers' training camp at Fort Myer, Virginia, called at teatime to say goodbye. He had orders for France. I gave him the helmet. On the next day Colonel House arrived from Europe. I sat in the study while he gave his first report on the critical situation abroad. The next day, our second wedding anniversary, my husband gave me a lovely bracelet. It was a happy, busy day. In the morning I sat in the study while the President, Colonel House, Secretary of War Baker and General Bliss, the Chief of Staff, discussed the military situation.

Meantime a serious home problem had arisen. The railroads, confronted with labour troubles and an enormous increase of all kinds of traffic, had fallen down. Neither materials nor troops were moving as they should. The President held many consultations, none of which seemed to reach the seat of the difficulty. One night he went alone to consult Mr. Justice Brandeis and shortly thereafter, on December 26th, took over, in the name of the Government, the control of the railroads, appointing Mr. McAdoo to operate them. Then he prepared a special message to Congress asking legislation fixing the

SEPTEMBER 28, 1918: PRESIDENT AND MRS. WILSON ARRIVE IN NEW YORK FOR OPENING OF FOURTH LIBERTY LOAN

Left to right: President Wilson, Mrs. Wilson, Miss Margaret Wilson (back to camera); Mrs. W. H. Bolling, Mrs. Wilson's mother; Mrs. W. G. McAdoo.

compensation to be paid the roads. A copy of the rough draft was sent to Colonel House for suggestions and comment. Reaching the White House about five one afternoon, the Colonel found the President in a meeting of the War Cabinet. He would not be free until dinnertime. Colonel House approached my door, which was open. I asked him to come in and ordered tea sent up. We sat before the fire, and, taking the paper from his pocket, he literally waxed eloquent over a thorough disagreement with the entire policy outlined, bringing up some very good reasons for his side. I said: "Well, we will have an interesting session after dinner, when you take this up with Woodrow." His answer was: "Suppose you tell him about it first and let him think it over." "Very well, I will," I said.

Then the Colonel went to dress for dinner. In a few moments I heard my husband's quick step and ran to meet him at the door. When he saw the tea-things he said: "Oh, you and House have been having a talk. What does he think of my message?" "He doesn't like it at all," I said. Then I took up point by point his comments. Woodrow listened thoughtfully and said: "Oh, I am sorry; but I will be glad to have him go into his reasons; that is really where he gives me help."

We had dinner, following which we three went to the study for a conference. The President sat down at his desk, and, taking out his own copy of the message, said: "Well, Edith tells me you don't agree with me on this, which is a disappointment, for I have weighed every word of it and put a lot of hard work on it. But let's have it. I want your reactions."

The Colonel was walking about the room, and imagine my surprise when he said in his low voice: "Yes, I did tell Mrs. Wilson that, but she fought so well for your side of the question that I sat down and re-read the entire paper before dinner, and agree with every word of it."

I sat perfectly aghast at this, and finally said: "Why, Colonel, you couldn't! You said—" "Yes, I know I did," he interrupted, "but I have changed my mind."

I do not like people to change their minds so quickly, and was never able to forget this little scene. On January 4, 1918, the message was delivered as the President had written it.

On the afternoon before Christmas, the President had hoped to go with me to Virginia to distribute presents among the children who

habitually greeted us on our way to the golf course where we played.
The year before we had distributed, I think, seventeen presents. This
year the list had grown, and it continued to grow, until the last year
we were in the White House I think it totalled nearly a hundred. A
glance at his appointment slip showed the futility of expecting my
husband to accompany me:

"2:30 Mr. Daniel Willard [President, Baltimore & Ohio Rail-
road]
"3:00 Senator Kellogg
"4:00 Dr. Garfield [Fuel Administrator]
"4:30 Swiss Minister
"4:45 Secretary of War."

So Dr. Grayson and I distributed the presents. After dinner the
whole family went into the Oval Room and trimmed the Christmas
tree.

Christmas morning we all breakfasted together in the small dining
room. The tree was lighted afterwards, and we had lots of fun
opening the gifts. The Sayres and Madge Elliott were house guests,
and later in the day the Joe Wilsons came over from Baltimore. Late
in the afternoon there was a special performance for soldiers at
Keith's Theatre which the President wanted to attend. Mother,
Margaret, Frank Sayre, and I went with him. The matinée lasted
until 7:50, so we had to get into our dinner clothes hurriedly. There
were twenty of us—all family: the McAdoos, and my mother,
brothers and sisters, in addition to the guests in the house. On December 27th my brother-in-law, Matthew Maury, came from Roanoke
with his daughters Anne and Lucy. Their mother, who was my sister
Annie Lee, had died just under a year before.

A few days later we entertained at luncheon the British Ambassador and Lady Spring-Rice and the Governor General of Canada and
the Duchess of Devonshire, the affair giving me a variety of pleasure
which I think any housewife can understand, because we had a
"new" dining-room table. When I was married and first came to the
White House the state dining room contained two tables, exactly
alike—square, and large enough to seat two or three persons on each
side. Enlarged and put together the tables would accommodate a very

much greater number; but when we were a small party the empty table in the room always depressed me, and I constantly wanted to change the arrangement. But there were always so many immediate demands that things like this were apt to be put off. On the day before this lunch, however, I began rummaging the room on the first floor where discarded things were stored to see if I could find another table. Great was my joy to discover—not there, but in the old kitchen in the basement—a handsome round table with a rope edge which would comfortably accommodate fourteen or sixteen people. It was in good condition, and after a few minutes' polishing was substituted for the two square tables, which were not used again so long as we stayed in the White House.

For some time Mr. Wilson had been trying to get the Allies to join in a statement of their war aims, which should not only constitute a diplomatic offensive by rousing liberal thinkers in enemy countries against their imperial masters, but pave the way to a just peace. These efforts failing, he decided to undertake the task himself. He went to work, with Colonel House as his only confidant.

The result was the Fourteen Point Address before Congress on January 8th, giving the terms on which the United States would make peace. No public utterance Mr. Wilson had ever made was received with such general acclaim. Men who, like Theodore Roosevelt, had opposed the President all his public life, praised it. The New York *Tribune,* hitherto a consistent critic of Mr. Wilson, said: "The President's words are the words of a hundred million. . . . Today, as never before, the whole Nation marches with the President, certain alike of the leader and the cause."

For me, the burdens of the War seemed lighter after that.

CHAPTER 13

*T*HE beginning of summer, 1918, saw American troops streaming to the ports for embarkation overseas, while recruits by the hundreds of thousands came from farm and village and city street to take their places in the great training cantonments at home. In France our men were in the thick of the greatest of battles as the Allies countered the offensive of the Central Powers who had thrown their all into one more effort to break through to Paris. The dreaded casualty lists darkened the columns of our newspapers.

The President was signing letters and bills with his left hand, the flesh on the inside of his right having been literally burned away in an accident. He had been urged to enter an English tank that was being exhibited on the streets. The crowd was clamouring for a sight of him. Being unfamiliar with the interior of the tank, he was looking about for some way to climb up so he could be seen when one of the men inside said: "Just take hold of something above you and swing yourself up." Above him was a series of pipes, one of them nearly red-hot and the others cold. The President grasped the hot one. He reached the White House with the flesh of his palm fairly cooked—and his teeth set in agony. The hand was useless for weeks.

An insurance company in which my husband had carried an accident policy for years refused to pay indemnity on the ground that he was not incapacitated, being able to transact public business as well with his left hand as with his right. I thought the case should be taken to court, but Mr. Wilson, thinking his office might prejudice the court in his favour, refused.

I had joined a Red Cross unit which fed soldiers passing through to the ports. Our canteen was located near the old Baltimore & Ohio freight depot which is under a hill in what I believe to be the hottest spot in Washington. Shifts were on duty day and night. I chose the afternoon shift because that was the only time I could arrange, free from other duties.

We wore striped blue and white wash uniforms, with large bib aprons, and dark blue hats with white patent-leather bands bearing a red cross in front. Freshly laundered and pressed these habits looked very businesslike. But after several hours of hard work in the heat they lost some of their crispness, and so did we.

On an especially hot day in July we had had train after train of soldiers to feed, and were hot and tired, when one of the men came up to me and said: "Am I right in thinking this is Mrs. Wilson?" I said: "Yes, you are, and I am mighty glad to tell you how proud the President is of all you boys." He asked if he could introduce some of his "pals," and, collecting a dozen or more, he brought them up. Among them was a tall, rawboned fellow, who stood stock-still and looked at me silently for a few minutes until it became embarrassing. Then he drawled: "Well, buddy, you can't string me. That's not the wife of the President of the United States." Before his friend could answer I went towards him and said: "Oh, you don't think I look the part?" "I certainly do not," was his honest reply. This made us all laugh, and I said: "Well I agree with you; but when you come back from France if you will come to the White House I will do my best to 'look the part' and give you such a warm welcome it will convince you."

What a splendid lot of youngsters they all were—never a complaint, always a smile. Having eaten, they could go into the big room and write cards to the loved ones at home. One of the requirements of the War Department was that no hint be given as to when or where they were to embark. A part of our duty was to censor all cards before they went into the mailbags we had ready to fill. In the months I worked at that canteen hundreds of thousands of these cards were read. So far as I know not one contained a word or a sign as to the writer's destination. What a fine insight this is into the honour and glory of our draft army, made up of every stratum of society and every national ancestry. It quickens the pulse just to recall it! The boys wrote what would please the home people and cheer them up, which I think a rather splendid form of deception. Here is a sample of what we read so often:

"Got to Washington this A. M. Drove to White House where we shook hands with The Old Man [meaning the President]. This is a picture of the room he was in. Feeling fine. Love."

What actually happened was something like this. A long, closely-packed train would wind itself onto a siding. Officers would issue sharp orders for disembarking. Out would pour streams of khaki-clad boys. Forming in line they would pass as rapidly as possible by a file of canteen workers where we stood with great buckets of hot coffee and trays of sandwiches. Each man would take a cup of coffee and a sandwich. Sometimes only seven minutes were allowed for the entire halt. If they had more time they would troop into the canteen and write, or get tobacco and candy.

Sometimes the President would come for me just before dinner. He was always glad when a train was in and he could really see the boys. If possible he shook hands with each one and if there was not time for that he would wave them farewell and good-luck, and as the train got in motion a great cheer would go up.

Everything was being done now to release man power, as that was the great essential to winning the War. For this reason we decided to get a small flock of sheep to graze on the White House lawn and thus take care of the grass without having to cut it.

On April 30, 1917, eight sheep arrived and were put out to graze. Every tree and flower bed and bush had been carefully protected beforehand, so that the sheep could not injure them, and they added a very picturesque touch to the grounds. So much unjust criticism of having sheep on the White House lawn has been circulated that I am glad to testify to the splendid service they rendered, and to state that they did no harm.

Of course it was not long before the sheep obeyed the command given after the creation that they "increase and multiply"; and the lambs were so white and pretty they claimed the attention of visitors, especially children, who would stand for hours outside the fence to watch them.

When shearing time came, and the sheep furnished ninety-eight pounds of wool, the question arose how best to dispose of it, so that it might yield the most for the cause. We decided to send the wool to the Red Cross, and they in turn evolved a very clever plan to give two pounds to each of the forty-eight States in the Union, and the two extra pounds to the Philippine Islands, to be sold at auction as "White House wool." In that splendid desire all over the country to help in every way and give through every channel, the response was wonderful, and the prices paid unprecedented. The Philippine Islands led the list by selling the two pounds allotted them for fifteen thousand dollars a pound. The total sum from the ninety-eight pounds of "White House wool," as I recall it, was nearly a hundred thousand dollars; so I feel the sheep, installed on the lawn as a war measure, need no apologies from me, and certainly did their bit to help win the War.

One day in June Frank Sayre arrived early in the morning quite unannounced. We were at the breakfast table in my little dressing room, and after our welcome and questions concerning Jessie and the children, he said he must go straight to the War Department to get his orders as his boat was to sail that night. Woodrow asked: "What sort of orders, Frank?" When he answered he had applied for and received a Government appointment in France, the President said: "Why, my dear fellow, you can't take that position. It carries a Government salary, and you are my son-in-law. I cannot allow you to put either yourself or me in that position." Poor Frank looked as though the earth had opened before him for, of course, neither he nor Jessie had thought of it in that light, only welcoming the opportunity to serve. It was a tremendous disappointment to them both, which they accepted in the finest spirit, and he afterwards went over as a Y.M.C.A. worker without remuneration.

Since the War, George Creel has mentioned this episode in one of his amusing stories published, I think, in the *Saturday Evening Post*. He stretches the truth a little to make a good story, saying that as Frank was going up the gangplank of a transport the President took him by the collar and yanked him off.

There was also the case of Margaret. From the moment of our entrance into the War the dream of her life had been to go over and sing to our soldiers. Her father was unwilling, saying that she would be another person to feed on the other side and that, being the President's daughter, she would put a responsibility on the French Government. Tearfully Margaret accepted this decision. She told me that she felt herself a slacker. The fact is that few women could match the contribution she had made in money alone, remitting to the Red Cross every penny earned on two long and profitable concert tours.

As the War drew near the end, however, I am glad to say that the President yielded to her prayers. She came down from New York, bringing her music teacher and her accompanist, Mr. and Mrs. David, for a short sojourn before sailing. It was a pleasure to see one so happy and radiant as she went about the house singing, busy with preparations for departure. It was impossible not to share her enthusiasm when we drove to the train to see her off.

This brings back the memory of still another complication along the same line. The husband of a relative of the President petitioned the War Department for contracts in connection with the building of cantonments. Some of these had been granted when a friend of the President brought the matter to his attention. Mr. Wilson's caller said that no matter how remote the family connection or how just the contracts the situation might give rise to criticism. Years later this friend told me the story of the interview. "I felt I owed it to the President to go and tell him, but—boy, it took all the nerve I had! If he had not seen the thing as I did I would have been thrown out of the White House head first. It turned out that I knew my man. The President rose, put out his hand, and thanked me. That jaw of his was set as he said, 'It must be stopped at once.'"

Unhappily the family of the man whose contracts were cancelled could not accept things as Jessie and Frank Sayre did. The President's action made a breach that has never been healed.

I mention this only to show the small worries and misunderstandings which increased the burden of the man who so wearily said to me over and over:

"You see, everything that comes to me is a problem. Things that go right take care of themselves."

Nothing was harder for him than hurting or reproving anyone he cared for, but, obedient to a sense of duty, he put the personal grief aside and steered a straight course. I think this side of my husband's nature has never been fully understood. He could mark a line of cleavage between what was personal and what was official, and no matter whether the decision was against family or friend, it must stand. No one who knew him needs my testimony of the sorrow such

PRESIDENT WILSON AND KING GEORGE V IN CARRIAGE LEAVING STATION FOR BUCKINGHAM PALACE, DECEMBER 26, 1918

Spartan courage gave him, but to the stranger I hope it will explain why friendships were terminated, or close contacts checked.

The phrase for which he was so criticized, and misunderstood—"too proud to fight"—surely applied to himself; for he kept silent under attack, often preferring to bear the blame rather than expose a false friend or bungling member of his official family. When I would sometimes remonstrate, he would say: "Truth is no cripple. She can manage. But had I done otherwise I could not have lived with myself; and you must admit it is wiser to have the consent of my own conscience than to stoop to justify myself at the expense of the other fellow."

Despite the fact that official entertaining was reduced to the minimum required by good manners, the White House was a veritable kaleidoscope of arrivals and departures. Leaving aside those who were running the War—Cabinet officers, Baruch of Industries, Hurley of Shipping, Herbert Hoover of Food, Garfield of Fuel, influential Senators and Congressmen and the whole array of foreign Commissioners—the twenty-four hours of the day would have been insufficient to see all the others who sought audiences or pressed on the President, and on me, the acceptance of invitations. Would we attend this, inspect that, address the other? My husband did as much of this sort of thing as he could, and so complete was the discipline of his mind that often it afforded real recreation. I recall a visit of motion picture stars including Mary Pickford, Marie Dressler, Charlie Chaplin and Douglas Fairbanks. Again, a trip to the theatre to see *Over There,* a war charity play in which the actors gave their services without compensation. And a Red Cross baseball game, played by big-league players.

Mr. Wilson was a dyed-in-the-wool baseball fan. He has told me how, when a young man at Princeton, he would climb the fence and watch games when he could not spare a quarter for a ticket. Once I took my knitting—war knitting—to a game and he was scandalized. How one could knit and watch a baseball game was beyond him. Returning from the Red Cross game he found Dr. Garfield waiting with ominous news about the shortage of coal for the ships. "Oh, hang it all, Garfield," he said. "I have just been to a ball game and I wish I could say three strikes and out to this job."

On July 4th there was a great celebration at Mount Vernon, with foreign-born citizens as the guests of honour. We took as many of them as we could accommodate aboard the *Mayflower* for the trip. My husband spoke, after which John McCormack, the Irish tenor, sang "The Star-Spangled Banner." He sang as one inspired and when he had finished a hush hung over the multitude.

On our way back, Colonel Harrison H. Dodge, the custodian of Mount Vernon, gave us an amusing account of McCormack's request that, to accompany him, a grand piano be placed in front of the tomb of Washington. The Colonel thought this out of the ordinary, but on the singer's insistence he consented in the spirit of the French, who could explain anything with a shrug of the shoulders and their terse *"C'est la guerre!"* This was the second precedent established in connection with that shrine, the first being when the British War Mission, visiting the spot, reverently unfurled the Union Jack above the tomb.

About this time I received a note from M. Jusserand saying the French Government wished to present to me a small piece of Gobelin tapestry made at the State factory. After consulting my husband I wrote the Ambassador of my appreciation, adding that while we did not usually accept valuable gifts, this was such a gracious tender on the part of his Government that I would be pleased to accept it in the spirit offered. M. Jusserand replied that when the parcel arrived he would ask for an appointment in order to present it in person.

Two or more weeks passed, and in the press of other things I had forgotten about the tapestry when the Embassy telephoned that the package had arrived. I sent a note asking the Ambassador and Madame Jusserand to tea the next day, if they should be free. They were, and I asked if we could send for the package and have it opened at the White House before they came.

This was arranged, but I was at the canteen that afternoon and did not get home until just time to change and receive our callers. We had tea in the Green Room, and I remember how cool and serene it seemed after the heat and bustle of the canteen. About six the President joined us. I said to the faithful Hoover, who had just announced my husband: "Please bring the piece of tapestry to the Ambassador." Hoover's face was a study. "Oh," he said, "I took the liberty of having it put in the East Room, and it is difficult to move." Taking in the situation at a glance the Ambassador said, in his quizzical way: "You did not see the package? I think it is easier for us to go to the mountain than for it to come to us." So we all moved through the door leading into the East Room where on the floor, stretching eighteen and a half by fifteen feet, lay a royal piece of Gobelin tapestry. Aghast, I exclaimed: "But you said a *small* piece, Mr. Ambassador!" "Yes, I did," he replied, "but I had not seen it." Then I said: "But I could not accept this. It is far too valuable. Perhaps your Government meant it for the White House—surely not as a personal gift for me." "No, not at all," he answered. "My instructions are that it is absolutely for you."

The President suggested that M. Jusserand be kind enough to explain to his Government the mistake on our part in thinking it only a small piece, and say that with their permission I would accept it and leave it in the White House when his term expired. Fully understanding our position, the Ambassador agreed to do this. My husband added: "As a matter of fact, any gift to the White House must be approved by the Congress, but I am sure there would be no difficulty there, so we won't take that up until we get the consent of your Government."

Accordingly, I had the tapestry hung in the East Room just opposite the double doors. It made a beautiful vista from the long corridor as one approached from the dining room.

Personal matters were not acted on promptly in any country during the War. So it was late in September when I received a letter from the Ambassador saying he had instructions from his Government to the effect that *"in no circumstances* is the tapestry to be left at the White House." It was sent, and accepted beforehand, as a personal gift; and they would be deeply hurt if it were now rejected. This was a surprise, and an embarrassment, but there was too much at stake in the world to risk hard feelings or a misunderstanding. So the gift was mine, and has been a source of genuine pleasure to me ever since.

Mr. Burleson, the Postmaster General, sent us a pass and, on May 15, 1918, the President and I went to Potomac Park to witness the inauguration of the first air-mail route—between Washington and New York. I sent to Mrs. William A. Bartlett, an aviation enthusiast of New York, a thimble which weighed one ounce. The postage was forty-eight cents. After taking off, the plane circled the White House grounds and the pilot dropped a cluster of roses, with a nice message of greeting. On his return from New York he brought me a post card from a friend which carried a twenty-four-cent air-mail stamp; also a stunning corsage of orchids from the firm of J. H. Small & Sons, florists.

On August 5th I christened one of the hundreds of ships for which I had the honour to select names during the War. It was the first ship to leave the ways at Hog Island, a war-built shipyard. Following the Indian nomenclature this one was named *Quistconck,* which in the Indian tongue means "Hog Island." As I stood on the platform and thought of the fate it might meet at the hands of a submarine I could not help a little catch in my voice as I said: "I christen you *Quist-conck.*" Then I swung my bottle of champagne, which was so hot that Mr. Charles M. Schwab, who stood beside me, and I received a baptism in white foam.

That was the hottest day of the year—105 and not a speck of shade. Coming home our train was delayed for a few minutes in the tunnel at Baltimore, and I thought I might die. Many times after that day, when the sun was beating down on us in Washington, I thought of those shipbuilders toiling at their tasks and felt they were as heroic as many who carried a rifle.

When we got back from Hog Island there was just time for a blissful tub before we greeted the first guests to arrive for the wedding of Alice Wilson, the President's niece. The ceremony was not to take place until the evening of August 7th, but guests began arriving on the 5th. Alice's parents lived in an apartment in Baltimore and a wedding would have been such an undertaking for them that I suggested it be held in the White House. The President's daughters, thinking only of their father's comfort, opposed this, but Woodrow wanted the girl to have a nice wedding. Only relatives of the bride and the groom were asked, but these were sufficient to fill the White House.

Nearly all of them were there by the evening of the 6th, which was dreadfully hot. They seemed ill at ease, and so, in view of the event of the morrow, I proposed early bed for everyone and got them all off to their rooms at 9:30. Then I ordered a car sent around to the Treasury entrance and my husband and I stole out through a basement door and had a lovely ride.

Next day was worse than ever. Heat shimmered on the surfaces of the streets and the buildings. Guests were still coming and Margaret

Edith Bolling Wilson Woodrow Wilson George R.I. Mary

IN GARDEN OF BUCKINGHAM PALACE, DECEMBER 28, 1918

Left to right: Mrs. Wilson, Queen Mary, President Wilson, King George V, and Princess Mary.

generously volunteered to meet the trains. I shall never forget one relative of the groom. She arrived in a tailored suit, skirt and coat, with a starched high-collared waist, and not a hair turned from the heat. While we were all suffocating in the thinnest of white dresses with open necks, this lady really seemed comfortable as she sat bolt upright on the edge of a chair, and said she preferred hot tea to iced lemonade!

Evening brought no relief from the torrid temperature. So, as there was none but family guests, my husband and I suggested the gentlemen wear their white clothes, instead of formal dress; for it did not seem humanly possible to put on a stiff shirt and black, long-tailed coats. Our suggestion was scouted. No indeed; full dress was essential, decreed the mother of the bride.

My poor, long-suffering husband and all the other men yielded, but I should hate to speculate on what their thoughts must have been! Photographers were on hand, and as the light was still good at seven o'clock, they insisted upon photographing the bride on the south portico. In all her white mystery of tulle, she was posed. Just as they were ready to snap the cameras, out of the quivering heat came a perfect tornado! It was alarming. Without premonition the wind caught Alice's veil and wrapped it around a railing, stripped the green awnings from their iron frames, and sent men and cameras flying in every direction.

The poor bride was rescued and repaired. The wind was followed by torrents of rain, and forks of lightning and ominous thunderbolts. By the time the ceremony was over, the delicious coolness which follows such storms made us all feel that life was still sweet and worth-while.

The White House observed wheatless and meatless days and all the rest. On September 1st a request from the Fuel Administrator to conserve gasoline brought a Presidential plea for "gasless Sundays"— no pleasure driving. This was on Saturday and the following day we set forth to church in an ancient victoria, found in the White House stables and hastily polished up. But the Secret Service men were put to it to discover anything to carry them. Finally an old-time surrey, with fringe around the top, was procured. The two smartly uniformed motorcycle policemen, who since the declaration of war had been detailed to escort the President's car, were mounted on bicycles.

Thus it was we started for the Presbyterian Church, through silent, empty streets—no noise, no traffic. Sidewalks were filled with churchgoers who could not help staring at the unfamiliar procession, but their greetings were warm and generous. The bicycle men had the hardest part, for our journey was uphill, and we told the coachman to slow up his horses. My husband said he loved the leisure and quiet of the streets, and sometimes, on subsequent Sundays, we would drive in Rock Creek Park. The first time none of us thought of the ford until we missed our police escort, for the water was far too deep for bicycles and they had to make a long detour. After that we were more considerate and chose another road.

That autumn the President and I witnessed our first demonstration of wireless communication with an airplane. A wireless set was established on the White House grounds. Mr. Wilson was asked to direct the manœuvres of a fleet of planes overhead. He spoke into the microphone and his orders were obeyed by the planes. "Well, I have seen it, and taken part in it," he said. "But still I can't believe it possible."

What I have undertaken in this chapter is to describe a few personal everyday things in order to convey some idea of the intimate life of the occupants of the White House during the most thrilling weeks of the World War. The trivial incidents here related took place against the heroic background of the greatest of all American military efforts. Two million men were in France, half of them on the fighting front. In July the German advance upon Paris was stopped and since then the enemy had been in retreat. Every day brought glorious news— glorious until one turned to the casualty lists.

At eleven o'clock on the morning of Monday, October 7th, the Swiss Minister delivered a note from the German Government asking for an immediate armistice and requesting the President of the United States to initiate peace proposals on the basis of his Fourteen Points.

This *was* glorious news.

We were giving a luncheon that day for the British Ambassador and a party of thirteen. The afternoon was filled with appointments up to six o'clock. At nine Colonel House arrived from New York. Despite the fact that every moment of his time seemed to have been filled, the President had ready the trial draft of a reply to the Germans which he discussed with Colonel House and the Secretary of State until after midnight.

I believe the next four weeks were the most hectic of the War. There was a catch in the original German proposal by which they hoped for an armistice in order to re-form their armies and resume fighting to better advantage. The Allies' job was to avoid this pitfall and yet end the fighting, permanently, at the earliest moment. All the negotiations on the Allies' side were conducted by the President. Colonel House left for Paris at once to represent him at the scene of action. Cables flew between them constantly and I worked early and late coding and decoding. The tension was not lessened by the fact that we knew the end was near.

On Thursday forenoon, November 7th, whistles and sirens began to blow and people to flood the streets. Newspaper headlines proclaimed the signing of the Armistice. A jubilant throng stormed the White House with bands playing and hats thrown into the air. I ran to the President's study and begged him to come to the portico and greet the people. He said that he could not. He knew that no Armistice had been signed. The German representatives were only setting out for the rendezvous with the representatives of the Allies. He could not make himself a party to the celebration of false news of victory. Of course I, too, knew that the news was premature. But the President's decision, right though it was, greatly disappointed me.

Nell McAdoo came in for lunch. Making her way from the Treasury, just across the street, had been a thrilling adventure. Caught in a whirlpool of dancing, singing men and women, she had been swept about like a chip on the waves. One enthusiast had thrown his arms around her and kissed her.

As the day lengthened the excitement grew, and I simply could stand no longer having no part in it. In an open car I picked up Mother and my sister Bertha at the Powhatan Hotel, thinking we would drive down Pennsylvania Avenue and watch the crowds. No sooner was the car recognized than the throngs surged around us. I was glad that I had come out, to take my place among all the other Americans who had stood behind their President during the War. My only regret was that he was not there.

Sunday, November 10th, was very quiet. We went to the Presbyterian Church for the morning service, had luncheon alone, and

waited anxiously for the confirmation that the Armistice had actually
been signed. In the evening Mother, Bertha and Randolph came to
dinner, but we were all too excited to settle down. About ten o'clock
they decided to return to their hotel. My husband and I went out to
the elevator with them, and Mother said to Woodrow: "I do wish you
would go right to bed; you look so tired." "I wish I could," he
answered, "but I fear The Drawer; it always circumvents me; wait
just a moment until I look." He came back in a minute or two with
four or five long code cablegrams which he handed to me, saying:
"This is your task, and I have many others; so there is no rest in
sight for either of us yet." Randolph said: "Let me stay and help
you, Edith." Before I could answer, Woodrow said: "Indeed you can
help her, and I will be very grateful." So after seeing Mother and
Bertha in the car Woodrow went to the study, and Randolph and I
to the big table in the west hall, where we worked out the messages,
taking the last one to the study about one A. M. The President was still
at his desk, and eager for the news we brought. My recollection is
that this principally concerned the expressed desire of M. Clemenceau to work in harmony with the United States during the peace
negotiations that would ensue.

Two hours later, at three A. M., Monday, November 11th, came
the long awaited news—the Armistice was signed! The guns were
still! The World War was ended!

Many persons have asked me what we did, and all I can answer is,
we stood mute—unable to grasp the full significance of the words.

When confirmation of the actual signing reached the public, pan-
demonium broke out afresh in Washington and all over the country.
At 12:45 we left for the Capitol where the President made the formal
announcement of the Armistice. At four o'clock we reviewed a parade of war workers and at 8:30 drove out again to watch the cele-
brators as I had done two days before. The Secret Service men were
powerless to stem the crowds which swamped the car until soldiers
locked arms and formed a ring about us, in the centre of which we
moved slowly back to the White House.

November 11th happened also to be the birthday of the King of
Italy. The Italian Ambassador and Countess Cellere were giving a
ball to celebrate the event. It is not the custom for the President to
be invited to foreign embassies, but, in the exhilaration of the mo-

ment, my husband proposed going. We dressed and left the White House again at 10:50, driving unannounced to the Embassy on Sixteenth Street. The ball, colourful with uniforms, was in full swing when our surprised hosts rushed down to receive us. The President toasted the health of the King, and we stayed for about an hour. The day had been so crowded with emotion that we were too excited to sleep when we got back to the White House. So kindling up the fire in my room we sat on a big couch and talked until the early hours of morning. Then my husband read a chapter in the Bible and went to bed.

Early in the days after we entered the War, the President had publicly urged our troops to keep alive their faith in God, and feel that they were crusaders in a just and holy cause. Once he received a company of soldiers at the White House and talked along the same lines to them. One man spoke up: "You wouldn't promise us to read a chapter in the Bible every day, no matter how busy you are, would you?" "I will, with all my heart," the President answered. Then the boy said: "Well, I know it will make it easier for us to do it if we can count on you."

I wonder how many of those gallant young souls kept the faith as scrupulously as my husband. The Y.M.C.A. got out a pocket edition of the Bible covered with khaki, a copy of which the President used, for it had been sent to him by a soldier. No matter how late the hour, or how weary the brain, he never slept until he had kept the promise made.

CHAPTER 14

THE forenoon of December 4, 1918, my husband and I stood on the bridge of the *George Washington,* watching the fluttering flags on the Hoboken pier grow smaller and the music fainter as we dropped down the river to the sea. There were some carrier pigeons aboard and, tucked under the protecting wing of one, I sent a message to Admiral Gleaves, thanking him for all his care and for the beautiful arrangements he had made on the docks.

We had left Washington at midnight, having passed into the huge railway station through what is known as the President's Entrance the rooms of which my husband had turned over to the Red Cross for care of the home-coming troops. Here they had established a first-aid station, reading rooms and a canteen to which I had belonged. They were busy as ever, serving troops who were returning from, not going to, the front. We were the "troops" who were going to the front—to the Peace Conference in Paris.

After the excitement of departure we had an early lunch with Dr. Grayson and my secretary, Miss Benham, in the dining room of my suite. Formally speaking, Dr. Grayson was now Admiral Grayson, though I shall rarely refer to him as such in these pages which do not, I hope, comprise a formal book. The lunch was marvellous, as were all the meals, and on our first return trip, in February, we learned the reason. The Hotel Belmont, in New York, had placed aboard one of its best chefs who prepared everything for us quite independent of the menus served in the main dining saloon. My husband was put out to learn this. His disbelief in special privilege was aroused, and on our second trip to the Conference this culinary artist was left behind.

Lunch over, the President crossed to his suite, on the opposite side of the deck from mine, and lay down. In a minute he was asleep. I was so happy. The long strain of war was lifting. For three hours he slept without stirring, and got up looking refreshed and renewed. Those naps were daily occurrences during the voyage. Sometimes he would sleep four hours, without moving or apparently breathing; and then sleep again at night undisturbed, storing up energy for the trials ahead.

Our quarters on the *George Washington* were very comfortable. We had found them a wilderness of flowers and good-will messages. My suite consisted of three rooms—cozy dining room, done in English chintz, with a table large enough to seat six persons, or eight with a little crowding; a homelike sitting room, in cretonne, with a writing desk, telephone, comfortable chairs and a centre table; a bedroom in ivory with a pink bedspread and curtains and soft cushions; and beyond this a big bath.

In the President's suite one entered, first, an office as large as my dining and sitting rooms combined. It contained a handsome flat-topped mahogany desk, on which were two telephones, one a deep-sea instrument to communicate with the U.S.S. *New Mexico,* our escort, which steamed just ahead, and the other an inside 'phone. Adjoining was a bedroom whose sombre green curtains gave it a gloomy look, to my mind; but it was comfortable. Soldiers on twenty-four-hour duty patrolled the decks on which the windows of both suites faced. This may have been necessary, but it seemed useless to me, and really it got on my nerves to have those young things pacing back and forth all day and all night. If I could I would have done away with it.

After the President had finished his siesta on the first day we went for a walk around the deck where we found many members of our company: the French Ambassador and Madame Jusserand; the Italian Ambassador and Madame Cellere; the Secretary of State and Mrs. Lansing; Mr. and Mrs. John W. Davis—Mr. Davis being on his way to succeed Mr. Walter H. Page as our Ambassador to the Court of St. James's; Mr. Henry White; Mrs. Benson who was going over to join her husband, the Admiral; many experts and advisers attached to the Peace Commission; newspaper men, and so on. We went into the big saloon which had been fitted up as a chart-room. The walls were hung with huge maps and tables covered with charts and technical information.

Captain McCauley, who was in command of the *George Washington,* offered to show us over the boat. There were two theatres equipped with moving picture projectors—one for the troops below decks, known as "The Old Salt Theatre," and another on the upper deck for the Peace Commission. This last one we never went to, my husband preferring the company of the boys at "The Old Salt." Every night after dinner we would go down. Beside the picture there would be much singing of all the catchy war songs, such as "Pack Up Your Troubles," "Keep the Home Fires Burning," and "Over There." The words were thrown on the screen, with a new verse or two added nearly every night. These verses were written by the soldiers and generally had some reference to the "Big Chief," or "the Old Man." They made the welkin ring, almost shaking the sturdy boat's timbers.

Life was serene and the sea calm. We had one or two guests to lunch or dine with us nearly every day. Once we had a long table built into the study where there was more space and gave a real "official" dinner party. Then there was shuffleboard on deck, and morning meetings of the Commission and the experts, in the President's study, to clarify and discuss future questions.

Despite the smooth waters, many were seasick, among them several of the Secret Service men. This interrupted a French class organized with Mr. Murphy, head of the Secret Service, as teacher. Poor Miss Benham was another casualty. She longed for terra firma with a longing that would have made her admiral father blush.

The ship was steady but slow, giving us ten full days aboard, which I loved, for I felt better with every new day. It was a real holiday, life-giving to my husband, though he worked every morning. The discipline of boat drills and other precautions used during the War were still rigidly observed, for there was danger from floating mines. In every cabin was a notice of the life boat to which each passenger was assigned, and directions how to put on life jackets, together with information regarding signals to which all passengers must respond without delay. On our second day out shrill calls of the siren summoned all on deck. We rushed for our jackets and to our places. It makes me laugh even now to think how we looked! But every one was on deck except Mrs. Lansing and Mrs. Davis, and when asked where they were the Secretary said: "Too sick to get up." An officer replied: "But how did they know this was not a serious alarm?" "Well," Mr. Davis answered, "their only fear is we are not going to the bottom, for at the present moment that is what they most desire."

On Sunday we went to the service held for the troops, where all sang not with their lips alone but with their hearts. In the evening we attended their song service after which the enlisted men formed in line to shake hands with the President. On December 10th we passed the Azores, steaming near enough to see with glasses the very interesting contour of the islands. At dinner that night we entertained the French and Italian Ambassadors and their wives, Secretary of State and Mrs. Lansing, Mr. and Mrs. John W. Davis, Mr. Henry White and Captain McCauley—and took all our guests later to the Old Salt Theatre.

The last day out, December 12th, we had early breakfast and a busy morning at our desks. In the afternoon the President had his picture taken with the crew. We dined with Captain McCauley in his quarters and again went to the moving pictures with the boys. After the picture they all stood and sang "God Be with You Till We Meet Again."

Early on Friday, December 13th, we went on the bridge to see the arrival of our escort of French destroyers. It was a radiant day, just cold enough to be exhilarating. After a very early lunch various officials came aboard, for we had already dropped anchor. There were French officers in every arm of the service, besides General Pershing, General Bliss, Admiral Benson, and their aides, until our rooms were crowded. After much kissing of my hand by the foreigners, and clicking of heels, presenting of bouquets, and general good humour, we left our good ship to go ashore in a tender, called *The Gun.*

From *The Gun* we got a fine view of the port of Brest, greatly enlarged by the United States for the landing of our troops. As seen from the water the town is picturesque to a degree, rising sharply from the sea in a series of natural terraces, the streets appearing to double on themselves, each turn mounting higher. As we drew nearer we could see the people, arrayed in their charming native costumes, lining the streets. The men wore velvet trousers, short jackets and very flat hats with gay neck-scarfs and sashes; the women crimson petticoats, peasant bodices laced over white guimpes, big black silk Breton bows as headdresses, and many gold ornaments.

On shore we were met by the city officials. Margaret also had come to Brest to welcome us. Poor child, the food or the climate had not agreed with her and she was really quite ill. We were glad to take her under our care. In open motor cars we climbed those steep roadways we had viewed from the water and soon were driving under triumphal arches which canopied the streets, amid steady choruses of *"Vive Vil-s-o-n!"*

At the railroad station a crimson carpet was spread to the very steps of the train. The President of France had sent his own train, and it was impressive as coach succeeded coach each painted a dark blue and bearing the letters "R. F."—*République Française.* We entered a luxuriously appointed saloon car, with comfortable armchairs, writing desk, small adjustable tables under large plate-glass windows. Again there were flowers presented to all of us and much formal leave-taking—this despite the fact that it seemed as if we were carrying with us every official in France, each with several aides, as well as newspaper men, photographers, Secret Service guards, and many very important-looking personages who, as far as I could see, had no reason for being there. All these, besides our big ship's company, made a formidable body for a single train to dispose of. The French Ambassador had, for example, brought back with him eight servants; the Italian Ambassador two children and four servants. So there may have been some excuse for the mixup in rooms which followed.

The day before landing we had received a wireless asking for the full names and family relationships of those comprising the President's party. This information had been furnished in detail. Nevertheless the printed list found in each compartment designating the disposition of our party was a trifle eccentric. It read: "Secretary of State Lansing and Miss Edith Benham in Room A; Honourable Henry White and Mrs. Benson in Room B; Mrs. Lansing and Miss Margaret Wilson in Room C," etc. This caused all sorts of amusement, and some hardships. Serious-looking Frenchmen in charge of the train had placed all baggage in rooms according to the lists. When such consignments were disputed, they would solemnly produce the list, point to such-and-such a name and say: *"Oui, oui, voilà."*

This confusion did not apply to the President or to me, for at our disposal was an entire car, consisting of two compartments, with a washroom between, a valet's room and a maid's room. We were told that this was the French President's own car. While much better than many of the others, it was far from being modern or luxurious. For instance, the "beds" were very narrow, hard berths, running cross-way of the car, with only room for a folding chair at the side. No part of the train was clean and the sheets felt damp as though just washed. The dining-car service was terrible. All this attested the results of war.

Leaving Brest towards five o'clock, the train moved out slowly and a great cheer went up from American soldiers who had gathered to see us off. Among them were a number of coloured soldiers, assigned to stevedore duty on the docks. We had talked to some of them, and, while they were cheerful as could be, they said that this was the first bright dry day many of them had seen at Brest, for it usually rained all of every twenty-four hours. Judging from the seas of mud on every side, we could well believe it.

We reached Paris next morning at ten, coming into the station near the Arc de Triomphe. Again the sun shone a golden welcome, and when the train stopped we found President and Madame Poincaré, the French Cabinet, and members of the American Embassy, on hand to greet us. Troops were drawn up, bands playing the "Star-Spangled Banner," and flags flying everywhere. After formal welcome addresses and replies had been made, the two Presidents entered an open victoria drawn by perfectly groomed horses. In a double carriage Madame Poincaré, Madame Jusserand, Margaret and I came next; and so on, until a procession of carriages was filled.

The mounted Garde de Républicaine escorted the two Presidents, making a picturesque head of the parade with their brass helmets, long black horsetails down their backs, and the polished hoofs of their horses striking sparks from the stones as they went at a gallop. As a mark of honour, the chains barring the road beneath the great Arc de Triomphe were withdrawn, and we passed under it. The next day a Paris paper said that this was the first time this had happened in forty-seven years. The Champs Élysées was cleared all the way to the Place de la Concorde, with solid lines of French soldiers standing like sentinels on either side. Captured German cannon, hideous in their spotted camouflage, sent a chill down my spine. But today there was no place for them in a gay world, for Paris was wild with celebration. Every inch was covered with cheering, shouting humanity. The sidewalks, the buildings, even the stately horse-chestnut trees were peopled with men and boys perched like sparrows in their very tops.

Roofs were filled, windows overflowed until one grew giddy trying to greet the bursts of welcome that came like the surging of untamed waters. Flowers rained upon us until we were nearly buried.

From the Place de la Concorde, our route took us past the beautiful Madeleine, and ended at the handsome palace of Prince Murat, 28 Rue de Monceau, which was to be our home in Paris. The property was one of the finest in the city and so private, with its great wall in front, broken by two large entrances, double doors looking solid and massive enough to defy an army. These were abutted by two gate-houses, through one of which a small door admitted tradesmen and servants, and was always attended from within by the concierge. Beside the gatehouses stood two blue and red sentry boxes; and the entire street was cut off and guarded by a detail of French soldiers.

On our approach the great street doors were thrown wide, and we swept up a semicircular drive to the steps of the palace. Extricating ourselves from the flowers, we entered the house. I found it charming in every way. On the lower floor were three formal drawing rooms, a lovely ballroom with a gleaming polished floor, tall mirrors between long French windows hung with flame-coloured brocade curtains, gilt benches and chairs. There was also a formal dining room, and a grand sweeping stairway that had a small entresol halfway up on which was located a sort of *cabinet de travail,* or secretary's room.

The second floor had a broad central hall, with suites of rooms on either side and a very comfortable library opposite an informal dining room, which we preferred to the big one below. On opposite sides of the hall were two enchanting suites for the President and me. On his side, one entered first a large square room. The walls were hung in crimson damask and the same material curtained four large windows opening on the garden. There were a few choice pictures with lights to bring out their rich tints and leather-bound books in wall cases of carved cedar. An open fire and low comfortable chairs formed a background for an exceedingly handsome Napoleonic writing table fitted in tooled leather.

From this cheerful workroom opened the door into a rather austere bedchamber. The walls were dark green, with bees embroidered thereon in gold, and the bed covering and curtains the same. The bed itself, a single one with high head and footboard, was placed with the side against the wall. By this stood a bed-stand which, like the dressing table and large flat desk, was ornamented with fire-gilt Napoleonic eagles. There were heavy velvet carpets, so not a sound could be heard at any time. This room communicated with a dressing room and bathroom.

My own quarters opposite followed a different plan except the first big sitting room which duplicated the one opposite in size and crimson hangings. It was furnished in more affluent fashion, however—cabinets filled with *objets d'art,* low sofas, smaller chairs and so forth. Beyond was the bedroom with a complete set of ivory-tinted furniture; the bed regal with a canopy of delicate blue, and an elaborate lace covering over blue; a chaise longue of blue, a bed table with gold and crystal decanter of orange flower water. An open fireplace afforded the only heat in this room, though the rest of the house was furnished with central heating.

Next was a dressing room, panelled in soft grey wood. Behind these panels were cupboards for every possible use—one for hats, one for shoes, another for lingerie, one for stockings, one for gloves, and, of course, one for gowns. Each was lined with quilted blue satin, with hat rests, shoe trees or slipper pads, coat and dress hangers—everything complete and so dainty. There was a toilet table in front of a great mirror, and a small telephone table near by with a low armchair.

The bathroom beyond had a tremendous built-in stationary double washstand with two basins, one equipped with a shower for shampooing hair. The entire toilet set was gold with the Murat crest on each piece.

Of course I did not have leisure to take in all these details that hurried first morning for, as I have said, we did not reach Paris until ten. By the time we got to the house and had received all the officials who accompanied us, there was hardly time to rush up to our rooms and change before starting to the Élysée Palace for a lunch given by the President and Madame Poincaré.

As we approached, the Presidential palace gates were thrown open revealing a guard of honour standing at attention and a sort of drum corps beating a salute on small drums. Henri Martin, the Chief of Protocol, whose long, lugubrious face was to become so familiar in the coming months, rushed to open the carriage door, and preceded us up a few steps to the main entrance where our hosts were waiting.

We were taken into a large reception room and the guests were presented to us. The world and his wife were there, all in their smartest attire with uniforms and medals conspicuous in the foreground. Members of the Cabinet, and the President, wore long old-time-looking tightly-buttoned frock coats, which reminds me that as we were hurriedly going to our rooms to change for this function a young American officer dashed up with the information that no one in Paris wore cutaways, or morning coats, as we do in America, "frocks" being the only coats used for formal wear. They were so out-of-date at home that I said: "Oh, but I am afraid the President did not bring such a garment." The faithful Brooks, his valet, saved the day by assuring us he had brought two, as "one never knows different customs in different countries." So my husband appeared at the lunch as he should, and we seemed suddenly to find ourselves in the act of being introduced to the whole of France.

When all the guests had assembled, we moved towards the long saloon room where the tables were placed. The President of France escorted me, and my husband Madame Poincaré. Instead of a perfunctory escort, such as is our custom when a gentleman takes a lady in to dinner or to lunch, the French take the office seriously. When the arm is offered and accepted, the lady finds a viselike hold fastened upon her, which apparently nothing but death can relax before the goal at the table is reached. Thus, when I accepted Monsieur Poincaré's arm, I was towed along through room after room, and being a head taller than he I felt like a big liner with a tiny tug pushing her out from her moorings.

Thus the dining room was finally achieved. Tables were set in a hollow square and our places were at the far end, to which the approach was through a narrow aisle lined with liveried attendants. Single file there was ample space, but two abreast made it an adventure. However, mowing down waiters as we went, we arrived breathless and panting. This was my first experience, but as time went on I got so expert that I felt I could qualify for a football rush.

The table was very French in its appointments. There were set flower pieces at intervals all down its long length, alternating with slender Sèvres china figures in graceful poses. The flowers in front of me were violets formed in an airplane with the wings spreading two or more feet. Then there were mounted guns, ships, flags of the Allied countries, and so on, all made of different flowers of every colour.

To me one of the most interesting features of the occasion was a sight of the heroes of the War—Joffre, Foch, and of course our own Pershing, Bliss, and many, many others. When the lunch was over we were escorted in the same formal fashion, with drum accompaniment, back to our carriage.

About an hour later the President and Madame Poincaré formally called on us, and within another hour we returned their call, again heralded and speeded on our way by the rat-ta-tat-tat from the troops.

That afternoon a parade of women had been scheduled. One of the organizers, a lady of extremely cultivated appearance, called and requested to see my husband. When he received her she was in tears as she told her story, which was that a body of working women had desired to march to our house to express their approval of Mr. Wilson's Fourteen Points, and ask him to address them. They had procured the necessary permit to parade and hundreds of them had gathered ready to start when an officer appeared and rescinded the permit. Naturally my husband said he could do nothing, as he was a guest of the Government.

The next day being Sunday we went in the morning to the Presbyterian Church in the Rue de Berri, and immediately afterwards drove to the old cemetery where La Fayette is buried to place a wreath on his grave. This is in the old part of Paris in an enclosure which looks as if it had been a part of a convent. Dr. Grayson, General Harts, formerly military aide at the White House and now in charge of all troops in Paris, and the two French aides, General Léorat and Lieutenant Colonel Loher, accompanied us. As we walked from the gate to the grave eerie-looking old women came out of an ancient building and gazed at us. They were dressed in a sort of habit of white heavy worsted, with queer headdresses of white shaped like sunflower petals, from which peered their little wizened faces.

In a Paris paper containing a long account of this visit, we were amused to read the following:

"When the President went to the tomb he insisted on taking his wreath with him, contrary to the custom here, by which the florist delivers the wreath and the donor makes his visit later and leaves his card. The President sent Admiral Grayson to buy the wreath, and after some difficulty in explaining to the florist, who could not understand why the traditional custom should be broken, he got it. On his personal card the President wrote this inscription: 'In memory of the great La Fayette from a fellow servant of liberty.' "

In the afternoon we went to the Episcopal Church of the Holy Trinity. Later my husband again received the President of France; and afterwards the Premier, M. Clemenceau; then Mr. Herbert Hoover, who came to tell him of the food situation.

The next morning was filled with appointments, one caller after another, among them Ambassador and Mrs. Page whom we kept to lunch with us. Immediately after this a big delegation arrived to escort us to the Hôtel de Ville where, with due ceremony, the President was given the freedom of the city. We went in open carriages, and again the entire way was thronged with people shouting and acclaiming. We had the escort of the Garde de Paris, and when we reached the beautiful building an open square had been cleared for the carriages to approach, but otherwise the whole world seemed to be massed with people. On entering we found still another reception committee which accompanied us through the long stately rooms. A gold medal was presented to the President, with speeches and all the graceful compliments to which the French language lends itself. After Woodrow had responded, we imagined that would end the ceremony.

But to my surprise, the master of ceremonies then turned to me and presented a beautiful Lalique box containing a most unusual pin composed of six doves of peace made of rose quartz. The setting was in tiny diamond chips outlining slender fronds between which rested the doves. It was a pretty conceit, and the workmanship was unique. The pin rested on a green satin pad inside the box. "A gift from the City of Paris" was the presentation phrase. To the President was also given a gold pen with the following presentation: *"Le peuple Français offre la plume avec laquelle il signera la paix juste, humaine et durable"* (The people of France offer the pen with which to sign the peace, just, humane and lasting).

After this second ceremony we were asked in to another great

TELEGRAMME OFFICIEL

M. PRESIDENT OF THE UNITED
STATES PARIS

Hotel Murat
28, Rue Monceau

À DÉCHIRER

Indications de réception.

SSSS   SANDRINGHAM 0081 79   31   5-35 S   =
= I HASTEN TO EXPRESS MY SINCERE THANKS FOR YOUR KIND
MESSAGE JUST RECEIVED YOUR VISIT HAS AROUSED GENERAL
ENTHOUSIASM AMONG MY PEOPLE WHILE THE STAY OF MRS WILSON AND
YOURSELF UNDER OUR ROOF HAS BEEN A SPECIAL PLEASURE TO THE
QUEEN AND ME IN OFFERING YOU OUR GOOD WISHES FOR A HAPPY
NEW YEAR I HEARTILY RECIPROCATE YOUR HOPES THAT IT MAY BRING
PEACE AND HOPPINESS TO BOTH OUR COUNTRIES = GEORGE R I =

Official Telegram from King George V to President Wilson, December 31, 1918

room where a long table was set with every dainty in the market. Much champagne was opened and toasts again offered.

Arriving home very late we found M. Venizelos, the Premier of Greece and head of the Greek delegation, waiting. The two guards who always attended him were among the most picturesque of the many figures which made the Paris streets so colourful. Their uniforms were an exquisite clear blue, like the sky, and heavily embroidered in silver. The caps, which were small and round and set far back on their heads, had long black horsehair tails depending from them, and their shoes were turned up at the toes with big rosettes of black bear skin on them. They carried silver swords, and were young and lithe, with fine dark eyes and dark hair.

After the Premier had left, General Pershing came. My husband tried to express the gratitude of our people as well as his own pride in the way our commander in the field had conducted the War.

Each day brought more interesting people, and every hour was parcelled out. Marshal Foch arrived early the following day, and that evening we went to the American Embassy for a dinner, followed by a large reception, given for us by the American Ambassador and Mrs. Sharp.

This was all very pleasant, and we were touched and gratified by the tremendous ovations and welcome; but my husband was anxious to get things working. We had now been in Paris four days with nothing done. So he called a meeting at the Crillon Hotel where our delegates were housed, and met them to discuss plans. He was told that the English did not think it possible to open the Conference until after their elections were over; that Mr. Lloyd George said his political fortunes were at stake, and he could not leave; that both England and Italy felt a personal visit from the President to their countries would do much towards smoothing out domestic differences and making it easier for their representatives at the Peace Conference.

The British and Italian Ambassadors urged the President to visit London and Rome at once. This was confirmed the following day by a personal visit from the King of Italy who came to Paris especially to extend the invitation. With few attendants he arrived at our house wearing his field uniform with a queer double-decker cap, and looking tiny and unimpressive. But he was so free from ostentation and so genuine that no one could fail to respect and like him. Gazing around the beautiful room in the Murat Palace he exclaimed: "My God, I couldn't live in a place like this!"

That same morning M. Clemenceau brought me a small piece of the flag of truce which the Germans had carried when they came to sign the Armistice terms. It is a square about two and one half inches large of what looks like an old piece of damask tablecloth. The French Premier wrote a few lines on a sheet of paper and pinned the bit of cloth to it: a very gracious thought on the part of this old man, who always had a black skullcap on his head, and grey cotton gloves on his hands to cover the eczema which must have added to the pessimistic view he took of life.

In the afternoon we went to the French Academy which was that day honouring lovable old "Papa" Joffre. The big blue-eyed Marshal appeared in his uniform, wearing the Médaille Militaire, the Croix de guerre and the plaquette of the Legion d'Honneur. A burst of applause greeted him. He was very pale and walked heavily to his seat. Next day Signors Orlando and Sonnino, heads of the Italian Peace Delegation, called. These men were the antithesis of each other: Orlando fat, soft, poetic, idealistic and sweet-natured, with grey hair that stood up in a brush on the top of his head; Sonnino spare, bland, a nose like a hawk, little eyes. A shrewd, calculating Jew, he was always on the watch, suspected everybody and took nothing for face value. Thus it was that I obtained my first glimpses and registered my first impressions of some of the men with whom my husband was presently to spend grim hours and days. Following the Italian statesmen came several Ambassadors and Ministers from various nations; then the President of the French Senate and ten of the members; following them, M. André Tardieu; then the Spanish Prime Minister. After this my husband returned the call of the King of Italy. Margaret left Paris that day to keep her concert engagements, home fare and a good rest having quite restored her health.

The following afternoon, when we went to the Sorbonne where my husband was given an honourary degree, a funny incident occurred. Just as we were ready to leave the house a message came that Madame Poincaré wanted me to sit in her box, and would be there at a certain hour. So I went before the hour set and found poor, dreary M. Martin at the door awaiting me and looking his saddest over the failure of Madame to appear. He begged that I would be so gracious as to pause for a few minutes before ascending to the box as he was sure she would be delayed only a moment. So I waited a few minutes, but my secretary, always jealous of the prerogatives, protested against my waiting longer, saying she felt Madame should await me, as I was the guest. So at Miss Benham's insistence we went up to the box where we found Mme. Poincaré seated in state and furious with Martin that he had not been on hand to attend her arrival. She was so angry at him that she almost forgot to be polite to us. I decided not to let her ill temper mar the afternoon for me. After dryly observing it was her own fault if she came ahead of time and so inconvenienced every one, I ignored her and settled down to enjoy myself. This I did thoroughly—for it was a very interesting occasion.

We got home in time for a brief rest before dressing for a dinner given for us by the British Ambassador and his wife, Lord and Lady Derby. The Embassy, a beautiful old palace which was the home of Napoleon's favourite sister Pauline, was filled with tradition and many beautiful things. The host is a genial, easy-to-know gentleman. Their lovely daughter, who has since met a tragic death hunting, was among the company.

On the way home my husband confessed that he was afraid Lady Derby thought him dull, for she had asked while at table: "Do you in America arm after dinner?" And he, whose thoughts had been so concentrated on war and armaments, could not for a moment focus his mind on the social amenities and recall whether after dinner the gentlemen escorted the ladies from the room or merely stood while they withdrew. He said he tried after that to rally his wits and follow her more closely.

The next day was Sunday and instead of going to church we started early with a car filled with flowers for Neuilly to visit the American Hospital. What a vast place it was, and what tragedies of suffering and death those silent walls had witnessed. I am ashamed to say that I am peculiar about hospitals. Their very name depresses me, and I only visit my friends or family connections from the severest sense of duty, never losing the feeling almost of nausea which strikes me at the very door. I confess this with no wish to pose as a martyr, but only as an apology for that side of my temperament. Thus I went, and we spent five hours going from bed to bed, talking

to the boys who were getting well, and trying to comfort those whose
wan faces told the awful story of approaching death or helpless
invalidism stretching over difficult long years. My heart ached, and I
felt I would disgrace myself and burst into tears as we went up and
down the endless rows of neat white beds. We were being conducted by some of the nurses and the head doctor to whom it was
all so familiar that they were oblivious to the shock to me.

The hospital was one to make any American proud, for it was so
spotless and so well equipped. Having been through the wards we
were shown the very modern operating room. I was counting the
minutes until we could get away and breathe God's pure air free
from the odour of disinfectants and anesthetics, when the doctor
opened a door and stood back for me to enter. Never shall I forget
that awful sight! The room seemed to be turning upside down, and
through a mist I saw human forms with faces so distorted and mutilated that the place seemed an inferno. I think for an instant only
my will to hold on and not let them see my horror kept me from
fainting.

Suddenly I seemed to come back from a long distance, and heard
the doctor's even voice saying to my husband: "Yes, this is the facial
ward. You see we put them all up here together so they won't get
sensitive about seeing people, and sort of help each other. If each
were off to himself he would not know about the others, and would
get morbid and self-conscious." This brought me up with a jerk, and
I have never ceased to be grateful to that wise doctor. I felt so ashamed
that I should grow faint at merely looking at what these boys were
enduring without a murmur. There they were, some with their
entire noses blown away, some totally blind, others with chins and
half their faces gone. Well, I revived and shook myself free of
horror and stayed on and talked and told them how proud I was
just to touch their hands. My husband made a little talk to them as
they gathered around him like children.

To lighten this gloomy picture, I must recall one or two of the
little contacts we had in the hospital. A great giant of a fellow, with
his arm and shoulder in splints, came forward to shake hands with
the President. Mr. Wilson said: "Your face seems so familiar; have
I seen you before?" "You bet you have," roared the giant. "I was a
traffic cop at the Grand Central in little old New York."

A badly wounded private said his name was Thomas Wilson. Taking his hand, the President said: "I am proud to be the namesake of such a brave man." Not everyone is aware that my husband was christened Thomas Woodrow Wilson. The poor fellow replied: "It's an honourable name, sir, and I've tried to do it proud."

We got back home about four, but did not want lunch. Our hearts were too sad.

We had promised to go to Val de Grâce, the largest French military hospital, which was in the old part of Paris. We got there about five o'clock, accompanied only by our two French aides. Everything was run as it had been during the War, with the very least light possible. On the short winter day had already dropped the curtain of night.

The hospital consisted of a group of old buildings. Between them were ill-paved alleyways with evil-smelling overground sewers running through a depressed central part. Feeble electric globes of about twenty-candle power made it just possible to pick one's way through. The buildings were very little better lighted and so cold they gave one a chill. The nurses wore sweaters or capes, and the whole place seemed so comfortless.

To add to the eeriness of it, a gibbering old woman attached herself to me and insisted on clinging to my sleeve and going wherever we did. One of the nurses explained that she had lost her wits, but was harmless, and thought herself a doctor's assistant. The bed linen did not look clean, and neither did the patients. The doctors kept saying: "Of course we have not the modern things your rich country has put in your hospitals," but they added gratefully: "You have sent us many things we needed, saving many soldiers' lives." And truly, I learned afterwards, these doctors had performed some of the finest surgery done during the War, in spite of their poor equipment.

When we had finished the dreary round of the wards we were asked to come into the main room to see some of the convalescent patients who were having a little Christmas celebration. I wish I knew how to draw with my pen the scene in that room so you could see it as I do. It is as vivid today, twenty years later, as it was that Sunday, December 22, 1918! A low-ceilinged room, whitewashed walls, a cheap upright piano almost the only furniture; men in the blue French uniform standing close as they could be packed, many leaning on crutches or with bandages around their eyes, or shattered arms in slings; the whole lighted from one tiny bulb, dropped by a cord from the ceiling over which was a small bit of red paper and a French flag. Leaning against the piano was a big poilu with both eyes gone, just empty sockets, and a slender pallid boy with one leg was striking the keys in the accompaniment to the "Marseillaise." The big blind fellow in blue, wearing on his breast the Croix de guerre, was the only one who sang. It was one of the most dramatic moments of my life, for God seemed to have given him a voice in place of eyes. Its tones were so mellow that "only in Heaven shall I hear that chord again." There were tears in it—tears which had dropped from those sockets where eyes should have been; tears for all the suffering of his dear torn country under whose tiny flag he sang triumphant.

The next two days, December 23rd and 24th, were filled with appointments for the President; but finally in the afternoon on Christmas Eve he managed to slip off and we went shopping. We drove to the Rue de la Paix, and from there walked to Brentano's and to Perine's, the glovemaker's, on the Avenue de l'Opéra. The hurrying crowds gave us friendly greetings. We went also to the pretty flower market near the Madeleine, and here for the first time we saw mistletoe gilded. It was impossible to find a piece in its natural state, and while the gilded specimens were pretty they seemed so artificial.

At midnight we left to spend Christmas with our troops near General Pershing's headquarters at Chaumont. The special train of the President of France was waiting—the one in which we had come from Brest to Paris. Ambassador and Madame Jusserand were to go with us, and the two French aides, Dr. Grayson, General Harts and Miss Benham. We all stayed in the saloon car until the train started. There seemed to be no heat at all, but with heavy fur coats we managed to keep fairly comfortable. Alas, when we said good night and went to our sleeping compartments they were as cold as vaults. So we all spontaneously sought one another to see if all the cars were the same, which, unfortunately they were—not a speck of heat anywhere, and the sheets on the icy beds felt damp and dangerous. We sat up another hour and the French Ambassador was so funny and so indignant that such a state of affairs could exist in his country. At last from sheer weariness we again disbanded, but the hours between that and dawn were nightmares, and I have never understood why we did not all have pneumonia.

We did not mind having to rise at seven, for anything was better than that cold inaction. We found it was snowing fast, but closed army cars were waiting for us and we started on a long drive attended by General Pershing and his aides. We went where the boys were billeted, often in forlorn barns, where the mud came up to our shoe tops. Sometimes they were in a loft, reached by a ladder. Signs were posted prohibiting smoking or having a light for fear of fire—which, of course, was necessary, but how utterly dreary! In one place was a sort of cantonment where temporary shacks were put up, with a central canteen. This the boys had made a pitiful attempt to decorate for Christmas with a few green sprays, and little bits of red paper. Some faithful American women were there to minister to and try to entertain the boys, but they were all so brave, and things were so lonely and uncomfortable, that they brought tears to our eyes despite their efforts to pretend they were full of Christmas cheer. Again we found the billet of many of the soldiers in cellars of old houses, but everywhere they had won the affection of the French families, particularly the children, who hung about them as though they were their nearest and dearest.

The end of our long drive was near the village of Humes, where, in the centre of a great open field, was a small grandstand which we reached by a narrow plank walk raised above a sea of mud. The snow was still falling, its fleecy whiteness already showing on the boards; but the soaked earth seemed to absorb its moisture and melt away the mantle nature was trying to weave to hide its ugly furrows of mud. As soon as we were seated the impromptu manœuvres began—a sort of review of every branch of the army service. What a picture unrolled before us: the brisk marching and counter-marching of the troops through that mire, led by spirited music from a band; then the cavalry keeping a well-formed line in spite of the conditions underfoot, and sweeping in great waves across the country; then the artillery. Many of the heavy guns were drawn by stout army mules which, with characteristic mulish quality, at times stuck their feet firmly in the mud and refused to move, much to the disgust of their drivers, but to the amusement of the rest of us. And last came the highly camouflaged tanks crawling and bumping over hillocks and worming their grotesque shapes out of all difficulties. The drill ended with a procession of these disappearing over the hill. Then the infantry again came into action—thousands of khaki-clad figures with trench helmets on and full marching equipment. The flag was carried aloft as they followed double-quick in lines that would have done credit to West Pointers on a sunny parade ground.

The President and General Pershing made little talks to the troops and the commander of the 77th Division, from New York, made me a graceful little speech, saying that his boys had asked that I be made an honourary member. He presented me with the blue and gold insignia which I still keep among my treasures. It shows the Goddess of Liberty embroidered on a blue field, the same as worn by the soldiers on their left shoulders. After a prayer by a chaplain we got back in the motors and drove to where a big Christmas dinner was given for the troops.

It was a real traditional American dinner, with turkey, cranberry sauce, and pumpkin pie cut army fashion in slices large as this page, and plenty for each to have an encore if he wanted one. General Léorat, who was beside me, said he had heard of this pie but never seen it before. He looked dubiously at the great yellow square before him. Compared with French pastry, it was a little formidable looking, so I watched his approach to it. A very conservative corner morsel was his first and last tribute to good U. S. A. pumpkin pie. It was a merry meal with good stories and high spirits, and we were sorry to say goodbye to the boys when the time came.

Again we had a long drive to General Pershing's château where he and his staff lived. As we were all frozen to the marrow it was comforting to find open fires and steaming hot tea ready for us in this spacious house. We stayed long enough to thaw out and get an idea of the place and of the personnel of the General's staff, and at dark went again to the train for another night trip back to Paris.

The reports of delay in opening the Peace Conference had been only too true. To help fill in the time, on the day after Christmas we started for Calais to embark for England.

CHAPTER 15

SIR *CHARLES CUST,* Equerry to King George, met us at Calais. He was a delightful person, though possibly something of a martinet professionally, for from the moment he took charge things moved with excessive precision. Boarding the British hospital ship *Brighton,* we were escorted by French destroyers halfway across the Channel, where English destroyers took up that polite obligation. The change was made in a pretty manœuvre, which we went to the bridge to witness. The officers of the *Brighton* seemed to watch Miss Benham and me more closely than they did the destroyers, courteously explaining that they expected us to be seasick. Well, we disappointed them!

Vice Admiral Keyes was talking so pleasantly and so modestly about his war service that I was really sorry when the chalk cliffs of Dover came into view. On shore Duke Arthur of Connaught, sturdy old soldier-uncle of the King, was the first to greet us. Lord Reading, the Ambassador to the United States, and our envoy to Britain, Mr. John W. Davis, followed him. Then came my first view of a lord mayor in his robes of office. This particular gentleman, being small and delicate-looking, was not as impressive as some I saw later, but he wore the crimson gown with mock ermine and the chain and great seal of office. It was his function to greet the President and offer him the freedom of the city. This he did in timid fashion, and my husband thanked him, before we were taken to the luxurious train of the King, and whisked away towards London.

It was one of those rare winter days in England with radiant sunshine. We were immediately asked in to lunch which was quite informal, and with good conversation. At Charing Cross station Their Majesties, King George and Queen Mary, were at the step of the train to greet us. A crimson carpet had been spread, and palms arranged to line the way on either side. His Majesty and my husband reviewed the troops, going up and down the seemingly endless

191

ranks. Beautiful flowers were presented to me, and we were escorted through the station to the royal coaches, each drawn by four horses. His Majesty and the President went in the first one, preceded by a stunning mounted guard. The Queen, Princess Mary and I came next. The coaches were alike—high-slung, with the royal arms emblazoned on the doors. When these swung open the steps let down to the ground. Two men with bear grease on their wigs were seated high on the box, and two more at the back wearing high hats and crimson livery, mediaeval in style, but so English and so picturesque.

Every inch of space from the station to Buckingham Palace was filled with people and, as in Paris; roofs, windows, trees and posts were laden with humanity. Bands played and soldiers stood in unbroken lines all the way. There was wild enthusiasm, though perfect order, the Queen bowing graciously from side to side but insisting the hurrahs were for us. As we were passing Marlborough House, my eye was caught by the figure of a lady waving an American flag. She had on no hat and around her shoulders was a little shawl. The Princess Mary, startled out of her silence, exclaimed: "Why, it's Grandmama." Sure enough, it was the Dowager Queen Alexandra kissing her hand to my husband and waving the Stars and Stripes.

Every foot of the way was an ovation, and when finally we passed through the Albert Gate, instead of around it as is the custom, and turned into the courtyard of the Palace, there ended a great experience.

But only for another to begin. The courtyard was crowded with American troops, and the foreground reserved for those on crutches or in wheel chairs. What a gracious and thoughtful act on the part of our hosts!

A great shout of welcome went up as the President got out of the carriage, bared his head and greeted them. Our coach followed, and when we entered the Palace the lords and ladies of the household were in waiting in the great entrance hall. Their Majesties presented them, one by one, and we paused for a few moments to talk and acknowledge their welcome.

After this, the King and Queen personally escorted us to our rooms which are known as the Belgian Suite and overlook the gardens at the back of the Palace. They are on the main floor. We entered a big square living room with great windows reaching to the floor. The loveliest flowers were everywhere. I remember one gorgeous basket from Mr. Balfour, all vivid crimson roses and white heather, with a card bearing a gracious message. An open grate of glowing coals gave a note of cheer, and on the handsome writing table was a *printed* programme of the entertainments and official things planned for us.

Our hosts then showed us our other rooms, which were separated by a hall. My husband's bedroom had a large alcove cut off by heavy red curtains. His Majesty lifted one of these to disclose a well-equipped bath and a small electric heater. This last proved a lifesaver, on account of the shortage of coal. My room was enormous, with the largest bed I ever saw. It contained no heat at all, but in a cozy dressing room was a tiny grate fire and red hangings, which looked very homelike. A couch was drawn up between the fire and a big table on which lay magazines and newspapers. My bath, at the end of our hall, had a marble tub, beside which stood a high-backed chair as big as a throne and covered with a double blanket for which I was grateful after a plunge in the marble tub.

After acquainting us with our surroundings, Their Majesties withdrew but returned almost immediately to say that the people outside had requested that we appear on the balcony. They explained that it was their custom never to refuse such requests.

They escorted us upstairs and through long corridors until the balcony in the front was reached. Before us, extending as far as the eye could reach, was a sea of faces—thousands upon thousands of people, giving us welcome and calling, "Speech, speech." My husband responded, displaying a Union Jack which the Queen had given him. The King and Queen waved small American flags. When this was over they insisted upon returning with us to our suite, leaving with the promise they would be back to dine with us there at nine o'clock.

As soon as they had withdrawn, Sir Charles Cust appeared to know how soon we could be ready to start on a round of calls on the members of the royal family. We said in twenty minutes. I had travelled in a black tailored suit with a big rolling sealskin collar, and a small black tricot hat. I changed to a black crêpe gown, with skirt of broadtail and collar and long bands of the same on a Russian blouse effect. With this I wore a big black beaver hat with three soft grey ostrich tips at the side. We were ready on time, the President in morning coat, grey trousers and silk hat. We had two English aides besides General Harts and Admiral Grayson, and I took my secretary, Miss Benham, whom the British insisted upon calling a "Lady in Waiting"—despite my insistence that in our country we had no lords or ladies.

Our first call was on the Dowager Queen Alexandra. That gracious lady met us at the threshold, kissed me on both cheeks, and introduced all her household who were assembled about her. After presenting them to us she performed the same ceremony to those who accompanied us, after which she asked that my husband and I go upstairs and the rest remain below.

When we reached the top of a long stairway she led the way into a large drawing room packed with furniture—pictures, bric-a-brac of all sorts, statuary, lamps, books, etc., etc. Here we were joined by the Princess Royal whom she introduced as "Victoria," and the Queen of Norway whom she presented simply thus: "And this is Maud."

Then seating herself on a sofa she beckoned to my husband to sit beside her. "Victoria," "Maud" and I talked together while I surreptitiously kept my eye on my watch; for I had asked Sir Charles how long we should stay and his answer had been: "Fifteen minutes—not longer, but not less." Both of these ladies wore dark dresses, as did the Queen, but, to my surprise, all had on long *brown* suede gloves to the elbow, and no hats.

The Princess Royal was stout and not very tall, but Queen Maud was slender and tall. As we talked, the Princess said she had a great favour to ask of me, and when I wonderingly inquired what it was she said: "Would it be asking too much if I requested you to sign my book?" Whereupon Maud clasped her brown suede hands together and said: "Oh, I so wanted the same thing, but, alas, my trunks have not come; so I have no book and must miss this great opportunity." Of course, this struck my sense of humour—for these two royal ladies to want the signature of a little Virginia girl whom fate had picked out to share a great man's career. I did not let them see what I was thinking, but told them heartily how glad I was to do what they asked, and followed Victoria to a desk where a beautifully tooled leather book was open ready for signing. They both stood over me as I wrote. Instead of stopping after writing my first name "Edith," as royalty does, I added "Bolling," and then "Wilson." Their eyes nearly popped, and they said: "Oh, you sign *three* names." I could not determine whether that stamped me in their eyes as three times more royal or deducted in like proportion from my social status. But as Maud seemed even more desolated at the loss of such an autograph I asked if she would like me to sign on a sheet of the paper bearing the royal crest which was on the desk, and she seemed enchanted by the suggestion.

I then looked to see how my husband was faring with Queen Alexandra. I had been told that deafness made it next to impossible for her to carry on a conversation, and, being sensitive regarding her affliction, she talked incessantly, producing the effect of a monologue. This being hard for both parties to sustain for fifteen minutes, I thought it would be tactful to ask if they would not also like to have the President's signature. They answered in concert: "Why, of course, but we could not think of troubling him." I assured them he would be happy to give it. So I approached the sofa and asked if Her Majesty would excuse him and give me the great honour of being with her while he wrote.

We exchanged places, and she was so gracious and sweet to me. When the signing was over our time was up, and I rose to go. But the Queen said we must not leave until we had seen "Maud's child." So he was summoned and, while we waited, she said: "Oh, then you have not seen the picture," and turning to her daughters she added: "Do light the picture." They ran to do her bidding and pushed a number of light buttons near the door until at last the right one was discovered which illuminated a picture in a far corner of the room. We all followed her to where a painting about two by three feet was hung. It was the interior of Westminster Abbey at the time of the funeral of Queen Victoria. I stood gazing at this, not knowing just why it was designated as *"the* picture" in this room where all four walls were covered with what seemed to me much finer paintings. Then it occurred to me that its importance must lie in the fact that Queen Victoria's death marked the accession to the throne of King Edward and Queen Alexandra—for which they had waited many years. Therefore it was a symbol that marked a new epoch not only for England but in the life of this lady who held my hand in hers as we stood and looked upon the painting. So I pressed the thin hand and said: "It is certainly very interesting." My husband said afterwards that the comment was an inspiration, for he was wondering—just as I was—what comment to make.

From there we made a tour of the other royal relatives, but Sir Charles would leap out and sign the books and not permit us to move. So we were soon back at the Palace. He escorted us to our suite, saying he would leave us to rest before dinner which would be at nine. Remembering the brown suede gloves, I asked if he could tell me whether, as the dinner was to be informal and in our suite, I should wear gloves—explaining that during the War we, in America, had not worn gloves even on formal occasions. He said he did not know, but would find out immediately. He was back in no time with this information: "Her Majesty will not wear gloves but she and Princess Mary will carry a new pair with the string still keeping them together, held with fingers up, in their left hands." Even such an insignificant detail as this was thought out and arranged in this marvellously ordered country of England. After all, it makes for a sense of stability and relieves a stranger of the embarrassment of running counter to social custom.

Promptly on the hour Their Majesties arrived, accompanied by the Duke of Connaught, Princess Mary, the Duke of York (now the King) and his younger brother. The two ladies carried stiff, long white gloves held upright like our old game of "Simon says 'Thumbs up,'" and I greeted them with a similar pair held in the same way. Her Majesty wore a peach-coloured evening gown with simple jewels. The young Princess was in white, and I in blue and silver.

We went in to dinner informally and what I had dreaded as a difficult meal went off merrily. My husband told a good story which broke the ice, and the King responded with several that concerned our doughboys, who seemed to have delighted him. One of these I give as nearly as I can in his own words:

"I went to France and to one of the sectors near the front where many of the Americans were billeted with our troops who were standing in line for me to review them. As I went up and down the lines I was followed by many of your boys and I saw them staring at me. Finally I heard one say to another: 'Who is that bug?' And the other said: 'Why, man, that's the King of England.' And the first shrugged his shoulders and said: 'Hell! Where's his crown?'"

His Majesty added, in his very British accent: "I did not mind at all being called a 'bug,' but I hated to think that I was expected to review my men with a crown on my head."

Another of his stories concerned the time Her Majesty and he had attended the opening of the Liberty Hut in London. "One of your privates," said the King, "came forward and said: 'Excuse me, but am I right that this is the King of England?' I said 'Yes,' at which he extended a horny hand and said: 'Put it there!' " This true American praise, His Majesty said, was "most extraordinary," but he liked it.

When the dinner was over we had a brief talk around our fire and then Her Majesty asked if I would like to see her own rooms, and thus give our husbands an opportunity to talk over serious things. As we went through the long corridors, she called attention to historical objects and other interesting things. Her apartments were spacious and furnished with taste. As I recall it we went through nine rooms, each perfect in period. There was a French salon, dainty and exquisite; a Chinese one, the furniture covered with marvellous Chinese embroidery, and wonderful with red lacquer, jades and crystals. Even the lighting in each room was in harmony; so here, in the Chinese rooms, hung lanterns. On and on we went. I found that antiques and interior decoration were her hobby, and that she is an authority on both. She showed me many things which had belonged to Queen Victoria. She said that august lady never threw away anything, but that while much of it was worthwhile and beautiful, nothing was well-arranged, but all thrown together haphazard. For instance, the house at Brighton she said was so awful that they gave it up after the Queen's death, many of the furnishings being removed to Buckingham. I remember her pointing to a child's enchanting silver tea set of English design, which she said had been made for the old Queen when she was a little girl. This was in a tiny alcove off the English drawing room, each piece being placed with meticulous care.

Our tour ended in what she said was the room she loved best and where she spent most of her time. It was stamped as none of the others with that lived-in quality which a formal room always lacks. Instantly I knew a real personality was reflected in this room, which was large, and longer than wide, with big windows overlooking the garden. An orderly but much-laden writing table, easy chairs, books and personal things proclaimed her presence everywhere. There were many photographs, and a full-length portrait of the brother of the King to whom she had been affianced, but whose death had put King George first in the line of succession to the throne and had made her his queen instead. My thoughts were filled with this romantic story, and I wished I could know more about it. The only thing this and, indeed, all the rooms lacked was warmth. There was no heat in any of them, and I had to hold tight whenever I spoke to keep my teeth from chattering. It was December, and we wore evening gowns. How I longed for my fur coat, but it was too far away to get, and so I tried not to shiver and shake. Oh, the joy of our fire when we returned to join the gentlemen!

This ended our first day in London.

The next was equally delightful. My husband lunched with Mr. Lloyd George, and I with Lady Reading, the wife of the Ambassador to the United States. With reference to the lunch given my husband the London *Times* said:

> "It is not extravagant to say that this luncheon at No. 10 Downing Street is one of the most historic which has ever taken place in that House. It was a happy thought of the Prime Minister to invite the leaders of all political parties to meet the President of the United States. . . . But it was the unveiling by the President of the portrait of George Washington in the dining-room which will appeal to the imagination of the whole of the Anglo-Saxon race."

At Lady Reading's luncheon occurred my first meeting with Margot Asquith, and I found her about what I had pictured— clever, egotistical and exceedingly plain. I sat between her and my hostess. She smoked one cigarette after another, striking the matches as I have seen certain men do, on their own anatomy. She wore a severely tailored coat and a tight skirt. Her first question to me was: "Do you know all these women here?" I replied I had just been introduced to most of them. "Well," she said, "then I will tell you about them. This one on my right is Countess ——, the biggest liar in London; the one next is an American, but ashamed to let anyone know it until lately. Since Wilson's Administration it has become fashionable to be an American, and now she is disgusting in proclaiming it. Then of course Mrs. L. G. doesn't count," etc., etc. This remarkable conversation I endeavoured to get into another channel by asking her if she was to be at the great dinner that night at the Palace. This proved another unfortunate topic, for she said: "No, I. was not invited," adding that she had sent word to the King that she did not want his food but did want to meet President Wilson who, she was told, "really had brains"—a quality she had never yet found in any American man, though she had met many. She said they talked only of themselves, and that she made it a rule during these long eulogies to plan her future life and think her own thoughts, for she never listened. "How can you know then they have no brains?" I asked innocently. To this she only sniffed, and I turned to try to talk to Lady Reading, who was a lady in every sense, but so deaf it was very hard to carry on a prolonged conversation.

This left me rather at the mercy of Mrs. Asquith who attacked me again with this: "As you and I are both second wives I am interested in what you think of your stepdaughters. Are they very awful? Of course, you would say nice things about them generally, but to me you can tell the truth." "Thank you," I said, "for that privilege—" But before I could finish she was off again: "Instead of hearing about them I think I would rather hear how you met the President, and all about your romance." By this time I had decided Mrs. Asquith had taken a leaf from what she said was our American "men's book" and wanted to talk only about herself. So I countered: "Oh, I am sure your own romance is absorbing, so tell me about that." She beamed, and launched into a detailed and intimate narrative to which she warmed as she proceeded; and by the time luncheon was over the veil had been stripped from the most personal and sacred things, and I felt a sense of dismay that any woman could be quite so devoid of reticence.

From the Readings' we went to Mrs. Lloyd George's for tea, and all the gentlemen, including my husband, who had been there for lunch and the conferences which followed, joined us. There was much excitement as the returns were just in from the elections.

When I got back to the Palace the wife of the Lord Chamberlain, Lady Sandhurst, asked to see me. I found her unaffected and sweet.

After a few moments' conversation, she said the object of her coming was to learn if I would wear a tiara at dinner, as all the ladies had given up wearing them during the War, and put most of their jewels in bank vaults for safekeeping. I told her if I had a tiara I would certainly wear it on so great an occasion, but I did not own one. I think the fact of not having one had never occurred to her, but she said: "Oh, then of course no one else can wear one." I assured her I would not consider it in any way lacking in courtesy if they did, and I personally would love to see them.

After she was gone I rang for my maid. Susan arrived breathless with delight. She had just been taken up to see the throne room where the tables were spread for dinner. Her eyes were popping out at the gorgeous gold service which had been brought up from Windsor Castle, and all the beautiful things which the room contained. With true Southern darky genius for getting words wrong she called it the "thorn" room. From there she had been taken to see the Queen who had asked her if she had seen the table and what she thought of it. She said she had told her: "It was *jes'* beautiful," and that she did not believe there had ever been anything so lovely "since the Queen of Sheba danced before King Solomon."

I had instructed her before we came that, should she be in the presence of the Queen, she must curtsey, but I had had no idea she would be accorded an audience. Later, at the dinner, His Majesty asked me if the Queen had told me that she had met Susan and how much she enjoyed her. So I hoped from this that she had acquitted herself creditably, notwithstanding the fact that her Bible knowledge was a little mixed.

But I myself am mixing the sequence of events by taking my readers to the King's and Queen's dinner too soon. Earlier in the day there had been a conference with my husband as to what style of dress was to be worn. Mr. Wilson explained that our Chief Executive never wore uniforms, as is the custom abroad, and that regular evening clothes were suitable on every occasion. Accordingly, the King decreed that he and all members of the household would wear the same. This caused much scurrying around, as during the War only military uniforms had been worn by His Majesty and the members of his suite. Consequently there was a very perceptible odour of moth balls when the gentlemen appeared.

Returning from Mrs. Lloyd George's tea we found in our rooms a printed diagram of the great table, with the place of each of the ninety-six guests designated. At the proper hour the Lord Chamberlain, Sandhurst, and Lord Farquhar appeared to escort us to the royal family, and this is how they did it. As we emerged from our suite the gentlemen stood facing us, each holding in his two hands before him a slender wooden wand, which was his badge of office. In perfect unison they bowed until the wands almost touched the floor—from an athletic point of view a really creditable performance for gentlemen of their years in dress suits. Then they stepped backwards one pace and bowed again. Then one more step—backwards, remember—and another bow. I began to wonder how long this was going to keep up, for judging from the length of the corridor we had a long way to go.

But we made it, with one bow about every three feet, and our acrobats still apparently in good trim. Then we turned and confronted a great stair. Up the steps tripped our escort, backwards, still making their bows at the correct intervals. I was both alarmed and amused and had some difficulty keeping a straight face. Another long corridor and finally we reached our destination, Lords Sandhurst and Farquhar having had as much exercise as they could have got in a cricket match. Which was not a bad idea, for those royal corridors were cold.

Later, on better acquaintance, I asked Lord Farquhar the origin of the custom. It was very old, he said—just how old he did not know—and was used only in the case of heads of States. I expressed my admiration for his agility. Lord Farquhar laughed. As there had been no formal entertaining for four years he said he had really feared for his form, adding: "My dear lady, had you looked out of your door late this afternoon you would have seen two elderly gentlemen practising, up and down. Even the maids who were placing flowers in the corridors could not disguise their amusement."

The progress described conveyed us to a white drawing room, oval in shape, where our hosts received us. With them was the jovial old Duke of Connaught and his lovely daughter, the Princess Pat, who at once made me the recipient of a feminine confidence. She said that, although her engagement had not been publicly announced, she wished me to know of it, adding that to be engaged, and to have the first new slippers in four years, not to mention meeting the President of the United States—was all very exciting. I recall this to show how informal and unostentatious these people were: the Princess Royal, in velvet and marvellous rubies; the Queen of Norway; the Duchess of Sutherland, the tall and very lovely Lady in Waiting to the Queen; the Princess Mary, etc., etc.

We lingered long enough to talk for a few moments to each one. Then the doors leading to another large room were thrown open and the company of guests was ranged in long rows—the ladies on one side, opposite their dinner partners. The men made a much longer line as there were many more of them. Most of the men were resplendent in uniforms and orders and medals, looking even more decorated than the ladies.

The Queen was stunning in a white gown with the blue Order of the Garter across her low bodice, a coronet of diamonds, and other magnificent jewels. I loved looking at her. My own gown was very simple—a princess black velvet with long train and no jewels. We seemed unconsciously to represent the difference between a monarchy and a democracy.

His Majesty presented the ladies to my husband, and the Queen performed the same act with the gentlemen and me. Introductions over, the King took me in to dinner and the President escorted the Queen.

How I wish I could bring that vivid picture to this paper! The room was vast, with tables forming three sides of a hollow square. Tall golden candelabra ablaze with wax candles alternated with vessels of gold holding tall stems of the Christmas crimson poinsettias. Everything on the table—service plates, goblets, etc.—was gold, and huge formal gold pieces adorned the racks on the walls. At the far end of the room was a minstrel gallery where musicians were playing our loved Southern airs—"Suwanee River," "Maryland, My Maryland," "My Old Kentucky Home," and at last, "Dixie." At the other end was the throne, almost hidden by magnificent flowers.

To add to the colourful scene were dozens of men in livery. Some wore uniforms of the time of Queen Anne, in a heavenly shade of blue with silver. Others were in crimson. All had white wigs and short trousers, with great buckles on their shoes. Ranged around the room at intervals of a few feet were the Yeomen of the Guard, such as one sees at the Tower of London, in their picturesque Tudor uni-

JANUARY 1, 1919: PRESIDENT WILSON WITH MEMBERS OF AMERICAN PEACE DELEGATION

Left to right: Colonel E. M. House, Secretary of State Robert Lansing; President Wilson; Honorable Henry White and General Tasker H. Bliss.

forms of crimson and gold, with their mediaeval hats and pointed beards. Armed with ancient halberds, they stood like statues, without moving a muscle.

During the course of the dinner, a man with pink coat, white breeches, high hat and boots appeared through the doorway, carrying a slender wand. He went to each of the "statues" and touched its toes with the end of the wand, and thus all around the great room. I asked the King why he did this, and he explained that the man was the head of the "Beef-Eaters," who are all old soldiers receiving a pension from the Government, their only duty being service at the Tower of London, and at very formal dinners at the Palace. The one requirement is that they maintain the cut of beard and hair in harmony with the period of the costume. The King went on to say that on an occasion, hundreds of years ago, when they were first used as they were tonight, their commander came to see if they were maintaining their military postures. He found one man had relaxed, with one foot out in front of the other. He touched the offender's toe with the wand of office, and seeing the blood mount to the face of the man, and feeling sorry for him, the kindly commander went the rounds touching each man on the foot as though it were a ceremony. Ever since, this has been the custom—a sort of memorial to a kind heart. I think this is a pretty story, and so am doing my small part to preserve it.

During the dinner His Majesty rose and offered a very graceful little toast to my husband, but before doing so he confided to me that he was always so nervous when he had to speak that he dreaded it. As the address was typed on small sheets of paper and put before him, I wondered why he should feel nervous. But when I saw how the paper shook in his hands, I realized he was sincere. The President rose to thank him and to propose the King's health and, as was his custom, he had no notes but spoke spontaneously. His graceful speech made me thrill with pride.

After dinner we went into another large drawing room where we stood while each of the guests was brought up for a few minutes' talk. Two of the gentlemen of the household were detailed for this— one to me, and one to my husband. There were so many guests that it was a long ordeal standing, which I did not mind but which was trying to many others. One of the Ladies in Waiting fainted and was carried out. But as Her Majesty still stood, of course everyone else did. But I saw the Princess Royal looking so fatigued I asked her if she could not sit down, and she said: "Oh no, not while the Queen is standing." I then suggested she rest against the end of a large davenport, which she said she was happy to do as her slippers hurt her feet and she had not stood so long since before the War because there had been no formal entertaining. The dear lady looked over at the Queen, who was apparently as fresh as though the day had just begun, and shaking her head, said: "Oh, she never gets tired. She stands for hours, but for me it is terrible." The distinguished people present interested me so much I did not feel the least weary, and I loved every moment of it.

The next day was another thrilling one. We left the Palace in one of the great coaches drawn by four horses with outriders on either side, to go to the Guild Hall where the President was to be given the freedom of the City of London. This time Their Majesties did not accompany us, but we were attended by the Master of the Horse, Lord Chesterfield. Again the streets were thronged with people, and shouts of welcome sounded on every side.

When we reached the Guild Hall we were met by the Lord Mayor in his robes of office. His coach was magnificent, and I felt all the time as if I were taking part in some splendid pageant. We were escorted to a platform and given large, high-backed chairs. On one side of the dais sat many gentlemen, all wearing frock coats and looking very official. I asked Lord Chesterfield who they were and his reply was so English that I quote it. To get its real flavour you must imagine a very broad "a": "Oh, all of those gentlemen have *passed* the chair"—meaning they had all been lord mayors!

After this ceremony the Lord Mayor gave a splendid luncheon for us at the Mansion House. So we had another drive of a few blocks in our coach, escorted by him in his.

The "freedom of the city" presented to the President was enclosed in a beautiful gold casket, on one side of which is his own portrait and that of the King, done in coloured enamel; and on the other side an eagle in blue, with the English and the United States arms.

The luncheon was colourful and impressive, carrying out mediaeval customs. It was laid in the Egyptian Hall, with its stained-glass windows and rich silken banners. A man stood behind the Lord Mayor's chair with a great gavel, and beat three times on the wood, calling: "Oyes, oyes, oyes." The Lord Bishop of London pronounced a blessing, and when the toasts were drunk the wine was poured into a great tankard, which was first given to the functionary responsible for the wine to taste, with the happy idea that had poison been put in it he would be the first to suffer. Then it was passed from the chief honour guests to those next in rank.

Following the lunch we received in a smaller room, and here Mrs. Asquith first met my husband. As I watched her putting her pinched, small face closer and closer to his, as is her habit when she talks, I wondered if she were trying to see his brains as well as test them. Whatever her purpose, she held on, claiming his attention by her persistence, when many others were waiting to be presented.

In the afternoon a charming reception was given for me at the Women's Club, where I met, among others, Viscountess Harcourt, Lady Farquhar, Lady Sandhurst, the Countess of Stafford, Lady Ward, Lady Northcliffe, Lady Paget, Lady Randolph Churchill, and Mrs. Skinner, wife of the American Consul General.

An event not on the prepared programme was another tea with Mrs. Lloyd George at 10 Downing Street. Tea was served in the big drawing room and quite informal. The wives of the heads of government departments were asked, among them Lady Curzon, Mrs. Austin Chamberlain, Mrs. Jan Christiaan Smuts, Lady Geddes, and Lady Reading, Mrs. John W. Davis and Mrs. H. A. L. Fisher.

That night Mr. Lloyd George gave a men's dinner for the President, and I went to dine at our Embassy with Mr. and Mrs. John W. Davis.

At midnight we left London for Carlisle, where my husband's mother was born, and where he was eager to go to pay respect to her memory. It was a night's journey, but made comfortably on the King's own luxurious train. We reached the little town, almost on the border of Scotland, early Sunday morning, to find the rain pouring in torrents. As I looked from the window of my stateroom I had the impression of entering a forest of giant toadstools. All I could see was a mass of dripping umbrellas manœuvring for places nearer the train. The whole population had turned out, and a sturdy-looking lot they were. We were met by the town officers, and many flowers and speeches made us welcome. Closed cars bore us to the Crown and Mitre Hotel, where a large reception was held. Among the guests was an old gentleman of eighty, Mr. Thomas Watson, the only surviving scholar of the Sunday School during the days when Mr. Wilson's maternal grandfather was minister there. At eleven o'clock we went to the church over which Grandfather Thomas Woodrow had presided, finding it a quaint little edifice with one of the old-time very high pulpits. We were given the front pew, and the minister announced that the service would open with "the National Anthem of the United States." To our amazement the choir and people burst forth with "The Battle Hymn of the Republic"! After this the minister made some very nice remarks, winding up by saying he had not preached a sermon because he knew our time was limited and he was therefore only welcoming us, and would ask the President of the United States to speak. This was totally unexpected, and, when my husband rose, I wondered what he would say. Certainly I never heard him speak more eloquently or straight from his heart. There was not a sound except his voice accompanied by the steady, gentle patter of rain on the roof. As he stood there, I thought of that little girl, his mother, whose tiny feet may have rested on the same boards so many years before (for she came to America when she was only seven), and how proud she would have been of him. Someway her spirit seemed very near him there, and the tribute he paid her was to a real and gracious presence. Afterwards we were asked to come into the vestry to sign the book, and I was glad of the moment's seclusion for my husband, for he was profoundly moved.

From the church we drove to his grandfather's house, which is still in good repair—an unpretentious brick abode of two stories, but very well built, and comfortable. Then a large luncheon at the hotel, with more speeches, and back to our train and off to Manchester, where we were to spend the night.

By the time we reached there the weather had cleared and we found the Lord Mayor standing in his crimson robes, and great chain of office, at the steps of the train to greet us. The Town Constable was also on hand—a most resplendent figure in green and silver uniform with cocked hat—and strutting like the bird whose name he bore, for he was introduced as "Mr. Peacock!" Beside his six-feet-two impressiveness trotted a little man in a black gown, wearing in place of a hat a funny grey wig that sat high on his cranium, showing his own hair at the back, over which fell two little white braids tied with black. This dignitary was presented as "the Town Clark," and he quickly assured us that the Lord Mayor had so recently ascended from the lowly estate of a farmer that he knew little of the solemn ceremonies he should perform; so he, "the Town Clark," on whose ability and discretion we could always rely, would have to coach him.

We were to be guests in the Town Hall, where the Lord Mayor resides, which we found to be a very handsome building with offices and formal reception rooms on the lower floor, and a grand stairway, twelve feet broad, carpeted in crimson, leading to the private apartments above. We were escorted up and given very pleasant rooms, and I found my maid already there unpacking my bags. In the room with her was a woman wearing a white shirtwaist and dark skirt and without a hat. Thinking her probably the housekeeper, I introduced myself and said I was very much obliged to her for coming in but as the maid would take care of all my things I would not bother her. Imagine my surprise when she replied: "Oh, me name is McKaig, but they call me now 'the Lady Mayoress,' so you need not trouble to remember me name!"

Then she said there was to be a dinner that night, but before that she would like me to have tea with her in the living room.

When I got the travel dust off, I appeared. The dear lady was very ill at ease, but she soon found herself, and we were quickly chatting like old friends. She said she would show me her Seal and Chain as Lady Mayoress, for she was the only woman in England who had one. The reason was that the State furnished one only for the mayors and not for their wives, but that a rich Manchester man, who had great pride in his city, provided the one she had. She confided that it was "kept by the *mon*," meaning the general factotum of the Mansion, who always put it on for her. "Sometimes," added her ladyship, "he gets it right over my breathing apparatus, which is painful, for it is heavy. But he is very kind and changes it if I tell him!"

What a really pathetic picture I got of this good soul trying to live up to the artificial formalities of her husband's new office. She told me they had always lived in the country where she did all her own work and loved her garden and flowers. She almost whispered this information to me: That here the "mon" watched her all the time and would never let her go out as she wanted to, alone, but always in a car or carriage, while he sat on the box to attend her.

I found her frank conversation interesting and instructive. For all the glamour and pageantry of royalty, this simple, genuine woman and her good husband had risen by means of unadorned merit to their high positions—showing plainly what a democracy England is. She poured her woes into my sympathetic ears until we were both recalled to the lateness of the hour by the sudden appearance of the "mon," who said it was time to dress for dinner.

Realizing that she probably had never observed the custom of dressing for dinner, I said: "Shall I put on an evening gown, or just change to another dress like this?" One look from her ogre "mon" settled the question, and she replied: "Oh, do wear the pretty dress your maid laid out for you." So I did, and when I came out again to dinner I was sorry I had, for my hostess had not even changed. She said that the dress she had hurriedly ordered when she knew we were coming had failed to arrive; so we must excuse her.

Dinner was served in the formal banquet room downstairs, and the table was long enough to have seated forty or fifty guests. We were a company of only ten, however, and so a short cloth was used on the far end of the great mahogany expanse, and looked like the tail wagging the dog! The funny little Town Clerk sat on my right, and the Lord Mayor on my left. It was a ponderous English meal, and our hosts so ill at ease that I was glad when it was over.

The next day we were taken down the Manchester Canal which is so important to the city's trade. Of great interest to me was one of the "mystery ships" used against submarines during the War. On board a large boat we passed what looked like an old freighter and were told to look at it. Suddenly a tiny whistle sounded, and instantly she became a man-of-war. The false sides fell away, disclosing guns which rose like magic—fully manned, and ready to meet the enemy.

We got back in time for a formal luncheon at the Guild Hall where the President was tendered the freedom of the city. That night we left for London with the nicest impression of the people and of the importance of that great manufacturing place.

But I cannot close my tale of the visit to Manchester without repeating one of Admiral Grayson's stories—and here I fall naturally into the style of calling him "Admiral," for on this formal tour he looked the part in all his formal blue and gold. On leaving Paris my husband had asked the Admiral if he would take charge of that necessary but disagreeable part of a trip, that of gratuities, or in good old United States language, tips. In London, where we had access to banks, this was an easy task; but on the hurried trip to Carlisle over Sunday, and to Manchester, funds had to be provided ahead. Therefore the Admiral had taken considerably over a thousand dollars in cash. Now I will try to tell the story in his own language:

"In a Navy uniform there is only one pocket, which is in the trousers. So I folded the notes as flat as I could, and pinned them in the pocket with a safety pin. The night we spent in Manchester there was no way to lock the door of my room, and, the Town Hall being a semi-public building, I did not know who might come in. So I placed my trousers on the foot of my bed. With this on my mind, I suddenly woke up, thinking I had just dozed off for a moment, to see a man with my trousers in his hand going out of the door. Without stopping for slippers or dressing gown, I sprang out of bed and dashed after him. The hall was dark and empty, but I heard footsteps, just round a corner, so on I went—and ran full tilt into the Lord Mayor. He was in an old-fashioned nightshirt, and had his shaving brush and mug in his hand. Naturally he was as shocked as I, and when he got his breath, which I had nearly knocked out of him, he gasped: 'Oh, I say, Admiral, is there anything wrong?' 'No sir,' said I, 'I was just trying to find my trousers.' 'But my word, Admiral, the mon has just taken them to press, and by the time you shave he will have them ready.'"

The Admiral had to think quickly. Rallying his wits he said: "Yes, I know, but, Mr. Lord Mayor, I always shave with my trousers on." At this point other footsteps were heard and round the corner came the Lady Mayoress wearing only her dream robe. This made flight the only alternative, so the Admiral retreated to his room and looked at his watch to find that it was seven o'clock, and that he had slept soundly all night. Happily the trousers were returned with money and safety pin still in place. It was evident that the Lord and Lady had vacated their own comfortable rooms to give them to us, and were probably seeking a bath when the Admiral had his amusing encounter.

In London we had another delightful day, with a small dinner, of thirty, at Buckingham Palace. Next morning we were escorted by the King and Queen to the station where we were sped on our way towards France. This happened to be December 28th, my husband's birthday. Of course he had not intended that anyone should know this. To his surprise, before we left the Palace, the King came to our suite at ten o'clock to tender his congratulations, and to present Woodrow with a handsome set of books on the history of Windsor Castle.

I cannot leave England, and especially Buckingham Palace, even in retrospect, without again expressing my warm appreciation of the exquisite courtesy shown us by every individual, particularly our royal hosts.

We embarked at Dover amid flowers and cheers and with an escort of British destroyers we were soon in mid-channel where the English boats gave way to French which steamed along on either side until we reached the harbour of Calais.

ROME, ITALY, JANUARY 3, 1919

The Queen of Italy and Mrs. Wilson in carriage on way from railroad station to Quirinal Palace.

CHAPTER 16

*I*N Paris we had only a few hours before boarding the special train of the King of Italy for Rome. So on that day we rode on the trains of three heads of States—the King of England's from London to Dover, the President of France's from Calais to Paris, and now King Emmanuel's. To my surprise the Italian train was the most magnificent of all. I had never seen anything like it: servants in livery of royal scarlet; plate, china and glassware bearing the Italian arms; table linen and bed linen beautifully embroidered.

My husband was anxious to have these ceremonial visits over and to address himself to the work of the Peace Conference. He had not expected to do all this running around, and was greatly disappointed that the British had postponed the Conference until after their elections. As the opening of the Conference had been set for January 18, 1919, we planned to be back in Paris, with our social obligations fully discharged, well in advance of that time.

The Duke de Lante della Rovere represented King Emmanuel, and acted as host on the journey to Italy. He was a tall, lugubrious individual, wearing a long-tailed frock coat and looking like the undertaker at an important funeral. He insisted upon observing official etiquette in the seating at table, which for a long journey was exceedingly fatiguing. It meant that he sat next to me at every meal until we reached Rome where Prince Udine, cousin of the King, took his place. Fortunately we breakfasted in our rooms, but lunch and dinner were State functions.

At the frontier we were joined by Mr. Thomas Nelson Page, American Ambassador to Italy. Our party consisted of the very agreeable Italian Ambassador to the United States and Countess Cellere, Margaret Wilson, Miss Benham and Dr. Grayson. The presence of the Doctor was rather fortunate for two of the ladies who were taken quite ill on the train.

211

We stopped at Genoa a few hours where my husband wanted to visit the house where Christopher Columbus is said to have been born. In one room was a charming little marble statue of him as a boy. One could let one's imagination have full rein and enter into the dreams of the youth setting out to find a new world!

Our arrival in Rome will always be the most brilliant canvas in all the rich pictures in my memory. Before we left Paris it had been grey with constant rain, rain, rain. But here the sky was a dome of sapphire pouring golden sunshine over a radiant world. The ancient beauty of Rome needs no tribute from me, but those who know and love it must picture the added brilliance of streets covered with the golden sands brought from the Mediterranean Sea, a time-honoured custom accorded to returning military conquerors and to visiting heads of States. The long windows of every house along the way were open wide, and from each hung rare old brocades or velvets with arms embroidered on them. American and Italian flags were flying and the people crowding everywhere. Troops lined every street, wearing their picturesque uniforms and "two-story" caps. And the flowers! From the roofs, the windows and balconies, poured a veritable shower of purple violets and golden mimosa. From baskets filled with them, from white arms laden with them, they fell about our stately coaches, a libation fit for the gods.

Their Majesties had welcomed us at the station, and after the formal greetings and speeches, and review of troops, we had entered the royal coaches to proceed to the Quirinal Palace. I rode with the lovely Queen, who looks in every way her part, and I never had a greater thrill than that marvellous drive. At the Palace we were escorted to our gorgeous apartments. The President's suite was in the section known as the Manica Lunga Portide and looked out upon the gardens of the Via Settembre which were in full bloom like midsummer. His quarters consisted of a vestibule hung with ancient Flemish tapestries, a richly decorated salon in Florentine style, a Japanese smoking room, a luxurious bedchamber, dressing room and bath. Mine comprised a lovely bedroom in green and mauve, with bath adjoining, a study, and an enormous drawing room. These were much more formal than our rooms at Buckingham Palace, and were hung with priceless tapestries, carpeted with rugs worth a king's ransom, and filled with rare and beautiful treasures.

During the War, the Palace was used for hospital service and only the wing which housed us had been refurnished. The rest was still full of the wounded and suffering.

Our royal hosts asked if we would go through the hospital with them, as it would mean much to the soldiers, Her Majesty adding that many of them were her own patients as she had worked there in the X-ray department during the War. She said the constant exposure to the ray had affected her arms and fingers, but that she hoped to get over the trouble.

We followed them past long rows of iron beds holding wasted or mutilated forms. White, eager faces brightened. I could see that the gentle presence of the Queen meant much to them, and that through her service she had changed forever the popular feeling about her Montenegrin birth. When I had been in Italy a few years before many people had told me that Italians felt they were taxed for the benefit of the Queen's country since her father, the King of Montenegro, was constantly making demands on her to support his bankrupt land. I do not state this as a fact, but only as what I was told; and as a result of it, gossip said, the Queen was unpopular. From what I now saw, however, she seemed an angel of mercy to these soldiers.

Part of the hospital contained a sort of medical museum, in which were long cases filled with plaster casts of mutilated faces, showing the marvellous work of reconstruction achieved by the surgeons. In the last room we visited stood a line of soldiers wearing their green uniforms with buttons polished till they shone. As we entered they advanced to meet us, and held out their hands in greeting. They walked a little stiffly, but not very noticeably so, and not until we shook hands with them did we realize that some of the men had artificial hands. We were told that each of them had lost either a leg or an arm, and one poor fellow both legs, and they were now ready to be discharged as cured. They were covered with medals and honours, and some of them were very handsome, stunning-looking men.

Our visit ended here, but before we left His Majesty presented me with a beautifully enamelled Order of the Italian Red Cross.

We were to have lunch with Their Majesties at their Villa Savoia, just outside the city. So we parted at our suite, but a moment later our hosts reappeared to beg us to join them on the balcony to greet the people who had been waiting all this time. Facing us was an ocean of humanity—in all more than a hundred thousand persons. After this ceremony we changed, and had time to look at the programme of entertainment arranged for our visit. Then we were notified the cars were waiting to take us to the villa.

Happily this was an informal lunch, so we could dispense with the Duke de Lante and all our escort. Our drive out was quiet and restful. When we drew up to the entrance of the villa the door was thrown wide and down the few steps ran His Majesty, the King, bareheaded. Before the footman could dismount he had opened the car door and was greeting us in the most hospitable way. He speaks English without a trace of accent.

When we entered a low, broad doorway the scene before us made a very lovely picture. The Queen, wearing soft, filmy grey that brought out her brunette beauty, stood with four of her children grouped about her. The oldest daughter was dark, slim and tall, and wore a ruddy shade of red; the second daughter, smaller and very blonde, was in green; the charming little girl, only four, I think, was in velvet of violet colour with a big lace collar; and the heir to the throne, a handsome boy with fine dark eyes, was in black velvet with a lace collar. They were grouped in a sort of solarium at the back of the house, with the Italian sunshine illuminating a scene that should have been immortalized by a Vandyke. Near the family stood a great Russian wolfhound such as I always associate with portraits.

The only other guests were the old Duke of Genoa, uncle of the King, and an English governess who was responsible for the fluent use of our language by all the children. All there spoke English but the Queen, who used French. She presented each of us with a lovely souvenir. The President's was a charming painting of a church in Rome. To me she gave a silver reproduction of a pitcher which she herself had excavated at Pompeii, and to Margaret another rather interesting piece of silver on the order of a small loving cup. Miss Benham was given a very handsome ring with a ruby, a diamond and an emerald, reproducing the Italian colours.

Then His Majesty asked if we would like to see his apartments. He conducted us to a room on the main floor. For the bedroom of a king it was indeed a surprise. The floor was bare. A row of shelves ran round three sides. On these were war relics of every kind—muskets, shells, helmets, bullets, sabres, etc., each tagged with its history.

January 3, 1919: President Wilson Entering Royal Carriage at Railroad Station, Rome, Italy

A low flat-top desk, on which, in a silver frame, was a picture of the Queen—the one concession to ornamentation—an army cot, two chairs and a few toilet articles completed the furnishings of this democratic ruler's sleeping room. The King laughed when we exclaimed at his cot. He said he liked it, and therefore did not mind when he had to exchange it for one in the field.

We came away with a very vivid impression, not that of a king and queen living in lonely state, but husband and wife with mutual interests in a real home made doubly dear by the presence of lovely children. It was all so unostentatious and genuine. I noticed that the blonde daughter, who looked like her father, seemed his favourite. Both were keen on the war relics, and he told us that she was the curator and knew more about them than he did. After the luncheon we went to call on the Queen Mother and the Duchess of Aosta.

The State dinner was to be held at the Palace that night, and a splendid affair it was. Everything was as formal as possible. The table was laid in a long tapestry-hung gallery. The lords wore decorations and orders, the ladies splendid jewels. Beautiful china and glass, and gorgeous plate, adorned the table, and great high-backed crimson-cushioned chairs gave the impression of a series of thrones. Remembering what His Majesty had said to my husband at the Murat Palace in Paris—"My God, I couldn't live in a place like this!"—and seeing how much more magnificent the Quirinal was, I reminded him of it. Turning in his quick, jerky way, and encompassing the room in a glance, the King said: "Oh, but I do not live here, and all this"—with a wave of the hand—"does not belong to me any more than the White House belongs to you."

The one amusing thing which occurred at the table was a conversation between Margaret and the old Duke of Genoa, who was almost stone-deaf. He was seated between Margaret and me and we both had made unsuccessful efforts to talk to him. Among the guests was Signor Marconi, the inventor of wireless, and so Margaret said to the old Duke that she thought Marconi such an interesting man, and how glad she was to meet him. The Duke asked her to repeat this, which she did—a second and a third time. At this moment one of those strange silences which sometimes happen in a big company fell upon us, so poor Margaret found herself the centre of everyone's interest, even of Marconi himself at the other end of the long table. But still the Duke did not understand. Marshalling all effort Margaret fairly shrieked: "I am so glad to have this opportunity of knowing Mr. Marconi." The Duke's reply fell upon the ears of many listeners: "Yes, there are more tunnels in it than any other in the world, eighteen between here and Paris, I am told." Margaret wilted in her chair and left me to struggle alone with the old gentleman.

After the dinner we all went to the Capitol where a large reception was given for us, and the President received the freedom of the city. As a token of his citizenship, and the privilege of saying *"Civis Romanus sum,"* he was presented by the Syndic, Prince Prospero Colonna, with a bronze replica of the figure which surmounts the tomb of Hadrian. I received a gold wolf suckling Romulus and Remus—a gift of "the people of Rome."

After we had stood with Their Majesties to receive, the Queen, looking very lovely in a trailing gown of white, with a diamond coronet, asked me to go with her to see the illumination of the Forum. We stood on a balcony which overlooked the city. Above shone a full moon in a dark blue sky, and below lay all the beauty of those exquisite columns of ancient art, standing out in a soft, rosy light shed from invisible fires which burned around about. As I write I can see the scene in my memory, as unreal and mystical as it was on that marvellous night. The whole company felt the spell, for as they crowded to view it all conversation ceased and a silence of appreciation fell.

The cousin of the King, the Duchess of Aosta, was extremely tall, over six feet, and she was apparently appointed to companion Margaret, for they were always put together. Margaret, being small, laughed and said she always felt like the lesser end of Mutt and Jeff. The Duchess was the head of the Italian Red Cross and I heard glowing accounts of her ability and courage. Her husband, the Duke, said to be charming, was still away with the troops.

The next day there were many conferences with my husband. The afternoon before he had had a request from the people to address them in the great square surrounding the monument to Victor Emmanuel II. To this he had agreed gladly, and as the programme was arranged for him to be received by the Pope, he said he would repair to the square immediately after leaving the Vatican. Being a Protestant, and knowing the temper of many of our people at home regarding the Pope, the President decided he would also call on his old friends, Mr. and Mrs. Lowry, the former of whom was then in charge of the American Episcopal Church in Rome. I went with him. We were received in the vestry, where we had a very delightful little visit. Then we returned to the Palace where my husband was to be joined by a formal escort. Some of the White House Secret Service men who attended him were Catholics, and regarded this audience with the Pope as the climax of their lives. I had been asked to accompany my husband, but we thought it better for him to go alone. So Miss Benham, a duke whose name I have unfortunately forgotten and his wife, who had been assigned to me as a "Lady in Waiting," decided to follow along and see the crowds, on our way to tea with the Countess Cellere.

Never before had I seen so many people anywhere as were gathered in every street, and when we reached the region of the monument the way was blocked with humanity. They gave a great shout as my husband appeared on his way to the Vatican, and he had to stand in the car to greet them before the multitude would part to allow him to pass. The police could do nothing to control them. He finally got through, but our car was detained thirty or forty minutes. There was nothing alarming about it, the people were all so friendly. I regretted when we did get through, and wished I had an excuse to linger instead of going to the tea; for I was crazy to hear my husband speak.

Alas, this was not to be! It seemed that the Government, seeing the outpouring of the people, and especially the soldiers, feared that if the President addressed them he would say something which would enlist their support for his Fourteen Points. Though Italy had agreed to the Points as the basis of the Armistice, she had no intention of standing by her word in the Peace Conference. So, before my husband had left the Vatican the police were instructed to disperse the crowd. To do this without consulting the President was a gross discourtesy, and when I got back to the Quirinal he was already there and fairly blazing with anger. He expressed himself in no uncertain terms both to the press and to the officials who tried to explain their action by saying the crowd was so vast they feared it would get out of hand and cause a riot. Thus they tried to save their faces, but the veneer was too thin to fool anyone.

The next, or second, day of our sojourn, Their Majesties sent word to Mr. Thomas Nelson Page, our Ambassador, that they would lunch with us at the Embassy. The King and Queen having never before been entertained at an embassy, the President and his wife of necessity became the hosts *pro tem*. So we arrived at the charming old Palace, used as our Embassy, ahead of them. We found Mrs. Page and all the secretaries of the Embassy flustered and uneasy for fear everything had not been arranged as it should be.

The King and Queen arrived promptly with their suite, and as we were going into the dining room the Ambassador whispered to my husband: "It is the custom here to offer the health of the King just after the asparagus has been served."

The President waited for the asparagus to appear. Course after course of a most delicious and elaborate luncheon was served, until finally the table was cleared for dessert. Then the President rose and, addressing Their Majesties, said that one of the early precepts instilled into him as a small boy was, "When in Rome do as the Romans do." Certainly here, he continued, where he had seen and been the beneficiary of the gracious customs obtaining in Rome, he hesitated to depart one jot or tittle from such a standard. So he begged the indulgence of Their Majesties if in his ignorance he should offend the code. He said that the Ambassador had whispered to him: "It is the custom here to offer the health of the King just after the asparagus has been served." So he had waited, but as he saw this very delicious meal could not go on indefinitely, and, not knowing whether Roman customs included asparagus after ice cream, lest he lose entirely this unique opportunity of welcoming their gracious Majesties on American soil (as the Embassy was considered), he ventured to rise and offer a hearty welcome and a toast to the health of Their Majesties, the King and the Queen.

To this dear Mrs. Page said audibly: "Oh, but there was no asparagus in market!" This caused a hearty laugh and the meal was ended by a very happy little speech from the King, in the same spirit, which helped make the whole occasion informal and charming.

After we left Rome the next morning our first stop was at Genoa. Here my husband wished to place a wreath on the monument of Mazzini. We arrived just before a storm broke over the city, and by the time we had reached the monument the rain was pouring in torrents. I stayed in the car, but the gentlemen of the party got out and stood with bared heads while the Chief Magistrate of the city welcomed my husband. Attendants tried to hold umbrellas over the party, but the violence of the wind made their efforts futile, and it was a very wet set of tourists that returned to the motors.

Our next stop was Milan, where we arrived Saturday afternoon, and went straight to the Palace in the big square near the Duomo. By this time I was accustomed to great multitudes, and thought no larger ones possible. But Milan was a revelation. All the newspaper men who travelled wherever we went agreed there had never been in one spot so many human beings. The police estimated forty thousand in that great square alone. They begged for a speech from the balcony, and my husband responded briefly.

We were to go at once to a reception, and there was to be a State dinner at the palace that night. Having changed hurriedly to afternoon dress, I was leaving my room when I said to Susan, my maid: "It smells as though something is scorching." She said she did not think it was anything but very hot pipes. I thought no more of it, but when I returned two hours later I found the wall black from flames which had burst through the register just after I left, greatly alarming Susan and causing much excitement.

It seemed this palace had not been occupied during the War, and the flues had become overheated and set the wall afire. All of our clothing smelt of smoke, but nothing was injured and so we got ready for the dinner, which proved to be a grand affair.

The outstanding event was a gala performance the next night at the famous Scala Theatre. Though the best talent of Europe had been summoned, we knew nothing of it until a short while before curtain time. When the news came my husband spread dismay among the Italians by saying as it was Sunday night he regretted he could not attend a theatre; that he never did that in his own country on Sunday, and he could not do differently somewhere else. We were both so sorry it should have happened. The newspaper men all gathered around and asked the President what they should write in their home dispatches. He said: "Just write the truth. There is nothing else to do." Just then our dreary Duke de Lante appeared to ask if the President would come to the theatre to a sacred concert, adding that every seat was taken, and they could not disappoint so many people who had gathered from all over the country to pay honour to the President.

It would have seemed churlish to decline this. So the Duke left looking almost cheerful and my husband asked the reporters to send the news home that *Aïda* had been given up and instead there would be a concert of sacred music. Off they rushed to send their cables, and we had a few moments' rest before going to the dinner preceding the "concert."

I had always wanted to see this famous Scala Theatre, which is said to have the largest stage in the world, and where so many noted singers have attained their first fame. At first the building is disappointing if compared with the elaborate decoration of the Paris Opera House or others in Vienna or Berlin, for it is spacious, but plain.

The Royal Box in which we sat was directly opposite the stage on a mezzanine floor, and afforded a wonderful view of the great interior. There were many flowers and flags, and the uniforms worn by the men, and the handsome gowns and jewels of the women, stood out against the not overdecorated walls of the house. The audience rose when we entered, and gave us an unforgettable welcome, calling "Speech, speech." My husband thanked them in a few words, expressing our pleasure at being there.

When the great curtain was lifted revealing the depth of the stage it was like looking down a long vista. Again the audience rose when the American and Italian national airs were sung by a huge chorus. One or two solos followed, and then the great opera of *Aïda* was given with the finest effect I have ever seen. The promise to have a "sacred concert" had been filled in letter, but not in spirit, for *Aïda* could hardly be put under that title. But it was such a magnificent spectacle I have always been glad they did it. Secretly, I think my husband was too; and he made no comment regarding the elastic fulfillment of their promise. After leaving Milan we spent the next day in Turin where Mr. Wilson made five addresses.

After an official lunch my husband was given a degree at the University of Turin. He delighted the students by putting on one of their blue caps and wearing it while making his speech of appreciation. How young and virile he looked as he stood there!

But the most picturesque feature of our visit was the gathering of more than a thousand mayors from Piedmont to greet the President.

They came from the hills, the fields and the valleys, virtually every little town or crossroad being represented as well as the cities. Every walk of life was represented—prosperous bankers, merchants, shy countrymen, village blacksmiths and artisans. The President shook hands and spoke to each, and was deeply touched when some of them bent and kissed his hand.

From Turin we went direct to Paris again. These two journeys— to England and to Italy—were experiences that come to few Americans. Fate having chosen me for such a Cinderella rôle, I have tried to picture it for others, in an endeavour to make a return for this great privilege which was mine.

CHAPTER 17

O N January 7, 1919, we arrived in Paris once more. It lacked only six days of a month since we had landed in Europe. The Peace Conference was not to open until January 18th. This delay had not been anticipated by my husband, who was impatient to get on with the work. Intervening time was not wasted, however. There were conferences every day, and all day long—informal meetings of the Commissions of the various countries, and meetings between experts of different countries. On Sunday, January 13th, Mr. Wilson drove to the Quai d'Orsay for a long conference attended by Clemenceau, Pichon and Foch of France; Lloyd George, Balfour and Sir Henry Wilson of England; Orlando and Sonnino of Italy; Lansing and Bliss, United States. There was no ceremony. My husband said it might have been a meeting of bank directors. They sat very late; and so were put in motion the wheels that were to grind out the future status of the world.

This made it impossible to accept invitations, though they came in a stream. Only three or four times during our sojourn did we relax this rule, and then informally. Once we dined with our Ambassador, Mr. Sharp, who was retiring from the post; again with our old friends, Mr. and Mrs. Hugh C. Wallace, who succeeded the Sharps at the Embassy; and again at the British and the Italian Embassies.

More and more was the President caught up in the train of work until, after the formal opening of the Conference on January 18th, I scarcely saw him except at meals. My time was filled, at first, with visits to canteens, places of amusement for soldiers, French war industries, hospitals and rehabilitation centres for broken bodies.

The Petit Palais was a perfect hive of workers, where splendid women were striving to teach crippled soldiers new ways of self-support. I found the men typing, weaving and printing and operating hosiery knitting machines, and learning various other kinds of reconstruction work. The pupils were wonderfully patient and cheerful, doing their brave best to start life over with an arm or a leg, or sometimes both, missing. Then there was the fine work for the blind carried on by Miss Winifred Holt. She called her place "The Light House," and truly she brought light to those who must sit in darkness the rest of their lives, teaching them to see through the touch of their fingers. I went there many times and bought some of the pretty bags and scarfs woven by these deft hands. Once I was presented with a beautiful piece of Braille done by a blind soldier.

In one of the big factories outside the city, the places of men called to arms had been filled by women. It had been converted to a munitions plant, and these women, most of them young, had worked early and late to do their bit for their country. During those long, cold winters they had had no heat at all and their hands and feet were swollen and aching with chilblains. My hat goes off whenever I think of these and other women whose names are on no honour roll. When I saw this particular group, they were gay, and gave me the sweetest greeting. Most of them wore shabby mourning under the black factory aprons, but they joined their hard, pitiful hands and stood in a circle singing some of those charming French folk songs that have a lilt unlike any other airs I have ever heard.

Another day I went to the hospital which was the charity of Mrs. Whitelaw Reid. She had started it before the War as a home for American women students in Paris. But like nearly everything else during those tragic years, it had been given over to the soldiers. What a charming contrast it was to the long wards in hospitals where everything is glaring whiteness. Here there were small individual rooms with yellow window curtains, cozy cushioned seats, armchairs, reading lights and flowers; and everything was done to bring cheer to those who were fortunate enough to come there to convalesce.

One other "home"—in sharp contrast to this one—I must mention. After we had been in Paris a while, I had a letter from an English clergyman who asked if I would come to his house in the Montmartre district to see what he and his wife were doing for young English girls who came alone to Paris, seeking fame and fortune.

The writer was at his door to greet Miss Benham and me. Entering the small reception room of a very humble abode, we were presented to his wife who held a bouncing baby boy on her arm. Briefly the minister explained the origin and scope of his work. It was the result of several years of personal observation. The cheap cafés and dance halls in that part of the city were open all night. These places became the last barriers against starvation for girls, some of gentle birth and some who had come to Paris as young as fourteen, thinking they were artists and would soon make their mark, and too proud to write or to go home acknowledging failure. The consequences, he said, were terrible. The law was that girls employed to sing or dance in these low places had to accept any attention from the customers and never decline to drink with them. "But," added our host, "I have been much encouraged by a change I have got enacted into the law, by which the girls can leave the café after three o'clock, and come home."

They had accommodations for twenty-two girls, in a long dormitory room furnished with rows of single beds. At the foot of each bed was a small stand for the simple toilet articles; underneath was a drawer for clothing; a bag at the head of the bed, like a comfort kit; and one or two chairs completed the furnishings. In the hall was a cold-water tap by which stood a row of tin basins and two roller towels. A curtain hung on wire stretched tight at the back of the hall formed a closet for dancing costumes. A few photographs on the little dressing stands gave a pathetic touch to this picture of disappointed young lives.

The minister talked as he showed us around, saying they took these girls for eight dollars a month "when they can pay it." Often there would be weeks when they could not pay a cent. He explained that if a girl were fortunate enough to get in a chorus or ballet at the opera or at a theatre, she was never paid during rehearsals, which often took weeks. He said he gave keys to those who danced or sang in cheap places and told them when they were not on duty he would expect them home early. When I asked how early he said: "Well, never later than one o'clock."

Our tour of the second floor finished, we rejoined Madame in the tiny sitting room where about twenty of their "girls" were assembled. Most of them were painted and manicured and artificial-looking. Their clothes were cheap and shoddy. The one really natural feminine instinct that had survived their unnatural lives was the love for the fat baby. He was handed from one to the other as the *pièce de résistance* of the frugal tea which was served. Amid "oh's" and "ah's" they told me: "He comes to tea with us every afternoon, and we just adore him." If my impression of the girls was disappointing, my admiration for the minister and his wife was genuine and unbounded. I wish I could have added another figure to the check I sent him later to help him carry on.

Leaving this mean quarter of the city we drove home through the beautiful Place de la Concorde and up the Champs Élysées, flanked on either side with ugly cannon captured from Germany. Turning into the Rue de Monceau, where gendarmes constantly marched back and forth, we entered the precincts of our palace through a gate guarded by a sentry box of blue, red and white. The great gate slammed behind us, and we were in the house, and attended up the great sweep of the stairs by liveried lackeys to the second floor. If only some of the cost of this sort of useless attention could be diverted to those who stand in need of the necessary things of life, this would be a better world.

The door of the study was open, and there on the floor were spread maps, and on their knees before them were my husband and three or four experts trying to work out new national frontiers made necessary by the War. They called to me to come in, and I said: "You look like a lot of little boys playing a game." My husband replied: "Alas, it is the most serious game ever undertaken, for on the result of it hangs, in my estimation, the future peace of the world."

The days went on with unceasing work for him. Our house was a meeting place, and every day M. Clemenceau, Mr. Lloyd George and Signor Orlando came, often accompanied by secretaries or people doing special research work on the multitudinous questions which had to be solved.

My husband was usually busy night as well as day. Our Commission occupied the Hotel Crillon and there all the meetings were held which concerned our particular problems. These meetings, in some way that I do not know, were begun in the rooms assigned to Colonel House, and so they continued to be held there for several weeks.

One day I received a note from Mr. Henry White asking if I would allow him to take me to see some of the historic places in Paris of which he had a most interesting knowledge. As a young man Mr. White had been Secretary of our Embassy, and later had held many higher posts in the Diplomatic Corps, so it was a treat to have him as a guide. While we were going from one place to another he asked if he could talk to me as a friend instead of a member of the Peace Commission. "Why, of course," I said. Then in his courtly manner he turned and said: "Dear lady, then I am going really to avail myself of that permission, and tell you a few of the jealousies and sore spots in the Commission to which, I think, by a word to the President, you can bring balm. The first one is that Lansing is terribly sore because the meetings the President attends are held in Colonel House's suite instead of his. Since he is the Secretary of State, forgive me if I say I think he is right; for he is being ignored. Also all the newspaper men, in quest of information, are told by Gordon Auchincloss to see his father-in-law, Colonel House."

I told Mr. White that these things were so small I was sure they had never entered the President's mind, but that I knew he would appreciate his thought in telling me of them, and he would look into them. "Yes," Mr. White answered, "they are small things, but Lansing is a small man, and sometimes personal vanity makes or mars the success of large affairs."

I begged him to feel I would always welcome his confidences, knowing they came from interest and friendship. We had a delightful day sightseeing, and an opportunity to talk over many things; and I still recall the tour with pleasure.

I waited until the following Sunday afternoon, which was the one holiday of the whole week for my husband. After going to church in the morning we usually went for a motor ride in the country. This Sunday it was raining, but we bundled up and went in an open car with the top up, and I told him of Mr. White's conversation.

When I said that Lansing was hurt about the meetings, I can hear his voice now as he replied: "Why, I am very sorry about that; it never occurred to me and I am quite sure it never did to House." He then added: "I will see that it is changed, for White is right about it." I then told him about the newspaper matter, and to that he said: "I have been working out a plan in my own mind. It is this: I have decided to ask Mr. Ray Stannard Baker, for whom I have the highest regard, to act as an intermediary between our Commission and the other press representatives. It is highly important that the right news be given out, so I am going to ask Baker to accept this position, and come to see me every night at seven o'clock, when I will go over with him everything that has transpired during the day, telling him what is finished and what is unfinished business, and suggesting that the completed business be furnished all the papers, but that questions still under discussion be omitted."

This plan was followed to the letter, Mr. Baker never failing to appear at the stroke of seven, often having to wait an hour, or even more, if the President was still in conference; and as faithfully carrying out his contract with all the other newspaper men.

I always tried to be at home and ready for dinner in time to attend these interviews between the President and Mr. Baker. In this way I kept in constant touch with the work of the Conference, and made it unnecessary to burden my weary husband with questions. Mr. Baker's alert mind was always eager to grasp every subject. He kept up a continual fire of questions and never was satisfied until he had each point clarified. So it was a stimulating half-hour.

Mr. Wilson inaugurated these meetings purely out of justice to Secretary Lansing, and to compose any difference that may have threatened to arise between him and Colonel House because the newspaper men seemed to prefer the latter as a source of news. In the President's mind was not the least suspicion that Colonel House's sessions with the press were deliberate on his part, or calculated to magnify the Colonel's importance at the expense of his colleagues.

The Baker conference over, a quick bath and change put the President in a more rested state for dinner. As I have said, we attempted no official entertaining, though usually one or two interesting men would join us for dinner. As a little departure from the routine, we accepted an invitation to a performance at the Théâtre des Champs Élysées, by the Argonne Players of the 77th Division, of which I had been made an honourary member. It was an original revue written and first produced behind the Argonne Forest front. The players, most of them professionals before the War, had been recruited from the front lines and gun pits. They had formed a permanent theatrical unit which at this time was touring the A.E.F. Among my mementoes is a programme autographed by each member of the cast.

It was also about this time that I made the acquaintance of the old Duchess of R. The title is one of the oldest in France. The dukedom at that time was held by a little grandson around seven years old. His father had been killed in the War, leaving the elderly Duchess alone in a great house in the old aristocratic quarter of Paris. Like so many other courageous Frenchwomen, she tried to forget her own sorrow by doing for others, and had opened her beautiful house as a hospital.

This gives you the picture of the Duchess as it was given to me by the Serbian Minister, M. Vesnitch, who had sent me an urgent note begging an immediate audience. M. Vesnitch had headed the Serbian Mission which had come to America after our entry into the War. On our arrival in Paris I felt we were already good friends, but could not imagine what he wished to see me about, in such haste.

He arrived, and, with many apologies and real embarrassment, told me the following: "I was at a large dinner night before last and had the honour of taking in the Duchess of R. I asked her if she had met the President and Mrs. Wilson, and to my great surprise she answered: 'No, and I do not want to meet them. Paris has gone mad about President Wilson and I am sick of hearing about them. What are they? Only ordinary Americans with no claim to aristocracy or title.' 'Oh,' I said, 'Duchess, there you are wrong, for Mrs. Wilson is directly descended from a princess, and of the only aristocracy in America; her grandmother seven times removed was the great Princess Pocahontas. I have just returned a short time ago from the United States and there I read all of this in a paper which I kept and can show to you.' 'Why,' said the Duchess, 'this is very important, and I knew nothing of it at all. Of course I must go and call on Mrs. Wilson at once and give an entertainment in her honour.' So," said M. Vesnitch, "that is the reason I begged that you see me at once that I might tell you about this, so that you will be sure to receive the Duchess when she calls."

Alas, the grand lady had already come and written her name in our book but I had not seen her, and so I had to confess this to him. His face was tragic at this information, for he sincerely thought he was putting me in touch with what he considered a great social opportunity. I warmly appreciated his interest and friendship, but I could not help being amused just the same.

After he had gone I made an amusing story of the incident to tell my husband, adding that as my mother was then living at the Hotel Powhatan in Washington I thought I would get a picture postcard of it and send it to the Duchess as the photograph of "my ancestral palace, now used as a hotel for war workers." The Chief Powhatan was

Pocahontas' father. Woodrow laughed and said: "Please wait until I finish this job over here before you play jokes on any French lady."

I thought, of course, that I had missed the chance of knowing this *grande dame,* but a few days later Mrs. Wallace, wife of our American Ambassador, gave an afternoon reception for me, asking principally French ladies. Presenting them in her easy gracious way, she brought forward one who was not very tall, inclined to stoutness, and dressed in black far from modish. As she said: "This is my friend, Mrs. Wilson—the Duchess of R., who says she is very anxious to meet you," the lady fixed piercing black eyes upon me, and looked me over from tip to toe. Then she *curtsied,* as though I had really been of the royalty. She said she had heard much of me through a friend who had been in America, and wished to give a dinner for the President and me on any night we would name. I thanked her for her graciousness, but declined, saying my husband was working so hard we had to give up all dinner parties unless they were official. "Oh," she said, "then you, madame, must come alone." I explained that I did not dine out without Mr. Wilson. The Duchess said she was "desolated." Then suddenly she smiled and said: "Oh, but I learn that you visit the hospitals." "Yes," I said, "I do." *"Voilà!"* she cried. "My house is a hospital, so you will come now?"

I saw that Pocahontas, my "royal" ancestor, was fighting hard for my social prestige, so I replied: "I will with great pleasure do that." "Yes," she said, "I must have you under my roof; please write me a day when you will come."

Thus the plan was made, and I asked Miss Benham to send a note saying I would be glad to come on the following Tuesday. Miss Benham came with me, and upon our arrival the great gates swung wide and we entered a charming garden completely hidden from the street by a high wall. It was a large property in the centre of which was a great house typically French in architecture, with wide hospitable doorway opening on semicircular stone steps.

As the motor swung around the driveway, the door was open, and on the bottom of the three steps stood a small boy in black velvet with wide lace collar, holding in his small hands long sprays of pink apple blossoms. Behind him stood a Cardinal of the Church in his gorgeous red robes, and grouped about were the Duchess and the ladies who comprised her staff of nurses—all dressed in white, with long veils, and no colour save the Red Cross on the band that held the veils.

As I stepped from the limousine, the little Duke knelt on one knee, kissed my hand and presented the blossoms. Then the Cardinal held up his hand in silent benediction, after which we were greeted by the Duchess who presented her friends.

After we had been to the wards and greeted the soldiers, we went into the large dining room where a table was spread with all sorts of things for tea. To my surprise I was the only person seated, everyone else standing, as in the presence of royalty. Certainly M. Vesnitch had impressed the Duchess, and I will always recall that afternoon as a unique experience, and treasure a real regard for my hostess whom later I learned to know better.

I receive so many inquiries about Pocahontas that, with the indulgence of my readers, I will try to answer a few in these pages. She was born about 1595, was married in 1614 at Jamestown, Virginia, to John Rolfe, died and was buried at Gravesend, England, in 1617, leaving a son, Thomas. This half-Indian boy returned to Virginia with his father, where he married, and where hundreds of his descendants remain, bearing such family names as Archer, Bolling, Branch, Cabell, Grayson, Harrison, Randolph, Robertson, Skipwith, Tazewell, and many, many others. My own line of descent follows:

GENERA- TION	BOLLINGS	MARRIED	CHILDREN Sons	Daughters
	Pocahontas	John Rolfe	1	1
1	Thomas Rolfe	Jane Poythress	1	1
2	Jane Rolfe	Colonel Robert Bolling 1	1	
3	John Bolling	Mary Kennon 1	6	5
4	John Bolling	Elizabeth Blair 1	6	5
5	John Bolling	Mary Jefferson	11	
6	Archibald Bolling	Catherine Payne	8	
7	Archibald Bolling	Anne E. Wigginton 2	4	2
8	William H. Bolling	Sallie S. White 6	11	5
9	Edith Bolling	Norman Galt Woodrow Wilson		

Ambassador Jusserand asked me to go to the Gobelin tapestry factory. On leaving the house I asked the young American soldier

PRESIDENT WILSON AT RAILROAD STATION, CHATEAU THIERRY, FEBRUARY 8, 1919

Being saluted by American and French soldiers.

who drove our car if he knew how to reach the place. Having been there years before, I recalled that it was particularly difficult to find. "Oh, yes," he said. "You cross this *champ* and three *rues,* then turn . . ." Sure enough, he went directly to it. Although he did not speak the language, with the aid of a map and his native American wit that boy always "got there."

I met the artist who had designed the beautiful tapestry given me by the French Government; and in addition many officials and friends of the Ambassador. This made the visit something on the order of a reception, a little too formal to be enjoyable, but to watch the tapestry weaving, always a mystery to me, was fascinating.

A little later I had an afternoon reception for the many persons who had called to write their names in "the book." What a company! Diplomats, soldiers, politicians, statesmen, writers, artists, from the four corners of the world. To me the most striking figure in the colourful assembly was Prince Feisal of Arabia. His white robe swept the floor and over his head was a sort of drapery held in place by a fillet. His features were exquisitely fine. Long dark hair and a pointed beard completed a startling resemblance to pictures of Christ that I have seen. Later, during our second sojourn in Paris, I gave a reception for the full membership of the Peace Conference—and again Feisal was, to me, the most extraordinary-looking personage present.

Things like this are all right as spectacles, but I enjoyed more the tea we gave for the soldiers on guard duty about our house, the telephone operators and the stenographers. The soldiers were on duty in three eight-hour shifts. Shifts changed at four in the afternoon, so we had the party from three to five that everyone might be there.

Having obtained the names of each man we sent out formal engraved invitations, the same as used at the White House. Our one anxiety, however, was for the hardwood floors of the Murat Palace. Hobnailed shoes would be fatal to them. After much pondering we turned the problem over to young Mr. Garfield, a son of the president of Williams College and a grandson of a President of the United States, who was acting as an aide to Mr. Wilson. He promised to get tactful word to every man to procure other shoes for the occasion. He did more, personally inspecting the shoes of each of our soldier guests before he entered the house. The boys took it as a part of the fun, and not one had to be sent back for a change of footgear.

Two hundred strong, they were a cross section of the U. S. A., hailing from nearly every State in the Union. We had feared they would be shy or embarrassed, but not a bit of it. They called the President "the Old Man," and gathered around him like a lot of college boys. Each wanted a photograph to send home, so we got a photographer and had him make many trys at it, and it was funny to see the manœuvring of the boys to be taken standing with my husband. They sang songs, and how they revelled in the sandwiches, cake, ice cream, and other good things. Years afterwards we would get letters from some of them, asking if we could send them a duplicate invitation, because some calamity had overtaken the original. We complied as long as we had any left.

A number of the boys had made a confidante of Edith Benham, consulting her about various matters. One asked her what she thought would be nice for him to take home as a gift for his mother, who lived in the country in Iowa. She offered to go with him to the Bon Marché. When she got back she told me that his eye was caught by a pair of gloves with bright green stitching, and nothing could wean him from them, though she saw a dozen things more practical. She said that as she was coming back he told her his buddy was quite in love with an American girl who was in Paris doing war work. The friend was taking the girl sightseeing and had consulted his chum as to what to show her, saying he had thought of taking her to the Louvre, meaning the art gallery, not the department store. Miss Benham's escort had advised strongly against that, saying that as the girl in question had been very nicely brought up, he did not think she should go to the Louvre because there was "a lot of *rough* stuff in that place."

About this time the King of the Belgians arrived in Paris and called on my husband. What a fine, distinguished-looking man he was, and so delightfully interested in a funny thing he had seen in the White House as a very young man. It was a round, upholstered seat with a sort of pedestal in the centre, on which stood a palm. "Is it still there?" he asked with great eagerness. "Yes," I told him, "it is, but is now in the basement, kept as a relic of early Pullman style of furniture." I promised him if he would come back to the United

States I would show it to him, which promise I fulfilled a year later.

The grinding work of the Conference went on day after day, and late into every night, the only rest for my husband being Sunday, when he dismissed every care, slept later, and often went in the motor for a long drive with me.

The French papers and people kept commenting on the fact that he did not go to see the devastated regions, and the French Ambassador, M. Jusserand, visited us nearly every day to urge his going.

My husband had followed all this terrible destruction with knowledge and sympathy, so that to see it with his own eyes would have been only a tangible verification of what he already knew. Add to this that he was working eighteen hours a day, and was eager to finish and get home where the country must readjust itself to the normal conditions of peace.

When we first reached Paris his hope had been to get the major terms of the Peace completed so that when he came home for the closing of Congress on March 4, 1919, it would not be necessary for him to return to Paris. The month lost after our arrival he felt was a great waste, and so he was driving every hour to try to make up this loss.

His one hope was to get the Conference to agree on the inclusion of the Covenant of the League of Nations as part of the Treaty. Through this instrumentality he felt that any unwise or unjust terms of the Treaty itself could and would be adjusted in the future. He envisioned the League as the clearinghouse for all international disputes, providing pacific means of settlement for men to meet and talk over their problems as neighbours, and learn the value of complete understanding by personal contacts.

Many books have already been written of this tense period, dealing with M. Clemenceau, an avowed cynic, distrustful of humanity's ability to rise to unselfish heights; with Mr. Lloyd George, a political weather vane shifting with every wind that blew across the Channel lest it affect his personal fortunes; with Signor Orlando, whose ear was ever to the ground for fear Italy should not get all she hungered for. I will not go over that ground, but try to show what I saw with my own eyes. Amid all those complexities my husband stood practically alone—with very lukewarm support from some of his own Commission, such as Lansing who, over his own signature, has since admitted that he accepted a place on the Commission knowing he was antagonistic to principles which he would be called on to promulgate.

But Woodrow Wilson was a born fighter, and never let defeat turn him aside as long as a remnant with which to carry on was left. Seeing him growing grimmer and graver, day by day, how I longed to be a man so I could be of more help to him. All I could do was to try to "soothe him with a finer fancy, touch him with a lighter thought."

It was at this time that the pressure was strongest for him to visit the despoiled areas. Finally, from sheer weariness, he said he would go. It meant giving up his one day of rest, for he would not postpone the work of the Conference longer than one day, a Saturday. We were to be back late Sunday night.

Our first objective was Rheims where everything seemed desolation. At the door of the great Cathedral we were met by the old priest who had stayed on with his distraught people all through the awful bombing raids that had destroyed their homes and killed so many of them. I recall so vividly his small figure outlined against the vast interior of the building. He was very frail-looking, and wore a black cassock, and one of the flat black plush hats of his order, the only note of colour being gloves of crimson silk, much too large for his slender hands. A light snow was falling, and it drifted silently down through the great holes in the roof which had been made by the bombshells. Pointing to them he said, in tones as tender as a mother's speaking of an injured child: "My Cathedral stood through three other raids without any bad hurts, but the fourth one she could not withstand, and this broke her." My eyes followed the long red silk finger, but soon returned to rest upon this modest old hero who forgot his personal danger and courage in the desecration of his church.

The few people who were left in the town were now coming out of the great wine caves which had become homes to them, and a dreary picture they made. Women with shawls over their heads and thin shoulders; men in shabby clothes; all their faces pinched with cold and hunger.

From there we went to the Chemin des Dames and to Soissons to find the town virtually deserted. On leaving we took the regular

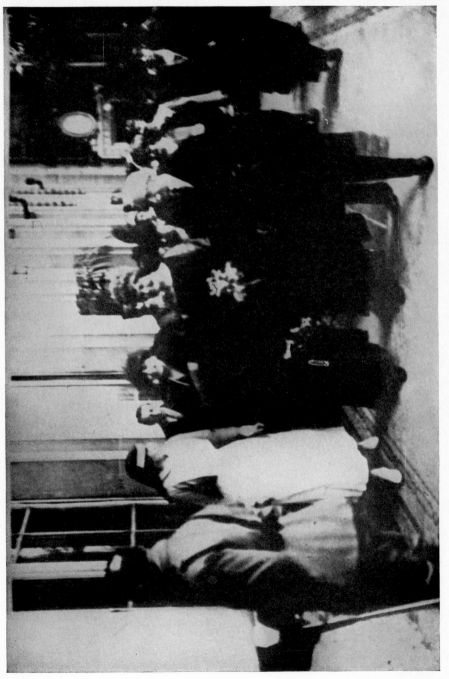

Mrs. Wilson Visiting Hospital in Paris (Grande Palais) in Spring of 1919

Left to right: Queen Marie of Rumania, Mrs. Wilson, Mr. Nelson Cromwell.

road out, but were soon warned to go no farther as an ammunition dump had been accidentally set fire to by two French Indo-Chinese soldiers and it was unsafe to go that way. When we retraced our route to Soissons, imagine our surprise to see the streets, which a few minutes before had been almost depopulated, alive with French troops. They swarmed about our car in the friendliest way, one soldier shouting that his comrades believed the peace Mr. Wilson was fighting for was not the peace their own Government was trying to gain. They called for the President to speak.

Where, we asked, had these soldiers been when we were in the town before? In their billets, they said, their officers having ordered them there on hearing that the President of the United States was coming. As soon as our car had disappeared, for good as they thought, the soldiers were set at liberty. "But fate has stepped in," the spokesman said, "and brought you back to us."

In these illuminating circumstances, there was nothing the President could say except to thank the men for their welcome.

The incident affected Mr. Wilson profoundly. So French soldiers, the men who had saved the Republic from disaster, were being shielded from contact with the author of the principles on which the fighting had been brought to an end. It was of a piece with the refusal of the authorities to permit the working women of Paris to see him, and the dispersion of the countless multitude gathered in Rome to hear the President.

On the ride back to Paris that night my husband was thoughtful and depressed.

CHAPTER 18

RETURNING from our eye-opening tour of the battlefields, the President resumed his labours to speed the work on the Treaty. He still hoped to get things far enough along to obviate the necessity of a second trip to Paris following his return home for the closing of Congress in March, 1919. As the days rolled on this became a vain hope. So we made plans to go, calculating on an absence of a little more than three weeks, allowing nine days for the trip each way and seven days in the United States.

This brought to my husband's mind the question of who should be in charge of the United States delegation during this absence. Mr. Lansing was next in official rank, but by this time the President had begun to feel that the Secretary of State was not in sympathy with the League of Nations ideal. At one time Mr. Wilson considered asking Mr. Lansing to resign. He discussed this with Colonel House and with me. There were many reasons against such a course. The disruption might hinder rather than help. In the end Mr. Lansing was not asked to resign. It was decided that he should remain as the titular *ad interim* head of the American Commission, though the actual authority should be in the hands of Colonel House.

Up to this time, Colonel House had been of inestimable help to the President. He had worked with and for him. But the one thing which had disturbed me was that Colonel House so seldom disagreed with my husband. Of this I had spoken to Woodrow, saying: "It seems to me that it is impossible for two persons *always* to think alike, and while I like Colonel House immensely, I find him absolutely colourless and a 'yes, yes' man." My husband said: "No, I don't think that is altogether true. You forget that it is my constitutional duty to formulate policies and take the responsibility for them. House thinks straight, and can gather public opinion and get the real views of men in a way that is impossible for me. I consider

236

one of the greatest handicaps of this office is the fact that few people are natural or frank with a President; they seem to feel they must flatter and fawn. So House brings to me something I cannot get in any other way."

I reminded my husband of the Colonel's behaviour with reference to the railroad message. I distrust the judgment of people who change sides as abruptly as he did then, and from that day on I had been inclined to question the worth of Colonel House's services as an adviser. In public life, however, one often is obliged to use the instrument readiest to hand. Since 1916, when the idea first began to take shape in my husband's mind, Colonel House had been a firm believer in a league of nations and had contributed much to the development of the President's thought on the subject. In Paris Colonel House had worked staunchly for the League, and Mr. Lansing had not.

The immediate fight was to incorporate the League of Nations Covenant into the body of the Treaty. With this done before he sailed, my husband could lay the tentative draft before the Foreign Relations Committee of the Senate, get suggestions for amendments and bring them back to Paris on his return. Thus Mr. Wilson saw a really fortunate circumstance, after all, in his journey home. He explained to me that he wanted to put everything squarely before the Foreign Relations Committee, and that it would be natural for the Senators to wish to study the first draft and make their own suggestions. The President was sure he would be able to accept any changes they desired. This, he said, would assure the satisfaction and co-operation of the Committee, making eventual ratification of the Treaty practically certain.

At length came the day he was to make his plea before the full Peace Conference for the inclusion of the Covenant of the League of Nations in the Treaty, and by the votes of the delegates that great question would be decided. It was February 14, 1919, and that night we were to leave Paris for home.

Of course I was eager to be there to hear him, but as the meeting was for members only, and not the public, this seemed impossible. Mr. Wilson always stood away from asking favours for himself or for anyone close to him; so I would not add to his cares by repining over my disappointment but went to our dear Dr. Grayson and asked if he thought it would be very dreadful if I should ask M. Clemenceau (who was president of the Conference) if there was any way in which I could be admitted. The Doctor was keen for it, and said he, too, was crazy to go, so if I would let him ask "the Tiger," saying he came from me, he was sure the old Frenchman would try to arrange it.

Before doing this, though, I decided to ask my husband if it would in any way embarrass him should my request be refused. He thought it over a moment, and said: "In the circumstances it is hardly a request, it is more a command, for he could not very well refuse you." "That being the case then I shall certainly make it," I said, and he looked up from his desk and laughed. "Wilful woman, your sins be on your own head if the Tiger shows his claws." "Oh, he can't, you know; they are always done up in grey cotton," I answered, referring to the gloves Clemenceau wore, even at table.

I knew from this that Dr. Grayson and I were free to make the request.

The meeting was in the great Room of the Clock, and under the huge timepiece from which that chamber in the Ministry of Foreign Affairs takes its name was a long table for the heads of the Commissions. The other delegates occupied seats with desks or tables in the main part of the room. At the far end, facing the clock and the Conference table, heavy red brocade curtains concealed a small alcove just large enough for two straight chairs, and seemingly made for eavesdroppers.

When the Conference assembled, hidden away in that tiny place were two unsuspected listeners—happy, but hot. We had been told that we must be in our places before any of the delegates came, to keep quiet, and to stay until all had gone before we came out of hiding. Dr. Grayson said that the old gentleman had added that if our presence were discovered, he would have the wife of every delegate pestering the soul out of him. So we were in honour bound to follow his directions. It is proverbial that foreigners, especially the French, hate drafts. Therefore every window was closed tight and our retreat grew stifling behind the heavy brocade; but I forgot it when the preliminary work, lasting an hour, was over and my husband rose to speak.

He was exactly opposite us and as every eye was centred upon him we ventured to part our curtains enough to see the whole scene. It was a great moment in history, and as he stood there—slender, calm, and powerful in his argument—I seemed to see the people of all depressed countries—men, women and little children—crowding round and waiting upon his words. He rarely made long speeches, and this was no exception. I could see it had made a great impression, and I longed to go to him and tell him all I felt.

Then the ballots were placed before the delegates. After the usual procedure, which takes much time, the result was in favour of the measure. The members rushed to grasp Mr. Wilson's hand. In the general noise and bustle, we felt free to stretch our muscles, for we had been motionless nearly four hours.

Outside, it was already dark, and the lights had been on for an hour in the room. Men were gathering up papers and briefcases, and in an incredibly short time the room was empty. Reporters were rushing off to wire their news to the four corners of the globe. We waited until the last coattail disappeared through the door, and then hastily withdrew.

Once outside the building we were only a part of the crowd that always stood there waiting. The long line of motors was breaking up. The flags on the front of the cars, designating the different countries, were flying to the breeze. Presently I saw the familiar blue one bearing the President's seal. The car was not in motion so I knew my husband was waiting for me. Oh, how glad I was to find him and tell him all the things that filled my heart!

He took off his high hat and leaned back in the car. "Are you so weary?" I asked. "Yes," he answered, "I suppose I am, but how little one man means when such vital things are at stake." Then continuing: "This is our first real step forward, for I now realize, more than ever before, that once established the League can arbitrate and correct mistakes which are inevitable in the Treaty we are trying to make at this time. The resentments and injustices caused by the War are still too poignant, and the wounds too fresh. They must have time to heal, and when they have done so, one by one the mistakes can be brought to the League for readjustment, and the League will act as a permanent clearinghouse where every nation can come, the small as well as the great."

Then turning with one of his radiant smiles, he said: "It will be sweet to go home, even for a few days, with the feeling that I have kept the faith with the people, particularly with these boys, God bless them."

I saw he was deeply moved, and we sat silent until the car turned in at our gates and the soldiers stood at salute as we went in.

In a few hours we drove to the railroad station where the usual official party was gathered and the train of the French President awaited us. A crimson carpet was spread, and with much kissing of my hand, and clicking of heels, and speeches and band music, we were on our way to the U. S. A.

One of the happiest members of our party was our soldier chauffeur, a big upstanding fellow from Pennsylvania and a marvellous driver. He had asked if it would be possible to go back with us, as he had come over with our First Division and was, of course, crazy to see home. "But," he added, "I don't want to stay there. I'll be on the dock ready to come back with you any day you tell me to." My husband said: "If you go I will arrange it so you will not have to do that; I will have you mustered out so you can stay." This he instantly refused, saying: "No *sir,* I'd rather not go than have to give up driving for you. Forget it!" (This was true "United States talk"!) After considering the matter several days, the President, who felt the boy had earned his holiday, gave orders that he was to go and return with us.

We also brought back many sick and wounded soldiers. Every day we would go up on the top deck of the *George Washington* where the sick bay was located to see the patients. Those who were able would be taken out on deck to lie all day in the sun. Near the Banks of Newfoundland we ran into a dense fog which lasted for hours. We almost stood still while the dreary fog horn of another ship came across the water. The next day when I went up to see our invalids I asked them if they were frightened. One of them said: "No ma'am, 'cause I knew if we hit anything and drifted into shore it would be our own country."

The Assistant Secretary of the Navy and Mrs. Franklin D. Roosevelt also came back with us, and we found them very delightful companions.

We landed at Boston on a marvellous day, February 24, 1919. Mr. Calvin Coolidge, the Governor of Massachusetts, and his staff, escorted us from the dock through the cheering throngs to Mechanics Hall. The place was packed to suffocation, and hundreds more trying to get in. This reception almost equalled those abroad—perhaps not so picturesque, but just as warm. The Governor rose to speak and the crowd grew quiet, only to break out again when he said: "We welcome him [the President] as the representative of a great people, as a great statesman, as one to whom we have entrusted our destinies and one whom we will support in the future in the working out of those destinies as Massachusetts has supported him in the past." My husband was deeply gratified by this. If Boston were a representative audience, the pulse of the Nation beat steady and true for what the President was working to attain.

In response to Governor Coolidge's introduction, the President made a vigorous address and got a real ovation when he finished. Mr. Coolidge accompanied us to the railroad station and when we departed for Washington, the concern foremost in our minds was for the health of I. H. Hoover, the head usher of the White House. Just after leaving France, Hoover had been taken very ill, and had developed pneumonia. Fortunately it was a light case. However, he could not be moved on our arrival at Boston, and so remained aboard the *George Washington,* which proceeded at once to New York.

A review of newspaper comment indicated that Boston's enthusiastic reception expressed the preponderant sentiment of the Nation on the League. On reaching Washington the first thing my husband did was to invite the Foreign Relations Committees of the Senate and the House to meet with him at the White House. At that conference he discussed the rough draft of the Covenant of the League of Nations, which had been accepted as a part of the Treaty, and asked for any and all comments and suggestions. Many were made, and all thoroughly talked over. As a whole they were not, I think, very different in substance. The President asked that they be submitted to him in writing so he would have them in proper shape. When the meeting was over he told me, as nearly as I can remember, the following:

That he had addressed himself to Mr. Lodge of Massachusetts, saying: "Of course you understand, Senator, I will have to go back to Paris and resubmit this to the Conference, for while it is not essentially changed, it is not what they accepted the day I left; and

I have some pretty stubborn men to deal with. However, I am going to do my best, and if this draft as it stands is accepted, do you think it will go through the Senate?" Mr. Lodge replied: "If the Foreign Relations Committee approves it I feel there is no doubt of ratification." "Very well then," my husband answered, "I consider that, armed with your approval, I can go back and work feeling you and your associates are behind me." Lodge bowed his head in assent.

As I now look back over twenty years and review the words of Senator Lodge—"If the Foreign Relations Committee approves it I feel there is no doubt of ratification"—I read into it a very subtle difference from its apparent meaning. Certainly the facts justify the impression that he already intended to block ratification, in the Committee and on the floor, for he attacked the League in a speech two days later and a few other Senators chimed in. Nevertheless, as far as anyone could judge at the time, this opposition did not represent the sentiment of the country. Mr. William H. Taft had just finished a long speaking tour in favour of the League, and believed the people for it. The press of the country confirmed this opinion.

On the night of our return departure for Paris the President answered his critics in a speech at the Metropolitan Opera House in New York. I have heard that there were one hundred thousand applications for tickets. To preside at the meeting, Mr. Taft interrupted a vacation ordered by his physician. In his speech introducing Mr. Wilson the former President took up the objections to the League one by one, refuting them so masterfully that my husband afterwards told me he wondered what would be left for him to say. The reception given my husband exceeded that in Boston, which, after a week of sniping at the League, was doubly heartening. When the band struck up "Over There" he said that he would not come back "until it is over, over there," and when he did come back he would bring a League Covenant that the American people could continue to support.

As soon as the President had finished speaking Mr. Cleveland H. Dodge, Woodrow's lifelong friend and classmate, and I left our box and made our way back stage. We found my husband facing Mr. Tumulty and looking very grim for one who had just received such a heart-warming ovation. "No," he was saying. "You can tell

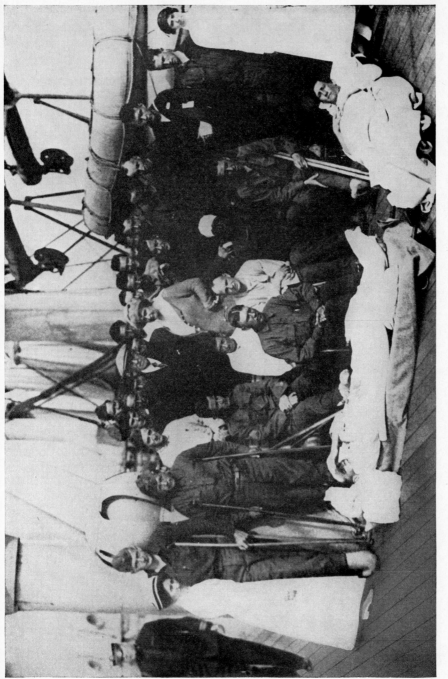

PRESIDENT AND MRS. WILSON WITH WOUNDED SOLDIERS ON S.S. *George Washington*, JULY 7, 1919

them I will wait five minutes. If in that time the rest of them want to come I will receive them; if not, I will go to the dock."

What had happened was this. The President had been asked to receive a group of Irish-American leaders who wished to present a paper. He had consented to do so, with the proviso that Daniel F. Cohalan should not accompany them. During the War Cohalan had been a great disturber. Nevertheless the committee had shown up, headed by Cohalan. Tumulty was urging the President to relent. "Oh, Governor," he pleaded, "this will make a terrible impression on his followers." Cohalan was an influential political leader. The President took out his watch. "That's just what I want it to do, Tumulty; but I think it will make a good impression on decent people."

It was then after eleven and we were due to sail at midnight. Tumulty reluctantly departed on his errand, and in less than five minutes he was showing in the committee minus their leader. As such things often happen, the mission, being leaderless, sort of petered out. They stood awkward and embarrassed, and though my husband tried to put them at their ease, his eyes were blazing at the trick they had tried to perpetrate by having this man run in at the last moment. They soon slunk away, and we immediately left for the steamer, having to run to get aboard in time. Mr. Dodge was so emotional that he kissed me goodbye, saying: "God bless you for taking care of this great man whom the world needs."

Our doughboy chauffeur, waiting at the gangway, greeted us warmly.

As on the previous voyage, marines patrolled the deck outside the windows of our rooms, marching back and forth, day and night, with their guns ready for use. It was monotonous and deadly dull work. One night I was awake and, missing the even sound of the feet that had become so familiar, I got up and looked out to see a very young boy leaning against the rail, with gun at rest, sound asleep. "Poor fellow," I thought, "let him sleep." Just then I saw, at the other end of the deck, the officer approaching on his round of inspection. I knew that if the boy were discovered asleep the penalty would be severe; also that if I spoke to awaken him the officer would hear. So quickly I gave a loud attempt at a sneeze, which had the desired effect. The young marine jumped, seized his gun, and like a machine operated by a spring resumed his march. The officer came along, and said kindly: "Not catching cold, are you, soldier?"

This reminds me of a story the Bishop of Washington, the Right Reverend James E. Freeman, has told me since. It is so characteristic of my husband that I venture to repeat it.

During the War Bishop Freeman was an Army chaplain. Two soldiers whom he had known in training camp as highly honourable and trustworthy had been given night guard duty near the front. They had been discovered asleep, tried by court-martial, and condemned to be shot.

The chaplain was so shocked that he immediately rushed to the War Department to beg the Chief of Staff, General Peyton C. March, to look into the case and see if there were not some extenuating circumstance. He met with a stern refusal. Nothing daunted, he insisted upon seeing Mr. Newton D. Baker, Secretary of War. There he again told his story, but the Secretary said: "No, I cannot interfere, horrible as it is; this is war and until it is over every humanity is adjourned where duty is concerned. Think of the other lives they put in danger; the whole course of the War might have hung on this one mistake."

Chaplain Freeman had to agree that was all true, but was determined to appeal to a higher court. He came over to the Executive Offices, and was given an appointment with the President for two o'clock.

On the minute, the Bishop told me, the President entered the Green Room. Knowing the overwhelming demand on the President's time the chaplain had expected to remain standing while he repeated his story as briefly as possible. "But," he said, "the President held out his hand and, after shaking mine, drew up a chair for me, and seated himself. There was no evidence of hurry or any but the most concentrated attention to every word I said. No one could have shown deeper sympathy than he, and, when the story was finished, he said: 'Of course this is a most serious offense, and what the Secretary of War says is true. But every man must have justice, and I will at once give orders for the delay in the execution until I have the facts before me.' Then rising, and again taking my hand, he said: 'And I pray they will be such that these young lives can be spared.'"

The sequel, the Bishop told me, was that the records showed the men had been without sleep for two days and nights, and that their previous records were splendid. Therefore, the President rescinded their punishment, saying the circumstances proved that only the limitation of physical endurance was responsible.

And now back to the boat. I am glad to linger on this scene, crossing the mighty deep, where my husband was as happy as a boy. For though there was still much work before him, it never irked him if he could see accomplishment ahead. And now there seemed every reason to believe that no matter how complicated national ambitions warring against one another made the terms of peace, with the League of Nations as part of the Treaty there would be set up the pacific means of readjusting any mistake. We used to walk the deck together, and he would tell me how much this eased his anxieties. "It is beyond human power to satisfy every one," he would say. "So the best we can hope for is not to satisfy any one entirely—strange as that may seem; for only so, with give and take, can we come to an agreement. As the United States wants nothing we are in a wonderful position; but by the same token my task is harder, because all these oppressed people look to me to fight for them. God knows I wish I could give them all they hope for, but only He Himself could do that."

Again we landed at Brest, but this time too late to make the night trip to Paris. The usual official party came aboard in a tender, and among them we were surprised to see Colonel House. My husband said that if I would do the courtesies to the French people, he would go to his compartment and talk to Colonel House and get in touch with what had been done at the Conference while he had been away.

I look back on that moment as a crisis in his life, and feel that from it dated the long years of illness, due to overwork, and that with the wreckage of his plans and his life have come these tragic years that have demoralized the world.

The welcoming officials said their speeches and departed. Passengers went to bed. My husband and Colonel House talked on while I waited in my adjoining stateroom. It was after midnight, and very still aboard, when I heard my husband's door open and the Colonel take his leave. I opened the door connecting our rooms. Woodrow was standing. The change in his appearance shocked me. He seemed to have aged ten years, and his jaw was set in that way it had when he was making superhuman effort to control himself. Silently he held out his hand, which I grasped, crying: "What is the matter? What has happened?"

He smiled bitterly. "House has given away everything I had won before we left Paris. He has compromised on every side, and so I have to start all over again and this time it will be harder, as he has given the impression that my delegates are not in sympathy with me. His own explanation of his compromises is that, with a hostile press in the United States expressing disapproval of the League of Nations as a part of the Treaty, he thought it best to yield some other points lest the Conference withdraw its approval altogether. So he has yielded until there is nothing left."

I was speechless, knowing the fact to be that the great majority of the press was for the League. Bursting with indignation, I stood holding my husband's hand. Before I got myself together, he threw back his head. The light of battle was in his eyes. "Well," he said, "thank God I can still fight, and I'll win them back or never look these boys I sent over here in the face again. They lost battles—but won the War, bless them. So don't be too dismayed."

We sat down and talked until early morning.

THE KING AND QUEEN OF THE BELGIANS, AND PRESIDENT AND MRS. WILSON
In garden of Palace, Brussels, June, 1919.

CHAPTER 19

A NEW home awaited us in Paris—a house on the Place des États-Unis, where Bartholdi's statue of La Fayette and Washington gives a friendly welcome. It was less ornate than the palace of the Prince Murat, and more homey. My first feeling was that here people had been happy. This I took as a good omen, and, to tell the truth, my spirit needed lifting that mid-March morning in 1919.

Our rooms were on the first floor, the President's in the back, looking upon the garden; mine on the street. My bath was a marvel. The tub was sunk almost like a small pool, and the walls tiled in rich cream. From the four corners rose the patterns of life-sized apple trees in bloom. On the porcelain of the tub were a few pink petals, as if they had dropped from the blossoms above. Where the branches of the trees met, in the centre of the ceiling, a chandelier hung like a bough, on which sat birds of various colours. Gay-hued butterflies, on slender wires, hovered over the blooms. The faucets of the washstand were of gold.

It was all so frivolous that I ran for my husband to come and see it. He smiled: "I think, like the King of Italy, I could not live in this place."

This house was suddenly transformed into a workshop as the President, without an hour's delay, laid about him to win back what had been surrendered by Colonel House. The chief compromise yielded by the Colonel affected the League of Nations, which now was in danger of being dropped from the Treaty and pushed off into the vague future. Many "insiders" thought the League dead. Calling Mr. Ray Stannard Baker to the house Mr. Wilson issued, through him, a statement to the press—dispassionate, but unmistakable and firm. "The decision made at the Peace Conference in its plenary session, January 25, 1919, to the effect that the establishment of the League of Nations should be made an integral part of the Treaty of Peace is of final force, and there is no basis whatever for the reports

247

that a change in this decision was contemplated." So much for the "trades" made in Wilson's absence. The statement caused a sensation.

My husband's study became the daily meeting place of the so-called Big Four—Clemenceau, Lloyd George, Orlando and Wilson. The walls of the antechamber connecting my apartment with my husband's were hung with huge maps on which new boundaries were traced. The room buzzed with experts, passing in and out of the study, and up and down the stairs. The ballroom on the second floor was converted into an office, alive with the clatter of typewriters.

"All to do over again," my husband had said to me on the night we arrived. So it was, and against increasing odds. The French and the English papers had taken up the cause of the opposition to a moderate, workable peace, and to the League. Partisan opposition was increasing at home. In addition to his fight to keep the Covenant of the League in the Treaty, the President had also to procure amendments to that instrument to allay critical opinion at home. Not all this critical opinion was hostile. The President was in communication, by letter and by cable, with Mr. Taft, whose attitude was helpful and understanding. He believed some of the changes advocated by friendly home critics in truth unnecessary, but his urging of their acceptance was to strengthen the League's case in the face of the hostile opposition.

To satisfy home demands without impairing the League's structure was one task. Another was to meet foreign opposition, particularly that of cynical old Clemenceau. Sessions lasted far into the night. The President grew thin and grey, but there was no resisting his determined purpose to hold the delegates to their pledge to incorporate the League into the Treaty, and to discover a formula for acceptable amendments. Under this terrific strain of work and anxiety a more robust man might have broken. But had not a severe attack of grippe laid him low the fight would have gone on without respite. When the dread disease struck there was little reserve to fight with. He was too ill to rise from his bed. However, things were at such a crisis that he would not relax his personal hold. Taking advantage of the President's dilemma, Clemenceau had pressed his demand for an uncollectable sum of reparations, and the Italians their claim to Fiume. The President opposed both.

With these great interlocked questions hanging fire, Mr. Wilson sent word that unless Clemenceau, Lloyd George and Orlando were afraid of the disease he wanted them to meet in his room, as usual. This they did, while Dr. Grayson and I sat outside fuming, for the President was sapping every drop of vitality left. Then came a night of burning fever. Finding the chest was involved, Dr. Grayson forbade further work. We went about on tiptoe as our patient lay utterly spent, fitfully asleep.

More days of tense anxiety. Getting better, the President insisted on knowing what had gone forward while he had been incapacitated. Alas, his absence had been taken advantage of again. The news that came to him was so grave we trembled for the effect on him. But the spirit was stronger than the flesh, and instead of causing a relapse it stiffened his will. Silently I sat beside his bed, knowing that he was formulating his course. At length he said: "I can never sign a Treaty made on these lines, and if all the rest of the delegates have determined on this, I will not be a party to it. If I have lost my fight, which I would not have done had I been on my feet, I will retire in good order; so we will go home. Call Grayson for me, please."

When Admiral Grayson came in the President said: "Grayson, I wish you would send word to Captain McCauley that I want the *George Washington* put in shape at once for my return home as soon as you think it is safe for me to make the trip."

These orders were forwarded promptly. As soon as the news got out the heads of Commissions began rushing to our house, consternation written on their faces.

From a standpoint of health, Dr. Grayson felt it unwise for the President to see them. As my husband was now anxious to get away as soon as possible, he accepted the suggestion of his physician. Though it was not done for that reason, this had the effect of further exciting the Conference. Failing to see the President, statesmen big and little began to write him letters, begging him to remain and holding out hopes for an adjustment of conflicting views. Clemenceau, Lloyd George and Orlando, for all their aggressive desires to get everything for their own countries, gave proof that they respected and trusted Mr. Wilson; particularly was this true of Orlando. Once more it was plainly demonstrated that without the President and the fight he was making for a just peace, the Treaty would be less acceptable than otherwise. The small nations looked to him as their one hope. Mr. Wilson did not want, or intend, to leave Paris if there was still a fighting chance for terms he could sanction. So the order regarding the *George Washington* was rescinded, and, as soon as the Doctor was willing, the President resumed his work.

Within a few days the amendments to the League Covenant were adopted. Mr. David H. Miller, legal adviser to the American Commission, has left an account of one of the meetings at which this occurred. I will quote Mr. Miller. "At the close of the debate, President Wilson replied to the French in an extempore speech of witching eloquence—a speech made after midnight, which left the secretaries gasping with admiration, their pencils in their hands, their duties forgotten, and hardly a word taken down."

Such efforts took their toll in strength from the man just up from a sickbed. I was dreadfully alarmed. The foreign press grew increasingly hostile. A section of the American press, reflecting the views of the "irreconcilable" Senators, attacked the League amendments as not being sufficiently broad. Certain English and American newspapers began publishing perfect eulogies of Colonel House. One afternoon when the President had walked across the street to Mr. Lloyd George's apartment, I opened a consignment of home papers that had just arrived. In one was an article saying that the only constructive work of the American delegation had been done while President Wilson was away and Colonel House in charge. The Colonel was described as "the brains of the Commission."

A tap at the door interrupted my reading. I said, "Come in," and Colonel House appeared.

"I came to see the Governor," he said, "and, finding him out, thought you would let me talk to you until he came back."

"Do come in," I said, "for you are all so busy I never see you."

He took off his overcoat and put it on the sofa; then drew up a chair near the fire, and began to talk over the difficulties of the work they were doing. As we talked in the old intimate way, without a thought beyond that of feeling he would be as distressed as I was over the article in the paper I had just put down, I picked it up and said: "Colonel, have you been reading these awful attacks on Woodrow, or have you been too busy? Just listen to this, which I know you will resent."

I read several paragraphs aloud. The Colonel's face turned crimson. "Has the Governor seen that article?" he asked. "No, it has just come," I replied. He sprang up, and taking his coat in one hand he held out the other saying: "Please let me have that to read. After all, I will not wait for the Governor." "Why," I said, "I thought you said you wanted to see him!" By this time he had reached the door, through which he fled as though pursued.

I was still sitting wondering about what had happened, when Dr. Grayson arrived and I told him how Colonel House had acted. "What do you make of it?" I asked.

"Mrs. Wilson," he said, "I did not want to worry you or the President with it, but everyone is talking about these articles, and the gossip is that Gordon Auchincloss [Colonel House's son-in-law] is inspiring them. Feeling just as you did that the Colonel would be the first to resent such a thing if he knew it, I went to him a week ago and talked to him about it, and came away feeling that the gossip was correct. Several of our friends among the newspaper people have told me that the man who writes these articles is always in the Colonel's room and gets his tips straight from him."

"I don't believe it, Dr. Grayson," I answered, "for if it were true Colonel House would be a traitor."

"Well," he said, "I don't say it is true, but that is what I hear. I even went so far as to mention the man's name to the Colonel and he said: 'There is nothing in it. I rarely ever see the man.' But, by a strange coincidence, the next day the newspaper man who had told me about it asked if I had done anything to draw it to the attention of the Colonel. I told him I had, and that the Colonel had said he rarely saw the man and there was nothing to it. At that, my newspaper friend said: 'Well, do you mind coming up on the roof with me?'"

This was at the Hotel Crillon where our Commission was housed. Dr. Grayson went to the roof where a photographer had his camera set up and was taking pictures of Colonel House and the writer of the articles standing with their arms around each other's shoulders. Dr. Grayson added: "When they saw me the Colonel dropped his friend and said: 'That is enough,' and quickly left the scene."

When my husband came in I told him of Colonel House's call and the incident of the newspaper article, but not what Dr. Grayson had said. "Oh, I am sorry you hurt House," exclaimed Woodrow. "I would as soon doubt your loyalty as his. All this is another attempt to misrepresent things at home."

All my husband had against the Colonel at this time was what he regarded as a grave error in judgment in failing to stand up against men with whom he wished to be on intimate terms. I remember having said: "Oh, if Colonel House had only stood firm while you were away none of this would have to be done over. I think he is a perfect jellyfish." To which Mr. Wilson had replied: "Well, God made jellyfish, so, as Shakespeare said about a man, therefore let him pass, and don't be too hard on House. It takes a pretty stiff spinal column to stand against the elements centred here."

Nevertheless, the conversation of the afternoon when he fled my drawing room proved to be my last with Colonel House. He did not come to our house again except for business meetings at which others were present; and on these occasions I did not see him. Some time later when I was recovering from an infected foot Colonel House sent me a cluster of my favourite orchids. As was our custom I thanked him by telephone instead of writing a note. That communication was our last word by mouth.

As I have said before, Sunday was the one possibly free day. So, on Sunday, March 23rd, the President suddenly decided to make another trip to the devastated regions.

We left by motor at 8 A. M., taking the Paris-Soissons road and pausing at Soissons where the magnificent Cathedral had been shattered almost as badly as the one at Rheims. Then on to the original emplacement of the "Big Bertha," in the forest near Crépy-en-Laonnais, from which the Germans had shelled Paris exactly one year before to the day. We saw where the rush of flame from the muzzle had withered the trees and killed vegetation in front of the monster cannon's position. There was a huge concrete base on which the gun had rested, and leading up to it a narrow-gauge railroad to carry ammunition. To show the very clever camouflage, this railroad led through a dense wood where the trees had been cut only in its course. Between the cross ties, metal receptacles had been sunk where the cut trees were placed except when the ammunition trains were in motion.

One day I went to a gala performance given for a French charity where Madame Sarah Bernhardt recited a poem by Fernaud Gregh. This was after she had lost her leg; so she was borne in on a sort of float with white draperies so arranged that she seemed to be emerging from clouds. Her voice was exquisite and as musical as that of Madame Tetrazzini who sang later on in the performance. The Queen of Rumania was there in a box, and I had as my guests Madame Poincaré and Madame Deschanel; also the wives of our Peace Commissioners. The performance was a sort of revue, and one scene represented the great literary men of France—Balzac, Dumas, and so on. When Dumas entered one of my French guests exclaimed: *"Voilà,* Dumas," at which a U. S. A. lady was instantaneously transformed from a languid, disinterested listener to a lion-hunter keen on the scent. "Oh," she exclaimed, "I didn't know he was in Paris; we must have him to dinner!"

On April 11th, there was a plenary session of the League of Nations Committee at 8:30 p. m., and one of the questions which came up for discussion was the permanent location of the seat of the League. Brussels had been recommended by a special committee consisting of Colonel House, Baron Makino for Japan, Signor Orlando for Italy and General Smuts for South Africa. I quote from the London *Daily Mail* for April 12th:

"Mr. Paul Hymans, head of the Belgian delegation, made an eloquent appeal in favour of his country; but the feature of the debate was the intervention of President Wilson, who, rising from his place at the table contrary to the usual custom, spoke with great eloquence of the reasons—in his opinion—which made it desirable that Geneva should be the seat of the League. He said the League must not be originated out of the hate and enmity which had marked the great war; its seat ought to be removed from the souvenirs of the conflict, and be located in a neutral country. No country seemed better fitted for this than Switzerland. He was also in favour of the League being established in a city which was not a capital, and thus removed from political influence."

Geneva was formally chosen.

Following this, a day came when there was no scheduled meeting of the Council of Four. The President devoted it to seeing people who had been waiting for an audience. He began at ten in the morning with the members of the Chinese delegation; next the French delegation to discuss the question of the left bank of the Rhine; the Foreign Minister of Switzerland; a delegate from Chaldea; two American women labour leaders; the patriarch of Constantinople; Mr. Bratiano, Foreign Minister of Rumania; Premier Pachitch of Serbia; the Portuguese Minister; Mr. Herbert Hoover; Mr. Newton D. Baker; and the chargé d'affaires of San Marino who called to present a certificate of honourary citizenship conferred on the President by that little principality.

With "holidays" like this is it surprising that I rejoiced when a free evening came and we went to a theatre called "A War Baby" (because it was built by the soldiers) to the opening of *Hello Paris?* The audience was made up of delegates from nearly every country. At least for a few hours my husband's thoughts could be diverted from Shantung, Fiume, reparations and all the other problems over which there was such bitter feeling.

How I wished there was some way I could share the ever-increasing burdens. Every hour of my husband's time was claimed and when the night conferences were over he would turn to a desk filled with demands from Washington. I waited up until the grind ceased and, as he ate almost nothing at table, I would have a glass of milk and some tiny sandwiches provided. At first the old maître d'hôtel brought three sandwiches, about the size of a silver dollar. After two or three nights he reduced them to two, saying the third was not eaten. Some nights, indeed, my husband ate only one, but, lest French thrift use this as an excuse for reducing our ration again, I concealed the true state of affairs by giving the extra sandwich to the doughboy on guard outside our door.

Italy's great grievance was Fiume. Mr. Wilson had steadfastly refused to give this port to Italy, on the ground that, by right of nationality, it belonged to the new Jugo-Slav State. France and England concurred, but let Wilson do most of the fighting. On a Saturday Orlando, Clemenceau, Balfour and my husband met at our house for a final discussion. Orlando remained obdurate in his opposition to the other three. The meeting adjourned with the understanding that Clemenceau, Balfour and my husband were each to give to the press a statement of his country's view of the question.

All Sunday forenoon the President worked on his statement, for, realizing the seriousness of the matter, he wished to make things clear not only at home but in Italy as well. I was quite resentful to see his rest day broken into. About lunchtime, when the draft was ready to be typed, a messenger arrived from Mr. Balfour saying, as he had not had time to write his statement, would President Wilson kindly permit him to have a copy of what he had written to use as an outline. This my husband did, and on the Wednesday following gave a copy to the press as agreed.

Next morning the President's statement was on the front page of every paper at home and abroad, but not one word from either Balfour or Clemenceau. A deluge of adverse comment came from the Italian Commission—all directed against my husband. He was white with anger. When an explanation was asked for, the smug answer was that, after seeing President Wilson's paper, Mr. Balfour had conferred with M. Clemenceau, whereupon both felt that Wilson had made such a fine exposition of the situation nothing they could add would strengthen the case against Italy: so they had agreed to make no statement. In other words, knowing it would be an unpopular decision in Italy, they decided to hide behind the President and shirk responsibility.

With all the dramatic ostentation of a scene from an Italian opera, Orlando summoned a train and prepared to abandon the Conference and go back to his people with this tale of outrageous treatment at the hands of the President of the United States. Just before he boarded the train a statement written by Mr. Balfour, confirming the stand of England and France in the denial of Fiume to Italy, was handed to Signor Orlando. Mr. Balfour did not give this to the papers, however. Orlando did not give it to the papers. Italy's fury, and that of the reactionary elements in France, England and even the United States, continued to be directed at Mr. Wilson alone.

Affairs of this kind prompted stories that Mr. Wilson did not understand European diplomacy and could not cope with Old World statesmen. I thank God that there is some truth in the statement. Never did he turn from the weapons of truth and right, as he saw them, and I think the world realizes now that the ends of all would have been better served if more of his views had prevailed.

Throughout Italy pictures of the President were torn down and the candles that were burning in front of them extinguished. Clemenceau and Lloyd George worked on Mr. Wilson to relent on Fiume. He refused, and there was nothing for Orlando to do but come back in case he wished to sign the Treaty which was then nearing completion.

His arrival was unheralded and as dramatic as his departure, though unconsciously so. Clemenceau and Lloyd George were in my husband's study. Mr. Wilson told me that at the moment Orlando was announced Lloyd George was loudly denouncing him as a quitter. The President really liked Orlando, and, on questions where Italy's interests were not involved, had received useful and enlightened support from him. The little Italian seemed so crestfallen that my husband tried to make his greeting seem casual and natural. Unlike Clemenceau, Orlando did not understand English beyond a few phrases.

On this occasion this was fortunate, for otherwise Lloyd George's words would have made the meeting more awkward than it was. After my husband's cheerful greeting, Orlando brightened up and asked innocently: "Mr. President, what subject are you met to discuss this morning?" The President answered: "Well, Mr. Orlando, we are still trying to get Fiume on the map." Orlando walked over to a window, and pressing his face against the glass began to weep. "Poor fellow," said my husband, telling me the story, "of course his Government had given him the devil, and I felt sorry for him. So I went over to the window and told him it was no lack of tact and ability on his part, but just the very stern necessity we were all under to try to give every country just treatment and to consider everyone's claim. I led him gently back to his accustomed chair, feeling as though he were a little boy, and that I ought to take out my handkerchief and dry his tears."

Not long after the meeting was over I received a basket of wonderful orchids—with Signor Orlando's card attached.

May 1st is always a day of tension in Paris and often of rioting and bloodshed. This year, with so much in the air, the papers had counselled citizens to keep indoors unless on essential errands. My husband had a meeting at the Quai d'Orsay and I drove over with him, finding the streets almost deserted except for soldiers. These stood guard at every bridge over the Seine, and great piles of sandbags were ready to form barricades if need be. An ominous silence hung over the Place de la Concorde. The day before it had teemed with traffic. Now it was empty—not even a cruising taxicab in sight.

Leaving my husband, I drove home and intended to stay there, but the weather was too enticing. So, getting Miss Benham, I drove to the Bois. Here, too, was absolute quiet—not even soldiers. We sent the car back and walked home. When my husband arrived he was shocked at the risk we had run. He said there had been serious riots in many places in the city, and reports that several persons had been killed.

To add to the excitement of that day, the German Peace Commissioners had arrived only twenty-four hours before. They had been conducted to the Hôtel des Réservoirs, in Versailles, which was closely guarded. The delegation was astonishingly large, numbering about one hundred and fifty, counting experts, secretaries and so on. They resented the guard which made them look like prisoners. Clemenceau was a bitter old man, and with reason; but in part, at least, the guard was for the Germans' protection and not merely to humiliate them.

At long last the Treaty was done, and on May 7th it was formally presented to the Germans at the Trianon Palace, Versailles. It comprised a book of two hundred and fourteen pages. The Germans were given fifteen days in which to submit comments and receive the Allies' answer in writing and to say whether they would sign. Immediately began the desperate effort of the Germans to obtain a relaxation of the terms—in some respects unmistakably harsh. On the matter of reparations, especially, my husband believed France and England had gone too far. They had imposed indemnities far beyond the capacity of Germany to pay, especially in view of industrial restrictions which would hamper the beaten nation's economic recovery. All these matters, my husband thought, would properly come before the League of Nations for adjustment after the passions engendered by the War had cooled somewhat.

At the expiration of fifteen days the Germans were given more time. Then the original delegation was called home to be replaced by another. While this change is being made I will go back a little to tell of the arrival in Paris of Her Majesty the Queen of Rumania. She stayed at the Ritz Hotel with her two daughters, then young ladies (afterwards the Queens of Jugo-Slavia and Greece), her sister the Infanta of Spain, and ladies and gentlemen in waiting. She immediately sent a message saying she would like to receive us as early as possible. We found Her Majesty in a soft grey dress which, with her blonde hair and blue eyes, was very becoming. She was alone, and at once plunged into the claims of Rumania at the Conference, insisting upon going into great details. She reviewed the new Russian laws concerning sexual relations, saying the proximity of Russia to her country made the menace very real. At first my husband listened courteously and attentively but presently he held up his hand and said: "Permit me to assure Your Majesty that all this was conveyed to me through dispatches long before I left the United States, and it has been thoroughly considered by the Conference. Also your Prime Minister, M. Bratiano, has faithfully presented Rumania's case. So it is useless for me to claim more of your time regarding it."

He rose to end the interview. She put her hand on his arm, trying to reseat him on the sofa beside her, and in dulcet tones said: "Oh, Bratiano! He is not getting anywhere with such men as you." When my husband did not yield the Queen tried another tack. Lifting from the mantelpiece a photograph of a dark-haired girl of ten or twelve years, she held it up to him, saying: "This, Mr. President, is a picture of my youngest daughter, Ileana. My love child I call her. Is she not lovely? My other girls are blonde, like me; but she—oh, she is dark and passionate."

By the time she had finished speaking we were all standing, waiting to say goodbye—which we did very promptly, and she escorted us to the elevator. When we got in the car, Admiral Grayson, who, as naval aide to the President, had accompanied us, said: "Well, in all my experience I have never heard a lady talk about such things. I honestly did not know where to look, I was so embarrassed." "Yes," I said, "I could not help watching you with great amusement, for you seemed to shrink with each new word she said until you grew smaller and smaller before my very eyes!"

My husband said nothing. So I looked around and seeing his jaw set, knew this very beautiful woman had met one man whom she had failed to charm.

A few days later I met her again at the Grand Palais, which had been converted into a hive of workers teaching the poor mutilates of the War how to start life again maimed or blind. She hailed me

· sweetly and graciously and I could not suppress an admission to myself that her beauty made her seem an ideal queen. "What day can
you and the President come to dinner with me?" she asked. I told
her that unfortunately we neither lunched nor dined out, so she must
excuse us. She insisted, and I firmly declined. "Then I will propose
myself to lunch with you," she said. "You can't be so rude as to tell
me not to come. Shall it be tomorrow?" "No," I said. "There is a
long and important conference for my husband tomorrow; let
us say the following day at one o'clock." "Good," she answered.
"I will be there with my two girls, my sister, and one or two of my
gentlemen."

This was unwelcome news to my husband, but he agreed it was
not possible to refuse her. In addition to our household which included, besides ourselves, only Dr. Grayson and my secretary, Miss
Benham, we had General Harts and two young aides for the young
princesses.

It proved to be a beautiful spring day, and, while we waited for
the Queen's arrival, the windows were open overlooking the little
park opposite the house where some lilac bushes were in their first
bloom. As usual, many things claimed my husband, but he had put
them aside to be ready to join me at the door to welcome the Queen.
We waited up in the drawing room, from which we could see her
car approach and have ample time to go down before she reached the
entrance.

We were talking, and happy to be together, and did not notice the
time until the big French clock on the mantel struck the first quarter
of the hour. "Surely," I said, "that must be wrong. I told her one
o'clock and that says a quarter past." My husband consulted his
watch. "Yes," he said, "that is right; and I have an appointment at
two-thirty."

At one-thirty she still had not come, and the President said:
"Come, let's go in to lunch. This is extremely rude, and we are not
called upon to delay any longer."

As we went out I found all the servants standing like sentinels on
either side of the door, at the top and bottom of the stairs, and of
course at the entrance. When we were halfway downstairs, with a
great throbbing of motor engines the party arrived—thirty-five
minutes late. There were five ladies and five gentlemen, led by the

Queen, who clasped both my husband's hands in affected repentance for being late.

However, lunch went off very pleasantly in spite of the bad start, and we all liked the Infanta of Spain very much. She was not as pretty as her sister, but had more dignity, and was very clever. The two Princesses, however, were very shy, uninteresting, and German in type.

On May 30th I went on crutches, owing to an infected foot, to the American military cemetery at Suresnes where the President was to make a Memorial Day address. The weather was perfect—one of those radiant days of spring when Nature is calling everything awake. As we drove out through Paris the world seemed truly a place of peace and beauty. But when we reached the cemetery the long endless rows of wooden crosses, around which grateful French women had twined flowers or placed the Stars and Stripes to flutter in the soft air, brought a lump to our throats. The picture is one I cannot forget. Back of the crosses marking the last resting places of so many of our boys was a hillside covered with boys in khaki who had been spared to live on in the world they had fought to make better. Many of them showed scars or an empty sleeve; and their young faces seemed mature and thoughtful that day.

In the centre of the cemetery on a small platform stood the President, his head bared—and how white the hair had grown those last few months—his tall, slight form tense with emotion, as he spoke to the living and for the dead in a passionate plea to end all wars and never again make such sacrifice necessary.

When the speech was finished people were sobbing. For myself I could not speak for the tears. We drove home in silence, for my husband's control had also broken and only by supreme effort had he been able to finish his speech.

This man, whom the world sometimes judged cold, had a heart that bled with every drop that was shed by the boys he had to send to their death in the hope of saving humanity! How many times I have thought of that May day in that city of the dead and wondered if men like Mr. Henry Cabot Lodge and his supporters in the Senate could have been there for just that hour would they have dared vote against any instrument, such as the League of Nations, to stop war! I wonder!

Now that the labours of the Peace Commissioners were done the French insisted they must give a gala performance at the Opera House for us. Although rest and quiet was what my husband most coveted, it would have seemed discourteous to decline. The night was decided on, and the opera was to be *Faust*. The splendid building was packed from pit to dome; everyone in evening clothes, and the women ablaze with jewels. We had a box draped with the Stars and Stripes and the tricolour of France. Between the acts, as is the French custom, the entire audience would stand and focus their glasses upon us with such unblushing stares that I felt like a new specimen of insect being studied under a microscope. To escape we retreated to the foyer, only to encounter the same thing at closer range. So it was a relief when the manager came to invite us behind the curtain to see the artists and their dressing rooms. This part was interesting, and particularly the room where the ballet dancers "warm up" before going on. It is a large room, and on either side were bars for exercising; also sets of pulleys for making arm and leg muscles supple. Mr. Henry White had told me much of this room, which he said was quite a rendezvous for the gilded youth when he was a young attaché in Paris. Though the room was interesting, the ladies of the ballet looked rather weatherbeaten, as though they might have been the same ones who had beguiled Mr. White before the naughty 'nineties.

The new German delegation arrived and continued to haggle about signing. We took advantage of the delay to accept an invitation of the King and Queen of the Belgians to visit their country. Margaret Wilson, Miss Benham, Dr. Grayson, Mr. Herbert Hoover, Mr. Bernard M. Baruch, Mr. Norman H. Davis and Mr. Vance McCormick accompanied us. At the frontier we were met by Their Majesties, who had come by plane.

At this point we transferred to automobiles, the King and Mr. Wilson riding in the first one, and the Queen and I in the next. These were Belgian cars, with the royal arms on the doors and upholstered with crimson brocade. The others were open touring cars, furnished by the United States Army. The Secret Service men followed the car in which I rode. Then came the other members of our party, followed by representatives of the press, photographers and so on. When we strung out we looked like a division of an army on the march. There had been little time to repair the war-torn roads, which were fearful in places and everywhere dust rose in clouds.

As our itinerary covered most of Belgium, we started off at a good clip. Her Majesty asked if I minded if she closed the car tightly for, as she had hay fever, the dust was very painful. I certainly did not mind. The Queen added that only two kinds of flowers, which she named, brought on her affliction. "I hope," she said, "we will have none of them given us today."

I found her easy to know, with a keen interest in affairs, a splendid sense of humour, and a happy way of telling of the things she had done and seen during the War, so that much of the horror of those awful days was touched lightly. When she was telling me of some of her work in the hospitals, I said: "But it is surprising that without training you could know what to do." "Not a bit," she laughed. "You see, my father was a German doctor. I had been much with him and learned more than I realized, and when I needed it, it all came back to me."

As we passed through villages, no matter how small, the streets were packed with people, throwing flowers and waving the Stars and Stripes together with their flag of orange, crimson and black. In many places where only wreckage met the eye, a few forlorn figures would emerge from cellars to smile a wan welcome. Our cars would stop at a shell-riddled old *hôtel de ville* and a gentleman in worn frock coat would be on the step to greet us and ask us to sign the *"Livre d'Or."* Usually this ceremony was celebrated by opening champagne where, in these desolated buildings, a toast was offered and returned. I always wished I could give my glass to one of the poor old women standing near, whom life seemed to have pushed aside and forgotten.

At the first stop of this kind, when we were re-entering the motors, Margaret ran to the one we were in and said: "Edith, may I not ride with you all? Our car is open and the dust back there is terrible." I asked Her Majesty if it would be agreeable, moving over to show there was plenty of room for three on the seat. As a matter of fact it would have been more comfortable for us all as we would not have rolled about so much. But apparently the Queen regarded the request as *lèse majesté*. None too cordially she leaned forward and said to the footman to put up the little seat for Mademoiselle.

LEAVING VERSAILLES AFTER SIGNING OF PEACE TREATY, JUNE 28, 1919
Left to right: Honorable Lloyd George, M. Clemenceau and President Wilson.

The little seat was properly termed, for it was about nine inches in the centre, tapering off to nothing at the ends, and so low there was no room for feet except straight out in front. There was nothing for Margaret to do but accept the decision. She got in, and after her came two huge bouquets of flowers for the Queen and for me. Then the door was shut and we bounded off at about sixty miles an hour, for this delay had left us far behind the car bearing the King and my husband. Alas! with the first leap of the motor poor Margaret leaped too and came down in a heap on the floor. Her heavy mesh bag shot off like a cannon ball against the Queen who, poor lady, was sneezing at about the same rate the motor was racing, for the bouquets were made up of the two flowers she had said she could never have near her.

It all happened so quickly I felt I was taking part in a nightmare. I took the flowers and suggested we throw them out of the window; but the Queen—between sneezes—said that would let in dust which would kill her. She signalled the chauffeur to stop. This was dangerous, for the cars in line behind us were coming at terrific speed; so on we tore with both men on the box trying to find a place to turn out, and signalling the other cars to stop. Finally we swerved into a side road and stopped so suddenly that again Margaret and her possessions went all over the floor. The footman solemnly helped her up, collected her things, took the two great armfuls of flowers, and was just closing the door when out of a white cloud of dust came a group of children who flung into our laps more sprays of the dreaded flowers. The door slammed, the footman climbed nimbly to his seat, and again we started—no better off than when we halted.

By this time our royal hostess reminded me of a conjurer, for handkerchiefs were being taken out of her sleeves, her bag, the pockets of the car, and from the mysterious folds of a woman's garments. She was red-eyed and weeping. Again I ventured to suggest that if Margaret could sit with us we could put the flowers in the front and cover them with the linen lap-robe. The Queen firmly shook her head and gasped: "No, if she prefers this car she must sit there." So I could do no more.

Conversation was adjourned, and our time was spent in restoring Margaret right side up and finding handkerchiefs. It was a joy to reach the place where we were to have lunch.

This proved a delightful experience, though somewhat unreal. Of what had been a great wood adjoining a prosperous, happy village, not one tree or building was standing. Interspersed among the stumps of trees were shell holes twenty feet deep. Round the edges of some of these waved red poppies—nature trying to hide the wounds with which the inventions of man had mutilated her.

Here was stretched a huge white canvas to shelter us from the sun. Under it was laid a long table set with rare china and glass and decorated beautifully. Around the table were placed chairs for the entire party. Liveried servants served a lunch such as one would expect only in a palace. It was a unique experience—to be eating and drinking here where such a short time ago there had been such horror of death and destruction.

Lunch over, I was glad for her sake that Margaret decided to go back to another car where, in spite of the dust, I knew she would be more comfortable.

From here on, as I learned long afterwards, a joke was played on Mr. Herbert Hoover by the other men. His car was in fifth or sixth place, and naturally the farther from the head of the line the worse the dust. But the idea occurred to these men, as they put it, to "kid Hoover a little." "Why don't you sit with the chauffeur," they said, "where all these people can see you? After sending food here and helping the Belgians, they naturally want to see you, which they can't possibly do here in this shut-up car." "No," said Mr. Hoover. "They came out to see the President." "Nonsense," answered one of these teasers, "they want to see you, and we think you ought to be willing to gratify them. Get out there and see if it won't please them a lot!" So at the next stop Mr. Hoover solemnly mounted the box with the chauffeur, and was soon so covered with dust his best friend could not have recognized him.

The most interesting place we went, I thought, was Zeebrugge where we walked upon the mole and heard a British officer, who had been there, tell of the intrepid attack and landing on the mole. Ypres seemed the most desolate of all the towns, and the people so pitiful. There were just a handful of them, but so poor and hopeless. At Ostend things were better, but how utterly unlike that gay resort of prewar days!

At Bruges we got on a train, and it was a comfort to get a good wash and freshen up. In a brief time we reached Brussels, and here we were welcomed by many officials, after which we drove to the Palace. The Queen apologized for its condition, saying the Germans had left it denuded and there had been no time to refit it. However, we found everything more than comfortable, the only inconvenience being that my apartment was on one side of a great hall, where officers and servants were on continuous duty, and the President's on the other side. We had to go through all these bowing and saluting men each time we wanted to speak to each other. So many things came up about which we wanted to talk that it seemed we were constantly shunting back and forth.

Almost as soon as we reached the Palace we were asked to join Their Majesties and receive the Cabinet and other civil authorities. The Queen said to me: "Please excuse me if I don't know the names of any of these people any more than you do; they are all new and belong to the populace." The reception was soon over, for which we were exceedingly glad, because everyone was dead tired and ready for bed.

My poor husband, and all the men in the party, started at seven next morning on a long motor trip through the factory district which the Germans had wrecked and which Belgium was rebuilding. They were to be back in time to dress and go to a luncheon given for us by the American Minister and Mrs. Brand Whitlock. Mr. Whitlock was a boyhood friend of my husband. The King and Queen had also sent word they would lunch with them, which, as in Italy, was without precedent. I stayed in my room with my secretary to take care of the mail, and did not go out until it was time to start to the Whitlocks'.

As the King and Queen were to be there, the President and I were the nominal hosts, and were supposed to arrive in time to receive the royal couple. But alas, the hour struck and the men had not returned. I waited ten minutes; then I decided to go on, as they might be indefinitely delayed, and the Queen might go on alone without waiting for His Majesty. I had reached the door and was ready to step into the motor with Margaret Wilson and Miss Benham when the men arrived. The cars were so covered with dust they looked like white phantoms. In spite of their long linen dusters the men, too, were covered, even their hair and eyebrows being heavy with dust. I went on, and they followed in an incredibly short time, immaculate in morning coats and high hats.

The lunch was a very brief affair as we were due at the Hôtel de Ville where the freedom of the city was given my husband. From there we went to their Parliament where the President addressed the body. After thanking Their Majesties, the officials and the people for their gracious welcome, he said he wished more substantially to attest his admiration for Belgium by recommending that Congress recognize its importance as a nation and raise our diplomatic representative, his old friend Brand Whitlock, to the post of first American Ambassador to Belgium. When the President finished, and His Majesty had replied, Mr. Hoover was asked to speak. When he rose there was great applause, and he made a very good address indeed.

From Brussels we drove to Malines to have tea with Cardinal Mercier. He was on the steps of his palace to greet us, his towering form in the gorgeous crimson robes, with the great gold cross on his breast, making a striking picture. He took us into a long lofty room, on three sides of which had hung huge mirrors, set in lovely soft panelling of carved wood. Alas, the mirrors had been shattered, and in the vaulted roof gaped a hole showing the blue sky. This he explained had been made by a German bomb. "But," he smiled, "although this floor was covered with pallets on which many of my poor children lay wounded, none of them was killed—thanks to *le bon Dieu.*"

We could stay but twenty minutes, for there was still another long motor ride to Louvain, on which the Cardinal joined us. At Louvain we found hordes of people, many of them presenting flowers. I was deeply touched by the unmistakable love and reverence in which these people held Queen Élisabeth, for as she passed in her trailing robe of white, old women and men would lift the hem of her gown and kiss it. It was a beautiful tribute, and one I am sure she had earned by personal service and sacrifice.

Thus we entered all that was left of that historic and wonderful library, whose loss to the world can never be replaced. The old stone walls shattered by shells were still standing. An attempt had been made to cover the wreckage by spreading flowers everywhere. At the far end of what had been a great entrance room a small platform had been built and on it was spread the inevitable crimson carpet. High-backed chairs were placed in a circle on this, and here we were seated. It was hard to keep back the tears as I sat facing this emptiness presided over by old white-haired gentlemen whose lives had been devoted to enhancing the glory of this library. I was reminded of a line I had read somewhere: "Now tottering thunderstruck from root to crest, where can the soul from such black misery flee?"

One of the gentlemen rose, looking very dignified in a long-tailed black coat, and made a gracious speech of welcome, and then conferred a degree of the University of Louvain on my husband. Old Cardinal Mercier's tall form made a vivid splash of colour among the sombre black of the other gentlemen. We drove back to Brussels almost in silence, everyone felt so deeply stirred.

That night a State dinner at the Palace brought our visit to a close. His Majesty presented my husband with a souvenir he always deeply prized. It was a complete file of the little paper *La Libre Belgique,* which had given the Germans such trouble during their occupation of Belgium. Repeatedly the German commander decreed its suppression but it went serenely on, defying orders, spies, threats, everything—and the Germans never could find where or when it was published. Editors and printers knew that discovery meant death. So they moved from place to place, and one edition was printed in an automobile on an old hand press. Such was the courage and unquenchable patriotism that held Belgium together and brought her triumphant through four years of horror.

Returning on the next day, June 22nd, to Paris, we received the welcome news that the Germans would sign. This came in the nick of time, for the French, British and American troops on the Rhine were under orders to march on Berlin on the following day in case the Germans had not given in.

The ceremony of the signing was set for three o'clock on June 28th. We made arrangements to leave immediately afterwards for Brest to board the *George Washington.* The whole household went merrily to packing, and "home" was the word on everyone's lips. In the midst of this cheery bustle M. Jusserand called. President and Madame Poincaré wished to give us a farewell dinner on the evening of the 28th at the Élysée Palace. Again it was a case of *noblesse oblige,* and the train on which we had fondly hoped to get an early start for Brest was ordered for midnight.

The historic day dawned gloriously bright and clear. All Paris was astir early. Flags waved everywhere, and the streets were patrolled by soldiers. The official route was policed all the way. As we left the house the President gave me a lovely beaded bag of grey and blue made by an old lady who lived at Versailles. He had ordered it for me to match my gown. With it was a single crimson rosebud—the nearest he said he could come to the red, white and blue of our colours. Early that morning he had brought my favourite orchids, which I was wearing with a grey dress and hat. I put the red rosebud inside the little silk pocket of the bag, where it has long ago fallen into dust; but the perfume of that hour will always be fresh in my memory, and the bag a precious souvenir.

I love to think of my husband as he looked that day, for already the sense of freedom from that unremitting labour was relaxing the look of strain, and the happy thought of going home made him radiate content. The delegates all wore frock coats and high hats. We reached the Versailles Palace without hindrance, driving through crowds of people who were cheering and waving flags. The order was perfect, and everyone seemed glad to do his part in preserving it. Car followed car in quick succession to the foot of the long stairway, and greetings were heard on every side.

Margaret Wilson and Miss Benham went with me to the Hall of Mirrors where the ceremony was held and, curiously enough, where the German Empire had been proclaimed in 1871. Four documents were to be signed: the Peace Treaty, the Convention concerning Alsace-Lorraine, the Convention relative to the occupation of the Rhine territory, and the protocol recognizing the independence of Poland.

The President joined the other members of our Commission in the room from which each Commission was to enter in a body. At last the doors opened and the French came first headed by the old "Tiger," Clemenceau; then my husband, leading our Commission. I felt a curious tightening of the throat as I looked at his dear figure, grown more slender in those months, but alert and alive. Following him were Colonel House, a small man and unimpressive, except for his intelligent eyes; General Tasker H. Bliss, in uniform, looking very much the soldier; Mr. Lansing, also small, with grey hair; Mr. Henry White, a tall, courtly man of the world, walking with a slight limp—the result of a knee injury sustained years before.

The other groups followed quickly, and all took their places. Then fell a silence, broken at length by the sound of footsteps as the German signatories were conducted to their places on the right-hand side of the room. They seemed embarrassed and ill at ease, and were uniformly stolid, uninteresting-looking men. I could not help feeling had I been sending men, I would have selected more impressive-looking ones. They reminded me of prisoners before the bar of justice. They were the first to sign. Their Teutonic faces changed not an iota as they approached the table. The gold pen used was the work of a poilu and a gift of Alsace-Lorraine. The mechanical click of cameras and motion picture machines was the only sound on air so tense that I sat with gooseflesh all over me. When the Americans were called the voice of Mrs. House awakened my sense of reality. "Please," she said, "just let me stand long enough to see my lamb sign."

At 3:40 the booming of cannon announced the long-looked-for Peace. Already in the great Hall of Mirrors the spectators were becoming restless when Clemenceau abruptly pronounced the ceremony at an end.

The President was asked to walk through a part of the grounds with M. Clemenceau, Mr. Lloyd George and Signor Orlando, so pictures could be taken. I stood at one of the great windows and watched them as they passed. The crowds would no longer be held back; they broke through the cordon of police and surged around the four men. For a moment the mass came with such force that it was alarming, but, laughing and cheering, those nearest joined hands, making a circle around the statesmen. The pictures were taken, but not in the sedate, orderly fashion which had been planned.

The rest of the afternoon was devoted to last-minute going-away details, and at eight we set out for the Élysée Palace. The great entrance gates were thrown wide, and the same solemn drum corps beat the rat-ta-tat-tat as though they had been there ever since the day of our arrival in Paris.

I wore an unusual evening gown by Worth. Long tightly draped skirts were in vogue, and my gown was of heavy black charmeuse, crossed in front from a low hip line, and wound tightly about the figure in lines ending in the back in a fish-tail train. From the knees up it was made entirely of sequins, black to begin with, and shading to gun metal, then to dark grey, light grey, and finally gleaming white at the bust and shoulders. With this, Worth had designed a sort of tiara of the sequins and rhinestones, which I wore along with the great pin with the diamonds and doves of peace which had been given me by the City of Paris. I carried a huge fan of shaded grey feathers with tortoise-shell sticks.

But before encountering the throng of the Élysée Palace, I must tell of an odd scene that happened at Worth's when he was making this dress. Too old for army service, M. Worth had opened his house as a home for those blinded in battle; which was a noble and splendid thing to do. But I think he made a mistake in bringing these poor mutilated men to his place of business. He called them his "children," and when I would go to be fitted he would bring them into the room, four or five men, some pitifully disfigured, and say: "My poor children, they are blind; so you will not mind if they sit while you are being fitted, as it gives them great happiness." Though this was not always agreeable, I would of course raise no objection. My pity was such that I could not bear to look at them. This very reaction made me realize the emotional strain Worth had been under for years; so I could comprehend what a hair trigger his nerves were on.

One morning I came in search of a certain shade of blue for an afternoon dress. We were in one of the private salons, with the usual attendants of five blind men, and had all sorts of blue stuffs piled around us, when a *vendeuse* came timidly in to ask if she could show Worth some material which a lady had selected for an evening coat and of which she was sure he would not approve. I said: "Certainly, let her bring it." So two others appeared, one bearing a roll of orange-coloured velvet for the coat, the other a piece of chartreuse green for lining. Worth took only one look, then covered his face with his hands, crying in French: "Take it away! I cannot stand it! My poor children, rejoice for once that you are blind. I am sick and cannot do anything more today. Oh, oh, oh!" Whereupon all the women rushed around as though he were dying. One said: "Oh, poor Monsieur, I will get you some brandy." The other ran to order his car, and a third knelt before him and held his head. With many apologies to me he was borne out in the arms of devoted employees and, after being revived, was put into a closed limousine. I was glad we had found the thing I wanted before this happened, and also glad I was neither French nor an artist.

Now let us return to the Élysée Palace. President and Madame Poincaré met us at the door and escorted us to the great drawing room where we stood with them to receive exactly as we had done seven months before on that December day when we first reached Paris. How many weary burden-laden weeks stretched between, and how glad I was that they were over! The rooms were brilliant with decorations and orders on the uniforms of almost every hue, worn by men from almost every nation, from our own men in khaki to the turbaned representatives of India—in fact the whole world in party dress.

Everyone was in holiday mood and happy, though the note of sadness too was felt in the severing of daily contacts and the saying of farewells. We left early and went for the last time to our Paris house in the Place des États-Unis. As soon as we could change and have our evening things packed we left for the station. For one last time we found the red carpet stretched, the lines of soldiers to be inspected, the palms waving, and the French officers lined up to bid us *bon voyage*. I was smothered in lovely flowers.

As the train moved out and the lights of Paris grew dim, my husband and I still stood at the open window, busy with our own thoughts, but united in our happiness of being together at last. I turned and saw he was looking at me. Before I could speak he said: "Well, little girl, it is finished, and, as no one is satisfied, it makes me hope we have made a just peace; but it is all on the lap of the gods."

At Brest next morning all was bustle and excitement. The great ship was flying the long home-coming pennant; the docks were filled with American soldiers, white and black; the natives, many in their picturesque costumes, were waving welcome and farewell. Out in the harbour, on either side of the *George Washington,* French destroyers were lined up as an escort.

Ropes were thrown off and as the ship slowly got under way a salute was fired. My husband stood on the bridge with his head uncovered while a band played "The Star-Spangled Banner."

CHAPTER 20

THE voyage home was leisurely, with many hours of sleep for my weary husband. The relaxation of nerves tense from unremitting labour and anxiety acted like a narcotic at first. But on the fifth day out, July 4th, the President consented to address the home-going troops with whom we shared the *George Washington*. Like ants they swarmed over the ship, climbing ropes and perching on all sorts of things the nautical names of which I do not know.

Among our other fellow passengers were about twenty French war brides of American soldiers. That some of our boys should marry in France had apparently not been foreseen by the authorities, who had made no provision for their brides' transportation to America. A tearful appeal to the President, signed by a number of the wives, solved at least a part of the problem.

The transport *Great Northern* met us at sea with bags of mail and official papers from the White House. These out of the way, my husband was drafting his message to Congress when, off Sandy Hook, a fleet of destroyers met us. In the harbour, Vice President Marshall, members of the Cabinet and Governor Alfred E. Smith of New York were on hand to bid us welcome home. After an exhilarating day how good it was to reach Washington and see the White House limousine, with Robinson at the wheel. And how good to be surrounded, once more, by the simple dignity of the White House, spick and span with cool linen on the chairs and flowers everywhere.

Fondly I had imagined that this would mean the resumption of normal ways of life. With the Peace Treaty ratified, my husband had planned to return to his programme of domestic legislation interrupted by the War. Alas, it *was* but a dream, with a tragic awakening!

On July 10th, two days after his return, the President laid the Treaty before the Senate. But already the partisans, bent on destroying him by defeating the Treaty at any cost, had drawn their lines. I shall relate little of the political part of that tragic story here, for my account is a personal one. Scholars of a new generation, men unknown to my husband and unknown to me, have written books on this subject in which much of the opposition to Mr. Wilson is called political and vindictive. I shall skip all I can skip and keep my story clear, lest otherwise I yield to the feelings of my heart and use harsher names.

Day after day there were long conferences with Senators—some of them eager to help, some "Irreconcilables," as they became known. Patiently the President clarified and explained, pointing out that in March some of the men who now opposed the Treaty had promised to vote for it if certain changes they suggested were made. These changes had been made. The President contended that neither he nor they had the moral right further to modify any Article unless every other country should be granted the same privilege. That, of course, would mean chaos, complete emasculation, for each country had amendments it wished to make.

Day after day, week after week, these conferences continued, but nothing seemed to result except increased fatigue for the President. He had, of course, many other problems to work out, and these, added to hours of fruitless arguments and explanations, were telling on his strength and resistance.

All of July and August passed. Aside from Treaty matters there were constant addresses to the Congress, one on the high cost of living, another urging co-operation of railway employees, another on railway wage differences, still another urging increased domestic production and economy.

Any one who knows the heat of Washington in July and August can picture the way energy is sapped, with no strain needed to add to that of the weather. The increasing demands on my husband's brain and body exacted a toll which pyramided, while I looked on with anxious heart. Towards the last of August, when there was apparently no more he could do alone to get the Treaty ratified by the Senate, he said that as a last resort he must go to the country to explain to the people what failure to ratify would mean. His hope was that an aroused public opinion would force the Senate to yield. This proposed trip was stoutly opposed by Dr. Grayson, who did not think the President could draw further on his strength without risking disaster. They had several talks, very serious talks, the Doctor pointing out the effect of the heat and discomfort of a month on the train, the perpetual strain of speaking and handshaking, the endless luncheons, dinners, parades and receptions—in short, all the noise and excitement and absolute denial of rest or privacy that attend a President wherever he goes.

"Yes," my husband said, "all that is true; but I feel it is my duty, and my own health is not to be considered when the future peace and security of the world are at stake. If the Treaty is not ratified by the Senate, the War will have been fought in vain, and the world will be thrown into chaos. I promised our soldiers, when I asked them to take up arms, that it was a war to end wars; and if I do not do all in my power to put the Treaty in effect, I will be a slacker and never able to look those boys in the eye. I must go."

To this neither Dr. Grayson nor I could find an answer.

On August 22nd I gave my first party since our return from abroad. It was a lawn party for the wounded boys at the Walter Reed and the Naval Hospitals. One soldier brought his camera, and, seeing the President crossing the lawn with two plates of ice cream and a platter of cake, he said: "One minute, please." My husband paused and the photographer snapped, remarking that he guessed that was the first time a President had ever been caught doing K. P. I am happy to relate that each succeeding Administration has maintained the custom of giving a garden party for the disabled veterans.

I would rather dwell on that scene, touching as it was in some of its aspects, than those that are to follow. A final appeal by Dr. Grayson having been rejected, on September 3rd the special train pulled out of the familiar Union Station and we were off. I do not believe that I have told how the President travelled on long trips, or "swings"; and I shall not have another opportunity. The itinerary agreed upon, the routing was worked out by Edward Smithers of the Executive Offices of the White House and everything moved with military exactness. Unlike the heads of the principal—and, indeed, some of the minor—foreign States, our Chief Executive has no private train, but for each long trip a train is made up to run on a special schedule. In our day this train was always in charge of Captain Dave Hardester, conductor. The President's car, the last on the train, usually was one called "The Mayflower."

Entering the car from the rear one came first to a sitting room, fitted with armchairs, a long couch and a folding table on which we dined. Next came my bedroom and then the President's, with a door connecting. Each room had a single bed and dressing table. Beyond this was a room which my husband used as an office. There was placed his typewriter, without which he never travelled, and there he and Mr. Tumulty worked whenever they could snatch a few minutes from the "local committees" which were usually aboard.

The next compartment was for my maid, on this trip a wonderful little Swedish girl named Siegrid. She carried an electric iron and all the necessary things for washing and pressing, which she had to do constantly. One more room was for Dr. Grayson. Brooks, the President's valet, slept on the leather couch in the sitting room. In the front of the car was the kitchen, presided over by a very fat and very excellent negro chef named Green. Green's assistant, Lancaster, and a porter completed the staff.

Other Pullman cars, a diner and baggage cars were added to the train to accommodate those making up the party. On this trip the train was a particularly long one, for the newspaper men and photographers alone numbered a hundred.

We left the station at eleven o'clock on a warm night. The President, Dr. Grayson, Mr. Tumulty and I were sitting in the lounge and someone rang for cool drinks. Imagine our surprise when, instead of the regular porter, who should appear bearing a large tray but "Little Jackson," a coloured messenger in the Executive Offices. Moreover he wore a white apron and the largest white cap, of the design usually worn by chefs, that I have ever seen. We all laughed heartily, while he showed his white teeth in a pleased smile.

The substitution of Little Jackson for the porter had been a prank of Mr. Tumulty's, who had also superintended the manufacture of the gigantic white cap which sheltered the small negro like a toadstool. Mr. Tumulty was a lot of fun on a trip. Before going to bed we generally gathered in the sitting room for a supper of sandwiches, as the President rarely ate dinner when he intended to speak early in the evening. Sometimes newspaper men or other guests from the front of the train would join us. The explosive Irish wit of Mr. Tumulty would garnish the incidents of the day as Dr. Grayson, with keen, quiet humour, drew him out.

Columbus, Ohio, was the first stop and the scene of my husband's first impassioned appeal to the people. It met with a tremendous response. Later from the rear platform of the train at Richmond, Indiana, he spoke for the second time. We reached St. Louis the following morning where he addressed a vast crowd gathered at the Statler Hotel for lunch, following which there was the usual stampede to "shake hands with the President," and the inevitable interviews with local politicians. Never a moment to relax and rest. And so on across the continent. From one city to the next "a small local committee" would accompany us, which meant constant entertaining even on the train.

The tour had not progressed far when serious headaches began to afflict my husband. He paid little attention to them, though I could see that each day, each meeting, each appearance, was calling more and more on his depleted reserve of nervous energy. The rising tide of approval, of course, helped him much. He felt he was winning his fight—stirring up in the country a force of popular opinion for the League that would sweep upon the senatorial opposition and break its force. This gratified me, naturally, though I could not remain blind to the physical sacrifice he was making and must wonder if it were not too great. I could see how closely Dr. Grayson watched his patient. The Doctor's disregarded warnings against attempting the tour haunted my sleep, and I do not think that I am one to borrow trouble or look without reason on the dark side.

Even at the time I got my share of amusement from the lighter incidents of each day—as, for example, in Columbus when a lady came struggling through the crowd holding aloft a Susan B. Anthony pennant and calling out: "Mr. President, don't forget Susie!"

At one place in the Dakotas there was no building large enough to hold the crowd. So they had pitched a tent, big enough for a circus. We proceeded thither in a cavalcade of motor cars, one of the Secret Service men going in advance to see the local police. His car broke down and by the time it was repaired we were already in the tent. The Secret Service agent was anxious to report to his chief, Mr. Murphy, who was inside with us, but a local policeman guarding the entrance was deaf to all entreaties. The plea that he belonged to the President's party was waved aside. When the badge worn under the coat was produced the local authority grabbed our poor agent, crying to his fellows: "Arrest this fellow. He has stolen a Secret Service badge." Fortunately one of the other members of our escort rescued our poor man from the clutches of the law. He told me afterwards it certainly gave him more sympathy for persons in like position, even if they were guilty.

At Billings, Montana, occurred an incident which touched us, and which my husband related later in an address at Tacoma, Washington. I give it in his words: "A number of boys carrying flags were chasing the train as it pulled slowly out, yelling all sorts of pleasant things to their friend 'Woody.' One youngster in his enthusiasm insisted I should take his flag and handed it up to me. The boy next to him did not have a flag and he looked a good deal disgruntled for a moment, and then he put his hand in his pocket and said: 'Here, I will give you a dime.' I would like to believe that that dime has some relation to the widow's mite—others gave something; he gave all that he had."

After my husband's death nearly five years later I found, in a little change purse he always carried, a dime wrapped in a piece of paper and put in a separate pocket. I am convinced that it was the dime that little boy gave him on that September day in 1919.

We made a brief stop, between stations, to see some wonderful falls, leaving the train to walk up and get a better view. On our return we found two of the worst looking tramps I ever saw, veritable Happy Hooligans, standing by our car and asking to shake hands with the President. One of the Secret Service men had found them preparing to stow away for a ride on the trucks underneath one of the cars. He told them they could not do that, and when they asked what he had to do with it he said it was the private train of the President of the United States. Without a word, he said, they crawled out and one of them said: "Well, I know he's got everything and we've got nothing, but we would not change places with him with the load he is carrying, and we will do nothing to add to it." The other one said: "Do you think he would shake hands with fellows like us?" After my husband and I had shaken their hands, Mr. Wilson offered them a lift on our train. They declined, saying, no, they would not trouble us but would "hang onto" the "regular" when it came by. From the rear of our train we waved goodbye to these unshaven knights of the road. They waved their shabby hats in return.

We watched their figures grow small and disappear: two homeless men who had refused a favour from the head of the Nation—a nation from which they seemed outcast, but so carefree.

We entered a Far Western State early one morning where the Governor was supposed to head the reception committee which welcomed us. Alas, His Excellency came up missing. After waiting for a while, the Mayor of the city said there was a fair going on and that the people were anxious to see the President, so he thought we had better start. When we reached the fairgrounds the crowd insisted the President should go up in the judges' stand. I stayed in the open motor. Just as a great shout of applause greeted the President's appearance in the stand, I saw a shabby old gentleman, dressed in a long-tailed coat and a battered high hat, and clutching a big umbrella, emerge from the crowd and start up the steps of the judges' stand. Instantly he was seized by two Secret Service agents and held struggling in their grasp. Finally he recovered his breath enough to gasp: "I am the Governor and I want to speak to the President." It was a funny sight, but we were all so sorry to have offered him such indignity. My husband insisted he should return to lunch with us on the train en route to the next stop. He did this, and proved a good sport whom we both liked and admired.

The first tragedy to a member of our party happened at Portland, Oregon, where one of the reporters, Mr. Ben F. Allen of the Cleveland *Plain Dealer,* was killed, and another one injured, in an automobile collision. It occurred when the whole party was taken in motors out the beautiful drive along the Columbia River. There were the usual mass of people, and thousands of cars. We knew nothing of the accident at the time and upon our return to Portland went immediately to a lunch given by the press. Noticing several vacant tables I inquired the reason and was told of the collision and asked to say nothing to the President, as they wanted him to enjoy the lunch. The empty places were those of special friends of the victims. As soon as my husband learned what had happened he went to see the injured man who, fortunately, was not seriously hurt and was able to go on with us that night on the train. His name was Small. He was given a drawing room on the train, and the President went every day to his car to visit him. He recovered entirely, and lived to write some very unkind things about Woodrow Wilson.

PRESIDENT WILSON AND PARTY IN BELGIUM, HOUTHOULST FOREST, JUNE, 1919

From Portland we went to Tacoma, and then to Seattle, where again we had a two nights' stop in the hotel. Here the President reviewed the great Pacific fleet. Secretary of the Navy and Mrs. Daniels were at the station to greet us when we arrived, and we drove through thronged streets to the dock. The barge of Admiral Hugh Rodman was expected to be ready to convey the reviewing party to the historic battleship *Oregon*. By some negligence the barge was not there. Commander Foote, personal aide to the Secretary of the Navy, promptly took over a naval launch, and we got aboard. With Secretary and Mrs. Daniels, Secret Service men, aides, reporters, etc., we constituted a large party. As Commander Foote ordered the launch shoved off, the small craft heeled over until the port rail was nearly under water. Then we ran bow-on into another launch. Personally I would not have excused the officers who had endangered lives in this way, though the President did.

Reaching the *Oregon* without further mishap, the old battleship moved down the Bay, passing the *New Mexico, Mississippi, Idaho, Texas* and *New York*. From each roared salvos of twenty-one guns, while above us circled airships. Then came twenty-seven destroyers spaced about three hundred yards apart, followed by every type of vessel—destroyers, tugs, submarine chasers, etc. On each vessel the sailors lined the rail at attention, and bands flung across the waters strains of the National Anthem.

The review over, we went to the Hotel Washington. There was time for a brief rest before going to the Hippodrome where the President spoke at a dinner, the third speech of the day. I was glad to get back to our suite on the top floor of the hotel which overlooked the harbour. Straight out as far as the eye could see, lay the entire fleet, every ship ablaze with light. Surely America should have been proud of such a sight. It awed us both as we sat on a little roof garden and gazed silently.

These weeks of travel, day and night, with their multitude of events, bring almost overwhelming memories as I sit here, nineteen years later, at this desk in a quiet room alone. My husband used often to say that he thought the worst writing in the world was done by historians who mentioned some sequence of events and compared it to things which happened later on, saying, for instance: "Little did they think that on that date two years later such and such thing would happen." He said such writing projected the reader's mind into the future and warped his judgment concerning the period immediately under review; for without omniscience no one could know what would happen "two years later." Each period of history should be judged in the light of contemporary events and not the events of subsequent years. Thus, in recalling these crowded years in my own life, I have tried not to anticipate the record, but let it unroll naturally and without light or shadow thrown upon it by the events of the future. So back I must go to the unceasing whir of the wheels that had taken our heavy train on, on, on, from coast to coast—and then from Seattle straight down to Oakland, California.

With each revolution of the wheels my anxieties for my husband's health increased. He grew thinner and the headaches increased in duration and in intensity until he was almost blind during the attacks. Coming in from a reception or dinner I have seen him sit with his head bowed on the back of a chair in front of him while trying to dictate and keep abreast of his mountainous correspondence. Wish being father to the thought, I had hoped against hope that the distress would prove temporary. Now I began to doubt this. Only rest, complete rest, and an escape from the maddening crowds, could restore my husband. But I was trapped. Arriving in Oakland on the morning of September 17th we were confronted by a two-day schedule before which my heart sank.

It is no imagining on my part when I say that the crowds grew larger and more enthusiastic. That is the statement of chroniclers of the tour whose judgment is certainly to be preferred to mine. One of the newspaper men said the receptions on the Pacific coast reminded him of our trip to Italy. But things ran in a vicious circle. The greater the crowds, the higher the enthusiasm, the worse the wear and tear on my husband. If only some of these ardent, well-meaning people who whittled away at our privacy until almost none was left could have had a glimpse behind the curtain of what admirers were beginning to call "President Wilson's triumphal tour."

Two days in Oakland, Berkeley, San Francisco and Palo Alto; five major addresses; luncheons, dinners, receptions, miles upon miles of driving in flower-laden cars; interviews, conferences, and twenty different committees of escort and entertainment. I have never seen such flowers. To mention one basket that came to our hotel suite: it was twelve feet tall and filled with yellow chrysanthemums. From it hung clusters of grapes which I was told weighed a hundred pounds. As usual, we sent them all to hospitals.

The weather was warm and enervating. These two days would have taxed the vitality of one who was rested and refreshed. My husband took them on top of twelve days and nights of travel, and twenty-odd speeches; and was worn out when he started. Dr. Grayson and I took counsel with each other. He said the President *must* have some rest each day. So on to San Diego and Los Angeles, with the Doctor and me trying to act as buffers. The crowds at every station, the local committees travelling from one stop to another, and politicians who must have "just a word with the President," rendered our efforts almost futile.

We counted, however, on Sunday in Los Angeles as a day of rest— and then we would head for home! We counted in vain. The morning was taken from us by visitors before we knew it. But, I stubbornly told myself, the President would sleep in the afternoon and then in the cool of the evening we would slip out and drive alone. I have related before how my husband could sleep almost any time he got the chance, and how that sleep would relax him and dissipate the poisons of fatigue. Mrs. Peck, whom my husband had known in Bermuda many years before, was to have lunch with us. Because of the work scandalmongers had done to make an intrigue of that friendship, I was glad to receive her, and show my disdain for such slander.

She came—a faded, sweet-looking woman who was absorbed in an only son. She told many stories of her struggle to maintain herself and help him get his start. So wrapped up was she in her own problems that I am sure she forgot how fast the time was flying, and had I not coveted every moment of it I would have enjoyed her. Presently some men came for an official conference. When my husband left the room to meet them Mrs. Peck said she would wait until he was through. Poor woman, weighed down with her own problems, of course she did not understand. Darkness had fallen when she finally rose to go.

After Los Angeles we stopped at Sacramento long enough for an address from the rear platform of the train. Then on to Ogden and to Salt Lake City.

At Salt Lake City the address was to be made in the Mormon Temple at eight o'clock in the evening. Before six Mr. Tumulty came in to say that the place was packed, even the standing-room, and that the police had locked the doors to prevent a stampede. From our windows at the hotel we could see what looked to be thousands of people still gathering. By eight o'clock when we went over we had to have a cordon of police on either side to get us through.

The fetid air we encountered on entering that great building was unlike anything I have ever experienced. Imagine fifteen thousand human beings in hot weather shut up tight with no ventilation for over two hours. I felt sick and blind. We were pushed through at last to the rostrum and seated on the long seats where the Apostles, I think they are called, sit during the Mormon service. These seats rose in tiers and of course the higher one went the worse the heat and human odours. To this day I cannot conceive how the President spoke under such conditions. I should have fainted dead away but for the merciful fact that Siegrid, my maid, had carried a bottle of smelling salts, which she handed me when she saw me getting deathly white. It seemed an intervention of Providence that I had taken Siegrid, for I had never done so before. But that day she told me she had never heard the President speak, and would it be possible for her to go just once?

I borrowed a large fresh handkerchief from one of the Secret Service men, soaked it in the lavender salts and had it taken to the President. At last the oration made by the head of the Mormon Church, Mr. Grant, introducing the President, was over, and Mr. Wilson was on his feet waiting for the applause to cease before he began his speech.

With conditions so unfavourable I was scarcely the one to judge of the merit of the speech itself. I quote, therefore, from the Salt Lake *Tribune:* "The President's sincerity, the care with which he weighed his words, and the ease of his address made his message simple and at the same time tremendously effective."

When it was over and we were back in the hotel I found that even his coat was soaked through with perspiration. We got him into dry things as quickly as possible only to find they in turn would be soaking wet in a few minutes. This exhausting state continued into the night, and the next day at Cheyenne found him too weary to pretend he was not ill. He spoke there in the afternoon and we started for Denver, arriving at 10:30 P. M. and going at once to the hotel. How I longed to cry out for a few days of rest. But when I suggested it he said: "No, I have caught the imagination of the people. They are eager to hear what the League stands for; and I should fail in my duty if I disappointed them." So downcast was I that he tried to cheer me up. "This will soon be over, and when we get back to Washington I promise you I will take a holiday." Then he added: "Is Small all right? Is everything being done for him?"

Up early after a poor night's rest, my husband's headache never leaving him. A motor parade through the streets winding up for a 9:30 A. M. meeting at Denver's auditorium. Then back to the train and on to Pueblo, arriving at the fairgrounds at three in the afternoon. "This will have to be a short speech," my husband said as he took the stand, and then nodding to the men in the press box who had followed him more than 9,000 miles and listened to thirty-nine of his speeches already: "Aren't you fellows getting pretty sick of this?"

Strangely, the speech that followed was one of the longest, one of the most vigorous and touching he made on the tour, and again I do not venture this opinion without consulting the impressions of more detached hearers. As he warmed to his subject, the President's weariness seemed to leave him. New and undiscovered reservoirs of strength seemed to reinforce his efforts. Tears were on my cheeks, and not mine alone, when he launched into this conclusion:

"Mothers who have lost sons in France have come to me, and taking my hand have not only shed tears upon it, but they have added: 'God bless you, Mr. President.' Why, my fellow citizens, should they pray God to bless me? I ordered their sons overseas. I consented to their sons being put in the most difficult parts of the battle line where death was certain. Why should they weep upon my hand and call down the blessings of God upon me? Because they believe that their boys died for something that vastly transcends any of the immediate and palpable objects of the War."

He recalled Decoration Day at Suresnes Cemetery. "I wish some of the men who are now opposing the settlement for which those men died could visit such a spot as that. I wish they could feel the moral obligation that rests upon us not to go back on those boys, but to see this thing through to the end and make good their redemption of the world."

Such was Woodrow Wilson's valedictory.

Naturally there was a reaction. The headache returned—if, indeed, it had ever gone. On the train that evening Dr. Grayson

thought perhaps some mild exercise in the fresh Colorado air would
help. After consulting the engineer it was arranged to stop the train
for half an hour and let us go for a walk. This we did, and came back
much refreshed. Dinner was a cheerful one, for my husband really
ate something and said his head was easier than it had been for days.
Dr. Grayson and Mr. Tumulty dined with us, and we all decided
to turn in early and see if a good sleep would not banish the pain
entirely.

My maid came to brush my hair and give me a massage. We kept
very quiet, as my room was next to my husband's, and I thought he
was asleep. About 11:30 I was surprised, therefore, when he knocked
at the intervening door and asked if I were through would I come to
him as he was very sick. I found him sitting on the side of his bed
with his head resting on the back of a chair in front of him. He said
he had tried to sleep but the pain had grown unbearable and he
thought I had better call Dr. Grayson. I sent Siegrid to the Doctor's
room. He was not there, and it seemed to me hours before he could
be located on the train. Of course it was only a matter of minutes,
but I realized that we were facing something terrible.

That night was the longest and most heartbreaking of my life.
Nothing the Doctor could do gave relief. Finally the President got
up and dressed. He said he could not stay in that tiny room; he must
move about. He went to the improvised study where we took pillows
to try to make him comfortable, but he could not stay quiet.

The Doctor and I kept the vigil while the train dashed on and on
through darkness. About five in the morning a blessed release came,
and, sitting upright on the stiff seat, my husband fell asleep. I
motioned to the Doctor to go on to bed, and I sat opposite scarcely
breathing lest I wake him. He slept quietly, and how I prayed that
when he woke all would be well. Alas! I knew that it could not be.
The dear face opposite me was drawn and lined; and as I sat there
watching the dawn break slowly I felt that life would never be the
same; that something had broken inside me; and from that hour on
I would have to wear a mask—not only to the public but to the one I
loved best in the world; for he must never know how ill he was, and
I must carry on.

He woke about seven and said he must shave and get ready as we
were to reach Wichita, Kansas, very soon. I knew he could not speak

there. After seeing him to his room Dr. Grayson, Mr. Tumulty and I talked over how the situation could best be handled. In the midst of our talk the President appeared, freshly dressed, shaven and looking, oh, so piteously ill. When we suggested that he cancel the rest of the trip and take a vacation he said No. We urged it, and he still said No. Dr. Grayson said any other course might bring disastrous, even fatal, consequences. "No, no, no. I must keep on." In the end it remained for me to "hold the mirror up to nature" and show him—that the fight was over. In justice to his cause he must stop for a while. I think it was about the hardest task that has fallen to my lot. At last, though, it was done. He accepted the decree of Fate as gallantly as he had fought the fight; but only he and his God knew the crucifixion that began that moment—to stretch into interminable years, during which the seal he put on his lips, never to repine or voice a syllable of self-pity or regret, remained unbroken.

Not until the train was slowing down for Wichita did the President come to realize the truth. The programme called for a stop on the outskirts of the city where the official party was to transfer to automobiles. The newspaper men and other members of the train's company were getting in their cars, the reception committee was waiting when Mr. Tumulty went out and said that the President could not make an address.

What a transformation took place! Wires clicked train orders and the reporters fell upon telephones to flash the message that the President was ill and that Dr. Grayson had ordered him to Washington for complete rest. Tracks were cleared and with a pilot engine running ahead of us we left Wichita at eleven in the morning—September 26, 1919—for Washington seventeen hundred miles away. People gathered at every station to see the train roar through. At the necessary stops they crowded around so that we pulled down the shades. The car seemed like a funeral cortège.

My husband and I sat in the office compartment, I trying to go on as though the structure of our life did not lie in ruin around us. I took some knitting and tried to work, and to divert my husband with small talk. But the air was so heavy with unspoken agony that all seemed a travesty. The hours dragged on; night came; brought no rest; another day; another bad night—and another dawn found me staring into the future, wide-eyed, wondering.

CHAPTER 21

AT eleven on Sunday morning, September 28, 1919, the train pulled its heavy way into Washington, forty-eight hours and seventeen hundred miles from Wichita. A great crowd filled the station and the plaza outside. Margaret and the motors were waiting and we were soon back in the blessed shelter of the White House. I was rather unstrung. All those people at the station—my first impulse was to escape them, to get away from what I regarded as prying, curious eyes, though I now realize that the gathering was a sympathetic one.

All the rest of that day my husband wandered like a ghost between the study at one end of the hall and my room at the other. The awful pain in his head that drove him restlessly back and forth was too acute to permit work, or even reading. Late in the afternoon we went for a short motor ride; but still the demon of pain pursued him.

I had asked ten of the newspaper men who had been on the Western trip to come to tea the following day. My husband was too ill to join us.

Next day came an urgent message from Sir William Wiseman, a secret agent of the British Government. He said he had important information for the President, and hoped Mr. Wilson would give him a private audience. I asked him to come at 11 A. M. when I told him my husband was ill and that I would receive the information and convey it to the President. If Sir William would return at two o'clock I promised that the President's answer would be available. I had never liked this plausible little man. So I was glad my husband decided his information was not important enough for further consideration. This was the only instance that I recall having acted as an intermediary between my husband and another on an official matter, except when so directed by a physician.

The next day, the third since our return, the President seemed a

286

little better. We went for a short ride, and I arranged for the showing of a motion picture in the East Room that evening. Everything
went off so well that Woodrow insisted he would read me a chapter
from the Bible before retiring, as he had done every night during the
War.

He stood under the centre light in my room with the Book in one
hand and the other resting on a table that flanked the big couch
where I sat. His voice was as vibrant and as strong as I had ever
heard it, and when he finished he put the Book on the table and stood
while he wound his watch. We talked a little, and after he had
gone to his room I saw the watch on the table and decided to carry
it in to him. He said: "That worries me—to have left that watch
there. It is not like me." "Nonsense," I said, "what difference does it
make? It is what I do all the time—forget things." I realized afterwards it was not the fact of leaving the watch, but that he did not
want to relax the tight hold he was keeping on himself.

I had been sleeping fitfully, getting up every hour or so to see how
my husband was. It was so on this night. At five or six in the morning I found him still sleeping normally, as it appeared. Relieved, I
dozed off again until after eight. This time I found him sitting on
the side of the bed trying to reach a water bottle. As I handed it
to him I noticed that his left hand hung loosely. "I have no feeling
in that hand," he said. "Will you rub it? But first help me to the
bathroom."

He moved with great difficulty, and every move brought spasms of
pain; but with my help he gained the bathroom. This so alarmed
me that I asked if I could leave him long enough to telephone the
Doctor. He said yes, and hurrying into my room I reached Dr.
Grayson at his house. While at the 'phone I heard a slight noise, and
rushing into my husband's apartment found him on the bathroom
floor unconscious.

My first thought was to keep him warm. From his bed I snatched
a blanket, and while I was arranging it over him he stirred and asked
for a drink of water. I got it, and also got a pillow for his head. I
did these things automatically, for I was utterly devoid of feeling. I
had a curious sensation of having lived through this very thing
before—and so knew how to act, and act quickly. I seemed to know
just what the Doctor would say to my husband and he to the Doctor.

Then came a knock on the door. It was locked; the President and I always locked our doors leading into the hall, leaving only our communicating door unlocked. The knock was Grayson's.

We lifted the President into his bed. He had suffered a stroke, paralyzing the left side of his body. An arm and one leg were useless, but, thank God, the brain was clear and untouched.

Such is the story of that tragic morning hour of October 2, 1919, as my memory presents it to me. So far as was possible I checked my recollections with the data of Dr. Grayson, before his lamented death in 1938. I did this because of a rather remarkable account of the same events which appears in the posthumously published "diary" of Mr. I. H. Hoover, the White House head usher. For example, the late Mr. Hoover is represented as seeing a long cut on the President's temple, which, late that afternoon, still showed signs of blood; also a cut lengthwise of the nose. Dr. Grayson and I did not see these things. As I recall, not even a bruise resulted from the President's fall. The fact is that he had just slid sidewise to the floor from a sitting position.

Nurses came and the house was organized as a hospital. Dr. Francis X. Dercum, the great nerve specialist of Philadelphia, Dr. Sterling Ruffin and Admiral E. R. Stitt of the Naval Medical Corps, were summoned. Margaret and Nell were called to Washington by telephone. For days life hung in the balance. Then the will to live, to recover and fight on for his League of Nations, almost imperceptibly at first, began to gain ascendency over the forces of disease, and the President got a little better.

Once my husband was out of immediate danger, the burning question was how Mr. Wilson might best serve the country, preserve his own life and if possible recover. Many people, among them some I had counted as friends, have written of my overwhelming ambition to act as President; of my exclusion of all advice, and so forth. I am trying here to write as though I had taken the oath to tell the truth, the whole truth, and nothing but the truth—so help me God.

I asked the doctors to be frank with me; that I must know what the outcome would probably be, so as to be honest with the people. They all said that as the brain was as clear as ever, with the progress made in the past few days, there was every reason to think recovery possible. Dr. Dercum told me of the history of Pasteur, who had been stricken exactly in this way, but who recovered and did his most brilliant intellectual work afterwards. He sent me a copy of a remarkable book, *The Life of Pasteur*.

But recovery could not be hoped for, they said, unless the President were released from every disturbing problem during these days of Nature's effort to repair the damage done.

"How can that be," I asked the doctors, "when everything that comes to an Executive is a problem? How can I protect him from problems when the country looks to the President as the leader?"

Dr. Dercum leaned towards me and said: "Madam, it is a grave situation, but I think you can solve it. Have everything come to you; weigh the importance of each matter, and see if it is possible by consultations with the respective heads of the Departments to solve them without the guidance of your husband. In this way you can save him a great deal. But always keep in mind that every time you take him a new anxiety or problem to excite him, you are turning a knife in an open wound. His nerves are crying out for rest, and any excitement is torture to him."

"Then," I said, "had he better not resign, let Mr. Marshall succeed to the Presidency and he himself get that complete rest that is so vital to his life?"

"No," the Doctor said, "not if you feel equal to what I suggested. For Mr. Wilson to resign would have a bad effect on the country, and a serious effect on our patient. He has staked his life and made his promise to the world to do all in his power to get the Treaty ratified and make the League of Nations complete. If he resigns, the greatest incentive to recovery is gone; and as his mind is clear as crystal he can still do more with even a maimed body than any one else. He has the utmost confidence in you. Dr. Grayson tells me he has always discussed public affairs with you; so you will not come to them uninformed."

So began my stewardship. I studied every paper, sent from the different Secretaries or Senators, and tried to digest and present in tabloid form the things that, despite my vigilance, had to go to the President. I, myself, never made a single decision regarding the disposition of public affairs. The only decision that was mine was what was important and what was not, and the *very* important decision of when to present matters to my husband.

He asked thousands of questions, and insisted upon knowing everything, particularly about the Treaty. He would dictate notes to me to send to Senator Hitchcock who was leading the fight for the Treaty in the Senate. Or he would tell me what Senators to send for, and what suggestions he had to make to them. These directions I made notes of, so, in transmitting his views, I should make no mistake; and I would read them to him before going to the interviews. This method of handling interviews was another suggestion of the doctors. It is always an excitement for one who is ill to see people. The physicians said that if I could convey the messages of Cabinet members and others to the President, he would escape the nervous drain audiences with these officials would entail. Even the necessary little courteous personal conversations that go with an official interview would consume the President's strength.

These instructions from the medical men were far from easy to carry out. Picture the situation when my husband was stricken: his tour a success; public sentiment which had been worked upon incessantly by the enemies of the League once more responding to Mr. Wilson's logic; the initiative again in the hands of friends of the Treaty; Mr. Hitchcock and the other pro-Treaty Senators eager to push their advantage. And then—the President laid low, ruled out of the fight which he would have continued though he knew it would cost him his life. Upon all sides I was literally besieged by those who "must" see the President. But I carried out the directions of the doctors—and my heart was in it. Woodrow Wilson was first my beloved husband whose life I was trying to save, fighting with my back to the wall—after that he was the President of the United States.

In that other battle, in the Senate, the first victory was for the Treaty's friends. A series of crippling amendments, called the Lodge and Fall amendments, had been introduced. They were defeated—all the friends of the Treaty, Democrats and Republicans, voting together.

Then Mr. Lodge dropped the word amendment and began the gradual introduction of "reservations," until a whole stack of them were before the Senate. The difference between these "reservations," some harmless enough in appearance, and the original Lodge-Fall amendments was the difference between Tweedledum and Tweedledee.

A workable system of handling matters of State had scarcely been evolved when a terrible complication interrupted the progress of our patient. A stricture occurred, blocking elimination from the bladder. Its continuance meant death. A consulation of specialists was called— Dr. Hugh Young of Johns Hopkins, Dr. H. A. Fowler of Washington, Dr. Dercum, Dr. Ruffin, Dr. Stitt and Dr. Grayson. It was the seventeenth day of October. After an unsuccessful attempt to relieve the patient by means of local applications, the doctors retired to come to a final decision. As I waited by the bedside I longed for and yet dreaded their return. At length Dr. Grayson beckoned me to the door. I went into my room, finding him so overcome that he could not speak at first. We stood at the window, looking over the green lawn and on toward the towering Washington Monument, neither seeing anything. Finally the Doctor said: "Well, Mrs. Wilson, all agree there is no alternative but an operation, and I feel sure the President can't stand one. Since we came to this conclusion, I went out and walked around the block trying to get myself together before coming to you. This is the situation: Drs. Young and Fowler, who are specialists, agree that this condition cannot be relieved without an operation. I think the others are of the same opinion. I feel an operation will be the end. Therefore, while I hate to put the responsibility on you, there is nothing else but for you to decide."

I felt that another chasm had opened at my feet, and that this time I did not know how to bridge it. Automatically I spoke: "Then we will not operate. You know more than anyone else of the real chances of recovery. So go down and tell them I feel that Nature will finally take care of things, and we will wait."

In a moment Dr. Grayson was back with Dr. Young who said he felt that if I understood I would see things differently. Dr. Young followed me into my dressing room and, taking pencil and paper from his pocket, he proceeded to draw diagrams which my blinded eyes could hardly see. His arguments were supplemented by Dr. Ruffin, my personal physician long before I met Mr. Wilson, and by Dr. Dercum. But something kept me steady and I would not agree. Perhaps all this took only minutes, but it seemed hours to me. Finally the nurse came to say that the President was asking for me. When I rose to go Dr. Young called after me: "You understand, Mrs. Wilson, the whole body will become poisoned if this condition lasts an hour, or at the most two hours, longer." With this note ringing in my ear like the tolling of a funeral bell I went back to the sickroom. No matter what he was suffering, my coming was always greeted with a smile; and the thin hand would reach for and take my own. I stayed there, watching the coming and going of the nurses; the visits of the doctors; but with every fibre of my being noting the fast moving of the hands of the clock. My own life seemed suspended; even Nature herself seemed listening; for there was not a sound outside. The temperature and respiration were taken at frequent intervals, and each time the former got a little higher. Local treatments were again applied.

The two hours had gone by and we were well into the third when, suddenly, the tense condition relaxed and Nature again asserted her power over disease. The temperature receded, and the weary patient slept. The doctors went home to rest, and again peace descended upon my spirit.

This crisis proved a serious setback, however, taking much of my husband's vitality. Patiently we went to work to build him up again.

Our patient improved so that on October 30th we could receive informally the King and Queen of the Belgians. The royal couple were on the ocean when the President was stricken. On reaching these shores they behaved exactly as would considerate friends who find themselves inadvertently in a house of sickness. A ceremonial tour of the country was abandoned and the King and Queen contented themselves with visiting, incognito, some of the things they wished most to see.

When Mr. Wilson had recovered somewhat from his setback they came to Washington. Through the State Department Mr. and Mrs. Breckinridge Long placed their home at the disposal of the visitors. Vice President and Mrs. Marshall did the official entertaining.

The day of their arrival we had flowers sent with a note of welcome, and I went immediately to call upon Her Majesty, finding her the same gracious sympathetic woman I had learned to admire a few short months before when we had had such royal entertainment in Brussels. As a welcoming gift I took her a fan with shell sticks, and her name on it in gold. I explained our regret that the circumstances made it impossible for us to have them with us at the White House and that I wanted them to come for a cup of tea, when I hoped the President would be able to greet the King in his own room.

They came the following afternoon, with only their young son, the Prince, and two aides. We had tea in the Red Room. When it was over I asked His Majesty if I could take him upstairs where my husband was waiting to receive him. I excused myself to the Queen, but she, with all the naïveté of a girl, said: "Oh, but he must not go yet. We have a present for the President, but in spite of all our care it has never come, and we must wait here until it does so we can present it ourselves." She then explained that on their arrival in New York she wanted to bring "the box" with their personal bags but was persuaded to let it come with the big luggage. In some way it had been overlooked and she was desolated. I expressed regret at the mistake, but nothing would persuade her to let the King go up until "the box" came. Finally the head usher announced its arrival. Two men brought in and set carefully down a beautifully made box of polished wood, about three feet long and two feet wide, with mounted brass handles and raised metal lettering, reading:

> *Souvenir du Roi et de la Reine*
> *des Belges à Son Excellence*
> *Monsieur Wilson President des*
> *États-Unis d'Amerique*

When the box was opened with a key it revealed a case lined with crimson velvet and containing three trays holding eighteen exquisite plates. On every plate was a hand-painted representation of an historic place in Belgium—some of the places had been destroyed during the War—each framed in an identical border of rich black and gold. The back of every plate bore the same inscription as that on the handsome case. Truly it was a royal gift and one that gave us lasting pleasure. After this Her Majesty handed me a small case of grey suede which held a fan of Belgian lace mounted on amber sticks. On the supporting large stick is a garter of small diamonds enclosing two letter "E's" in sapphires. She explained that the initials were for her name and mine, Élisabeth and Edith, "in a circle of friendship." The lace was specially woven, and very beautiful. The main motif represents the angels of peace chasing the dragons of war, and in the background stand, as a sort of guard of honour, the national emblems of all the Allied countries—the American Eagle, the English Lion, the French Cock, the Russian Bear, etc.

I was overcome by the thought and care all this represented, for both gifts must have been months in the making.

After I had tried to express my gratitude, His Majesty said he would like to go upstairs. I asked if he wanted the plates to go, and he said he would like it very much.

My husband was ready to receive him, and the King was as gentle as a woman in his sincere sympathy and solicitude. After they had talked a while he presented the gorgeous china and we took out each plate for the President to see, and His Majesty recalled our visit to several of the places—Ypres, Bruges, Limoges—and then told of the wrecking of many others.

When he rose to go he made a very gracious speech, and my husband replied. When we got in the elevator to go down the King recalled his visit to the White House when he was a young man and my promise to show him the queer piece of furniture he had spoken of in Belgium. I told him that while it was too Victorian to do away with, it had been demoted and was in the first floor Oval Room. He begged to take Her Majesty down to see it. So we got her, and all descended to the ground floor. She was much interested, and then they wandered through the other rooms, winding up in the one where the cabinets of china used in preceding Administrations are located. I told them after the artistic plates they had brought some of our early specimens would seem crude, but the interesting thing about them was that few, if any, were domestic china, nearly all having been imported. So if an ice-cream plate of bright pink, having a snowshoe superimposed on it in gold, was an exhibition of poor taste on the part of some one of our predecessors, at least it was a personal and not a national one. They laughed at this and wanted to identify the origin of each piece.

All this made the time slip away. When we got in the elevator to go upstairs again, the Queen said she must go up to see the President for she wanted her son the Prince to know him. There was no gainsaying her request, and we went on to the second floor. Of course, my husband had put on his dressing gown to receive the King. But a gown was clumsy and uncomfortable when lying in bed and so he

President Wilson with Paris White House Honour Guard on S.S. *George Washington*, July 7, 1919

had changed it for an old soft woollen grey sweater he had bought years before in Scotland and which was the joy and comfort of his life.

When I took the party into his room he apologized for the sweater and assured them had he known he was to be so honoured by Her Majesty he would have worn his dressing gown. She was such an understanding person one could not feel embarrassed in her presence. And she was so pleased because we found him surrounded by the beautiful china they had given him, studying the details with a large magnifying glass.

When we left his room I escorted them to the front door where we found the usual flock of newspaper reporters waiting to ask questions. The Queen laughingly told them of her unannounced call on the President, and said he had made himself comfortable in a *worn* Scotch wool sweater. The next day a long account came out in the papers, quoting what she said, only using the word *torn* instead of *worn* sweater. By the next mail I began to get letters from old ladies telling me how shameful it was for me to allow the President to wear a torn sweater; that I could at least mend it—and some of the dear old souls even sent me grey wool to darn it with.

The Prince of Wales visited Washington a fortnight later. Naturally his coming caused a greater flutter in the younger element of society than in the older. Personally I saw him only twice—when he came to tea with me, and again when he came to say his formal adieux. He was ten minutes late to tea, but said he knew I would forgive him when he told me the reason. He was returning by motor from Mount Vernon and "a very charming young lady" stopped him to present some flowers, and of course he had to pause a few minutes to express his appreciation properly. We laughed, and I told him I was only sorry his visit was so brief and that he could not take all the time he coveted for unofficial entertainments, which are generally the most interesting.

After we had had tea I took him upstairs to see the President. At first he seemed as embarrassed as many another young boy would be to go to see an older man in his sickroom. He sat beside the great bed nervously pleating his trousers. My husband recalled their former meeting in Paris, and then spoke of the visit of our caller's grandfather, King Edward, to the White House when he was Prince of

Wales. The boy left off his nervous gestures and I knew he had forgotten himself. Mr. Wilson told him the bed he occupied was said by some to have been made especially for King Edward; others, however, claimed it was made for Lincoln. But all agreed that the King had slept in it, and, after a busy official day, had arisen one night and slipped out by the window to go to a dance which was not on his official programme. This captured the Prince's imagination and, springing up, he moved quickly to the window, saying: "Do you think it was this window, sir?" Unfortunately we could not say.

When he arose to go all embarrassment had left him. In a courtly, easy way he made his adieux and was again the representative of one Government addressing the head of another. I was interested in this transformation from a boy to the responsibilities of a prince.

These two visits from royalty over, Washington relapsed into a less excited social state, and the routine of things began again.

On November 11th, the first anniversary of Armistice Day, the President issued a short statement to the country. To my husband and to me this brief year since the world had laid down arms after four weary years of war seemed a lifetime. So many and so varied had been the experiences crowded into those three hundred and sixty-five days that I could hardly believe it had been only one year.

All this time the fight for the reservations to the Covenant of the League was being pressed in the Senate. Deprived of Executive leadership because of the illness of my husband, friends of the Treaty were on the defensive. The ground gained on the Western tour had been gradually lost until things were worse than when he started. Friends, including such a valued and persuasive friend as Mr. Bernard M. Baruch, begged Mr. Wilson to accept a compromise, saying "half a loaf is better than no bread." I cannot be unsympathetic with them for in a moment of weakness I did the same. In my anxiety for the one I loved best in the world, the long-drawn-out fight was eating into my very soul, and I felt nothing mattered but to get the Treaty ratified, even with those reservations.

On November 19th the Senate was to vote on the reservations. Senator Hitchcock came to tell me that unless the Administration forces accepted them the Treaty would be beaten—the struggle having narrowed down to a personal fight against the President by Lodge and his supporters. In desperation I went to my husband.

"For my sake," I said, "won't you accept these reservations and get this awful thing settled?"

He turned his head on the pillow and stretching out his hand to take mine answered in a voice I shall never forget: "Little girl, don't you desert me; that I cannot stand. Can't you see that I have no moral right to accept any change in a paper I have signed without giving to every other signatory, even the Germans, the right to do the same thing? It is not *I* that will not accept; it is the Nation's honour that is at stake."

His eyes looked luminous as he spoke, and I knew that he was right. He went on quietly: "Better a thousand times to go down fighting than to dip your colours to dishonourable compromise."

I felt like one of his betrayers to have ever doubted. Rejoining Senator Hitchcock outside, I told him that for the first time I had seen the thing clearly and I would never ask my husband again to do what would be manifestly dishonourable. When I went back to the President's room he dictated a letter to Senator Hitchcock, saying:

"In my opinion the resolution in that form [embodying the reservations] does not provide for ratification but rather for nullification of the Treaty. . . . I trust that all true friends of the Treaty will refuse to support the Lodge resolution."

That same day the Senate voted. The Administration forces, voting against ratification *with* the Lodge reservations, defeated it. The vote was then on the ratification of the Treaty without reservations—the Treaty as Mr. Wilson had brought it from France. The result was defeat. When the word came from the Capitol I felt I could not bear it, and that the shock might be serious for my husband. I went to his bedside and told him the fatal news. For a few moments he was silent, and then he said: "All the more reason I must get well and try again to bring this country to a sense of its great opportunity and greater responsibility."

How like him! From that moment he accepted the inevitable, turned the page and began a new chapter. As will I.

CHAPTER 22

SINCE the early days of my husband's illness, the necessity for shielding him from visitors had given rise to the myth that the President was insane, or at any rate greatly impaired in mind. Senator Moses of New Hampshire gave currency to the story that Mr. Wilson had suffered a brain lesion, which brought the prompt statement from Dr. Grayson that his patient's mind was "clear as a bell." Nevertheless, the whispering campaign continued and the statement appeared in print that bars had been placed on the windows of his room, the implication being that they were to keep him from jumping out. True enough, there were bars on a bedroom window of the White House. But they were not on the windows of the room occupied by the President and they had been placed there, I was told, by Colonel Theodore Roosevelt to protect his little children.

Two senatorial allies of Mr. Lodge made speeches about the "millions of dollars' " worth of gifts royalty had showered upon us in Europe. One of these Senators, a provincial Westerner of small intelligence, may have actually believed this, but it is difficult to imagine that the worldly-wise Mr. Boise Penrose of Pennsylvania could have believed it. Even newspapers ardently opposed to Mr. Wilson declined to take stock in such cock-and-bull stories, but the sinister rumour of Mr. Wilson's mental impairment persisted. Republicans alone were not responsible for the spread of this tale. Mr. Lansing had been the first, so far as I know, to raise the question as to the extent of the President's "disability," and to try to force him from office.

This, of course, was grist for the mill of Mr. Lodge and some of his associates on the Committee on Foreign Relations. After the Treaty vote in November some little incident with Mexico developed. Senator Albert B. Fall engineered a manœuvre in the Committee by which a subcommittee was named ostensibly to confer with the

President on the Mexican situation. The real object was to see whether the President was mentally capable of administering his office. The subcommittee was composed of Mr. Fall and Mr. Hitchcock. Senator Hitchcock had opposed the whole business, but he consented to accompany Mr. Fall to the White House. When this intelligence was received, the President appointed the morning of the following day to meet the subcommittee.

Senator Fall entered the room looking like a regular Uriah Heap, "washing his hands with invisible soap in imperceptible water." He said to my husband: "Well, Mr. President, we have all been praying for you." "Which way, Senator?" inquired the President with a chuckle. Mr. Fall laughed as if the witticism had been his own.

I had taken the precaution to carry a pad and pencil so I would not have to shake hands with him. I sat on the other side of the bed and carefully wrote down every word that passed between them. Finally Senator Fall said: "You seem very much engaged, madam." "Yes," I said, "I thought it wise to record this interview so there may be no misunderstanding or misstatements made."

When the Senators rose to leave, Mr. Fall was fulsome in his adieux. Reaching the front door he assured the reporters that the President was mentally fit and had waved both arms in talking and that he had the use of the left as well as his right side which, of course, was an overstatement of the case for Mr. Wilson's left side was nearly useless. When the oil scandals sent Mr. Fall to the penitentiary I could not but recall that this was the man Mr. Henry Cabot Lodge had delegated to pass on the mentality of Woodrow Wilson.

My husband took much to heart the disappointment of not being able to deliver in person his annual message to Congress—another "turning of the knife in the wound," as Dr. Dercum said. But, on the whole, he continued to gain and by Christmas he was able to sit up for a few hours each day in an easy chair. Both the Wilson and the Bolling families were at the house during the holiday season. I did my best to observe the time-honoured forms of that holy festival, but it was an effort.

The fight for the League and for the Treaty was revived in the Senate. The President agreed to certain interpretive changes and once again hope flared in the breasts of those who were fighting for the Treaty. By this time the Covenant of the League had been ratified by a sufficient number of nations to make the League operative, and Mr. Wilson was accorded the singular honour of issuing the call for the first meeting. This cheered and pleased him very much. He drafted a call for the meeting, appointing January 16, 1920, as the date and Paris, France, as the place.

He was now able to do more each day, but I eased things in every way possible and never left him if I could avoid it. In order to insure absolute quiet the house and grounds remained closed to the public. I got exercise by walking on the south side of the house where I could be reached in a moment if he needed me. Sometimes I would go for a short drive in Rock Creek Park.

A nurse can make or mar a house of sickness and in Miss Ruth Powderly we were fortunate in having one of the most efficient nurses I have ever known. She was with us nearly two years. Other nurses came and went, but the memory of the ministrations of Miss Powderly stand out in sharp contrast to some of the others whose pretensions were monstrous. They recalled what has been said of people who come as new officials to Washington: they either grow or swell.

By normal standards these were petty annoyances, but a house of sickness cannot be judged by normal standards, as everyone knows who has been through the experience. In our case to have good nurses was almost as important as to have good Cabinet officers. Two changes in the Cabinet were made during the President's illness. Mr. Lansing should have retired long before. In Paris he had been a hindrance rather than a help. The same situation continued after we reached home and my husband was expending the last ounces of his strength for the Treaty. As soon as the President became ill, Mr. Lansing started agitation to put his Chief out of office. He began calling the heads of other Departments to his office to confer on the direction of public affairs.

When at length the President was told of this he acted promptly. On February 7, 1920, he sent a letter to Mr. Lansing reminding him that under our Constitutional law and practise, as developed hitherto, no one but the President has the right to summon the heads of Executive Departments into conference, and no one but the President and the Congress has the right to ask their views or the views of any one of them on any public question.

In reply Mr. Lansing tendered his resignation, which my husband accepted at once, dictating a letter in which he let it appear that the reason was the Secretary's infringement on Executive prerogatives, rather than an accumulation of disloyalty in discharging the great trust he had accepted at the hands of the President.

I begged Mr. Wilson to state both reasons for his acceptance of the proffered resignation, protesting that the letter as written made him look small, because, unless people knew, as I did, all the other things he had suffered at Lansing's hands, the precipitating incident would seem the first offence, whereas it was the last and almost the least of many. At this my husband laughed: "Well, if I am as big as you think me I can well afford to do a generous thing. If not I must take the blame. I like Mrs. Lansing, and had great respect for her father, old Mr. John W. Foster [a Republican and a former Secretary of State]. The disloyalty is a personal act; the calling of meetings of the Cabinet is official insubordination; it is my duty to put a stop to that."

Mr. Bainbridge Colby was appointed Secretary of State to succeed Mr. Lansing.

The other Cabinet officer to retire was Mr. Franklin K. Lane, Secretary of the Interior. Shortly after our return from Europe, Mr. Lane discussed with Mr. Wilson the leasing of certain oil properties. The President did not regard this as a wise thing, and told Mr. Lane a more exhaustive study of the case would have to be made before he could permit any release of Government property to private capital.

While he was first ill, many leases or transfers came to the President's desk for signature. It was my habit to acquaint myself with the context of each matter and put the papers in convenient stacks before carrying them to him for his signature. We would prop him up in bed, and he would sign as many as he could before growing exhausted.

The first time I took him one of these oil leases, and explained what it was, he laid it aside and said: "That will not be signed, and, please, until I am able to study that situation do not bring me any more of them. It is better to let things wait than do a thing that to my uninformed judgment seems most unwise."

So insistent did Secretary Lane become when there was no action that he finally asked me "if it were possible the President is not going to sign them." I told him just what I have written above, and he became very angry, saying he was responsible for his Department and had gone very carefully into every detail before himself signing the leases which now lacked only the President's okeh; and that he felt the President's inaction a reflection on him. To this I said: "I am sorry, Mr. Secretary, but, after all, the final responsibility is the President's, and it is not like him to delegate his responsibility to anyone."

When I look back upon what occurred in the Harding Administration oil scandals I thank God for my husband's wisdom. While these were different contracts applying to different oil reserves, there was a possibility that Secretary Lane might have been misled. Anyway, on March 1, 1920, Mr. Lane sent in his resignation, which was accepted; and my husband told me to send for Judge John Barton Payne and convey to him an offer of the portfolio of the Interior.

At the hour appointed for the interview with Judge Payne, before meeting him in the Red Room, I went to get my instructions from the President as to what to say. He told me to go thoroughly into the oil leasing matter with the Judge, and tell him exactly how the President regarded the leases. The first duty of the new Secretary would be to study them from every angle and furnish a report to the President.

Judge Payne accepted the Secretaryship.

The atmosphere of cheer and tranquillity which I tried to preserve about the White House was not attained, or kept, without strain on some of its inmates. On March 4th my secretary, Edith Benham, fell suddenly ill, and her physician brought me word that she had suffered a complete nervous breakdown and must take an indefinite leave. I felt terribly about it. I knew that she had many personal responsibilities and cares, but was so absorbed in my own I did not realize that her health was going. She was never able to come back to me, though fortunately she recovered and married her Admiral—James Helm. At first I hardly knew how to do without her, but in those days I had to act and not think too long about anything. Having tackled the first day's consignment of mail myself I summoned Mr. McGee, Miss Benham's typist, and had him copy a series of form replies I had written, numbered 1, 2, 3, 4, and so on. To communications which could not be answered in this way I would scribble replies in longhand which Mr. McGee copied. It often happened that I did not get at the mail until everyone else except the night nurse was in bed and I almost too weary to hold a pencil. I used to wonder how Mr. McGee ever managed to decipher my notes, but he did.

During all this while the Treaty was a live issue in the Senate. For a time it seemed as if a number of "League Republicans" might assert their independence of Mr. Lodge sufficiently to arrive at some sensible basis of compromise. The President indorsed the position of Mr. Hitchcock, who expressed a willingness to yield certain points. In February the Senate voted to reconsider the Treaty, but the very next day the Foreign Affairs Committee, packed by Mr. Lodge with a majority of opposition members, voted it out with the old Lodge reservations attached. Again the President was urged to give way and accept them.

He declined, and on March 19, 1920, the Treaty met its final defeat at the hands of the United States Senate. Mr. Wilson accepted the news calmly, believing that in the long run history would prove him right and Mr. Lodge wrong. It is hard, even now, for me to be that calm. My conviction is that Mr. Lodge put the world back fifty years, and that at his door lies the wreckage of human hopes and the peril to human lives that afflict mankind today.

When the spring opened we, my husband and I, spent hours in the garden, or on the South Portico, enjoying the air and sunlight. Being unable to walk, he was in a wheel chair, and we would take papers and work outdoors. Or if nothing was pressing I would read aloud to him. Often members of the Cabinet, Mr. Tumulty, or other friends, would join us, and nearly every day we had a welcome visitor in little Gordon Grayson, the two-year-old son of Dr. and Mrs. Grayson. This charming little boy was a great diversion to my husband. Sometimes he would arrive in a little pony cart, holding the reins in his own tiny hands under the guidance of Davidge, the hostler at the White House stables. After driving round and round for our benefit, the baby would be lifted out and brought to where we were sitting.

At eleven o'clock a glass of milk and a cracker or cookie were brought to the President. He would always give the cookie to Gordon. If, by chance, this young gentleman were late he would sit patiently for a while and then ask in a whisper: "Didn't anybody bring a tookie out here for me?" We so loved to hear him say this, that sometimes my husband would hold back the "tookie" until the little fellow asked for it. Often we had a moving picture show in the East Room, and here Gordon always sat on the foot-rest of the President's chair and beguiled him with childish comments.

The doctors still held to their insistence for no more work than was absolutely necessary. So we resorted to all sorts of devices to fill the hours which for so many years had been crowded with labour. The President's mind was so active he had to have something to claim its attention, and the moving pictures were a real boon. Producers from all over the country co-operated with Mr. Long, the manager of one of the Washington motion picture houses, to give a new reel any day if we should want it. Mr. Long himself came to operate a huge lantern that had been presented to the President by Douglas Fairbanks. When we left the White House my husband gave the outfit to Mr. Long together with a personal gift as an evidence of his appreciation.

Usually we would go for a motor ride in the afternoon, taking Gordon Grayson with us. These rides gave my husband the pleasure of seeing some of our "road acquaintances" again. One of these was the watchman who lived in a small frame house on the District side of the Chain Bridge. This old fellow was fat and most inert, and sat all day long on the tiny porch of his house. He occupied an armchair and rested his arms on his fat knees with hands hanging limply down, palms inward. As we approached he would make a tremendous effort, pull the hands up to rest on his knees, and when we passed he would slowly turn his wrists so the palm of the hand was exposed for a brief instant and then relax into his former and permanent position. This unique salute afforded us great amusement, and it never varied until the winter cold drove the old fellow into the house.

On the Conduit Road towards Great Falls, two little brothers kept a flag ready to raise to the top of a pole. These children knew about the time we would pass, should we drive that way. They must have kept watch day by day, for often it was weeks between our coming. But as the car approached, one or both were always there to pull the cord and send the colours flying to the breeze, while they stood at salute. The President always removed his hat and saluted the flag and the children.

One day, after he had been ill for months, my husband said: "Let's go and see if our two little soldiers are still waiting." So we drove out and, to my great disappointment, there was no one visible. Even the flagpole was gone. I got out and rang the bell to ask about our little friends. A gentle lady answered, and said the little boys no longer lived there, but she knew them and would tell them of our inquiry. I hope some day, now that they must be grown, I will learn that they are still letting their colours fly.

Another friend in Maryland, barely more than a baby, with a halo of curls around his head, would pause in his play, stand erect and, putting a tiny hand up in salute, say: "Hi, Wilson!" He was a real charmer, and we loved him. Another road acquaintance, Mrs. W. H. Green, lived near the reservoir on the Conduit Road. This old lady was a real character. She always saluted as we passed, and after Mr. Wilson's illness she came to the White House to bring him an afghan she had knitted "to go over his knees," she said.

The spring passed and June and July brought the two political conventions and the usual scramble of candidates for office. It seemed as if nearly every Democrat in the country wanted an endorsement from the President, and the demand for personal appointments grew daily. Tumulty was under great pressure, but he, like all of us, strove to protect the President as much as possible. This in itself was a task, and a particularly hard one for Tumulty; for politics was breath to his nostrils and he hated turning anyone down.

The conventions nominated Harding and Coolidge on the Republican side; James M. Cox and Franklin D. Roosevelt on the Democratic; and the campaign got under way.

One day we were on the South Portico when, just as the butler appeared with the tray of crackers and milk, Mr. Tumulty ran up the steps waving a paper. He had come over from the Executive Offices and could hardly wait for the coloured butler to leave before he said: "Governor, we've got 'em beat! Here is a paper which has been searched out and is absolutely true, showing that Harding has negro blood in him. This country will never stand for that!" Fairly bursting with glee, he waved the paper like a flag. My husband slowly finished his glass of milk. Then he said firmly: "Even if that is so, it will never be used with my consent. We cannot go into a man's genealogy; we must base our campaign on principles, not on back-stairs gossip. That is not only right but good politics. So I insist you kill any such proposal."

Tumulty wilted. He looked like a little boy who has been caught robbing a bird's nest.

A few days later Governor Cox and Mr. Roosevelt called on the President and we kept them to lunch. When my husband referred to the above episode and gave them his reaction, I think both gentlemen agreed with him. Governor Cox was so wholeheartedly in favour of the League of Nations that he cheered my husband greatly, saying he wanted to make the issue stand out in his campaign.

During the last summer in the White House I consented, much against my wishes, to have my portrait painted. Seymour Stone had met my sister Bertha at the hotel where she and my mother were living and pleaded with her to help him, saying that it had usually been the custom to employ foreign artists to paint the President or his wife, and that he thought it time an American had a chance. Of course this was a subtle argument, and so I gave in. On hot, busy days I would put on a black velvet evening gown and sit by the hour. The five hours Mr. Stone had said would be necessary, stretched out to many, many more. This was the second portrait painted of me while I was in the White House, Colonel House having presented one by a Swiss artist, Muller-Ury, as a wedding gift to my husband. For the Ury portrait I wore a dress of my loved shade of orchid, a brocade which was made for my trousseau by Worth. A dark violet velvet evening coat, with darker fur, deepened the background. This portrait has always hung in my husband's bedroom, both in the White House and in our own home.

On July 15th, Mr. Wilson issued the formal call for the first meeting of the Assembly of the League of Nations for November 15th at Geneva. Mr. Cox gallantly kept his promise to make the League his big issue of the campaign. On October 27th, the President received fifteen pro-League Republicans—men and women—and made an eloquent appeal to them on behalf of the League. But it was useless. Mr. Harding straddled the League issue, and the campaign shifted to a patchwork of other questions representing simply a reaction from the tremendous effort of the War. A will-o'-the-wisp plea for a return to "normalcy" carried the day and Mr. Harding was elected.

Nevertheless, a few days later, November 15, 1920 (I quote from a paper before me), "at eleven o'clock in the morning all the Church bells in Geneva were rung in honour of the first meeting of the Assembly of the League of Nations. A procession carrying flags of all Nations, except the recent enemy States, marched from the City Hall of Geneva to the Hall of the Reformation where the meeting was held." M. Paul Hymans of Belgium sent a message of greeting to my husband, to which he cordially replied. Thus began the great service at Geneva which, despite the limitation put upon it by the failure of the United States to take its part, the League of Nations has continued to render for eighteen years and will, God granting it, go on until our own flag flies with those who covenant to keep the peace of the world by discussions around a table instead of at the point of the sword.

In December, the Nobel Peace Prizes for 1919 and 1920 were respectively "awarded to Léon Bourgeois, French Member of the Commission which drew the League of Nations Covenant, and Woodrow Wilson, President of the United States."

My husband requested Mr. Schmedeman, then American Minister to Norway, to represent him in receiving the award, and to read his acknowledgment of appreciation of the honour paid him. The Norwegian newspaper *Tidens Tegn* called the award to Mr. Wilson "a great demonstration for the League of Nations and especially for its creator," adding, "without President Wilson there would be no League of Nations."

Another, and our last Christmas in the White House. As usual we had a family dinner party, but further than that, and the assembling of the usual gifts for the roadside children in Virginia, little celebration.

As far back as the Peace Conference, and before, my husband and I had amused ourselves with the speculation as to where we would live after leaving the White House. Now the question called for a practical solution. In his usual orderly way Woodrow suggested that we make a list of things we considered essential to a congenial home and opposite them put a list of the cities we liked best, and then see how each city rated. We made a sort of game of it and the box score came out as follows:

THE WHITE HOUSE
WASHINGTON

	Climate	Friends	Opportunities	Freedom	Amusements	Libraries
Baltimore	30	50	60	70	25	255 = 47
Washington	40	25	30	0	40	135 = 27
Richmond	40	50	30	30	0	150 = 30
Boston	15	10	60	55	60	200 = 42
New York	50	45	60	30	100	285 = 57

Eventually Washington was decided on for these reasons, mainly: (1) The Library of Congress afforded the facilities which my husband wished to use while writing a book he had long had in mind; and (2) it was home to me.

This book which Mr. Wilson wanted to write was on the subject of Government.

Before leaving the White House in 1921, I found him alone one day in his study, writing on his typewriter. When I expressed the happiness it gave me to see him there in his accustomed place, he looked up smiling and said: "I have written the dedication to the book on Government for which I have been preparing all my life and which now I will have leisure to do"—and he added, "I hope you will like this." Then slowly he drew a single small sheet of paper from the machine and handed it to me, on which he had typed:

A Dedication.

To

E. B. W.

I dedicate this book because it is a
book in which I have tried to inter-
pret life, the life of a nation, and
she has shown me the full meaning of
life. Her heart is not only true but
wise; her thoughts are not only free
but touched with vision; she teaches
and guides by being what she is; her
unconscious interpretation of faith
and duty makes all the way clear;her
power to comprehend makes work and
thought alike easier and more near
to what it seeks.

Woodrow Wilson

The tragedy is that this was the only page of that book ever written. The city in which we were to reside having been selected, the search for a house began. In this my brother Wilmer, who had been in the real-estate business, was of untold help. He undertook the first inspection of houses that came to our attention, weeding out those he knew would not do.

At the same time my husband was eager to build a house that would be simple and yet adequate to our needs, and with this in view we rode often to the Conduit Road to view a beautiful site overlooking the Potomac River. Mr. Wilson was so enamoured of the location that he asked an architect to spend a day and night at the White House discussing the feasibility of building there. The architect agreed with me that while the view was fine, the lot was too shallow, owing to a sharp drop at the back. A street railway franchise prevented the acquisition of enough ground for the type of house he wanted. So we turned to another and, to my mind, finer site on top of a hill, where stood an old brick house that could be remodeled and made very lovely. This was a place I had wanted for years, and I was deeply disappointed to find it had no connection with the city water, sewage or lighting systems, and the cost of these, in addition to rebuilding and purchase, amounted to a large sum. However, the architect said he would make some sketches of both places and submit them with estimated cost.

My husband found much pleasure in hunting through architectural magazines for details, lovely doorways, windows, etc. I still keep many of these which he cut out and asked me to put away for reference. We talked over all of these, and sketches submitted by the architect. Of course this took time, and meanwhile I pursued my search for a house in case we decided not to build or rebuild; but the hunt was discouraging. We cast longing eyes at an old house between Washington and Alexandria, which belonged to a Congressman, but he did not want to sell.

Finally we decided it would cost too much to build. I had about begun to despair of finding anything when I stumbled onto a beautiful place of some twenty-six acres opposite the Bureau of Standards. There was enough ground to secure privacy, the place was accessible to everything, had marvellous oak trees, and a musical, rippling little stream. The addition of a two-story library would have made the

President and Mrs. Wilson in Bismarck, N. D.

On western trip, September 16, 1919.

house all that we were seeking; and the price was well within reach.

I was so excited when Mr. Wilson set out with my brother and me to see it—and so crestfallen when he dashed my hopes by saying he did not feel he could buy the property that must necessarily be needed by the Government in a few years. The Bureau of Standards must soon expand, he added, and this was the logical way for it to grow. He felt it would embarrass the Government to condemn the property owned by an ex-President, and embarrass him to keep it when the Government he had served needed what he owned.

As I write I understand there is an agitation to acquire that land as my husband foresaw. Another example of his vision concerned the Volstead Act which he vetoed while he was ill, but which was passed over his veto. In his judgment prohibition represented a restriction free people would resent and defy. He believed that the country, through orderly processes in each State, could handle the matter without Federal control, that the law was impossible of enforcement, and must therefore lead to crime and nefarious practises. Certainly no one who lived through the years of bootlegging, speakeasies, and the tyranny of gangsters can deny he assessed this situation accurately. Just as, I believe, another ten years will show that he was right in his vision of the machinery necessary to insure the peace of the world. The Hitlers, Mussolinis and Japanese imperialists, now threatening the peace of the world, are products of evils I think America's entry into the League would have corrected. When they have had their bloody day, I believe the world will return to the Wilson ideals of 1918.

To go back to my search for a house: My habit was to make my inspections of possible places very early each morning when my husband needed me least. Generally I would leave the White House at eight o'clock while he was having his bath and shaving—a ceremony he never omitted, though it was a slow and tedious process since the loss of the use of his left hand.

One of these mornings I came to S Street to see two houses in the 2300 block—one of which was later bought and occupied by Mr. Herbert Hoover. Neither house met our needs. I was about to get in the car, feeling more time had been wasted, when the agent who was showing the properties asked if I would go directly across the street to see another.

The owner, Mr. Q., had just extended the invitation, saying that if his house suited us he would sell. I found an unpretentious, comfortable, dignified house, fitted to the needs of a gentleman's home. I felt, however, that it was hardly worthwhile going through, for Mr. Q., having built it for his own use, was probably acting on impulse when he said he would sell. Reaching the bedroom floor, where everything was in perfect order and the whole atmosphere so serene, I refused to look further, not wishing to encounter another disappointment.

I returned to the White House and told my husband that this was the one house I felt would qualify in every particular, but I did not think we could get it. We still had under consideration a house on Wyoming Avenue, afterwards bought by Chief Justice Taft. But, as the owners did not want to sell it without the furniture, which we did not want, we had about decided against the place.

Perhaps I am giving too much detail on this subject, but to us it was an all-important one, and so naturally bulks large in my memory. A house known as Villa Rosa on Massachusetts Avenue was investigated, also a very lovely one owned by Mrs. Wetmore in Massachusetts Avenue Park. Mr. Wilson was always distressed when he had to differ with me, and, try as I would, I could not help showing my great disappointment over the giving up of the place near the Bureau of Standards. So when I said I liked the house on S Street, he himself took over the negotiations without my knowledge. He got my brother to have the agent get the price, and have the title searched. When this was done, the afternoon of December 14, 1920, he insisted that I should go to a concert by the New York Philharmonic Orchestra. Since he had been sick I had given up all such things, but he was so urgent about it I consented and took Mrs. Thomas R. Marshall, my mother, and one or two other friends.

Upon my return I found him in the Oval Room sitting by an open fire, and to my amazement he handed me the deed to the S Street property, saying he had bought it as a gift to me, and hoped it would compensate in some way for the loss of the Bureau of Standards place. Bless his dear heart! I was overcome.

Then the horrible thought came that I had looked at the place superficially and there might be things we would not like. However, my husband had arranged to go with me the next day to see the house. When we reached the door Woodrow's man brought a small piece of sod, which, with the key to one of the doors, my husband presented to me—the sod representing the land, and the key the house. Woodrow said that it was an old Scotch custom.

We went through the rooms, deciding which each should have for his own, what alterations we must make, and so on. I searched for hidden defects, for some skeleton in a closet. There was nothing. And as I sit here in my own den looking back over the years it has been our home I know that we made no mistake.

I think I have mentioned that Congress makes a special appropriation for each Administration for the purpose of buying china for the White House. Owing to the World War, this appropriation was not made until 1920, and so came after my husband's illness.

As Mrs. Taft merely supplemented the china known as the Theodore Roosevelt set, the need for additional things was real for, with constant entertaining, there is much breakage. But when word came that the appropriation had been made, I was so overburdened and weary I dreaded a new responsibility. As usual, however, Mr. Wilson had a definite suggestion to make, to the effect that, as our country had advanced so rapidly in the art of making real porcelain, we should have American china in the White House instead of imported as had been the custom. Therefore the Lenox china, made in Trenton, New Jersey, was selected. The design was simple, of creamy white texture with gold borders, and the President's seal like a gold medallion on each piece. Up to this time the china had all been marked with the United States seal, but we thought for the President's house his seal was more appropriate.

In later years Mr. Redfield, Secretary of Commerce under Mr. Wilson, told me an interesting story about Lenox china. Shortly after our entry into the War, one of the heads of the Lenox potteries had called on the Secretary to say that he was facing the direst tragedy. It seems that years of work and experimentation had been rewarded by a beautiful porcelain equal to that of the French. Overjoyed at this success, the pottery had filled its baking ovens, only to find it impossible to buy enough coal to keep them going. It meant the loss of thousands of dollars, and the closing of the plant, unless a carload of coal could be had to finish the baking. Mr. Redfield took the Lenox representative to see the Fuel Administrator, Mr. Garfield.

That official was unsympathetic, saying: "China is not essential to the winning of the War, coal is." So the ovens would have to cool.

As a last appeal, Mr. Redfield asked for a three-minute interview with the President, taking his friend along. Mr. Wilson instantly replied: "Tell Garfield I hate to disagree with him, but *one* car of coal will neither win nor lose our fight, and it means everything to these gentlemen." To keep the ovens hot until the coal could reach the plant the pottery people burned everything available, including some of their office furniture.

Our last month in the White House was a hectic one for me, not the least difficult of my responsibilities during these days of stress being to maintain about my husband the atmosphere of calm essential to his physical condition. A considerable number of alterations at the S Street house were necessary, chief among them being the installation of an electric elevator, construction of a brick garage, cutting of doors from the side driveway to the house and from the dining room to the terrace we were to have on top of the garage, and the installation of iron gates at the entrance to the drive. Inside the house some partitions were to be changed and stacks built for my husband's library of eight thousand volumes. As we were not to have possession until February 4th, exactly twenty-eight days including Sundays remained to accomplish these things plus furnishing the house. My husband's furniture had been in storage in Princeton for eight years and mine in Washington since my marriage.

About eight in the morning of February 4th, trucks which had been on the road all night drew up at 2340 S Street. Before the men could start to unload, Mr. Q. appeared on the doorstep of the empty house and, watch in hand, said the house was in his possession until noon and nothing could be moved in. The foreman of the movers telephoned the White House and I telephoned my brother Wilmer to see what he could do, thinking there had been some misunderstanding that could be easily straightened out.

There was nothing Wilmer could do—but wait. The agreement was that we were to have possession at noon and Mr. Q. sat tight on the agreement. I have no idea of the reason for his conduct unless he was irritated because we would not buy two Italian vases from him. In taking over the house we had purchased a number of things—carpets, furniture in the servants' rooms and two handsome lanterns in the

PHOTOGRAPH OF PRESIDENT AND MRS. WILSON MADE IN STUDY OF THE WHITE
HOUSE, JUNE, 1920

This photograph has never appeared in print before.

main hall. Especially did Mr. and Mrs. Q. wish us to take the urn-shaped vases which stood on either side of the door giving onto the garden in the back. He said he himself had imported them and would sell them to us for three hundred dollars. The only reason I did not take them was because, with the expense of necessary alterations, I did not think we could afford them.

The real-estate agent who had attended to the transfer informed me that inasmuch as the vases were set in concrete they constituted, according to common practise, a part of the house and that we could insist on their being left without extra compensation. Not for an instant did we contemplate doing any such thing; but we did decline to purchase. Mr. Q. sent men to take up the vases. They bungled their work and the vases were broken into bits, which would, of course, chagrin any lover of beautiful things. At the time, though, I resented his irritation against us.

As the hurly-burly of making over the house progressed I was delighted by the improvement in my husband's spirits. It seemed like old times when he accepted an invitation to see the Drinkwater play, *Abraham Lincoln,* at the National Theatre. Due to his lameness we entered by the stage entrance. The actors were drawn up to greet us and shake hands. The cheers of the audience as my husband entered the box was a heartening thing.

About the same time Mr. Colby, the Secretary of State, told me this story. He was besought to get an audience for an acquaintance who said he had something of "great importance" to tell the President. So, after the interview, Colby asked: "What impression did Mr. Blank make on you, Mr. President?" "That of a bungalow," came the quick reply. "How is that," asked the Secretary. "No upper story," was the answer.

Learning that President-Elect and Mrs. Harding were in Washington visiting Mr. and Mrs. Edward B. McLean, I asked Mrs. Harding to come to tea, suggesting the housekeeper could take her through the House so that she could know conditions and be able with that knowledge to make her plans. I sent the invitation by note to the McLeans' house early in the morning, and was starting downstairs to lunch when I met the usher with a reply saying that Mrs. Harding would be glad to accept and if agreeable to me would bring Mrs. McLean with her.

I sat down at the writing table in the hall and sent a second note suggesting that, since she was coming to go over the house and discuss personal plans with Mrs. Jaffray, the housekeeper, she should come alone. To this Mrs. Harding replied that she had not understood my first note, and that, of course, she would come alone.

She arrived on time, wearing a dark dress, a hat with blue feathers, and her cheeks highly rouged. Her manner was so effusive, so voluble, that after a half-hour over the tea cups I could hardly stem the torrent of words to suggest I send for the housekeeper so she could talk over her desires as to the house. I told her Mrs. Jaffray was very good in her position and that she had been first employed by Mrs. Taft. I said Mrs. Jaffray would take her through the house, except the President's own room where he was resting. Otherwise I hoped she would feel free to look at everything. The housekeeper, I added, would point out to her the things that were our personal belongings.

I rang for Mrs. Jaffray. The new mistress of the White House did not shake hands with the housekeeper, but gazed at her through eyeglasses which she put on over a black mesh veil fastened tightly about her face.

I said goodbye, explaining it was time for an appointment which would take me out of the house and so they would have the place to themselves.

I did not get in again until seven-thirty, and when I was going up in the elevator I heard a voice far down in the kitchen. It was Mrs. Harding talking to the cook. She remained until after eight o'clock.

I did not see her again until March 3rd when we asked that she and the President-Elect come to tea with us. My husband was already downstairs to join me in greeting them, and we had tea in the Red Room. As I recall it she wore the same hat as before but another dress. We tried to make things go, but they both seemed ill at ease and did not stay long. Mr. Harding sat in an armchair with one leg thrown over the arm.

That, of course, was a very crowded day. My maid and the President's valet packed our belongings and put them in place in the S Street house. I. H. Hoover, who had done all he could to assist us, came to me to beg that we leave everything in Mr. Wilson's room undisturbed until March 4th. When we left for the Capitol he said he would personally see that each article was carried and put in its accustomed setting in Mr. Wilson's room in the new house. In this way my husband would at once feel at home and would not be inconvenienced on his last night in the White House by the deprivation of the small things that make for the comfort of an invalid. This tender thought on Hoover's part touched me deeply. I was a little loath to adopt it, wishing to leave everything in perfect condition for Mr. and Mrs. Harding. But faithful Wilkins, the houseman, added his pledge to see that all should be in shape there while Hoover went to the new house; so I gave my permission.

I had been so busy at the White House I had not been able to go to S Street since the night of March 2nd. At that time only the bedrooms were in order. Our new servants were already installed; but on account of delay in getting all the inside work finished, particularly the elevator, dirt and rubbish covered the lower floors, no rugs were down or pictures hung.

For a week or more previous to this my habit had been to stay with my husband until he got to his room at night and then, about ten-thirty, go to the new house, where my brothers and the servants would be at work. I would help until two or three o'clock in the morning. Mr. Wilson's books had been catalogued before leaving the White House by Mr. W. T. Marshall who had rendered the same service for every President since Grover Cleveland; and this same kindly person came also at night to help unpack and place them on the shelves.

So the 4th of March dawned. We were up early, and by nine o'clock the house was filled with aides, Senators, Cabinet officers and their wives; and everything ready awaiting the arrival of the incoming President and Mrs. Harding, and the new Vice President and Mrs. Coolidge.

I was anxious about the effect of so much excitement on my husband. But I knew that, cost what it would, he would pay every respect to his successor, and go through the physical suffering without flinching. All the White House employees had been remembered, and we said goodbye to them with genuine appreciation of what they had done for us.

The cars were at the door, and I went up to tell my husband. I found him ready, dressed in morning coat and grey trousers. His room was in order with all his personal belongings around him as though he might return in a few moments. Brooks, the valet, held his high hat and gloves and gave him the cane which, alas, he could not walk without, and which he whimsically called his "third leg."

Slowly he walked with me to the elevator, where Hoover was waiting with the door open. We went straight to the Blue Room, reaching it just as the Hardings arrived. Greetings soon over, we moved towards the entrance door where the camera and moving picture men held full sway. The car stood under the porte-cochère and the President and President-Elect, accompanied by Senator Knox and former Speaker Cannon as escort, entered. Thus the man who had brought our country through war to victory and peace and had given his all in strength and health to make the peace permanent left the White House forever.

Mrs. Harding and I followed in another car. As we passed down the familiar drive she called out in hearty tones first on one side, then the other, greeting the newspaper reporters whom, she explained to me, she called "her boys." Our progress was slow as crowds cheered the car in which were the President and President-Elect.

At the Capitol the accustomed procedure was for the incoming and outgoing Presidents to drive to the front of the building and walk up the steps together. As this would have been too much for my husband's strength, he explained to Mr. Harding he would have to take the lower entrance out of sight of the crowd and use the elevator, and that arrangements had been made to this end. The Chairman of the Inaugural Committee had told us that he was sure Mr. Harding would accompany the President in the elevator. However, Mr. Harding alighted from the car and, smiling and waving his hat, ascended the steps, thoughtlessly leaving my husband to drive on alone.

Our car followed quickly and Mrs. Harding fairly raced up the steps. How I longed to follow the lonely figure just then making his painful way through the lower entrance! But I knew he would want me to play the game. With a heart hot within me, I followed Mrs. Harding, until I joined my husband in the room reserved for the President. At the close of each session of Congress it is the custom for the President to come to this room to sign the bills just passed, and when this is done a joint committee of both Houses notifies the Executive that the Congress has completed the business before it and now stands ready to adjourn unless the President has any further message to communicate. The spokesman of this committee is generally the Chairman of the Senate Foreign Relations Committee, an office at this time held by Senator Henry Cabot Lodge.

I quote the account which appeared in the Detroit *Free Press* of March 5th:

"Through a day that had taxed the President's broken physical powers greatly he came smilingly and with whimsical, humorous twist to his comments, yet with no hint at regret at his retirement from high office. There was only one incident of the day when that cheerful mood seemed to fail. As he stood in the President's Room, Mr. Wilson had been telling Senator Knox he would not witness in the Senate the inauguration of Vice-President Coolidge as he doubted his ability to negotiate the few steps he must climb. A moment later some one touched him on the arm to call his attention to the fact that Senator Lodge had arrived. Mr. Wilson turned toward the man who led the fight against the Treaty. His face lost its smile as he listened to the Senator's formal report and there was in his own tone a touch of cool formality as he said: 'I have no communication to make; I appreciate your courtesy; good morning.'"

This over we extended our congratulations to the new President and Vice President and departed. With Dr. Grayson, Mr. Tumulty and two Secret Service men we took the elevator and left the building.

Driving to our new home I expressed my indignation at the performance at the Capitol, saying just what I thought of it. My husband laughed at my fury. Where I was bitter, he was tolerant; where I resented, he was amused; and by the time we reached the corner of Massachusetts Avenue where we turned into S Street we were both happy and felt a great burden had been lifted from our shoulders and that we could return to our own affairs in a home of peace and serenity.

CHAPTER 23

ARRIVING in front of our house, we were amazed to find S Street packed with people. So unexpected and so friendly was this demonstration that we almost wept. Nor was that the only surprise awaiting us. This house, which forty-eight hours before I had last seen in utter confusion below the bedroom floor, was in perfect order—curtains and pictures hung, rugs down, and flowers, flowers, flowers everywhere. Every room a bower and a sense of home and peace pervading rooms that otherwise would have seemed unfamiliar. The place looked as if we had been there for years. This was the work of my brother Wilmer, our own and the White House staffs. I learned afterwards that they had been without a wink of sleep all night.

Margaret and my brother Randolph also were there to greet us, and they, too, had been a part of the conspiracy to have things ready for our coming. On our departure for the Capitol we had left them at the White House to see to the last odds and ends of our relinquishment of that residence. Moreover, lunch was ready and we were of good appetite. My husband sat down with us in the lovely dining room overlooking the garden. It was a happy meal, and when over Dr. Grayson said:

"Mr. President—"

"Just Woodrow Wilson," interrupted my husband, smiling.

"Mr. Wilson," the Doctor corrected himself, "I think you should excuse yourself and get some rest."

On the threshold of his room my husband leaned on his cane to survey another miracle. Every article was in the relative position it had occupied at the White House; all the little things: footrests, easy chairs with large castors to move without effort, pillows, the small tables conveniently placed to hold books and papers, reading lights, etc., etc.; and last of all the extraordinarily large bed that had been made to order, and which Mr. Wilson had especially desired. During his illness he had become accustomed to what, in the White House, is known as the "Lincoln bed," which measures eight feet six inches, by six feet two inches. Weeks before we had ordered a duplicate which had been delivered only the day before. On the wall above this bed hung a long silk banner my husband always valued. It had been presented to him in New York by an Italian artist on one of our trips there during the War. The banner, about six feet in length, shows the Stars and Stripes flung wide to the breeze from a standard running the length of the silk. Before this stands, with wings outstretched, a great American eagle. The whole is done with a bold brush, and the effect is exhilarating.

Over a door was hung the original of the Red Cross poster called "The Greatest Mother in the World." Every school child of the war era was familiar with that poster, which revealed a virile woman with arms outstretched to protect a wounded soldier, her crimson cape thrown back, showing the Red Cross on a white uniform, her eager compassionate eyes yearning over senseless suffering, her firm lips set, as though nothing should daunt them "till it's over over there."

On the mantel was the empty brass shell which had held the first shot fired by the American troops in the World War. And of course there were books and books.

But the finest surprise of all was Miss Ruth Powderly, in white cap and uniform, standing by the door to greet us. By rights she had no business there, being a navy nurse, paid by the Government. Once out of office, Mr. Wilson was not entitled to retain her, even though he should assume the expense. She had insisted, however, on coming "just to stay until you get settled." It was a comfort to have this capable, dignified girl; and a real loss to think of giving her up. But my husband was inexorable. Deeply as he appreciated her devotion, and much as her service meant to him, he said she could not stay except for the moment.

Both the Doctor and I had feared the result of so many changes for our invalid, though, characteristically, he was prepared to accept them and insisted there be no dallying. Brooks, the White House steward, and valet to the President, was so trained in Mr. Wilson's ways that he served without direction or friction. How to replace him seemed a real problem. However, Fate was kind. I had been able to get a couple I had long known and to whom I here pay a tribute of gratitude and affection. They are Isaac and Mary Scott, of the best of the old-time coloured Virginia stock. They are still with me and I count them high on my list of this world's blessings. Scott was my husband's personal servant, and Mary, his wife, was, and is, mine. From the moment Scott came in on that first day to assist my husband to undress and lie down, to the last tender service when Mr. Wilson was on his deathbed, there was perfect fulfillment of every intimate duty. Never flagging throughout those years, never failing in respectful sympathy, this gentle and understanding little servant became more and more essential to Mr. Wilson's comfort.

On that first day my husband's afternoon rest was brief. All the members of his late official family called, many of the Diplomatic Corps, and friends. Other friends, not known by name, thronged the street in thousands. They begged that Mr. Wilson address them. Twice he went to greet them from a window, but was too much stirred by their tribute to try to speak, fearing his voice would break. So he motioned to his throat, and waved to them, and I think they understood.

Ever since I first referred to this house, I have been wanting to describe it to my readers. One enters a hallway finished in ivory-tinted woodwork, with a floor of black and white marble. On the left is the office, presided over since the day we moved in by my brother John Randolph Bolling. This is a mannish-looking room— my brother calls it "the dugout"—and the first and last port of call for everyone coming to the house. There is an open fireplace, to the right of which is the typewriter desk which my husband bought while in the White House, and in which he kept under lock and key many of the most confidential papers relating to the War. To the left of the fireplace is my mahogany roll-top desk which I took with me to the White House, and used all the time I was there. Every morning when I come down to the office, I find on this desk all the mail which Randolph has opened and carefully sorted, with notes on some of the letters regarding replies, etc. In the centre of the room, between the two windows, is a long table on which rests the scrapbook of Wilsoniana upon which my brother is now working. His schedule calls for a page a day in this huge book, and the completion of a book a year. Back of the table, in easy reaching distance, is his radio, enabling him to keep in touch with happenings of the world through the

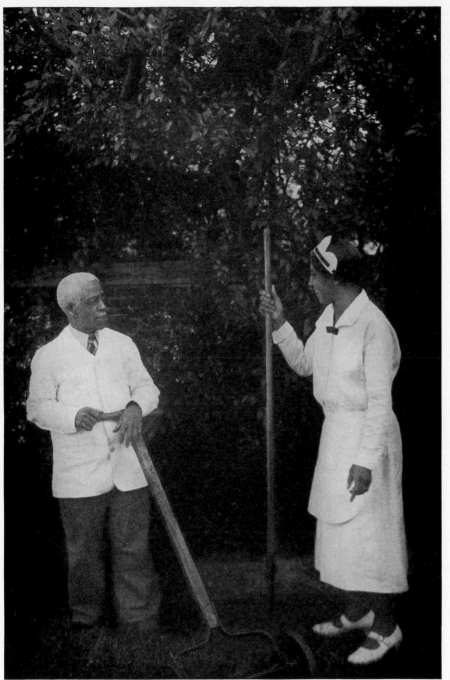

Photo by Lewis P. Woltz, Washington, D. C.

Isaac and Mary Scott

Servants of Mrs. Wilson.

news broadcasts several times each day, and also to listen to the baseball games and other sports events, as well as the wonderful music of
the New York Philharmonic, and the operas each Saturday afternoon from the Metropolitan in New York. On the mantelpiece, in a
glass case, is a baseball autographed "George R. I., July 4, 1918." This
baseball is the one that started the game between the U. S. Army
and Navy which was played at Stamford Bridge Grounds, London,
and which this democratic monarch (George V) attended on the date
indicated. It is said to be the only baseball he ever signed.

Across the hall is a companion room which we use as a dressing
room for ladies. Back of "the dugout" is a coatroom for men, a
trunk room which contains a bit of everything, including mementoes
of Mr. Wilson's life from his Princeton days onward, and a billiard
room. One end of the billiard room is covered with books from floor
to ceiling. My husband played a beautiful game of billiards, and
now the boys—my brothers—and their friends use the table. I never
learned to play billiards, but contented myself with pool.

Also on this floor is the elevator, which we installed in the shaft of
a trunk lift, the kitchen and servants' dining room.

From the entrance hall one mounts three marble steps to the main
hall, where again books overflow from the library. Once a visitor
asked Mr. Wilson if he had read all these books. "Not every line,"
he said, "but I believe I know what is in them all." From the main
hall a broad stairway carries one to the second floor.

There, in the front of the house, is the drawing room whose six
windows look upon the street. Back of this is the library, with windows facing the garden. It is in this room, by the fireplace in winter
and by the windows in summer, that we spend most of our time. The
dining room also looks upon the garden and opens upon a tiled sun
terrace on the roof of the garage. Between the dining room and the
library is a little solarium whose glass doors admit one to the garden.
Owing to the topography of our land the garden is almost on the
second-floor level. It is semi-formal in style, and surrounded by a
brick wall in the corners of which rise evergreens which have grown
quite tall.

On the third floor are four large bedrooms, one small one and five
baths. The arrangement of closets, which mean so much to a bedroom floor, is perfect.

On the fourth floor are the servants' rooms and a laundry that would delight any housekeeper's heart. The roof is surrounded by a parapet so we can hang our clothes to dry out of the neighbours' sight.

In excavating the basement the builders had struck rock and so it is only large enough to accommodate the furnace—no storage space, which is the one thing about the house I miss.

Relief from the burdens of official responsibility was such a boon that the first few days we simply basked in it, doing little except read the mail. This was heavy. Letters poured in from everywhere, from men and women of every walk and station in life. Someone sent a page from the Richmond (Missouri) *Conservator* dressed in black and containing an article headed: "The Wounded Soldier Who Never Surrenders." While reading this to my husband I had to pause because my eyes were filled with tears. Woodrow, too, was deeply moved, but his sense of humour came to the rescue. "I am having the unique experience of attending my own obsequies," he said, "and it has very nearly got me."

Soon we had to develop a daily routine or be swamped. After breakfast together upstairs, or in the little solarium below, we would read the papers, after which my husband would go down to the office. Randolph would have the mail opened and sorted. In the last chapter I forgot to mention that Randolph had spent the last few months with us in the White House where he had come to convalesce from a surgical operation. Due to a fall in childhood this younger brother of mine had never enjoyed robust health. Affliction contributing to a lifetime of meditation and study, he had evolved a self-made system of shorthand so that he could take dictation as well as operate a typewriter. When the question came up of finding a new secretary for Mr. Wilson on his retirement, my husband made a business arrangement with Randolph who came on to S Street in that capacity.

The mail finished, Mr. Wilson would take his daily walk back and forth across the hall. The doctors insisted upon this. When tired he would return to his room where Scott would be waiting with his shaving things on a small table by the window. Here he would sit and in winter take a sun bath while he shaved; for this, as I have said, was a slow and tedious process.

Intimate friends were often received in his room while he had his lunch. He enjoyed this and always lunched in his room unless we had guests he felt he must receive more formally. He preferred, however, to remain in his dressing gown and slippers until he went for his daily drive. After lunch he would retire for an hour's complete rest, then keep appointments until about 3:30. My brother would conduct visitors up to the library where my husband would be seated in his armchair by the fire. After this came our daily drive. As the reader knows, Mr. Wilson loved motoring and he was always cheered by the greetings that met him on every side. We would get home in time for his dinner at seven. Changing again to a dressing gown and slippers he dined on a small table, by the fire in the library, for nothing could induce him to enter the dining room unless properly dressed. As he ate I generally read aloud to him. He loved this quiet hour, with the curtains drawn and a low reading light which served for his table and my book, but did not destroy the flicker of the flaming logs. I would read on and on until he was tired and ready to go to bed. This was sometimes as late as nine or ten o'clock.

While he was getting ready for bed Randolph and I would dine. Then I would go up and read again until my dear one fell asleep. We had secured a splendid man nurse and masseur named John A. Ruppel, who became like a member of the family. He came on at seven at night and usually left early in the morning. He was not a timeserver, however, and stayed as long as needed. Besides his regular duties he would volunteer to do all sorts of things about the house—electric wiring, putting down rubber treads on the service stair, etc. This latter was no easy task, for the steps are metal and holes had to be drilled in them.

Sometimes in the evening we had movies in the library. Margaret now lived in New York, but she and Jessie and Nell and Helen Bones frequently came to stay with us. Stockton Axson, the first Mrs. Wilson's brother, the Graysons, and my family also often joined us for dinner and the pictures.

Our only other diversion was Keith's Theatre, where it became a custom for us to go every Saturday night. On account of my husband's lameness, Mr. Roland Robbins, the manager of the theatre, reserved seats at the back which were easily accessible from a side entrance. The public soon learned this habit of Mr. Wilson's, and the street would be filled. The theatre always had a Mr. William A. Carroll, a private detective, at the entrance. The manager and the assistant manager, Mr. Chevalier, stood at the door, and when we entered the entire audience would rise and cheer. Often one or two of the players (women generally) would bring great clusters of flowers and ask to be presented. If the girls were visiting us they went, and if not we would ask friends or Mother or some of my brothers or sisters, and so make a regular party of it. We always took Scott to assist my husband, and he would sit on the front seat of the car with the chauffeur, looking very solemn in black clothes instead of white which he wore in the house. When we left there would be another demonstration, even the actors coming out without taking time to remove their grease paint. At home a table of sandwiches and ginger ale would be waiting in my husband's room, where we would sit and talk over the evening's songs or jokes.

In the chapter before this I omitted something important. One morning towards the end of February the President, the Secretary of State, Mr. Bainbridge Colby, and I had been chatting in the White House. The Secretary invited me to come to the State Department and see the Declaration of Independence and some of the other historic documents. We made an appointment for the morrow, after which Mr. Colby, rising to go, delivered a very graceful little speech to the effect that now that the time was drawing to a close he wished to say what an honour it had been to serve my husband. Woodrow thanked him and after expressing his own pleasure in the personal association he asked: "Well, Colby, what are you going to do?" The Secretary stretched his arms out and said: "Oh, I suppose I shall return to New York and open a musty law office again which, after this experience, will be a dreary business; but I must make a living."

My husband smiled and said: "Well, I, too, must make a living. As I was once a lawyer, why not open an office together here in Washington?" Colby sprang forward and leaned on the desk saying eagerly: "Do you really mean that, Mr. President?" "Yes," Mr. Wilson said. "I can't face a life of idleness; besides, I must do something to add to my income." A moment later they were interrupted by a visitor.

Next day when Mr. Colby called for me we had hardly left the shelter of the porte-cochère when he said: "I can hardly wait to ask if

Mrs. Wilson at Wedding of a Niece, Richmond, Va., June, 1938

you think the President was serious about forming a law partnership with me here in Washington. What did he say after I left?" I told him that in the rush of things we had had no further talk about it and that, frankly, I felt it was said on the impulse of the moment and did not represent serious consideration. When he then asked me how I felt about it, I answered with the same candour. I told him there were two very divergent elements in it—one was that I thought some definite occupation would be essential to Mr. Wilson; that his mind must have something to feed on; and that I knew he dreaded idleness. But—that awful little word that destroys so many high hopes—I did not see how he could be active in the practise of law outside of the mere preparation of cases. Also that it had been many years since he had done that sort of work and I feared it would become irksome, and might not be good for him. The Secretary replied that he recognized all this but felt it could be so arranged as to obviate the objections. We were both so interested in this discussion that we stood several minutes outside the Department, forgetting the Declaration of Independence and everything else.

I returned home with mixed feelings, determined to talk at once to my husband. He was engaged; February was a frantic month for me; and it was not until one of our last days at the White House that I got a chance to bring up the subject. Very soon I realized that my husband had been turning it over in his mind, and that to him it was already a settled matter. At his request I telephoned the State Department on the direct line which connected with the Secretary's office and asked Mr. Colby to come over. Then I had to leave to keep an appointment and on my return learned that the Secretary of State had come and gone. Mr. Tumulty was in the study, standing by the desk and saying something about the newspaper men—when Mr. Wilson remarked: "Oh, that reminds me, Tumulty—you can tell them I have decided to open a law office in partnership with Colby." The announcement was so unexpected that Mr. Tumulty sank into the nearest chair.

On our removal to S Street the District of Columbia bar was more than courteous, Mr. Morgan Beach, Clerk of the Court, coming in person to present my husband's license to practise. Mr. Colby attended to the opening of offices in Washington and in New York, under the firm name of Wilson and Colby. The offices were luxuriously appointed, and I was happy at the thought of my husband's maintaining a place in the stream of active affairs, and also for a more material reason, as our expenses were running higher than I had calculated, and there were some unpaid bills.

Mr. Colby was to make his headquarters at the New York office, coming down to Washington once a week. The resident partner in Washington was to be Mr. Wilson, who expected to spend an hour or so each day in the office.

Dr. Grayson's advice was that Woodrow should not try to begin his office schedule right away. So Mr. Colby would consult him at the house. There was no dearth of clients. Case after case was offered, some with truly large retainers. Mr. Wilson listened while his partner outlined each one. All of them touched in some way the Government structure. My husband would not accept them, saying that his former official position, as well as Colby's, might tend to influence the deciding authorities in favour of clients of Wilson and Colby.

Poor Mr. Colby, too, had also to turn away from these lucrative cases. Time after time clients he could have represented with absolute propriety went elsewhere simply because my husband felt an ex-President's name should not be associated with the litigation. Mr. Wilson and I both worried over this, because it worked such a hardship on Mr. Colby, who was perfectly fine in accepting my husband's decisions.

One day the junior partner appeared at our house with his eyes sparkling and his step light. He had an offer of a case with a retainer of $500,000. "This time, Mrs. Wilson, I am sure we can appear in this case without scruples." My husband was waiting in the library. Mr. Colby came out of that room a different man. Again Mr. Wilson had felt he could not accept the case. Mr. Colby said: "Of course I want to go on as long as we can hold out, but day after day I sit in my office and see a procession walk through—thousands and thousands of dollars—and not one to put in our pockets. It is a sublime position on the part of your husband, and I am honoured to share it as long as we can afford it."

I realized that this was true and, much as I hated to do it, I urged Mr. Wilson to close the office and partnership, leaving Mr. Colby free to make a living. As always he was quick to respond and filled with regret that, instead of helping as he had hoped, he had been a drag on Mr. Colby who had so gallantly kept the doors open and bowed to the inevitable.

The Washington office was closed, the partnership dissolved, and nothing left to mark the anxious months of its existence save a beautiful closed electric car which my dear husband had bought with the one legal fee he received and which he presented to me on my birthday in October. In other years I had always had an electric, but after going to the White House I had given it up.

I am sure there was never anyone in the world who loved personal privacy more than Woodrow Wilson. Even the presence of a chauffeur was an intrusion, and he revelled in this car in which we could go alone. Speed never an object, we would wind our leisurely way through the park, or down by the river, even sometimes venturing as far as Alexandria, Virginia. But, on account of his lameness, I always feared to go too far afield lest the current should give out. As we turned from the driveway on our first ride I saw a small rusty horseshoe which I picked up. To this day it reposes where my husband put it on one of the side lights in my bedroom.

Towards the end of October, 1921, we received the following invitation:

"The Secretary of War extends an invitation to you to be present at the ceremony attending the burial of the Unknown Soldier at Arlington on Friday November eleventh at 11 o'clock."

My husband said he *must* go, and asked Randolph to go personally to the War Department and explain to the officer in charge of arrangements that Mr. Wilson wished to pay his respects to the dead by appearing in the procession, but, due to his disability, he could take no part in the service at Arlington. He also wished to drive in an open carriage in place of a motor. Brigadier General William Lassiter, Assistant Chief of Staff, was in charge. He said he would convey to the Secretary of War Mr. Wilson's wishes. On October 31st my brother received the following letter:

"It is proposed that Mr. Wilson, riding in a carriage, arrive opposite the main east entrance to the Capitol at 8:25 A. M. where an Officer will guide his carriage to the place appointed. In the procession his carriage shall immediately precede the Associate

Justices of the Supreme Court. When the procession reaches West Executive Avenue the President, Vice President, Members of the Cabinet, etc., will turn left and leave the procession proceeding afterwards by motor via the Highway Bridge to Arlington. It is planned that Mr. Wilson shall conform to this movement and leave the procession at the same point.

"[Signed] Wm. Lassiter."

To this my brother replied:

"I have laid before Mr. Wilson the contents of your letter of this date. He asks me to say he will be in the place designated by you on Armistice Day as near eight twenty-five as possible. That it is his wish to accompany the body of the Unknown Soldier all the way to Arlington and not drop out of the procession at Executive Avenue as you suggest.

"[Signed]   John Randolph Bolling,
"Secretary to Mr. Wilson."

One week later, on November 7th, the following was received from General Lassiter:

"I have communicated to the Secretary of War the contents of your note. . . . The Secretary directs me to say that the President and other dignitaries of the Government will retire from the procession at West Executive Avenue and . . . he is therefore constrained to ask that Mr. Wilson conform to the plans arranged.

"[Signed]   Wm. Lassiter."

At this we were amazed, but Mr. Wilson accepted in silence the dictum of the War Department.

We procured a victoria and put Scott on the box with the coachman. Though it was no little effort for an invalid to make such an early start, we were at the appointed place on time. However, the officer who was to meet us was nowhere to be found. The crowds were enormous, and the police had received no instructions. While they conferred we halted, a friendly crowd flowing about our carriage. A police sergeant conducted us to the place where the procession was forming. Here, again, no parade official could be found to take an interest in our plight. The place immediately preceding the Associate Justices of the Supreme Court was filled. The procession began to move and rather than be left out we wedged our carriage into the line as best we could—crashing the gate, as my brother Randolph would say. But "all's well that ends well." His obscure position in the parade served to emphasize the reception the people gave their wartime chief. Breaking barriers, the crowds poured into the street. American Legion men, some in their old service uniforms, formed an impromptu guard about the carriage whose progress, despite their efforts, many times was almost stopped by the press of humanity. We continued in the procession to West Executive Avenue where we were "retired" as per request, though Mr. Wilson had wished to follow the unknown dead to Arlington. Returning to the house we had an agreeable surprise. Thousands of persons were gathered in S Street to cheer the "Known Soldier," as one writer put it.

Large and small delegations periodically visited the house. In January, 1922, my husband addressed one of these from the doorstep, responding to a short speech by Mr. Samuel Gompers, the labour leader. On that occasion several hundred people were assembled. They had marched to the house from the National Theatre where one of the meetings to launch the Woodrow Wilson Foundation had just been held.

In February the famous Mrs. Asquith, wife of the former Prime Minister of England, arrived in Washington. Her visit was heralded in the papers and a list of her many engagements given. Though we had met her in London and in Paris, I saw no opportunity of adding anything to her already crowded programme. I decided to leave a card at the British Embassy and let it go at that. But, as usual with this lady, she made her own contacts. The White House called up to say she was lunching there and wanted to know if and when she could call on Mr. Wilson. As Mr. and Mrs. Hugh C. Wallace were calling that afternoon I said that we would be pleased to see Mrs. Asquith at the same time. Then I felt I must go before she came and leave my card. As she was lunching at the White House I thought I could do this and be back home in time to greet her. I ordered the car and dashed off, but again the energetic lady was before me; although I was gone only about twenty minutes I returned to find my shy bachelor brother, Randolph, standing in the hall with Mrs. Asquith's arms around his waist and her thin face almost against his as she reeled off her indignation that anyone could suppose she would visit Washington and not come to see "the great War President." Randolph was trying vainly to explain why we had not asked her, and how she had arrived before Mr. Wilson had come downstairs. But she kept up such a chatter he had to give it up. We were both relieved when the butler came to say Mr. Wilson was in the library. When I escorted her upstairs she rushed forward and knelt beside my husband. I left her pouring out the story she had overwhelmed Randolph with, while I went to greet the Wallaces.

I think, in spite of my explanation to them, they were surprised to find this amazing small lady still on her knees by my husband, laughing and gesticulating. Presently she had to rush off for another appointment, and as Randolph and I escorted her to the door she paused before a mirror and asked if we did not think her gown very chic. Then to my brother's embarrassment she released one snapper on the side and threw the whole dress wide open revealing very lovely French lingerie. "You see," she said, "how easily I can rid myself of it when I come in tired. Zip!—it's off!"

I did sincerely like the costume, including its then novel mechanical features: a coat dress of some handsome dark material with bands of fur at the neck and round the hem of the skirt. A small toque topped off the fetching ensemble.

You may be sure that Mrs. Asquith's visit provided a subject for family conversation. She reminded me of a hummingbird, the way she would dart about, always on the wing. I recalled a letter I had received from her asking for a photograph of the President. As it happened, he had only a large-size cabinet photograph mounted on a still larger mat. This he autographed and sent to her. The acknowledgment from her began: "The *vast* photograph came," etc., etc.; which shows how frankly this English lady expressed herself. My husband listened to these reminiscences and then said with a sly smile: "Well, of course, *I* think her a person of taste; for she told me I was the best speaker she had ever heard."

Constant endeavours were made to draw out Mr. Wilson on public affairs. What was, at the moment, regarded as just another such request came in a letter, under date of April 5, 1922, from Mr. Tu-

EX-PRESIDENT WILSON IN THE DOORWAY OF HIS HOME, 2340 S ST., N. W., WASHINGTON, D. C., NOVEMBER 12, 1923

Listening to address being delivered by Senator Carter Glass of Virginia.

multy, who was practising law in Washington. He wrote that on April 8th the National Democratic Club of New York was giving its Jefferson banquet. Messrs. Colby, Gerard, Elkus, Morgenthau, Frank Polk and others of the old Wilson guard would be there. Would Mr. Wilson send a message, taking the form of an acknowledgment of an invitation and expression of regret that he could not attend?

On April 6th my husband replied, thanking Mr. Tumulty for his thoughtfulness, and saying: "I feel that a message . . . would be quite meaningless unless I made it a serious expression of my views and feelings about the national situation, and I do not feel that the occasion is an especially appropriate one for breaking my silence."

Next morning Mr. Tumulty telephoned me. "Mrs. Wilson," said he, "can't you get the Governor to send a letter to this dinner in New York?" My reply was: "Why, Mr. Tumulty, he answered your letter yesterday; haven't you got it?" In a very fretted tone he replied: "Oh yes, I got it, but I think it very important he should write the letter; and won't you persuade him to do it?" "No, Mr. Tumulty," said I, "you know him well enough to know that when he has thought a thing out and decided it there is no use to continue argument; and besides, I thoroughly agree with him." Then Mr. Tumulty said: "Well, there is an important *personal* matter I would like to discuss with him, and which I must have his counsel about before going to New York; and could you arrange for me to see him this afternoon?"

While Mr. Tumulty held the 'phone I made an appointment for him to see my husband at three o'clock, just before we were to take our daily airing in the car. Mr. Tumulty arrived a few moments before Mr. Wilson got downstairs and stopped in the office to chat with my brother Randolph. My brother later repeated the substance of their conversation. "Did Mrs. Wilson get the Governor to write out that message to the dinner?" Mr. Tumulty had asked. Randolph replied: "No, I don't think she said anything to him about it, as I heard her tell you over the telephone this morning; and if I may make a suggestion, Mr. Tumulty, when you go upstairs I would not bring the matter up again, because Mr. Wilson isn't very well today and as you know it always tires him to go over the same ground twice." Mr. Tumulty then replied, in the same fretted tone he had used to me in the morning: "I have no idea of bringing it up."

Thinking that Mr. Tumulty had personal things to discuss, I left the house on an errand. When I returned, in about half an hour, I found Mr. Tumulty had gone—and Mr. Wilson coming down in the elevator to go for his ride. My brother having told me of Mr. Tumulty's conversation, I said to Woodrow: "Well, I hope that Mr. Tumulty didn't again annoy you with a request for a message to the dinner"; and he said: "No, I am glad to say he had the good taste not to mention it." As we took our ride Mr. Wilson went on to tell something of his conversation with Mr. Tumulty. It was a rather general one about American ideals, with some allusion to the hope that was in the hearts of both of them that America might yet lead the way to the salvation of the world.

The banquet was on Saturday. On Monday morning, April 10th, when we came down to breakfast the Baltimore *Sun* was, as usual, on the table. Before he could seat himself, a headline saying something about Mr. Wilson having endorsed Governor Cox for the Democratic nomination met Mr. Wilson's eye. My husband was thunderstruck. Reading the article, he learned that a message had been read at the Jefferson banquet in New York, purporting to be from Mr. Wilson and construed as an endorsement of Mr. Cox. The *Sun* had obtained its information from the New York *Times*.

My husband asked if I would mind calling Randolph. When my brother appeared Mr. Wilson asked him to write Mr. Louis Wiley of the *Times* requesting his authority for the publication. Randolph asked my husband if he would kindly dictate the letter so it would be exactly right. Mr. Wilson dictated a brief note saying any message read at the dinner purporting to come from him was "an absolute fabrication," and asking Mr. Wiley if he could discover its origin. Then we had breakfast while Randolph typed and dispatched the note, which he signed with his own name as Mr. Wilson's secretary.

What particularly distressed my husband was that the purported message should have been construed as an endorsement of Mr. Cox, who was present at the dinner. My husband had the kindliest personal feelings towards the Governor, who was such a loyal friend of the League of Nations. But Cox had been beaten in 1920, and Mr. Wilson thought the Party should have a new leader in 1924. He said it was that way with losing baseball and football teams at Princeton.

A new captain was one of the essentials for a victorious team the following year.

Entering my husband's room a little later I found him shaving. "It has just occurred to me," he said, putting down his brush, "that Tumulty was at that dinner. Would you mind taking down a letter to him, because he can find out just what I wish to know about that purported message from me?" Picking up a pad I wrote, at Mr. Wilson's dictation, the following:

"10th April 1922

"My dear Tumulty:

"I am deeply distressed to find in all the papers that contain an account of the dinner in New York last Saturday night a statement that a telegram was read that was said to be from me. This is particularly annoying to me because I understand that the dinner was interpreted as a boom for the re-nomination of Cox whose re-nomination would in my judgment be an act of deliberate suicide. I shall do everything that I honourably can to prevent it.

"Since you were present at the dinner it is possible that you may have had some means of judging, or may have been able to guess, what [was] the real source of the alleged message. If you are able to throw any light on the matter for me I would be very grateful. It is obviously my duty as well as my privilege to probe the incident to the bottom.

"In haste,

"Affectionately yours,

"WOODROW WILSON."

The next afternoon Mr. Warren Johnson, Mr. Tumulty's secretary, telephoned. He said that he had just read Mr. Wilson's letter over the telephone to Mr. Tumulty, who was still in New York. The secretary said that Mr. Tumulty was returning to Washington at once and desired an appointment with my husband at nine o'clock that night.

"Why, there is no urgency about this, Mr. Johnson," I replied. "The doctors think it is better Mr. Wilson see no one at night, but Mr. Tumulty can come in any time tomorrow—even as early as eight o'clock in the morning." Still Mr. Johnson insisted and I said that Mr. Wilson was asleep; that I could answer for him that there was no immediate hurry about the reply; and that I deemed it wiser for my husband not to be disturbed at night. In about five minutes, Mr. Johnson called again to say that Mr. Tumulty was taking an early train from New York. When Mr. Wilson awoke I told him of Mr. Johnson's messages and asked if I should call him back. "Oh, no," he said, "Tumulty will get in touch with me tomorrow; and there is no such desperate hurry about it after all." We went for our afternoon ride, and nothing more was said about it.

As my sister Bertha was ill, that night after Mr. Wilson retired Randolph and I went to see her at Mother's. We had been there a short time when my brother Wilmer arrived and motioned me into another room where he said: "I have just come from Mr. Tumulty's office, and you never saw anybody in such a distraught state in your life. He asked me to see if you could help him." "What about?" I asked in surprise. Wilmer said: "That telegram Mr. Wilson is supposed to have sent to that dinner in New York. Tumulty tells me it was written by him. He says he was so convinced that Mr. Wilson *ought* to send a telegram that after seeing him on Friday, he thought there could be no harm. So he wrote it out on yellow paper, making numbers of copies which he handed to the press, and which they 'stupidly published as coming from Mr. Wilson as a message.'"

Now this *was* a surprise. Wilmer went on: "I got a telegram from Tumulty this afternoon asking me to meet him at the train. There I found a big group of newspaper men, who rushed at Tumulty and began questioning him. Tumulty tried to ward them off by saying he must go with me at once and would see them later. Then he begged that I take him immediately in my car to your house. This I did, asking on the way, 'What in the world is it all about?' Tumulty then told me he had urged the Governor [as he called Mr. Wilson] to write a letter endorsing Cox for the nomination. The request was declined but, thinking he was acting for Mr. Wilson's best interest, Tumulty wrote out what he *thought* Mr. Wilson should have said and had a lady read it at the dinner. The next day came Mr. Wilson's letter to Louis Wiley of the *Times,* whereupon Wiley sent Tumulty a summons to inquire into the matter. On the heels of this Tumulty gets a long-distance message from Warren Johnson saying a letter has come from Mr. Wilson asking who is responsible for this faked message. Tumulty asked the *Times* to do nothing until he could see

Courtesy Washington Post

KNEELING THRONG ON SIDEWALK IN FRONT OF WILSON HOME SILENTLY BOWS IN PRAYER

Shortly before the death of the President.

Mr. Wilson and clear the matter up. So Tumulty is in this position: either he has to admit that he faked the message—for the New York *Times* is insisting on an explanation—or get Mr. Wilson to assume the responsibility.

"When Tumulty and I reached your house," continued Wilmer, "and they said you were here, he begged me to go to you with this message: 'For God's sake help Tumulty'—for, he says, if this is published it will ruin him and disgrace his wife and little children."

Wilmer delivered this message with genuine feeling, for he was sorry for Mr. Tumulty and trying to help him. "Have you left him at our house?" I asked. "No," said Wilmer. "I took him to his office where he is walking the floor like a crazy man while the reporters wait, like birds of prey, outside. I think if you saw him you would pity him yourself." I thought for a moment and asked: "What does he want me to do about it?" Wilmer said: "He wants you to ask Mr. Wilson to permit him to tell the reporters that Mr. Wilson did send the message, but not in just the form in which it was delivered— something like that, which would let Tumulty out." "But," I said, "Mr. Wilson did not send the message and repeatedly explained to Mr. Tumulty why he would not. So how can he say he did?"

Returning home, I took the rare liberty of awakening my husband from his sleep. I told him of Tumulty's plight as Wilmer had pictured it to me, putting in all the "sob stuff" (as Tumulty himself styled emotional displays in other people), the "disgrace to his wife and little children," etc. "Wilmer is downstairs," I concluded. "He says Tumulty is waiting in his office for him to bring your answer."

"Get Wilmer, please, to come up here," my husband said. "I will tell him what to say." My brother reiterated all I had said, after which my husband replied: "Tell Tumulty, Wilmer, that without stultifying myself I could not do what he asks; that he is entirely mistaken about its 'ruining' him, or disgracing his wife and children; that it is too small a matter to attract the attention of the public unless he himself dramatizes it, which he seems to be trying to do; and that if he were my own son I would act the same way. It is not the first time he has done things like this, and now it is better for him to take his medicine. It will all blow over in a few days, and he will be none the worse for it in the public estimation."

"Well, sir," said Wilmer, "Tumulty can't see it that way, and I hate to carry such a message." "Never mind," my husband answered. "Go and tell him just what I say. I know Tumulty. He is like a child, and will soon react."

Wilmer left, but came back later, as I had suggested, to tell me the result. He said he found Tumulty still nervous and excited, and when he gave him Mr. Wilson's message he said:

"My God, then I must do something to save myself!"

After this he showed that he wanted my brother to leave. As Wilmer took his departure Tumulty thanked him, saying he would never forget his kindness or that of his sister—meaning me.

Next morning the papers carried a statement from Mr. Tumulty to the effect that "the message read at the banquet came merely in a casual conversation with me at Mr. Wilson's home. . . . He sent no telegram. He simply gave a casual message to me in a casual manner."

The repeated use of the word "message" left Mr. Wilson under the implication of having used Mr. Tumulty to send up a sort of trial balloon which he now undertook to disavow. Having read Mr. Tumulty's words, my husband addressed the following letter to the New York *Times* under date of April 12th:

> "I notice in the issue of the *Times* this morning an article headed 'DOUBT IS CAST ON WILSON'S "MESSAGE" TO THE COX DINNER.'
>
> "I write to say there is no doubt about the matter. I did not send any message whatever to that dinner nor authorize anyone to convey a message."

This was published April 14th. Meantime Mr. Wilson had received two lengthy and remarkable letters from Mr. Tumulty, dated April 12th and 13th. They undertook to explain the circumstances of the delivery of the Wilson "message." With a wealth of detail Mr. Tumulty recalled his visit to Mr. Wilson on the Friday preceding the dinner. Quite accurately, so Mr. Wilson told me, Mr. Tumulty repeated the substance of some of their conversation. Then he went on to say that he left the house certain that Mr. Wilson intended the gist of this as a message to the dinner. The fact is that, having previously declined to send a message to the dinner, Mr. Wilson, in the account he gave me of that talk, complimented Tumulty on his good taste in not bringing the subject up again during their conversation.

Thus do men see things as they wish to see them. I should not, at this late date, mention the existence of those two letters had not Mr. Tumulty given them to Mr. William Allen White for publication in Mr. White's biography of Woodrow Wilson. Their appearance has conveyed to many an erroneous impression of what occurred, particularly as Mr. Tumulty closes his last letter (see page 509 of Mr. White's book) with words that speak of "this message" of greeting that he had delivered and assured Mr. Wilson that if it had embarrassed him in any fashion and a rebuke was in order Mr. Tumulty would not complain or wince under it.

"This message" again. There was no message. My husband had explicitly refused to send one. Had Mr. Tumulty been fair enough to give Mr. White the full correspondence between himself and Mr. Wilson that fact would have been made clear.

Indignant at this preposterous camouflage and at Mr. Tumulty's self-serving statement to the papers, I urged my husband to publish the full correspondence forthwith, thus providing the background for his brief and pointed repudiation of the dinner "message." He smiled and refused. "No, let the unpleasant affair fade out. Tumulty will sulk for a few days, then come like a spanked child to say that he is sorry and wants to be forgiven."

He did not come for ten months, and then on the day before Mr. Wilson died. The doctors would admit no one to the sickroom. I knew that people were coming in a continual stream, but I did not meet them and did not know that Mr. Tumulty was one of them until afterwards when I was told that Mr. Tumulty had said that I had refused to permit him to see his dying chief. After the end had come and the family had assembled Mr. McAdoo asked if I objected to Mr. Tumulty's coming to the house for the little private burial service. "No," I said, "not if he wants to come." Mr. McAdoo telephoned, and he came. Later I read in the papers that after this private service, when the names were read to follow the cortège to the Cathedral for the public services, Mr. Tumulty's was last, being preceded even by those of the domestic servants. That is something else I had not known before.

It is a pleasure to turn from this painful episode to some of the visitors we had that spring. One was the droll Mr. Christopher Morley. In his newspaper column Mr. Morley had written an article about how unpronounceable and unspellable were the Indian names I had selected for the emergency fleet. Right off, we started to tease him about this and in a way evened up the score of criticism. But we made our peace with him, and had another good laugh besides, when he told us of his personal memento of Mr. Henry Cabot Lodge. It seems that Mr. Morley got hold of a photograph of the Senator wearing light spats over dark shoes, but in the developing or retouching of the film the shoes had come out white and the spats black. Mr. Morley had cut off the feet from the figure, framed them, and hung this work of art above his desk. When people asked what these white shoes and black gaiters meant, he would explain that they were the feet of Senator Henry Cabot Lodge in mourning over their missteps.

Another enjoyed caller was M. Venizelos, the ex-Prime Minister of Greece, a big man from a small nation, and a congenial associate of my husband at the Peace Conference. A very friendly letter came from Mr. Justice Siddons, a descendant of the famous English actress Sarah Siddons, in which he offered to come and read aloud to my husband. We asked him and Mrs. Siddons to dine with us. After dinner we gathered in the library for our treat and were not disappointed. The Justice chose Poe's "The Raven" to begin with, and to this day I can almost see that ominous bird:

> ". . . never flitting,
> Still is sitting, still is sitting
> On the pallid bust of Pallas just above my chamber door . . ."

So dramatic did he make it that the lament of "Nevermore" seemed to ring through the entire house, and when his voice ceased we all paid him the tribute of complete silence—for no one would break the spell he had woven.

That summer and fall I was so happy to see our dear patient apparently gaining in health from the peaceful and congenial life with which we tried to surround him.

In December, Washington was honoured by a visit from "the Tiger" of France, the incredible old Clemenceau. Since his miraculous escape from death by an assassin's bullet—his car was fired on from the rear and Clemenceau wounded in the back—he said explosions made him nervous. As he had asked that no photographs be taken if it was necessary to explode a flashlight, we made every effort ourselves to protect him from such annoyance. However, he arrived at five-thirty for tea with us, and on a winter day it is practically dark at that time. Randolph and I were at the door to greet him as he got out of his car, and when he stepped over the threshold a loud explosion and flash of light startled the old gentleman so that I feared he would be ill. I was furious at the discourtesy to a foreign guest in our country, but M. Clemenceau's poise returned in a moment. How his familiar figure brought back the months in Paris when nearly every day he came to our house for those interminable conferences! In those days my husband had some memorable fights with the old Tiger, who claimed that idealism was not a thing Germans could understand. He looked younger than in 1919 and less grim and bitter. He wore a fur-lined coat, and the accustomed grey cotton gloves, and, scorning the elevator, tripped up the steps to the library to embrace my husband in the French fashion.

They had a long talk over old and new problems, and some genial general conversation. How merry the old man was! He said it was fifty-three years since he had last seen the United States and that he felt so improved by his visit, and had enjoyed it so much, he had decided to come back every fifty-third year to renew his youth.

Margaret came to spend Christmas. My husband felt strong enough to come to dinner with us and we had only Mother, Bertha and Stockton Axson, besides ourselves—quite a small circle by contrast with other years. After dinner the table was cleared and all our gifts brought in and opened. We let the servants go, and spent most of the evening around the board where the evidence of thought and long-planned surprises touched and warmed our hearts.

Three days later, December 28th, on my husband's birthday, he received four members of the Woodrow Wilson Foundation who came to bring him greetings from the Board. These were Mrs. Charles E. Simonson, Mrs. J. Malcolm Forbes, Miss Caroline Ruutz-Rees and Mr. Hamilton Holt. Such demonstrations of thought and affection touched Mr. Wilson very deeply, and he would say to me after friends were gone: "I wish I could have controlled my voice so I could really have expressed what I felt; but I could not trust myself lest I break down and cry like a schoolboy." Days afterwards he would revert to the subject, saying: "I am still worrying over my silence. Please make up for my omissions if you can and let them know why I can't express myself."

CHAPTER 24

THE only foreign decoration my husband ever accepted was the Order of the White Eagle, of Poland. During the War he could decline such honours by saying that under our laws a special authorization of Congress was necessary to their acceptance and that Congress was engaged with matters more important to the common cause. In 1922 when the Polish Government asked to present Mr. Wilson this medal, he could think of no polite reason for refusing and the Polish Minister brought it out to the house in November.

The only time he wore the decoration was on January 5, 1923, at a family dinner in honour of my dear mother's eightieth birthday. My husband put on full evening dress for the occasion. Diagonally across his chest was the broad blue ribbon with a big star on it. About his neck was suspended the gleaming insignia of the Order of the White Eagle. Mother and he received in the library, and she, bless her heart, was overcome when all the family presented themselves in fancy dress.

Randolph was an Indian chief with a splendid war bonnet of feathers which had been presented to my husband by the head of a tribe. The feathers hung to the floor, and, with a Navajo blanket and a raised tomahawk, his ancestral heritage from Pocahontas was most apparent. Wilmer was a sheik—a long silk robe, a green turban wound about his head in the front of which blazed my best jewel. My brother Julian was in an Abyssinian costume with headdress and shoulderpiece adorned with a lion's mane. Anklets, bracelets and a long spear made him a fitting match for Randolph with his tomahawk. Hunter Galt, my brother-in-law, was a Chinaman. He had a cap and long queue, a Chinese robe, and a small fan, and was an Oriental in every gesture. Bertha was a Japanese Geisha girl with gorgeous kimono, her hair dressed high, with flowers, and a wee fan behind which to hide her chalk-white face and painted brows. But

343

it would be too long a history to describe us all, so I will end with my own disguise—that of a Turkish lady with long veil, purple trousers and velvet cape. Dr. E. P. Davis, of Philadelphia, one of my husband's Princeton classmates, had arrived for a little visit, and no one entered more heartily into everything than he.

Mr. Norman H. Davis had asked to bring his friend Dr. Howard Chandler Robbins to call, and they came for tea the following day. Dr. Robbins, then Dean of the Cathedral of St. John the Divine, has since published an account of this visit from which I take the liberty of quoting:

> "Mr. Davis and I spoke of what appeared to us to be the more favorable trend of thought in this country with reference to the League of Nations. Mr. Wilson expressed agreement ... [and] then he said this: 'I am not sorry that I broke down.' We looked at him in surprise, and then he went on to explain that if, by his personal influence, he had been able to secure the acceptance by this country of the Covenant, and its entry into the League of Nations, it would have been a great personal and political triumph. 'But,' he added, 'as it is coming now, the American people are thinking their way through, and reaching their own free decision, and that is the better way for it to come.'
>
> "Those were his words, as nearly as I can recollect them. Nothing could have been more moving than the sight of that stricken figure, uncomplaining, so full of noble fortitude, looking forward with unshaken confidence to the time when his beloved country would in its own way vindicate his hope, and take its full and great and helpful place in world affairs."

Dean Robbins correctly recalled the words of my husband, which were uttered with no idea that they would reach any ears but those of the three of us in the room. He often said the same to me. He wanted the League to be the people's triumph, not Wilson's triumph. "Therefore," he would say, "it is better to wait."

And so he waited, cheered constantly by old friends and fellow believers. The roster would be a long one and I record here only the names that are on the tip of my pen: Senators Carter Glass and Claude A. Swanson, Mr. Bernard M. Baruch, Mr. Charles R. Crane, Mr. Henry Morgenthau, Sr., Mr. Cleveland H. Dodge, Mr. Norman H. Davis, the Charles Dana Gibsons, Senator John Sharp Williams,

Mr. and Mrs. Hugh C. Wallace, Mr. Edward Bok, Senator Joseph T. Robinson, Professor William E. Dodd of Chicago, Mr. Frank Cobb, Mr. Ray Stannard Baker, Mr. Henry Fisk, Mr. Cyrus H. McCormick—another classmate of Princeton '79, who, like Mr. Cleve Dodge and Dr. Davis, never let the years change the boyish friendship born at Nassau Hall.

Nor can I omit Lord Robert Cecil, a partner of my husband in the creation of the Covenant. He had been chosen to receive the first award of the Woodrow Wilson Foundation for his outstanding labours in behalf of peace. The presentation was made at a dinner in New York on April 2nd. To show our appreciation of the effort to honour Mr. Wilson by giving his name to this Foundation, I went as my husband's representative. Seated next to Lord Robert at a raised table, I could look upon the sea of faces which was like a mirror reflecting warm friendships—political associates, distinguished men and women from many places, editors, newswriters, and many, many more. The room was gay with flags and flowers; candles lighted the smaller tables, and an orchestra played. But my thoughts kept going back to a beloved figure in Washington, sitting alone, like a wounded eagle chained to a rock.

My one hope was that through the medium of the radio he could share some of the pleasures of the evening. Though up to this time Mr. Wilson had always said he did not want a radio, he had accepted our suggestion to install one so he could hear the speeches at this dinner. Before I left Washington that morning, the man was in the house working to have the apparatus in readiness. It is hard to realize now what an infant the radio was in 1923. Good reception between points as far apart as New York and Washington was a gamble. Lord Robert's speech of acceptance of the award of $25,000 was replete with appreciation, but what pleased me was a clear exposition of the League and his unfaltering endorsement of it as it stood. I knew this was what my husband hoped for and if he were listening, it would cheer him greatly.

I took an early train home next morning, eager to hear how the speeches had come over the radio. Alas, the operator had been overzealous and gone to the War Department to get a special kind of battery used during the War which he thought would bring more volume. These batteries worked perfectly for the preliminaries, but just as Lord Robert began his speech they suddenly went dead. It turned out that the operator had got an old set instead of a new one. My brother said the operator had worked so hard and taken such an interest that when the sound ceased and he could not bring it back he turned perfectly white. Randolph thought for a minute the man was going to faint. It was too late to do anything, and so all our high hopes fell in a heap and my husband had another disappointment. I was heartbroken, for the experience queered the radio with Mr. Wilson forever—just when I had hoped it would open a new interest in his life, now so circumscribed. Vainly I tried to interest him in the good programmes. He would listen for a while and then say with a whimsical smile: "Please ma'am, may I be excused from that infernal thing now?" And it did seem that a jinx was on it; for when we most wanted it to behave it would only sputter and roar.

But the opening of spring brought other diversions, luring us for long drives through the lovely country, and as summer came we often sat on the upper porch, or my husband would rest on a long chair-bed, invented by an ex-soldier and offered as a gift. Anything relating to the men of the A.E.F. was of deep interest to their ex-commander, and so I sent a check to the soldier and soon the bed arrived. It worked on the principle of the Morris chair, with the difference that the occupant could raise or lower the back by means of a lever on the side; and the mattress was covered with cretonne so as to convey the effect of an armchair or a couch. The inventor said he had tried to evolve something to help his wounded comrades. At the top of that list he put Woodrow Wilson.

My husband enjoyed resting on the sunlit little loggia at the back of the house overlooking the garden while I read aloud to him. I read so many detective stories that one day I told Woodrow in a state of alarm that I had suddenly found myself thinking in terms of crime. This amused him very much, and he said that he thought for his own safety we had better turn to something else. So we re-read Walter Bagehot and many biographies, and the magazines like *The Forum, The Living Age, The Atlantic Monthly*. Finally he proposed we turn again to Dickens and Scott, and we re-read almost every one of those authors' best books.

In the evenings Mr. Wilson took pleasure in looking over the illustrated magazines. These did not strain his eyes, which, however, became more and more impaired. We got all the architectural publications, such as *The House Beautiful, House and Garden,* the funny magazines—*Life, Punch,* etc.—and finally the moving picture magazines. I can see him now, seated in an armchair with a good reading light shedding its radiance on a small table piled with these publications. A rack beside him held his reading glasses as well as a magnifying glass so he could study details, a pocket electric light, writing paper and pencils. Wherever he sat this little stand was placed at hand. Thus I would find him every night after I had finished my dinner, for, his dinner over, he would set out to entertain himself until my coming. He always looked up and held out his hand to welcome me with a radiant smile. I would clear the table of books, and we would play double solitaire until he was ready for bed.

We played Canfield, a game I had taught Mr. Wilson during the War. Before that I think the only card game he played was old-fashioned whist. He played chess, and tried to teach me, but without success, and so I taught him Canfield—both the double and single games. During the War, I have seen him, with only five minutes to spare, relax his mind over a hand of Canfield. This diversion came to his rescue now. From day to day, week to week and month to month he kept, on ruled paper, a precise record of his running score. I have pages of these, showing the results of thousands of hands. Mr. Wilson developed considerable skill at play, one time being more than fifty thousand points ahead.

In that spring of 1923 Mr. Wilson began to betray anxiety over the signs of the times and to speak to me of calling the public's attention to the ills towards which we were drifting. It was a labour for him to write on account of a return of the old enemy neuritis, which had bothered him since the Princeton days. So he had his typewriter brought out. But this, too, was slow and tedious work, for he could use only his right hand. At length he gave it up, but the thoughts in his mind clamoured for expression and I undertook to write them down at his dictation. Often, when we believed him sleeping, his bell would ring and he would send Scott to ask me to come and take down a sentence or two.

Thus was written his last published message, which he called "The Road Away from Revolution." It is brief, but, even so, took its toll of his strength; for he pruned and polished the dictations over and over. Much of it was done in the night hours, when he would say: "I hate to disturb you, but I just can't sleep till I get this written down." When the article finally took form, Randolph typed it—after which more small changes were made. My husband then gave it to Stockton Axson, George Creel, and one or two others, to read. Mr. Creel begged that he be constituted an agent without pay to see publishers, and get a good price for the article. Mr. Wilson told him he had not written it with the idea of making money but just "to get it out of my system." Mr. Creel was so insistent, however, he allowed him to take the manuscript. A short while after a letter came from the "agent" saying he had an offer which ran into the thousands, but that if he could "shop around" he knew he could do better. The publication which had made the offer was one my husband said he did not care to have his name appear in; so he would not consider it. Neither did he want his work hawked about for the highest bidder. He wrote Mr. Creel to refuse the offer and return the manuscript.

My husband sent it to *The Atlantic Monthly* with which he had had long and pleasant relations, saying that if the editors cared to publish the article they could have it at their regular rate. Mr. Ellery Sedgwick, the editor, replied they would be honoured to publish the article, and that their regular rate was three hundred dollars.

Randolph and I were having pretty rough sledding meeting expenses, and the first offer would have been a godsend. But Mr. Wilson knew nothing of our financial troubles. His burden was already heavy enough, and, besides, I knew just what he would do—insist on dispensing with one of his nurses, or making some other personal sacrifice. The article came out in the August *Atlantic,* and was afterwards published as a tiny booklet. It is remarkable now as an evidence of Mr. Wilson's powers of premonition.

Now let me tell for what the reader may think it worth another story concerning unusual powers—extrasensory perception, I believe the learned call it. Summer was far advanced and I saw that the more than two years of constant service without a day's rest were telling on our faithful little Scott. More and more my husband depended on him, finding that Scott could arrange pillows, or do other personal services, more understandingly than the nurses; so he was always on call night as well as day. I knew he could not go on indefinitely, and that I must contrive some way of giving him a holiday. Like all invalids, my husband found a new person a trial; so my problem was a real one.

As often happens, it was answered from an unexpected source—the daily paper. Of course all the world knew that the President and Mrs. Harding had gone on the trip to Alaska which was to end so tragically for them both; but until I picked up the paper one morning I did not know that the White House was closed for repairs and all the servants off for a month. Here was my answer—to get Wilkins, who had been at the White House many years, and who had served my husband often when Brooks, the regular valet, was off duty. Of course I would never have thought of doing this had Wilkins not been on leave; but now that his time was his own I felt that I should be interfering in no way with the regular order of things at the White House.

Wilkins said he would be glad to come and do whatever I wanted. So Scott and Mary left for a two weeks' holiday. To my dismay I found that, though he tried hard to disguise it, the change in routine completely upset my husband from the first. He became frightfully nervous; could not sleep; and seemed physically failing. This alarmed me, and caused poor Wilkins to grow nervous too. This made him clumsy, and he became discouraged. Things got worse instead of better and I counted the days until Scott should return. He had been so faithful and so needed a change that it was not in my heart to recall him.

On the fifth day after Scott's departure my husband was looking really ill. I was in his room trying to do some small services myself. This also irritated and worried him, for while he loved to have me near, he said I was spoiling both him and the servants, and that I ought to make them relieve me and not I them. Poor dear! He could not see that the one thing I wanted above all else was his comfort.

This was August 2, 1923. I was reading aloud to Mr. Wilson when lunchtime came and I rang for Wilkins to place the table, etc. When the door opened I thought I must be dreaming, for in came Scott in his white uniform, ready to take charge of his work. "Why, Scott," I exclaimed, "what does this mean?" He said: "Well, madam, I had stayed long enough, so decided my duty was here, and Mary and I are both back on the job." I never was gladder to see anyone, and, indeed, his presence was a benediction. The nerves that had been crying out relaxed; the head that had ached constantly because of them was eased; and in a few hours the whole atmosphere seemed to clear. Wilkins was not at fault, and I was more than grateful to him for coming. It was just that he was different and that, despite fond hopes, my husband remained a very sick man.

Later that day I questioned Scott again as to why he had come back in five days when he had intended to stay fourteen. This is what he said: "I can only tell you, madam, what happened. I went to bed last night with no thought of coming back, and suddenly woke wide awake as though some one called me; and they seemed to be saying 'Mr. Wilson needs you, go home.' I tried to go to sleep again but could not. Then I called Mary and told her I was leaving on the bus at six in the morning for Washington. She asked what was the matter and I told her I did not know except I felt I was needed, and was going. So she said she would come too. Really, madam, I expected to find Mr. Wilson ill." Then he laughed and added: "But I'm mighty glad to see that is not the case."

This made me wonder if something ominous were hanging over us. The rest of the day passed quietly, however, and when I went to my room it was with the thought of peaceful sleep, until a few minutes later when there came from the street a chorus of voices calling: "Extra! Extra!" Then one voice more penetrating than the rest: "Death of President Harding!"

Hardly believing my ears, I rushed out to send for a paper. I had hoped my husband was asleep, but I found him propped up in bed and the night nurse already at the front door for the extra. Like the whole world we were shocked by this unlooked-for tragedy in San Francisco, and at once tried to express our sympathy in a telegram to Mrs. Harding.

Not until the next morning when I read in the paper that the servants had been hastily summoned to put the White House in order for the return of the official party did I connect this event with Scott's sudden return. Then the significance was plain. Wilkins having to return to his duties at the White House, Mr. Wilson would have been without an attendant. Thus had some psychic influence, which as yet we do not understand, conveyed a message to the humble little servant who had unquestioningly obeyed. This realization gave me a queer feeling, and I wondered if I myself should have been so receptive to an unknown voice.

When on August 8th the President's funeral service was held at the White House, Mr. Wilson and I, accompanied by Dr. Grayson, drove to the door in an open car. Owing to my husband's lameness, we did not go inside, but waited and followed the procession to the Capitol, where the President's body was laid in state.

The summer had been extremely hot, and in spite of my efforts to appear well, everyone told me I looked worn out. The fact is that I felt my splendid health deserting me, and could hardly drag myself around. Among the many friends who seemed concerned about me were Mr. and Mrs. Charles Sumner Hamlin who begged that I come to them for a visit at Mattapoisett, Massachusetts, where the air was cool and bracing. My husband endorsed their plea and Dr. Grayson told me plainly: "You will break down completely if you don't go." With his usual kindness, the Doctor said he would come and stay at our house to relieve me of anxiety over Woodrow.

At last I yielded. It was the first time I had left Mr. Wilson since illness had changed the current of our lives in September, 1919— except for the one day I went to New York for the dinner to Lord Robert Cecil. Four years lacking a month.

The Hamlins were ideal hosts, and the serenity of their home 'way off from every city sound, with life-giving air blowing in from Buzzard's Bay, made me a new being. We went for long motor rides through beautiful country; walked and read; but the real event of the day was the tea hour which in their house was almost a sacred rite. Mrs. Hamlin told me that throughout their married life they had kept this hour free for themselves and their friends; that none of the three—Mrs. Hamlin, her husband or their lovely daughter—allowed other engagements to interfere with this reunion around the kettle. All their friends knew they would find them in at this hour, so troops of them came, and it remains a happy picture in my mind. We would meet in a charming sunroom at the back of the house facing the blue waters of the Bay. The furniture was wicker, with bright cushions, and there were always flowers around. Mrs. Hamlin would preside over a table bright with silver and the steaming teakettle, while Anna, their daughter, would dispense dainty sandwiches and marvellous cakes. Mr. Hamlin had his favourite corner from which he would regale us with good stories. Each day some new and delightful thing was planned, and the house was kept gay by Anna and her young friends. This child was the darling of their hearts, and justly so, for she was intelligent, pretty, and full of interest in all the things they loved. My husband had selected Mr. Hamlin as the first Governor of the Federal Reserve Board, and all three of the Hamlins loved public affairs. So at their house were always interesting people and stimulating conversation.

A few years later the death of Anna all but made a wreck of this beautiful home and the life that flowed about it; but the healing and merciful hand of time has at last brought some solace, and Mr. and Mrs. Hamlin have carried on and found refuge in public service.

I returned to Washington early in September, much refreshed— and would to God I could have found my dear one so. Alas, no. In my absence of only a week he had grown more and more depressed, despite the efforts of Randolph and of Dr. Grayson to keep him from being lonely.

The day I got home Margaret and Jessie came, and the following day were joined by Frank Sayre, Jessie's husband. On the day before they left, Jessie's governess arrived with the three Sayre children. Frank had come to ask Mr. Wilson's advice about accepting the offer of an appointment as Adviser on International Law to the Court of Siam. Mr. Wilson advised acceptance. The appointment was for only one year. The experience would be valuable, Mr. Wilson said, returning Frank to his post at Harvard with increased prestige. They sailed soon after, and on his return to Harvard, Frank was raised to a full professorship.

Unfortunately the climate did not agree with the children, however, and Jessie had to bring them home before the year was out.

In October Mr. and Mrs. David Lloyd George, and their daughter, Miss Megan, came to tea. Mr. Lloyd George was always a charming companion, and he and my husband had an interesting hour, for while they did not agree very often on public questions their personal relations had been invariably delightful.

October also brought two other charming people into our lives— Mr. and Mrs. Bernard M. Baruch's oldest daughter, Belle, and her close friend, Miss Evangeline Johnson. These girls had been silent devotees of Mr. Wilson, and had worked steadily for the League of

Nations through an organization known as the Nonpartisan League, which is not to be confused with the former political movement in the Dakotas bearing the same name. Not only did they largely finance the entire organization, but each young woman was at her desk at 9:00 A. M. and worked through until closing time.

They had written to ask Mr. Wilson if they might come and tell him of a wonderful plan they had to promote interest in the League of Nations. That was the subject closest to his heart, though on account of his affection and admiration for Mr. Baruch he would have seen the girls anyway. So we asked them to come to dinner the following Saturday, and go to Keith's Theatre with us. They arrived promptly, and I shall always recall them as they looked that night. They are both over six feet tall, and were dressed in stunning velvet evening gowns of the latest Parisian stamp. Long earrings matched the costumes. In all they were two as stunning-looking young creatures as I ever saw; and so full of native vivacity and charm.

Their "wonderful plan" was to have Mr. Wilson speak over the radio on November 10th on "The Significance of Armistice Day." This meant a tremendous effort and a brand-new experience, for radio was then a strange instrument in the hands of ordinary mortals. The only time my husband had used it or, I believe, seen it used, was during the War when he had communicated with airplanes in flight—a feat that left him awed at the wonder of man's achievement. But who could have resisted those two gorgeous girls and their sweeping enthusiasm for the League? My husband granted their request.

Those girls stand out like birds of brilliant plumage against a dark sky, for since my brief visit to the Hamlins I had seen with clearer eyes how much my beloved invalid was failing. The eye and the mind accustom themselves to daily conditions, whatever they are; but after an interval of absence one sees with a fresh vision and comprehends with a fresh brain. Things hitherto unobserved, or imperfectly observed, stand out with startling clarity in their true significance. So after my return from the Hamlins I saw that, unmistakably, a decline had set in. I gathered my resources to arrest it if I could, and if not to accept the issue with such fortitude as my womanhood would allow.

About two weeks remained in which to prepare the radio address. For a well person that seems a long time. For the old Woodrow

Wilson it would have been an eternity in which to prepare a speech. The first summer we were married I never tired of watching him and Mr. Swem wade through a veritable haystack of papers, each presenting a different problem. On that last Western tour Mr. Wilson had boarded the train without a line of a single speech prepared in advance. Now, alas, failing vitality and eyesight made the creation of every sentence a problem. At length I suggested he abandon the speech, and that I write to the girls; but having once put his hands to the plough it was not in Woodrow's make-up to turn back. "No," he said. "I cannot disappoint those girls; I should feel like the most arrant coward."

He was greatly cheered when Evangeline Johnson, who was in charge of publicity for the Nonpartisan League, said she hoped to work up a debate for and against the League of Nations. She wrote to public men everywhere asking them to take one side or the other; and reported to Mr. Wilson that while pro-Leaguers were legion and ready to help, she could get no one—not even Senator Lodge—to take the negative side.

Work on the address continued every day. As when writing "The Road Away from Revolution," often my husband would call my brother or me to write down a sentence while he was resting in bed. The McAdoos arrived for a visit of ten days, and I was glad Nell could be with him. Always so bright and responsive, she cheered him greatly; for while he had urged Jessie and Frank to go to Siam— knowing it a rare opportunity for them—it was a new distress to him to have this gentle, lovely daughter so far away.

Mac was, as usual, busy all day, but would be back for dinner. Nell and I would read aloud, play cards, or drive, to rest my husband from his work. He thought we were resting him too much. "What are you and Nellie trying to do?" he asked. "Keep me from making any preparation for that radio talk?" In truth I saw the "talk" was doing much to increase his nervousness and sleeplessness, and so was grateful when the day for its delivery arrived.

The radio people came early in the morning, parking in the driveway at the side of the house a van which contained the paraphernalia they use. Wires were run up to the library. There a microphone was installed, after which the radio men asked Randolph to speak into it so they could make a test. This done, everything was in readiness;

but, as ill luck would have it, my husband was in bed all day with a nervous headache.

Mr. Wilson spoke at 8:30 in the evening. When the hour came he put on his dressing gown and descended to the library. He had always said he could not speak unless he was on his feet, and he stuck to that resolution now though he had to support himself with a cane. His head ached so he could scarcely see the words on the typed pages before him. I stood behind the microphone with a carbon copy of the address in my hand, ready to prompt him should he lose his place. For fear her presence would disturb her father, Nell waited in the next room with the others while he was speaking. Mr. Wilson left the library utterly discouraged, saying to Nell that he had made a perfect failure. We tried to cheer him, but it was no use. He said he wouldn't be fooled, and in low spirits—a thing most unusual for him—took the elevator to his bedroom where he spent a restless night.

This worry was needless. The address was splendidly received, one newspaper pointing out that Mr. Wilson had spoken to the largest audience ever reached at a given time by the human voice.

Next morning Mr. Wilson was cheered by the reception of his talk, but very weary. Armistice Day crowds early began to gather in the street about the house; bands of loyal supporters of the League formed in groups and marched to the door with banners afloat. Flowers came in baskets and clusters; telegrams and letters poured in. While these manifestations comforted my husband, he could not escape the emotional reaction such tributes deserve. The strain of the night before made him hardly fit to be out of bed, yet he insisted upon being dressed in his morning coat and grey trousers. When the delegations arrived Scott handed him his silk hat and his cane and assisted him to the front door where he thanked his many friends whose spokesman was Senator Carter Glass of Virginia. I wish I had a copy of Mr. Glass's moving little address, which stirred my husband deeply. Mr. Wilson's reply was taken down in shorthand by someone in the crowd, and a transcript later handed to me. I reproduce it verbatim, with the parenthetical remarks inserted by the shorthand reporter:

"MR. WILSON. Senator Glass, ladies and gentlemen (great applause): I am indeed deeply touched and honored by this extraordinary exhibition of your friendship and confidence; and yet

I can say without affectation that I wish you would transfer your homage from me to the men who made the armistice possible. It was possible because our boys had beaten the enemy to a standstill. You know—if you will allow me to be didactic for a moment—'armistice' merely means 'standstill of arms.' Our late enemies, the Germans, call an armistice *'Waffenstillstand'*—an armed standstill; and it was the boys that made them stand still. (Laughter and applause). If they had not, they would not have listened to proposals of armistice.

I am proud to remember that I had the honour of being the commander in chief.

A VOICE. The best on earth!

MR. WILSON (continuing): Of the most ideal army that was ever thrown together—pardon my emotion—though the real fighting commander in chief was my honored friend Pershing, to whom I gladly hand the laurels of victory.

Thank you with all my heart for your kindness.

(The band played "How Firm a Foundation.")

MR. WILSON. Just one word more; I cannot refrain from saying it:

I am not one of those that have the least anxiety about the triumph of the principles I have stood for. I have seen fools resist Providence before, and I have seen their destruction, as will come upon these again, utter destruction and contempt. That we shall prevail is as sure as that God reigns. Thank you. (Great and long-continued applause)."

He turned and moved slowly back into the house, and thus ended the long crusade. "That we shall prevail is as sure as that God reigns." As he said it, the fire came back to his eyes, the ring to his voice. There was no premonition that this was to be his last public utterance.

In fact hope kindled in my breast. Armistice Day behind us, the release from pressure seemed to bring new strength to my beloved patient. He brightened up to something like his old self, and took an interest in everything. My young niece, Lucy Maury, came from Virginia for a visit. At Woodrow's insistence I had two luncheon parties with ten or twelve persons present. Each day he joined us after lunch, and seemed to enjoy seeing old friends.

Delegations came every few days. I find in my brother Randolph's diary that on November 22, 1923, the United Daughters of the Confederacy came; and that on the 28th a little child selling the first Christmas seals to aid the Tuberculosis Association was photographed with Mr. Wilson as he sat in the car. That night Margaret arrived to spend Thanksgiving. To honour that festival and Margaret's coming, my husband had dinner with us. Mother, Bertha and Stockton Axson also came.

Margaret stayed several days, and we were diverted by what she had to tell of New York and her friends there. Following her going, Dr. E. P. Davis arrived for one of his week-end visits, which were always marked by a real literary treat; for he was a great reader and he knew the things my husband especially enjoyed. So he would have a bag full of gems, collected since his last visit, which he read aloud to us in his cultivated pleasant voice.

The next house guest was Helen Bones who arrived to spend Christmas. Margaret also returned, and the next three days were filled with the usual mystery and preparation for Christmas. We had just a family party for dinner at six-thirty, with the opening of gifts following. Woodrow was so weary that he had to go to his room by nine o'clock.

December 28th was always a red-letter day, for it was my dear one's birthday, and this year his friends had planned a wonderful surprise. It was a beautiful Rolls Royce car, with interchangeable touring and limousine bodies—the latter specially built for his needs, with an unusually high top and wide doors. The bodies were painted black with a narrow orange trim—the Princeton colours—with the monogram "W. W." on the doors. This magnificent gift was waiting at the door when he came out to take his daily drive. Of course everyone in the house except Mr. Wilson knew about it. We had been consulted as to every detail for his comfort. Also, the newspaper people had got word of it. So when he came out, the car was in the centre of photographers, reporters and onlookers. The surprise was complete, but a little too much—for it was almost a shock, which was something I always tried to avoid. He was overwhelmed by such a princely remembrance, and his poor nerves set so on edge that he could not restrain his emotion. We took only a short drive, as it was a cold, windy day; but the chauffeur, George Howard, who was with us eight years, was proud as Punch of the beautiful car, and almost wept when we returned to the house.

Among the last letters Mr. Wilson wrote were those to the group of friends who had done this gracious act. Here I want to express our deep gratitude to them again, and to record the other gift these same friends had made to my husband some time before. It was a check which covered the entire amount we had spent in putting in the elevator and other necessary changes in the house and for building the garage, driveway and wall. This came at a time when it eased things for us, making my husband's last days free of financial anxiety—for which I can never be sufficiently grateful.

Several of the family came to see the old year out and 1924 in. The next day Margaret went back to New York. We had another little party for Mother's birthday on January 5th. By a coincidence, Dr. Davis again arrived in time to help us celebrate in her honour, and we all went to Keith's Theatre.

A few days later Mr. Cyrus H. McCormick had luncheon with us. On January 16th Mr. Wilson received the members of the Democratic National Committee. There were about one hundred and twenty-five of them. He shook hands with each one and said a few words of greeting. Another friend came in for lunch, Mr. George Foster Peabody.

The following day the Spanish Ambassador and a colleague called to pay respects. On January 18th I had to keep to my bed with an attack of grippe. For five days I was in high fever and afraid to let my husband come near me, fearing the disease would strike him. Several times a day he would come to my door expressing the tenderest solicitude. Knowing how he missed and depended on me, I found it hard to stay in bed. On the sixth day I was up, but afraid to go out, though I persuaded my husband to take a short motor ride.

Dr. Grayson had planned to go to South Carolina for a week's shooting with Mr. Baruch. After a visit to the sickroom he came to tell me goodbye. My heart sank, for though things seemed normal I had a feeling that a subtle change had taken place, as if the improvement Mr. Wilson had enjoyed in November had spent itself. An ebbing of strength and energy was apparent. Each morning, as before, he dictated replies to his mail, but sometimes the letters would lie on his table for days unsigned. I tried to attribute this to the state of his eyes which were so bad that he could hardly see where to affix his signature; but actually I knew that the reason lay deeper than that. I asked the Doctor if he shared that fear. "No," he said. "If I did I would not leave him, and if you want me to give up the trip, I will; but I think you are mistaken."

I wanted to think myself mistaken, and was cheered by what Dr. Grayson said. Still, I could not rid myself of a premonition, though I told the Doctor he knew better than I; and that I knew he would not leave if he thought he was needed.

How vividly it all comes back. The Doctor, himself fatigued, took my hand in parting and descended the stairs. I went to Mr. Wilson's room, finding him seated with his head bowed, deeply depressed. I asked if he felt badly. He said wearily: "I always feel badly now, little girl, and somehow I hate to have Grayson leave." I said: "He is still downstairs. Let me run and tell him, and he will stay." Woodrow caught my hand to stay me. "No, that would be a selfish thing on my part. He is not well himself and needs the change." Then he added, slowly: "It won't be very much longer, and I had hoped he would not desert me; but that I should not say, even to you." Though the words were like an echo of the death-knell that had already sounded in my own heart, I set myself to divert and cheer him.

Mr. Wilson spent a restless evening on January 29th. At 1:00 A. M. (January 30th) he was not asleep and I asked Randolph to telegraph Dr. Grayson. About that time Scott readjusted our patient's pillows and he dozed off. On waking after daybreak he did not leave his room but had Randolph bring his mail to which he dictated no answers, only indicating the replies my brother should make. On his table lay, unsigned, letters dictated on other days.

By nightfall he was very ill. I called in Doctors Ruffin and Fowler. The next day, when Dr. Grayson reached the bedside, there seemed little hope. We sent for Margaret and Nell. Jessie was in Siam.

Dr. Grayson called Miss Ruth Powderly, my husband's favourite nurse, to help Miss Hulett who had taken Ruppel's place when he had to leave us a year before. Bulletins were issued. People thronged the street outside, friends began to call, flowers and messages to pour in. My dear one lay in a stupor, but when I would leave the room for a moment and return, he would lift his hand to take mine. Night succeeded day, and the day the night, the hours ticking on unheeded. Thus passed Friday and Saturday, the first and second of February.

The nights were chill, but throughout them both, knots of men and women remained in the street. Sunday, February 3rd, dawned radiant and beautiful. While church bells called people to worship, and crowds were kneeling in the street watching and praying, the frail body which had been racked with pain for so many years relaxed, and the enduring spirit took its flight.

The peace which passeth all understanding had come to Woodrow Wilson.

THE END

To My Husband

WOODROW

WILSON

who helped me build from the broken timbers of my life a temple wherein are enshrined memories of his great spirit which was dedicated to the service of his God and humanity.

INDEX

INDEX

363